DATE DUE

SEP 26			
			PRINTED IN U.S.A.

11/9/18

ISHIRO HONDA

ISHIRO HONDA

A LIFE IN FILM, FROM GODZILLA TO KUROSAWA

STEVE RYFLE AND ED GODZISZEWSKI

With YUUKO HONDA-YUN   *Foreword by* MARTIN SCORSESE

WESLEYAN UNIVERSITY PRESS   Middletown, Connecticut

Wesleyan University Press

Middletown CT 06459

www.wesleyan.edu/wespress

2017 © Steve Ryfle and Ed Godziszewski

Manufactured in the United States of America

Designed by Rich Hendel

Typeset in Utopia, Klavika, and Industry types

by Tseng Information Systems, Inc.

Library of Congress Cataloging-in-Publication Data

Names: Ryfle, Steve author. | Godziszewski, Ed author.

Title: Ishiro Honda : a life in film, from Godzilla to
    Kurosawa / Steve Ryfle and Ed Godziszewski ; with
    Yuuko Honda-Yun ; foreword by Martin Scorsese.

Description: Middletown, Connecticut : Wesleyan
    University Press, 2017. | Includes bibliographical
    references and index. |

Identifiers: LCCN 2017007286 (print) | LCCN
    2017024649 (ebook) | ISBN 9780819577412 (ebook) |
    ISBN 9780819570871 (cloth : alk. paper)

Subjects: LCSH: Honda, Ishiro, 1911–1993. | Motion
    picture producers and directors—Japan—
    Biography.

Classification: LCC PN1998.3.H68 (ebook) |
    LCC PN1998.3.H68 R94 2017 (print) |
    DDC 791.4302/33092 [B]—dc23

LC record available at https://lccn.loc.gov/2017007286

5 4 3 2 1

CONTENTS

Illustrations appear after page 118.

FOREWORD

I had the honor of working with Ishiro Honda when I appeared in Akira Kurosawa's *Dreams*. It was extremely moving to me to see Honda, in his late seventies at the time and an internationally acknowledged and celebrated filmmaker, working as an assistant director to his old friend and acknowledged master, Akira Kurosawa. It taught me something about Japanese culture, but it also gave me an enriched sense of Mr. Honda, as a wonderful human being and an extraordinary artist and craftsman.

This carefully researched and detailed book gives us a full picture of the man and his life—his early love for cinema; the terrible trials he endured as a soldier, a prisoner of war, and then as a veteran returning to a devastated world; his relationship with his wife, Kimi; his devotion to Kurosawa; his gradual rise within the studio system from assistant to director of documentaries to features; and his remarkable run of science fiction and monster films from the 1950s through the 1970s. Of course, that includes *Gojira* (known to American audiences as *Godzilla*) as well as *Rodan*, *The Mysterians*, *The H-Man*, and *Mothra*, pictures that haunted the imaginations of young moviegoers like myself and millions of others for years to come.

—*Martin Scorsese*

ACKNOWLEDGMENTS

Steve Ryfle and Ed Godziszewski wish to express their deep gratitude to the family of Ishiro Honda for helping to make this book possible. To Kimi Honda, for inviting us into her home and sharing many stories of her husband's life and work; to Ryuji Honda, for entrusting us with his father's story, for navigating many legal and logistical hurdles, and for facilitating research, interviews, and information gathering; to Yuuko Honda-Yun, our partner, who spent countless hours supporting this project by performing translation, conducting research, engaging in discussion, and providing an invaluable perspective, ideas, insights, and friendship.

Special thanks to Shinsuke Nakajima, our research associate in Japan, whose contributions are immeasurable; to Kenji Sahara, who arranged interviews with his fellow actors; to Mariko Godziszewski for translating many Japanese texts; to Stuart Galbraith IV for assistance with research and critiquing the manuscript; to Mark Schilling for reading and critiquing the manuscript; and to Parker Smathers, Suzanna Tamminen, Marla Zubel, Peter Fong, Elizabeth Forsaith, and the staff of Wesleyan University Press.

Two of Honda's longtime assistant directors granted lengthy interviews and offered unique insights. The late Koji Kajita generously met with us numerous times and answered many follow-up questions. Seiji Tani was likewise extremely generous. The contributions of both men are greatly appreciated.

Special thanks also go to Toho Co. Ltd., Kurosawa Production Co., and Honda Film Inc. for their cooperation and assistance.

———

The authors also wish to thank many individuals and organizations that provided assistance and support:

- The interviewees, who also included (in alphabetical order) Yasuyuki Inoue, Shusuke Kaneko, Hiroshi Koizumi, Takashi Koizumi, Akira Kubo, Masahiko Kumada, Hisao Kurosawa, Linda Miller, Kumi Mizuno, Haruo Nakajima, Minoru Nakano, Teruyoshi Nakano, Yosuke Natsuki, Teruyo Nogami, Kenji Sahara, Yumi Shirakawa, Akira Takarada, Masaaki Tezuka, and Yoshio Tsuchiya.
- For providing access to their interviews with Ishiro Honda, film director and producer Yoshimitsu Banno, journalist James Bailey, and writer David Milner.
- The staffs of Margaret Herrick Library of the Academy of Motion Pictures, University of Southern California Cinematic Arts Library, University of Wyoming American Heritage Center, California State University Northridge Oviatt Library, Nihon University Department of Cinema, UCLA Film and Television Archive, Los Angeles Public Library, County of Los Angeles Public Library Asian Pacific Resource Center, Rialto Pictures, American Cinematheque, Japan National Film Classification and Rating Committee, Sikelia Productions, and Storm King Productions.
- Friends, family, and colleagues, including Takako Honda, Naoto Kurose (Honda Film Inc.), Bruce Goldstein, Dennis Bartok, Michael Friend, Chris Desjardins, Jeffrey Mantor, David Shepard, Raymond Yun, Hinata Honda-Yun, Sergei Hasenecz, Norman England, Oki Miyano, Jenise Treuting, Gary Teetzel, Erik Homenick, Glenn Erickson, Richard Pusateri, Keith Aiken, Bob Johnson, Nicholas Driscoll, Stephen Bowie, Bill Shaffer, Stig Bjorkman, Edward Holland and Monster Attack Team, Akemi Tosto, Joal Ryan, and Stefano Kim Ryan-Ryfle.

INTRODUCTION

[Japanese] critics have frequently dismissed Honda as unworthy of serious consideration, regarding him merely as the director of entertainment films aimed at children. By contrast, they have elevated Kurosawa to the status of national treasure. As for the men themselves, by all accounts Honda and Kurosawa had nothing but respect for one another's work. Prospective studies of the history of Japanese cinema should therefore treat Honda's direction of monster movies and Kurosawa's interpretation of prestigious sources such as Shakespeare as equally deserving of serious discussion.
– Inuhiko Yomota, film historian

In August 1951, as Japan's film industry was emerging from a crippling period of war, labor unrest, and censorship by an occupying foreign power, the press welcomed the arrival of a promising new filmmaker named Ishiro Honda. He was of average height at about five-foot-six but appeared taller to others, with an upright posture and a serious, disciplined demeanor acquired during nearly a decade of soldiering in the second Sino-Japanese War. There was something a bit formal about the way he spoke, never using slang or the Japanese equivalent of contractions—he wasn't a big talker for that matter, and was usually immersed quietly in thought—yet he was gentle and soft-spoken, warm and likeable. A late bloomer, Honda was already age forty; and if not for his long military service, he likely would have become a director much earlier. He had apprenticed at Toho Studios under Kajiro Yamamoto, one of Japan's most commercially successful and respected directors; and he hinted at, as an uncredited *Nagoya Times* reporter put it, the "passionate literary style" and "intense perseverance" that characterized Yamamoto's two most famous protégés, Akira Kurosawa and Senkichi Taniguchi, who were also Honda's closest friends.

"Although their personalities may be similar, their work is fundamentally different," the reporter wrote. "Ishiro Honda [is] a man who possesses something very soft and sweet, yet . . . his voice is heavy and serene, giving off a feeling of melancholy that . . . does not necessarily suit his face. The many years he lost out at war were surely a factor. . . . The deep emotions must be unshakeable."

Honda's inclinations, it was noted, were more realistic than artistic. He didn't share the "Fauvism" of Kurosawa's painterly compositions.[1] He took a dim view of the flashy, stylistic film technique that some of his contemporaries, including Kurosawa and famed director Sadao Yamanaka, with whom Honda had also apprenticed, borrowed from American and European cinema of the 1920s and 1930s.

"I do not want to deceive by using superficial flair," Honda said. "Technique is an oblique problem. The most important thing is to [honestly] depict people." A beat later, he was more introspective: "This may not really be about technique. Maybe it is just my personality. Even if I try to depict something real, will I succeed?"

The newspaper gave Honda's debut film, *The Blue Pearl*, an A rating, declaring it "acutely magnificent." And with a bit of journalistic flourish, the paper contemplated the future of the fledgling director, admiring his desire to "practice rather than preach, [to] cultivate the fundamentals of a writer's spirit rather than being preoccupied with technique, a fascination with the straight line without any curves or bends. . . . How will this shining beauty, like a young bamboo, plant his roots and survive in the film industry?"[2]

———

A tormented scientist chooses to die alongside Godzilla at the bottom of Tokyo Bay, thus ensuring a doomsday device is never used for war. An astronaut and his crew bravely sacrifice themselves in the hope of saving Earth from a wayward star hurtling toward it. Castaways on a mysterious, fogged-in island are driven mad by greed, jealousy, and hunger for a fungus that turns them into grotesque, walking mushrooms. A pair of tiny twin fairies, their island despoiled by nuclear testing, sing a beautiful requiem beckoning the god-monster Mothra to save mankind. Invaders from drought-ridden Planet X dispatch Godzilla, Rodan, and three-headed King Ghidorah to conquer Earth, but an alien woman follows her heart and foils their plan. A lonely, bullied schoolboy dreams of a friendship with Godzilla's son, who helps the child conquer his fears.

The cinema of Ishiro Honda brings to life a world of tragedy and fantasy. It is a world besieged by giant monsters, yet one in which those same monsters ultimately become Earth's guardians. A world in which scientific advancement and space exploration reveal infinite possibilities, even while unleashing forces that threaten mankind's very survival. A world defined by the horrific reality of mass destruction visited upon Japan in World War II, yet stirring the imaginations of adults and children around the world for generations.

Honda's *Godzilla* first appeared more than sixty years ago, setting Tokyo afire in what is now well understood to be a symbolic reenactment of Hiroshima and Nagasaki. It was a major hit, ranking eighth at the Japanese box office in a year that also produced such masterpieces as *Seven Samurai, Musashi Miyamoto, Sansho the Bailiff,* and *Twenty-Four Eyes.* It was subsequently sold for distribution in the United States, netting sizeable returns for Toho Studios and especially for the American profiteers who gave it the exploitable new title, *Godzilla, King of the Monsters!* If the triumph of Akira Kurosawa's *Rashomon*—which took the grand prize at the 1951 Venice International Film Festival, and subsequently received an honorary Academy Award—had brought postwar Japanese cinema to the West, then it was Honda's monster movie that introduced Japanese popular culture worldwide.

Only fifteen years after Pearl Harbor, *Godzilla, King of the Monsters!* (famously reedited with new footage starring Raymond Burr, yet featuring a predominantly Japanese cast) surmounted cultural barriers and planted the seed of a global franchise. It was the forerunner of a westward Japanese migration that would eventually include everything from anime and manga to Transformers, Power Rangers, Tamagotchi, and Pokémon. *Godzilla* became the first postwar foreign film, albeit in an altered form, to be widely released to mainstream commercial cinemas across the United States. In 2009 *Huffington Post*'s Jason Notte declared it "the most important foreign film in American history," noting that it had "offered many Americans their first look at a culture other than their own."[3]

An invasion of Japanese monsters and aliens followed in Godzilla's footsteps. With *Rodan*, *The Mysterians*, *Mothra*, *Ghidorah the Three-Headed Monster*, and many others, Honda and special-effects artist Eiji Tsuburaya created the *kaiju eiga* (literally, "monster movie"), a science fiction subgenre that was uniquely Japanese yet universally appealing.

Honda's movies were more widely distributed internationally than those of any other Japanese director prior to the animator Hayao Miyazaki. During the 1950s and 1960s, the golden age of foreign cinema, films by Kurosawa, Mizoguchi, and other acclaimed masters were limited to American art house cinemas and college campuses, while Honda's were emblazoned across marquees in big cities and small towns—from Texas drive-ins to California movie palaces to suburban Boston neighborhood theaters—and were also released widely in Europe, Latin America, Asia, and other territories. Eventually these films reached their largest overseas audience through a medium they weren't intended for: the small screen. Roughly from the 1960s through the 1980s, Godzilla and

company were mainstays in television syndication, appearing regularly on stations across North America. Since then, they have found new generations of viewers via home video, streaming media, and revival screenings. Today, the *kaiju eiga* has gone global. It continues to be revived periodically in Japan, while Hollywood, via Guillermo del Toro's *Pacific Rim* (2013) and two big-budget *Godzilla* remakes (1998 and 2014), has fully co-opted it.

Honda's remarkable achievement went entirely unnoticed in the early years, because of several factors. First, there was a critical bias against science fiction films; in the 1950s, even exemplary genre pictures such as Howard Hawks's *The Thing* (1951), Don Siegel's *Invasion of the Body Snatchers* (1956), and Fred M. Wilcox's *Forbidden Planet* (1956) "were taken to be lightweight mass entertainment, and even in retrospect they have rarely been credited with any substantial degree of aesthetic or intellectual achievement," observes film historian Carl Freedman.[4] Critics tended to focus on technical merits, or lack thereof, rather than artistic value or content.

Stereotypes about Japan and its then-prevalent reputation for exporting cheap products were another obstacle, compounded by US distributors' tendency to radically alter Honda's films by dubbing them into English (often laughably), reediting them (sometimes very poorly), or giving them ridiculous new titles such as *Attack of the Mushroom People*. This process could marginalize Honda's authorship, or render it invisible: he sometimes shared a director's credit with the Americans who had chopped up his movies, and overseas theatrical posters often excluded his name entirely.

As Christopher Bolton, Istvan Csicsery-Ronay Jr., and Takayuki Tatsumi note in their survey of Japanese science fiction, *Robot Ghosts and Wired Dreams*:

> In the U.S., the Japanese monster film became the archetype for cheap, cheesy disaster movies because of . . . cultural and technological interference patterns . . . In many cases, the original films' anamorphic widescreen photography, which lent images greater scale and depth when properly projected, was reduced for American showings to a smaller format; the original stereophonic soundtracks (among the most technically innovative and musically interesting in the medium at the time) were [replaced] and rearranged; and additional scenes with American actors, shot on different screen ratios, were added . . . The American versions inevitably stripped out the stories' popular mythological resonances, their evocation of Japanese theater, and the imaginary management of postwar collective emotions.[5]

Such distractions and biases were evident in the writings of American reviewers. *Variety* called *Mothra*, one of Honda's most entertaining genre films, "ludicrously written, haphazardly executed"; of *The Mysterians*, it wondered if "something was lost in translation." Japanese film critics, meanwhile, tended to dismiss *kaiju eiga* as juvenile gimmick films. The genre's domestic marginalization as an *otaku* (fan) phenomenon was cemented in 1969 with the *World of SF Film Encyclopedia* (*Sekai SF eiga taikan*), a landmark volume covering sci-fi films by Honda and his contemporaries. Though published by the respected *Kinema Junpo* film journal, its author was not a mainstream critic but "monster professor" Shoji Otomo, editor of *Shonen Magazine*, a weekly children's publication.

Thus, Honda's career is one of contradic-tions. In Japan he was an A-level director, but abroad he was known only as a maker of B movies. Despite his large output and the popularity, longevity, and influence of his work (director Tim Burton once called Honda's genre pictures "the most beautiful movies in the whole world"), there has been relatively little study of it beyond *Godzilla*. Honda never had a number-one hit, but his films consistently performed well at the Japanese box office and netted substantial foreign revenue; yet even commercial success did not lead him to make the projects he was most passionate about.

Not unlike the English director James Whale—who, despite making war dramas, light comedies, adventures, mysteries, and the musical *Show Boat* (1936), is most widely remembered for directing Universal's *Frankenstein* (1931), *The Invisible Man* (1933), and *Bride of Frankenstein* (1935)— Honda became known for one genre even though his output included documentaries, dramas, war films, comedies, melodramas, and even a *yakuza* (gangster) actioner and a sports biopic. Of Honda's forty-six features, nearly half had nothing to do with sci-fi, and more than a few of these films are excellent, though underappreciated. The "shining beauty" who planted his roots in the business in 1951 would prove a versatile craftsman driven to, as he said, "depict something real."

Honda's career began with four subdued dramas about young people navigating the changing postwar landscape, with themes common to *gendai-geki* (modern drama) films reflecting social friction in contemporary Japan. After *The Blue Pearl* came *The Skin of the South* (1952), *The Man Who Came to Port* (1952), and the teen melodrama *Adolescence Part 2* (1953). Then a pair of dramas about the human cost of Japan's wartime hubris, *Eagle of the Pacific*

(1953) and *Farewell Rabaul* (1954), presaged the cautionary tale Honda would tell next in *Godzilla* (1954).

As Japan's harsh economic conditions slowly improved, Honda entered a second, more optimistic period, and through the early 1960s he would frequently incorporate music and humor in both his monster and mainstream films. Although the press had initially raised lofty expectations, Honda now became a member of Toho Studios' stable of contracted program-picture directors, craftsmen respected for their commercial durability and their ability to deliver films on time and on budget, while largely toiling in the critical shadows of the resurgent early masters (Yasujiro Ozu, Mikio Naruse) and rising auteurs (Kurosawa, Kon Ichikawa, Masaki Kobayashi, among others). As such, Japan's critics essentially dismissed him; of his films, only *The Blue Pearl* made *Kinema Junpo*'s annual best-of list. It would be decades before *Godzilla* would earn worldwide critical acceptance as a significant entry in Japan's postwar cinema, and even longer before several of Honda's nongenre films would begin to be reappraised.

Though he was instrumental in creating iconic films known around the globe for more than sixty years, Honda has been overlooked as a director deserving scholarly attention. That his talents and interests went far beyond the narrow limits of the monster-movie genre, and that he effectively had two overlapping but very different careers, one invisible outside Japan, remains little known. And so his story has not really been told, and his body of work not fully considered. This book looks at Honda's life, reexamines his films, recognizes his substantial achievements, and casts light on his contributions to Japanese and world cinema. Through a combination of biography, analysis—including the first study, in any language, of his entire filmography—and industrial history, it not only tells how Honda created a world of fearful yet familiar monsters, but also recalls the experiences and relationships that informed his movies, including his long years at war and the endless nightmares that followed. And it explores a lasting mystery of Honda's legacy: why, for reasons difficult to understand, he did not parlay the broad popularity of his genre pictures into the freedom to make the films he most wanted to; and why, while close friends and colleagues Akira Kurosawa and Eiji Tsuburaya used their own successes to gain independence from the studio system, Honda remained committed to it and accepted the constraints placed on his work and career.

————————

"I've always felt that films should have a specific form," Honda said. "Cinema should be entertaining, and should give much visual enjoyment to the public. Many things can be expressed by literature or painting, but cinema has a particular advantage in its visual aspect. I try to express things in film that other arts cannot approach. . . .

"My monster films have met with a great commercial success in Japan and elsewhere [but] that doesn't mean I'm strictly limited to this type of film. I think I make too many monster films, but that's because of the direction of Toho."[6]

In this excerpt from a 1968 interview, Honda indicated his simple and unaffected philosophy toward film, but also hinted that his creativity was stifled by the studio's business strategy. Despite his statement to the contrary, by this time Honda was exclusively making monster movies, a source of frustration largely responsible for his eventual departure from Toho. It was Honda's personality—a quiet and gentle spirit, a self-effacing and selfless tendency to put the needs of others before his own, a desire to create harmony and avoid conflict, and his strong sense of loyalty—that enabled him to thrive under the Toho system, within the parameters set by the company. Honda's reserved nature was a great asset, the reason he was so beloved by colleagues, but also a liability.

While Kurosawa reinterpreted Shakespeare and Dostoevsky in a postwar Japanese context, Honda was similarly inspired by Merian C. Cooper's *King Kong* (1933), George Pal's *War of the Worlds* (1953)—two films he frequently cited as influences—and the productions of Walt Disney to create his world of tragedy and fantasy, resembling the Hollywood prototypes but distinctly Japanese in viewpoint. Honda considered himself an entertainment filmmaker, and he admired fellow travelers; in later years, he would prefer the works of George Lucas and Steven Spielberg to Stanley Kubrick's *2001: A Space Odyssey*. He was unabashedly populist, putting the viewer's experience before his agenda behind the camera.

"No matter how artistic a film can be, if no one can appreciate it, it is no good," he said late in life. "Maybe that was my weak point, that I never thought that pursuing my theme was absolute. That is the way I live. I was never actually in the position where I could say or push my idea on everybody . . . like, 'No matter who says what, this is my movie.' After all, I grew up in the film studio system . . . I had to make my movies in that system. That's one reason why I wasn't completely strict about my theme, but at least I tried to show what I wanted to say, as best I could under the circumstances.

"I have a really strong [connection] with the audience. It's not about treating the audience just as my customer . . . I always thought about how [I could make them] feel what I was thinking about. I always tried to be very honest with myself. I tried to show my feelings directly and have the audience feel my excitement. That's how I tried to make my films."[7]

Honda's loyalty showed in many aspects of life. He remained loyal to his country even when war pulled him away from the job he loved, and even when he was unfairly, unofficially punished for an act of treason with which he had no involvement and was forced to serve much longer than usual. He was a reluctant soldier who avoided fighting unless necessary, but he carried out his duties, motivated to survive the war and return to his family and his work. He remained loyal to the studio even when it nearly fell apart, while others were revolting and defecting, and while younger men were promoted before him. He resolved to continue making feature films even as colleagues joined the rise of television. And he stayed with the studio even after it pigeonholed him as a sci-fi man.

Still, he wasn't the stereotypical Japanese employee blindly serving his company. Honda saw the director's role as a collaborative one, as a team leader rather than an author. "There is a great deal of discussion during the writing of the script," he said. "But once filming starts, the discussions are ended. Once I became part of Toho, I no longer had reason to complain [to] my employer. One may have objections before joining a company, but once you are inside, you really cannot. That is my opinion. [But] if I have the least objection to a script, I certainly do not make the film."[8]

————

With hindsight, Honda would express misgivings about his place in the film hierarchy. "The best way to make a film is . . . how Chaplin did," he said, after retiring.

"You have your own money, you direct, and act and cast it by yourself. That is a real moviemaker. [People] like us, we get money from the company and make whatever film they want. Well, that is not quite a real moviemaker."[9]

For Honda's generation, the studio was the only path to directing. It wasn't until the late 1940s that Kurosawa and a handful of directors would begin to challenge the status quo and pave the way for independent cinema to come later. And it's not difficult to understand Honda's allegiance to the system, for he entered Toho during the 1930s, when by one measure, film output, the Japanese movie business was the biggest in the world, a position it would regain during the 1950s and 1960s, coinciding with the peak of Honda's career. Japan's system was modeled after Hollywood, with each studio cultivating its own contracted stars, directors, and writers, and building audience loyalty by focusing on key genres. Just as Warner Bros. became famous for gangster pictures, or MGM for musicals, Toho became known for big war epics during the 1930s and 1940s, and later it would excel in white-collar comedies, lavish musicals, film noir–type thrillers, women's dramas—and science fiction films, most directed by Honda. Japan's apprenticeship program was, by some accounts, better than Hollywood's, with fledgling directors being assigned a mentor, who taught them the techniques of the craft and the politics of the business. Each studio was a tight-knit family of highly talented creative types.

Inuhiko Yomota, perhaps Japan's most highly respected film historian, believes Honda was "regarded as an artisan filmmaker capable of making various types of movies ranging from highbrow films to 'teen pics' within the restrictions of the Japanese studio system." Honda was among those studio-based directors who did not possess the truly individualistic style of an auteur, yet succeeded because of their ability to use genre conventions as guidelines to be embellished and blended, rather than strict rules. To that end, Honda improvised: *Mothra* is part fantasy, *King Kong vs. Godzilla* incorporates salaryman comedy, *Atragon* contrasts a lost-civilization fantasy with Japan's lost wartime empire, *The H-Man* combines monsters with gangsters, *All Monsters Attack* turns its genre inside out, and so on. Often the theme was a reflection of Honda himself. He would describe making films as the culmination of a lifelong process of observing and studying the world around him. "Only if you have your own [point-of-view] can you see things when you direct or create something," he would say. "Seeing things through my own eyes, making films, and living my life in my own way . . . I try to gradually create the new me. That is what it is all about."[10]

————

Honda's personality was evident in his approach to filmmaking and in his self-assessment. In a preface to a memoir published posthumously, he wrote, "Ishiro Honda, the individual, is nothing amusing or interesting. He is really just an ordinary, regular old person and a regular movie fan." In the same text, he said, "I am probably a filmmaker who least looks like one." And still later, he described himself as "A weed in the flower garden . . . Never the main flower." He preferred not to command the spotlight, but to be noticed for his achievements. "People who come to see the main flower will notice [me]. 'Hmm, look at this flower here.'"

In outlining his directing philosophy, Honda emphasized collaboration and cooperation. "The most hated word is 'fight,'" he said. Dialogue and understanding were keys to successful filmmaking: "Talk to each other. That's the way to get an agreement."

Like Kurosawa, Ingmar Bergman, and John Ford, Honda had his de facto stock company of performers, many of whom called themselves the "Honda family." There were major Toho actors such as Ryo Ikebe and Akira Takarada, and sirens such as Kumi Mizuno, Mie Hama, and Akiko Wakabayashi, plus a host of character players. They became the faces of Honda's body of work, appearing in both genre and nongenre films. Without exception, they would describe Honda as quiet and even tempered. He rarely coached actors directly about their performance; his direction consisted of subtle course correction rather than instruction.

"Actors have many 'drawers,' with many things inside, and he was good at pulling open the exact drawer he needed each time," said Koji Kajita, Honda's longtime assistant director. "He always suggested what to do, but he never demanded, so he could pull the best out of each actor. I'm sure the actors have no memories of being yelled at or anything like that. That wasn't his way.

"The biggest thing for him was how to maintain the concept that he had for the script," Kajita continued. "He had this concept in his head, and when the filming would start to stray from it, he didn't yell. Instead he very calmly spoke up. It was very firm.

"He had his own style, this way of thinking . . . he never got mad, didn't rush, but he still expressed his thoughts and made it clear when something was different from what he wanted, and he corrected things quietly. He persevered. That was his style. I was with him for seventeen films, and I never saw him get mad. His facial expres-

sion and manner was gentle and calm . . . He was that kind of director . . . He made each film as he wanted, like rolling the actors around in the palm of his hand."

"[Honda] never forced anything on the actors," said actor Hiroshi Koizumi. "If there was something he didn't like or that needed to be changed, he had this soft manner to let us know what he really wanted. He didn't like it when there was a prearranged result . . . he always wanted to discuss things and then decide how to do something."

To those who worked for him, he was Honda-*san*—literally, Mr. Honda; to those who knew him well, he was the more familiar Ino-*san* (derived from *inoshishi*, the first Kanji in his name), or Honda-*kun*. Whether on the film set, out in public, or at home, he treated everyone as equals, just as his mentor Kajiro Yamamoto had taught him.

"Everything I do is based on humanism, or love towards people," Honda would say. "My way of life is all about love towards people. I look at others that way . . . what is their idea of human love? When I make films, it is the same thing . . .

"Making people obey me is not my idea [of directing]. The entire staff understands what we are doing, and they direct all their energy and skill towards the screen. The director should put all those people together . . . that is how a good film [is made]. I really believe that my Honda group had lots of fun, always. When people have fun, they enjoy their work. When they enjoy their work . . . they try their best. I think my workplace was always that way. Maybe each person had personal likes and dislikes each time, but once the camera started rolling, everybody tried their best. There may be some other directors who have a really strong personality and show that through their films . . . That's why all movies come out differently . . . That's the process of creation."[11]

———

Susan Sontag's 1965 essay "The Imagination of Disaster" brought science fiction cinema to the intellectual fore, and was one of the first American writings to critique Honda's body of work in a serious manner. Sontag wrote, "Science fiction films are not about science. They are about disaster, which is one of the oldest subjects of art. In science fiction films disaster is rarely viewed intensively; it is always extensive. It is a matter of quantity and ingenuity. If you will, it is a question of scale. But the scale, particularly in the widescreen color films (of which the ones by the Japanese director Inoshiro [*sic*] Honda and the American director George Pal are technically the most convincing and visually the most exciting), does raise the matter to another level."[12]

In surveying the genre, Sontag identified recurring motifs, citing *Rodan*, *The Mysterians* and *Battle in Outer Space* as displays of "the aesthetics of destruction, with the peculiar beauties to be found in wreaking havoc [that are] the core of a good science fiction film." Sontag also noted themes that Honda's work shares with American genre films of the period: concern about the ethical pursuit of science; radiation casualties and mutations resulting from nuclear testing; moral oversimplification; a "U.N. fantasy" of united international warfare, with science as "the great unifier"; war imagery; and the depiction of mass destruction from an external and impersonal point of view, showing the audience the thrilling awe of cities crumbling but not the death and suffering that result.

Sontag failed, however, to detect the culturally specific subtleties that separate Japanese science fiction films, informed by the atomic bombings, from American ones, influenced by fears of nuclear war with the Soviet Union. Perhaps the lone Western scholar to define this difference was Donald Richie, the distinguished historian of Japanese cinema, who saw *Godzilla*, *Rodan*, et al., not simply as a Cold War–era phenomenon but part of a unique film cycle that expressed the prevailing national attitude regarding the bomb in the 1950s: a lamentation for the tragedy of Hiroshima, an acceptance of its inevitability, and an awareness that the sense of melancholy would pass. Richie identified this feeling as *mono no aware* (roughly translated as "sympathetic sadness").

Richie wrote, "This is the authentic Japanese attitude toward death and disaster . . . which the West has never understood. The bomb, like the war, like death itself, was something over which no one had any control; something which could not be helped; what we mean by an 'act of God.' The Japanese, in moments of stress if not habitually, regard life as the period of complete insecurity that it is; and the truth of this observation is graphically illustrated in a land yearly ravaged by typhoons, a country where the very earth quakes daily. The bomb, at first, was thought of as just another catastrophe in a land already overwhelmed with them."[13]

Richie's analogy helps explain why the arrival of Godzilla, Honda's monster manifestation of the bomb, resembles both a war and one of Japan's extreme weather events; indeed, when it first comes ashore, Godzilla is obscured by a fierce storm. No one questions why the monster attacks Tokyo, though it has no apparent purpose other than destruction, nor why it returns again, just as typhoons predictably hit Japan's capital every summer. It also explains why people respond as they would to a natural disaster. An electrical barrier is built around the city, like sandbags against a flood, and citizens seek safety at high ground, as if fleeing a tsunami. Similarly, Rodan creates a metaphorical hurricane, and the Mysterians cause a giant forest fire and landslide. Sometimes, like a sudden earthquake, Honda's monsters disrupt the humdrum of everyday life: Godzilla's footfalls come while a family idly passes time in the living room, a giant insect bursts into a home and frightens a young mother, or a woman taking a bath spies a giant robot outside the window.

For Honda, the monsters' suggestion of natural disaster was also rooted in things he witnessed on the battlefront. "During the war, the Chinese people did not run away when there was shooting between soldiers near their fields," Honda said. "To them, we were just like a storm. They thought of us as [like] a natural disaster, otherwise they would not have continued living there in such a dangerous place . . . For me, the monsters were like that. Just [like] a natural disaster."[14]

———

"I am responsible for tying Honda to special effects movies," producer Tomoyuki Tanaka once confessed. "If I hadn't, he might have become a director just like [Mikio] Naruse."[15]

Like the respected Naruse, and like all fine directors, Honda made films chronicling his time and place. Postwar Japan was a crucible of social, political, and economic change, as the veneer of Westernization continued to obscure centuries-old culture. Honda's early work followed what scholar Joan Mellen calls "the major theme in Japanese films . . . the struggle between one's duty and the individual desire to be independent and free of traditional values." His protagonists were young people, torn between their parents' ideals and their own, and the conflict often centered on an arranged but unwanted marriage. During the second half of the 1950s, Honda was groomed as a specialist in women's stories, and made a number of films about independent-minded young women and their changing roles at home and at work. Honda's handful of women's films, like Naruse's, question Japan's gender norms and depict female passions and disappointments; but Honda's world is a far more hopeful place, his characters less tragic. Honda had apprenticed with Naruse briefly and admired Naruse's "sturdy rhythm" and talent for "[showing] people's thinking in very special, quiet times." Honda didn't believe he was directly influenced by the melodramatic Naruse style, but acknowledged, "I had the same kind of things in me."[16]

Some of Honda's recurring themes and motifs were evident even before *Godzilla*. For instance, *The Skin of the South* offers images of a natural disaster and the destruction of a town, and presents a scientist as the trustworthy authority in a crisis and a greedy villain exploiter of indigenous people and the environment, two frequent Honda archetypes. From *The Blue Pearl* through *Terror of Mechagodzilla*, his last feature, and many times in between, Honda's drama hinged on a character's sacrificial death, self-inflicted or otherwise, to restore honor, save others from harm, express deep love, or a combination thereof. Japan's beautiful and dangerous seas and mountains served as visual and thematic symbols of nature's power from the very beginning; a mountain boy himself, and an avid hiker, Honda would frequently show a sort of reverence for Japan's majestic bluffs by having his characters trekking uphill, a visual motif reappearing in numerous films. And throughout his filmography, Honda utilized regional locations, culture, and minutiae to enhance authenticity, from local pearl divers and Shinto ceremony dancers in *Godzilla* to the *obon* festival signs written in reverse script, as per regional custom, in *The Mysterians*. Honda's preference for a trio of protagonists—sometimes a love triangle, often just three friends—was also there from the first.

The uneasy postwar Japan-US alliance underlies many of Honda's science fiction films, and while *Godzilla* and especially *Mothra* might be interpreted as somewhat anti-American, Honda was increasingly optimistic about the relationship. In his idealized world, America and the "new Switzerland" of Japan are leaders of a broad, United Nations–based coalition reliant on science and technology to protect mankind. Scientists are highly influential, while politicians are ineffective or invisible. The Japan Self-Defense Forces bravely defend the homeland and employ glorified, high-tech hardware; but military operations often fail, and force alone rarely repels the threat. Assistance comes from monsters, a deus ex machina, or human ingenuity. Honda was also frequently concerned with the dehumanizing effects of technology, greed, or totalitarianism.

Honda relied on his cinematographers and art directors to create the look of his films; thus the noirish style of *Godzilla*, made with a crew borrowed from Mikio Naruse, is completely unlike the larger-than-life look of the sci-fi films shot in color and scope just a few years later by Honda's longtime cameraman Hajime Koizumi. He was less concerned with visual aesthetics than with theme and entertainment. Therefore, in analyzing Honda's work, the authors weight these and other story-related criteria, such as tone, characterization, actors' performances, editing

(under the Toho system, editors executed cuts as instructed by the director), pacing, structure, use of soundtrack music, and so on, more heavily than technique or composition. The magnificent special effects of Eiji Tsuburaya are discussed in this same context; detailed information about Tsuburaya's techniques is available from other sources.[17]

Honda believed in simplicity of theme. "Yama-*san* [Kajiro Yamamoto] always used to say . . . the theme of a story must be something that can be precisely described in three clean sentences," Honda said. "And it must be a story that has a very clear statement to make. [If] you must go on and on explaining who goes where and does what [it] will not be entertaining. This, for me, is a golden rule."

————

Research for this project was conducted over a four-year period and included interviews conducted in Japan with Honda's family and colleagues; archival discovery of documents, including Honda's annotated scripts and other papers, studio memorandums, Japanese newspaper and magazine clippings dating to the 1950s, and other materials; consultation of numerous Japanese- and English-language publications, including scholarly and trade books on film, history, and culture; consulting previously published and unpublished writings by and interviews with Honda; locating and viewing Honda's filmography, including the non–science fiction films, the great majority of which are unavailable commercially; and translation of large volumes of Japanese-language materials into English for study.

Only the original, Japanese-language editions of Honda's films are studied here, as they best represent the director's intent and achievement. As of this writing, all of Honda's science fiction films are commercially available in the United States via one or more home video platforms, in Japanese with English-language subtitles, except for *Half Human, The Human Vapor, Gorath, King Kong vs. Godzilla*, and *King Kong Escapes*. For these films, the authors viewed official Japanese video releases when possible, and the dialogue was translated for research purposes.[18] Honda's dramatic and documentary films were another matter. To date, only three, *Eagle of the Pacific, Farewell Rabaul*, and *Come Marry Me*, have been released on home video in Japan, and no subtitled editions are available. Many others, however, have been broadcast on Japanese cable television over the past decade-plus; and with the assistance of Honda's family and research associate Shinsuke Nakajima, the authors obtained and viewed Honda's entire filmography except for two films, the documentary *Story of a Co-op*, of which there are no known extant elements, and the independent feature *Night School*; in writing about these two films the authors referred to archival materials and published and unpublished synopses. Yuuko Honda-Yun performed the massive undertaking of translating film dialogue for study. (As this book went to press, it was announced that the rarely seen *Night School* would be issued on DVD in Japan in 2017.)

Though none of Honda's non-sci-fi films are currently available in the West, they are analyzed in this volume—admittedly, to an unusual and perhaps unprecedented extent—because they reveal an invaluable and previously impossible picture of the filmmaker and the scope of his abilities and interests, exploring themes and ideas that his genre films often only hint at. And with the advent of streaming media and new channels for distributing foreign films, it seems not unlikely that some of these rare

Honda pictures will appear in the West before long.

One pivotal part of Honda's life that remains mysterious is his period of military service. Honda rarely spoke openly about his experiences, but it is clear that multiple tours of duty and captivity as a POW left psychological scars and informed the antiwar stance of *Godzilla* and other films. "Without that war experience, I don't think I would be who I am," Honda once said. "I would have been so much different had I not experienced it."[19]

Honda had collected his war mementos, such as correspondence, diaries, documents, and artifacts, in a trunk that was locked away for the rest of his life. It was his intention to return to this trunk and assemble the material in a memoir, a task never completed. Sources for the account of Honda's military service in this book were limited to Honda's writings, interviews with family members, and other secondary materials. The Honda family has decided that the contents of the trunk should remain private. A small number of the trunk's materials were shown in a 2013 NHK television documentary and subsequently put on limited public display in a museum exhibit. However, the contents have not been archived and made available for research; thus, it is unknown what further details may eventually come to light about Honda's lost years at war.

————

The book concludes with the first detailed chronicle of Honda's third career phase, in which he reunited and collaborated with Akira Kurosawa. Beginning with the production of *Kagemusha* (1980) through Kurosawa's last film, *Madadayo* (1993), this period was a rejuvenating denouement for both men, a return to the free spirit of their early days as idealistic Toho upstarts, with

Honda rediscovering his love of filmmaking while providing a bedrock of support for "The Emperor," his oldest and closest friend.

It is a little-known fact that Kurosawa once ranked *Godzilla* number thirty-four on his list of one hundred favorite films, higher than acclaimed works by Ozu, Ford, Capra, Hawks, Fellini, Truffaut, Bergman, Antonioni, and others. In doing so, Kurosawa wrote: "Honda-*san* is really an earnest, nice fellow. Imagine . . . what you would do if a monster like Godzilla emerged. Normally one would forget everything, abandon his duty, and simply flee. Wouldn't you? But the [authorities] in this movie properly and sincerely lead people [to safety], don't they? That is typical of Honda-*san*. I love it. Well, he was my best friend. As you know, I am a pretty obstinate and demanding person. Thus, the fact that I never had problems with him was due to his [good-natured] personality."[20]

Honda's story is about a filmmaker whose quietude harbored visions of war and the wrath of Godzilla, whose achievements were largely unrecognized, and whose thrilling world of monsters was both his cross to bear and his enduring triumph.

"It is my regret that I couldn't make a film that I would consider [the greatest] of my life," Honda said. "Each time I did my best, so for that I have no regret. But when I see my films later, there is always a spot where I feel like I should have done it this way, or I should have stood up for myself against the company. I do regret that.

"[However] it was definitely my pleasure that I was able to make something that people can remember . . . If I had not made *Godzilla* or *The Mysterians*, even if I would have received some kind of [critical] prize, it wouldn't be the same. There is nothing like the happiness I get from those things."[21]

NOTES ON THE TEXT

For familiarity and ease of reading, Japanese names are printed in the Western manner, with the subject's given name followed by the surname, e.g., "Ishiro Honda" rather than "Honda Ishiro." Macrons (diacritical marks) are not utilized in the text.

Foreign films are referenced by their official English-language title at the time of this book's publication. This may be different from the title under which a film was originally released in English-language territories. For films with no official English title, a translation of the Japanese title is given.

For Ishiro Honda's films, the original Japanese-language titles and their translations, if different from the English titles, are provided in the filmography following the text. For other films, the English title or translation is followed by the native-language title in parentheses on first reference in the text.

Japanese terms are presented in italics, followed by their English meaning in parentheses. Terms familiar to Western readers, such as anime, kabuki, manga, and samurai, are not italicized.

ISHIRO HONDA

I
DREAMS AND NIGHTMARES
1911–45

Only the dead have seen the end of war.
– George Santayana

Ishiro Honda is running.

Chinese resistance fighters are approaching fast. An ambush. His ears fill with the cacophony of gunfire and the screams of flying bombs. All around him, fellow Japanese soldiers dive for cover.

He is no longer a young man, but his body remains fit from years of marching, walking, hiking, climbing over the hills and through the valleys of China's interior. And he is not ready to die. He has endured too much, made too many sacrifices not to return home. So he runs.

Then it happens. Right in front of him a mortar hits the earth, scattering soil. And in that instant, he knows: within milliseconds, thousands of iron fragments will tear him to shreds.

Time freezes. An eternity. Then, as if a miracle, no explosion comes.

Cheating death, he runs on.

1

A BOY FROM THE MOUNTAINS

Ishiro Honda's birthplace no longer appears on the map. It was a tiny rural mountain village called Asahi, the meaning of which, "morning sun," attests to the vivid natural beauty that appeared with each new day. Asahi was located within the Higashitagawa District of Yamagata Prefecture, a densely forested province of rolling mountains and deep valleys on Japan's main island of Honshu. Spanning 9,300 square kilometers and situated about 375 kilometers north of Tokyo, Yamagata is a world apart, a place of thousand-year-old cedars, ageless shrines, and rich agricultural land. Its abundant, unspoiled wonders have inspired poets, novelists, and artists: the fragrant rainbows of spring foliage; the serenade of cicadas and frogs cascading over rice fields during humid summers; the autumns that turn the mountains into a kaleidoscope of yellows, reds, and oranges; and the snow sparkling under winter moonlight. Located one hundred kilometers northwest of Yamagata City, the provincial capital, Asahi village was home to just a few hundred residents in the early twentieth century, when Honda spent his formative years there; it has since been annexed into Tsuruoka, a modern town of more than one hundred thousand. Indeed, signs of progress are evident throughout the entire region, which today is accessible by car, plane, or bullet train. And yet, it is not so completely different now than it was back then, when people lived off the land, were in harmony with their natural surroundings, and had little contact with the outside world. In this idyllic, remote setting, Ishiro Honda was born on May 7, 1911.

Honda was the fifth and youngest child of Hokan and Miho Honda. He was close to his brothers, Takamoto, Ryokichi, and Ryuzo, and he also had a sister, Tomi, who passed away in childhood. As was tradition, the kanji characters of Honda's given name, Ishiro, indicated his place in the family order. As Honda explained: "'I' stands for *inoshishi*, the boar, the astrological symbol of my birth year. 'Shi' stands for the number four, the fourth son.[1] And 'ro' indicates a boy's name. Literally, it means the fourth son, born in the year of the boar."[2]

Honda's father, like his father before him, was a Buddhist monk at Churen-ji, a temple located on Mount Yudono, the holiest of the three sacred mountains that lord over central Yamagata. This majestic trio, which also includes Mount Gassan and Mount Haguro, is the epicenter of Shugendo, a feudal-era folk religion of mountain worship and extreme ascetic rites. In centuries past, Shugendo's most dedicated practitioners would mummify themselves, a ritual involving a long, slow demise. Today, Churen-ji temple still houses the mummy of Tetsumonkai Shonin, a revered monk who underwent this process in the early 1800s.

Hokan, however, had no such aspirations. He studied more traditional Buddhist teachings and was content with the simple life of a monk. The Hondas lived in a dwelling on temple property with a chestnut grove, rice field, and gardens on the grounds. They grew rice, potatoes, daikon radishes, and carrots, and made and sold *miso* (fermented soybean seasoning) and soy sauce; they also received income from a silk moth farm run by one of Honda's brothers. Hokan earned money during the summers, taking long trips north to Iwate, Akita, and Hokkaido prefectures to sell devotions and visit temples. He would return home before the beginning of winter, when the village might be snowed in. Honda would liken his father to *Koya Hijiri*, lower-caste monks from Mount Koya south of Osaka, traveling peddlers who preached Buddhism across Japan.

Honda remembered his father as "a living Buddha," a gentle soul with a long, white beard and an ever-cheerful disposition. Hokan led by quiet example, rarely lecturing his children and never raising a hand to discipline them, and the boy was strongly influenced by the man's patient, peaceful ways. Later, as a film director, Honda would be described by colleagues as patient almost to a fault, and his hushed assurance was a product of Hokan's serenity and the Japanese cultural qualities of *muga* (selflessness) and *kokoro* (mind and heart). When asked, however, Honda would say he believed his own personality was closer to that of his mother, whom he also remembered as "a very patient person, never scary, and always nice."

———

Honda was born one year before the death of Emperor Meiji, who reigned from 1868 to 1912 and oversaw Japan's transformation from a feudal society under the Shogunate into a modern, highly centralized, Western-style state. During the Meiji era, most every aspect of the nation was reformed: government, politics, military, economy, industry, transportation, agriculture, and education. The formerly isolated Japan embraced ideas from Europe and the United States and became the dominant economic and military power in Asia, victorious in wars against China (1894–95) and Russia (1904–5) and taking Taiwan and Korea as colonies in the process. Many feudal ways were abolished, and a new, Prussian-style education system encouraged the study of science and technology.

Sons followed in their fathers' footsteps, but such customs began fading in the new era. Honda's three brothers received religious tutoring at age sixteen, but Honda never did. "None of us really wanted to take after my father and be a monk," he would recall. "So we started learning about science instead." Hokan did not try to persuade the boys to live monastic lives, instead urging each one to follow his own path. Though hardly well off, the Hondas made sure their sons were educated. Even with the new reforms, compulsory elementary school was just six years; after that, children from poorer backgrounds often worked to help support their families while students of higher economic or social status continued to middle school (roughly equivalent to present-day high school, spanning ages thirteen to eighteen), and then finally to high school, vocational school, college, or military academy. The Hondas were able to send their son Takamoto to medical school and pay half his tuition; the boy worked to pay the rest and became a military doctor afterward.

Asahi was an agricultural village of about thirty families, mostly rice farmers and silk makers. The roads to the nearest town were narrow and treacherous. There was no library or bookstore, and newspapers were rarely available. Takamoto, a product of the new Meiji ideals, encouraged his little brother to study and regularly sent him books and magazines such as *Japanese Boy*, *Boys' Club*, *Kids' Science*, and *Science Visual News*. Thus, Honda developed a lifelong love of reading and a curiosity about things scientific, despite being all but cut off from the quickly modernizing outside world.

Childhood was a time of simple pleasures. With two middle-aged parents—Honda's mother gave birth to him at forty-two—there was little supervision, and Honda played from dawn until dusk. When it was hot, he and his friends would swim in the river or build a dam; when snow fell, they went sledding. Sometimes they played hide-and-seek in the temple, ducking behind the mummy's tomb. There was folk music and dance at village festivals throughout the year, and the Honda brothers all performed with a local youth troupe. Honda was not mischievous, though he once hiked to his cousin's house across the mountain without telling his parents. When he returned days later, his mother was upset—not that he had gone without permission, but that he wasn't dressed properly for the visit.

With his stable and happy home life, Honda didn't develop a strong competitive streak. "I never thought that I had to beat someone else, only that I had to do my personal best," he recalled. "I never gave thought to being on top . . . if someone else did better, I would still think and work at my own pace. I was very stubborn in that regard. [But] once I decided to do something, I just had to do it."[3]

2

TOKYO

The city of Edo was already one of the largest in the world when, in 1868, Emperor Meiji took power and the capital's name was officially changed to Tokyo. Its modernization continued as Western influence increased; and by the early 1900s, the rapid expansion of railroads to the plains beyond the city center gave rise to suburbs, with residential neighborhoods "scattered in the fields and wooded hills around long-established farming villages," according to historian Jordan Sand. These developments became home to people from central Tokyo and, in large numbers, from other parts of Japan.

In 1921 the Hondas uprooted from their tiny village and transplanted themselves to this burgeoning metropolis. Hokan was appointed chief priest at a Buddhist temple in Tokyo, and the family settled in the Takaido neighborhood of the city's Suginami Ward, a fast-growing suburb on the western side. In 1919 Suginami's population was roughly 17,000; by 1926 it would soar to 143,000 as families of modest means moved into newly built homes, displacing the area's rural peasant population.[1]

Honda was in third grade when his life abruptly shifted from the bucolic mountains to the bustling city; he'd never even seen a train before boarding one for Tokyo. Still, he adapted quickly to his new surroundings. When his classmates at Takaido Elementary teased him about his mountain dialect, he took it in stride and learned to speak like a Tokyoite. He'd been an honors student back home; but the city schools were more difficult, and he faltered briefly before his grades rebounded. His favorite subjects were Japanese, history, and geography; and he continued to cultivate a love of the natural sciences, saving his allowance to buy more science magazines.

(Later, in middle school, he would struggle with chemistry, biology, algebra, and other subjects involving equations, but he still liked the scientific mindset.) Despite a drastic change of scenery, many things in his life—family, school, play—were basically the same.

Then he experienced something entirely different. Before Tokyo, Honda had never heard of *eiga* (movies), but one day at school the students were assembled to watch one. Though Honda would forget the title, it was likely one of the Universal Bluebird photoplays, a series of mostly Westerns that were considered minor pictures in the United States, but were extremely popular in Japan from 1916 to 1919.[2] Honda described the film this way: "It was the story of a girl who was kidnapped and raised by Indians. She grew up and found out that she wasn't one of them. There was a dispute over her, who[m] she should live with . . . she got on the back of the horse and went off fighting . . . against her real brother, something like that. I saw it at the schoolgrounds. I still remember that girl, she was a little on the chubby side, not quite pretty, she had long dark hair, sort of looked like an Indian, and there was a situation where she was surprised by being told that she was actually a white person, not Indian . . . That was quite shocking, a machine that projected something like that, and people were moving around in there. I was so interested, and I definitely wanted to see more."[3]

Tokyo offered a multitude of ideal diversions for a "science boy," such as air shows and invention expos, which Honda would sneak off to see all by himself, without his parents' permission. But more and more, he was drawn to the movie houses. By the third and fourth grade he was reading newspaper critiques and asking friends which movies were worth seeing, and begging his big brothers to take him. "If you had the money, you'd just go to the movie theater and watch whatever," he said. "It was that kind of time."

————

Two minutes before noon on Saturday, September 1, 1923, a seismic fault six miles beneath the sea floor off Tokyo unleashed a magnitude 7.9 temblor, mercilessly shaking the Kanto Plain. A forty-foot-high tsunami came ashore and swept away thousands of people, and fires engulfed the city's wooden structures for days. Nearly 140,000 of Tokyo's roughly 2.5 million residents were killed and about half the city was destroyed in the Great Kanto Earthquake, Japan's deadliest natural disaster. Fortunately, the Hondas lived in the low-density western suburbs, where many people survived by escaping to nearby forests and farmland, away from burning debris.

Tokyo's rapid postearthquake reconstruction created a cosmopolitan, urban environment, where leisure activities now included jazz clubs, modern theater, and cinema. Film was by this time known as *daihachi geijutsu* (the eighth art), and its form and content had greatly evolved since Thomas Edison's kinetoscope had arrived in Japan in 1896. The earliest Japanese movies were essentially filmed stage plays that borrowed the conventions of Noh, kabuki, and *Shinpa* (a style of melodrama popular in the late 1800s) and featured stars of the theater. By the 1920s filmmakers were embracing new narrative styles, and their movies ranged from lowbrow sword-fighting adventures to high-minded studies of the human condition. The quake had leveled all but one of Tokyo's studios, resulting in a shortage of domestic movies.

Films were imported from abroad to fill the void, and Japanese audiences and filmmakers were influenced by Western methods, techniques, and stories.

Thus, the first films Honda saw ranged from ninja shorts starring Japan's first movie star, Matsunosuke Onoe (nicknamed "Eyeballs Matsu" for his big, demonstrative eyes) to the German expressionist horror masterpiece *The Cabinet of Dr. Caligari* (*Das cabinet des Dr. Caligari*, 1920). Honda's parents forbade him from going to cinemas alone, but he often did anyway, usually sneaking away to the nearby Nikkatsu theater in the Sangenjaya neighborhood of Setagaya Ward. Japan's silent-movie cinemas, unlike those in the West, did not employ screen titles; instead there were *benshi*, narrators who stood beside the movie screen and provided live running commentary. Some *benshi* were such great orators that they were considered artists, as popular as movie stars. "I was more interested in them than what was happening on screen," Honda later recalled.[4] After spending an afternoon at the cinema, he would often visit the nearby home of a young male cousin, who was blind. Honda recounted each movie for the boy, acting out the story and describing the actors, the action scenes, even the backgrounds and sets; it was his first real experience as a storyteller. Sometimes he'd perform this routine for his father.

One of the *benshi* whom Honda admired was Musei Tokugawa, among the most famous in Tokyo, known for his erudite delivery and for working in finer movie houses where foreign films played. It was at the high-class Musashinokan cinema in Shinjuku, during a showing of F. W. Murnau's *The Last Laugh* (*Der letzte mann*, 1924) narrated by Tokugawa, that young Honda experienced a small epiphany that

helped him begin to understand how films were created. *The Last Laugh* follows an old doorman at a fancy hotel, who is demoted to washroom attendant. Ashamed, the man hides his plight from family and friends, but soon everyone finds out and he is ridiculed. In the surprise happy ending, the doorman inherits a fortune from a hotel patron. Explaining this turn of events to the audience, the *benshi* Tokugawa said the filmmaker, Murnau, had taken pity on the protagonist.

At that, Honda's brother Ryuzo, sitting next to him, remarked, "Wow, I'm really impressed by this director." That word—director, *kantoku*—immediately grabbed Honda's attention. He knew directors were important because their names were prominent in the credits; he enjoyed the comedies of director Yutaka Abe or the action films of directors Yoshiro Tsuji and Minoru Murata, but he didn't know what these people did. He'd always thought movies were made by the actors, but now he began to understand there was someone else offscreen.[5] (The *benshi* Musei Tokugawa would go on to become one of Japan's most famous actors of the 1930s; Honda, perhaps recalling this pivotal childhood moment, years later would choose Tokugawa to narrate his documentary film *Ise-Shima*.)

After his father transferred to another temple, Honda enrolled in Tachibana Elementary School in Kawasaki, just southwest of Tokyo, and then Kogyokusha Junior High School, later a prestigious prep school for the Imperial Japanese Naval Academy. Athletically inclined, he studied kendo and archery and became an accomplished swimmer, but quit the swim team after tearing his Achilles tendon. Around this time, his brother Takamoto completed his service as a military physician and settled

High school portrait, c. 1927.
Courtesy of Honda Film Inc.

Kendo training, late 1920s.
Courtesy of Honda Film Inc.

in Tokyo with plans to open a clinic, hoping Honda would become a dentist and join him there. Honda half-heartedly promised to attend dental college, but soon witnessed something that changed his mind.

One day Honda was walking down a neighborhood street frequently used by filmmakers for location shooting when he saw a crew from Shochiku Kinema Kamata, predecessor of the modern Shochiku Studios. Tadamoto Okubo, mentor of Yasujiro Ozu, was directing action star Goro Morino in a *jidai-geki* (period drama) film.[6] Honda would always remember the scene: Morino stood atop a cliff, threw a rope, and captured the bad guy. Okubo, the man barking out orders, was addressed by a familiar word: *kantoku*. Little by little, Honda's understanding of the filmmaking process was growing. "That was a big deal for me, to see a location shoot," he recalled. "I realized that the true author of the movie is the director. Watching this . . . really made me want to enter the world of cinema."[7]

"The most attractive part of movies was that they engaged entire audiences," Honda later said. "It was not just one-to-one, artist to viewer, like ordinary art before it. For example, you could show paintings in an exhibition, but the experience is personal, one-to-one. Stage plays and concerts play to an audience, but even then, the audience is limited to the venue. Movies play on a much bigger scale . . . and this was when they began to appear before many people."[8]

There was no clear path to a career in film. Formal education in the field was nonexistent. Then, just before graduating high school, Honda learned that the art department of Nihon University (Nihon Daigaku, often abbreviated as "Nichidai") had recently established a film major program. It needed warm bodies; there were no entrance requirements. Instead of dental college, after graduating from middle school, Honda secretly applied to Nihon University and was accepted. Despite the broken promise, and even if Honda was opting for a nontraditional career path in a young, unstable industry, his family was not upset.

"My father never told me [what to do with my life]. My brother was much older, and he told me to do whatever I wanted, but he also said I must be responsible for whatever I chose. Back then, most people looked down on [working in the movie business], but my family was never like that."[9]

"[So] I thought, OK, let me try studying this thing called the cinema. That was when I bet my life on this field," Honda said.[10] As more and more new cinemas were built and traditional theaters were converted into movie houses, young Honda saw Tokyo entering a cinematic boom. "I realized there could be a pretty well paying future for me in the business. It all came together: I enjoyed telling stories and could find work in an industry that was financially successful and artistic to boot."[11]

3

FILM SCHOOL LESSONS

Honda entered Nihon University in 1931 with dreams of a career in the cinematic arts, but he was confronted with some rather unpleasant realities. If he was betting his life on a movie career, the odds didn't look good.

"Nothing [at the school] was well prepared," he remembered. "It was all brand new . . . The classes were not really that good, and there was not enough equipment. There was not even an actual campus . . . they rented space in a nearby school building and held classes there. A lot of the professors were well-known, good teachers, although they canceled classes all the time."[1]

The film department was a pilot program and, as such, it was disorganized and erratically run. The school's administration wasn't fully convinced that film could be taught at a university, thus there were no studio facilities or practical training. Many of the two hundred students in the inaugural class got frustrated and quit.

Still, when class was canceled, Honda had time to visit local cinemas, many in converted kabuki theaters and Buddhist temples (and some still bearing signs of earthquake damage), and there his education continued. He took copious notes on silents such as Edward Sloman's adventure *The Foreign Legion* (1928) and early talkies such as René Clair's classic romantic comedy *Under the Roofs of Paris* (*Sous les toits de Paris*, 1930). He watched Josef von Sternberg's *Morocco* (1930) more than ten times, noting all its cuts and dialogue for further study; the wartime romance between a legionnaire (Gary Cooper) and a cabaret girl (Marlene Dietrich) may have influenced Honda's *Farewell Rabaul* two decades later. He was impressed by Lubitsch's *Broken Lullaby* (1932), admired Frank Capra, and watched as many Charles Chaplin, Harold Lloyd, and Buster Keaton films as he could.

Early on, Honda and four classmates rented a room in Shinbashi, a neighborhood south of Ginza and a few kilometers from the university. It was a place to hang out after school, talk movies, and discuss the latest issue of *Kinema Junpo*, Japan's first journal of film criticism, founded in 1919. Honda hoped the group might collaborate on a screenplay, but mostly they socialized and drank. He also attended an occasional salon of film critics and students, though he rarely participated. "I couldn't pound others with my opinion, so I just quietly listened . . . I was the type of student who didn't stand out at all," he later recalled.[2] Still, even if school was not all he'd hoped, it introduced Honda to Iwao Mori, an executive in charge of production for an upstart studio called Photographic Chemical Laboratories, or PCL. Mori would become an influential figure in Honda's life.

Born in 1899, Mori was a film critic and screenwriter who emerged in the 1920s as a leading advocate for the improvement of Japanese films, which he considered far behind those produced in the West. Mori had entered the movie business in 1926 at Nikkatsu Studios, where he formed the Nikkatsu *Kinyokai* (Friday Party), a think tank of executives, producers, writers, directors, advertising staff, theater operators, and so on. Young and hungry, they discussed how to make better films and run a better operation, and were credited with helping reestablish Nikkatsu's Tokyo studio after the earthquake had crippled it. Mori would become known as an innovator, collecting ideas from his travels to Hollywood and Europe.

Mori taught a class at Nihon University called "Creating Movies," but he was too busy to show up often. His main interest

lay in recruiting young talent for PCL; so in September 1932 he created a new Friday Party with about ten promising students from various colleges, and paid them a small stipend as an incentive to attend. Honda was one of just two Nihon University students accepted. The group also included Senkichi Taniguchi, an ambitious young man who'd just quit Waseda University to join the film industry and who would become Honda's close friend. The group's discussions might focus on critiquing a particular film or on the montage theory of Russian directors Sergei Eisenstein and Vsevolod Pudovkin. Not one to stand out from the crowd, Honda wondered why Mori had included him in the group. Honda later learned that he was recommended by Hiroshi Nakane, a Russian music scholar who had befriended him; Nakane was impressed by Honda's curiosity about classical music and his interest in how music might enhance motion pictures in the coming age of sound film.

PCL was founded in 1929 as a film laboratory, but with the arrival of talkies it began providing state-of-the-art recording services to the big studios. Soon it moved into film production, starting with musical advertising shorts for beer, candy, and record companies. PCL made just two films in 1933, then quickly expanded production and released fifty-one features from 1934 to 1936.[3]

In August 1933, Mori offered entry-level jobs at PCL to a select few members of the Friday Party, including Honda and Taniguchi. It was a tremendous opportunity; industry jobs, even bottom-rung positions, were highly coveted, and it was nigh impossible to get hired without an inside connection. For roughly a year, Honda simultaneously completed his college studies while working at the studio.

PCL's innovative business model, largely Mori's creation, introduced a Hollywood-style, producer-centered system. It was markedly different from other studios, where production was a big bureaucracy run by an executive and built on the star power of famous directors and actors. Instead, PCL emphasized quality filmmaking and the latest technological advances. It abolished the feudal system of lifetime contracts and hired filmmakers, actors, and other personnel on short-term deals that could be renewed or canceled as warranted. Mori put producers in charge of individual projects, leaving directors free to concentrate on the work.

"PCL was just a dream place for young people who were aiming for the movie world," Honda recalled.[4] After some basic training, the young recruits were put on dif-ferent tracks—management, screenwriter, cameraman, sound, and other business and technical areas. Honda became a *jokantoku* (assistant director) trainee, and his first jobs involved working as a scripter in the editing department, which required logging and memorizing every cut, arduous tasks for an absolute beginner. Finally, Honda made his debut on a film set, working at the bottom rung as a third assistant director— or *kachinko* (clapperboard), as they were nicknamed—on director Sotoji Kimura's *The Elderly Commoner's Life Study* (Tadano bonji jinsei benkyo, 1934).

Then, suddenly, good fortune ran out. Immediately after the film was completed, Honda received a red postcard calling on him to serve his country and his emperor. A draft notice.

4

A RELUCTANT
SOLDIER

From the 1890s to the 1920s, Japan was governed under a hybrid system of democracy and imperialism. The British-style constitutional monarchy and the newly established parliamentary system fostered an era of social and economic plurality, which flourished during the reign of Emperor Taisho (1912–26). Simultaneously, a fast-burgeoning military was expanding Japan's reach across Asia, pursuing international influence and economic gains. In 1895, the armed forces counted seventy thousand men; a decade later, in the Russo-Japanese War, it had surpassed one million.

Victory over Russia created a foothold in Manchuria, rich in natural resources such as iron, coking coal, soybeans, salt, and developable land, which was in short supply within the Japanese empire. Factories were opened, and people migrated in search of prosperous new beginnings. In 1906 Japan began work on the massive South Manchuria Railroad, which forged the route for Japanese colonization across the province and fomented the Chinese nationalist resistance to it.

The reign of Emperor Hirohito, known as the Showa period (1926–89) or the "period of enlightened peace," began rather ironically with domestic and international upheavals threatening Japan's delicate balance of liberal democracy and rising military power. The 1929 US stock market crash and ensuing global depression pinched international trade and highlighted Japan's lack of territory and resources compared to the Western powers. The pretext for a full-blown invasion of China was fabricated on September 18, 1931, when Japanese soldiers bombed a railroad they were purportedly guarding, and blamed Chinese nationalists. This staged provocation enabled the Japanese army to invade the northeast provinces of China and Inner Mongolia,

Honda (right) with a fellow army recruit, mid-1930s.
Courtesy of Honda Film Inc.

establishing the puppet state of Manchukuo in February 1932, which became the Empire of Manchukuo (Manshu Teikoku) from 1934 to 1945. Japan's civilian government couldn't stop the generals for fear of a coup d'etat, and Hirohito proved unable to restrain the armed forces. Public euphoria over annexing Manchuria further cemented the military's political power, and condemnation from the West only fed rising nationalism. Thus began the period known as the Fifteen Years' War, encompassing the Manchurian Incident (1931–32), the Second Sino-Japanese War (1937–45), and the Pacific War against the Anglo-American powers (1941–45).

Japan's Kwantung Army in Manchukuo needed able-bodied young men, and so Honda was drafted in the fall of 1934. He was twenty-three years old. "It was only a year after I had entered PCL, and it was the saddest thing for me. I heard some

people drank a whole bottle of soy sauce to raise their blood pressure in order to avoid serving, but I gave up on that."[1]

Honda received an "A" grade on his physical examination, but was not required to report for duty immediately. Several months passed while he waited for his call-up, during which he continued working at PCL. His ascension through the assistant director ranks began, and he had been promoted to second assistant director by the time he worked on *Three Sisters with Maiden Hearts* (1935), a technically sophisticated early talkie from Mikio Naruse, who was emerging as a major talent.

Duty called in January 1935. Honda was enlisted in the *Dai-ichi rentai* (First Division, First Infantry Regiment), which was garrisoned in Tokyo and was one of the oldest divisions of the Imperial Japanese Army. He began his military training at the entry-level rank of *ippeisotsu*, the rough equivalent of petty officer first class. As weeks passed, he endured by focusing on his eventual return to the studio. Tensions were rising in China, but there was no indication yet of massive troop deployments. Honda believed he would complete his service without being sent overseas.

The opposite would prove true. Events far beyond his control would doom him to a long military career.

————

Snow blanketed Tokyo on the morning of February 26, 1936. Just before 5:00 a.m., Lt. Yasuhide Kurihara of the First Division overpowered the sleeping policemen guarding the prime minister's residence. Once inside, Kurihara opened fire—a signal to his comrades outside, who stormed in, guns blazing. A coup was under way, engineered by a rebel faction of young, right-wing army zealots determined to rub out government leaders whose support for the military they considered lacking.

Honda, stationed just a short distance away, was awakened by the shots. Confused, he wondered if the conflict with China had made its way there. Soon the

In China, late 1930s.
Courtesy of Honda Film Inc.

gravity of the situation was apparent: The rebels occupied a square mile of central Tokyo, including the Diet Building. Dubbed the Restoration Army, they railed against the civilian government and invoked Emperor Hirohito to expand Japan's imperial conquest all the way to Russia. Hirohito, in a rare display of authority, instead denounced them. Soon the 2/26 Incident, as it became known, fizzled; its leaders were soon court-martialed. The rebels had killed a handful on their hit list, but they missed the prime minister and other targets.

Honda had no knowledge of the plot, but he could easily have been swept up in it. Kurihara, one of the primary instigators, was Honda's former commanding officer. Sometime before the event, Honda had overheard Kurihara talking to sympathizers about "revolution," though Honda had no idea what it meant. The night before the coup, Kurihara visited Honda's barracks, looking for a machine gun. Honda later recalled that Kurihara had hesitated there—perhaps considering whether to recruit these young soldiers for his nefarious mission—before moving on.

Only a small faction within the First Division had participated, but everyone associated with Kurihara was tainted. Their unit was now considered dangerous; the brass wanted them gone. And so in May 1936 Honda and his regiment were sent to Manchukuo under questionable pretenses, on a mission to track down the leader of a Chinese resistance group who, as it turned out, wasn't in the area.

If not for the 2/26 Incident, Honda would likely have completed his compulsory military service within eighteen months, as was customary. But by the time he came home in March 1937, he had spent two years in the military; and as the war in China escalated, he would be recalled again and again in an apparent series of tacit reprisals against those connected, even tangentially, to the coup.

And yet, even though the revolt had failed and its leaders were duly punished, the violence instilled the fear of further assassinations and terrorist plots. The Diet subsequently increased military spending. The march toward totalitarianism was on.

5

FORGING BONDS

With its progressive acumen, PCL attracted filmmakers more concerned with their craft than with becoming studio power brokers. From 1934 to 1935, several big-name directors left larger, established studios for the young company. Two of these men became dominant figures on the PCL lot: Mikio Naruse, who defected from Shochiku, would develop into one of Japan's most celebrated directors, a master of sophisticated *shomin-geki* (working-class drama) films focusing on the plight of women; and Kajiro Yamamoto, from Nikkatsu, was a skilled technician, whose work would achieve tremendous commercial success. Naruse and his staff were considered the artistic group, while Yamamoto's team was a versatile bunch who developed the type of program pictures that would come to define the studio's brand. Yamamoto had a paternal attitude toward his devoted corps of assistants, a commitment to pass on the craft to the next generation. Bespectacled, handsome, and perpetually well dressed, Yama-*san*, as he was fondly called, became Honda's greatest teacher.

Born in Tokyo in 1902, Yamamoto was unimpressed with early, theater-influenced Japanese cinema, but he was inspired by pioneering director Norimasa Kaeriyama's work, including *The Glow of Life* (*Sei no kagayaki*, 1919), considered revolutionary for its lack of stage conventions and its use of actresses over female impersonators. In 1920 Yamamoto dropped his economics studies at Keio University and joined Nikkatsu's Kyoto studios. For the next few years he wrote screenplays, worked as an assistant director, and acted under the pseudonym Ensuke Hirato. He began directing films in 1924.

Yamamoto had caught Iwao Mori's attention as a member of the old Nikkatsu Friday Party, and Mori lured him over to

PCL in 1934 to direct the first of many films starring Kenichi "Enoken" Enomoto, known as Japan's "king of comedy." Yamamoto was naturally curious and enjoyed genre hopping; he made musicals, melodramas, and later crime thrillers and salaryman comedies. At the height of World War II he would direct several big-budget, nationalist war propaganda films that were highly successful at the box office. His career would last well into the 1960s.

Honda became one of Yama-*san*'s most trusted disciples. From Yama-*san*, Honda learned all aspects of the craft with an emphasis on writing, as Yamamoto stressed that directors must write screenplays. While shooting, Yamamoto often scribbled in a journal, a practice that Honda adopted.

Honda also learned from Yamamoto how to treat his staff. Yama-*san* would throw parties at his home for cast and crew as a way of creating a family atmosphere; when Honda became a director, he would do the same for his charges. Yamamoto had a soft, quiet demeanor and always treated his protégés in equal terms. He called them by name: It was always Honda-*san* or the more familiar Honda-*kun*, never "hey you" or the condescending language other directors often used. He never sent them to buy cigarettes or do menial errands. Years later, Honda would show the same respect to his own crew members.

"He didn't want yes-men around him," Honda recalled. "We always went drinking with him, though. But he was never an autocrat . . . Since [Yamamoto] was so knowledgeable, his stories were always interesting. He was also frank on the set and would ask me to write parts of the script. And then he would use it."[1]

Honda described Yamamoto as a connoisseur. "He was more like a free spirit. He was not like us, he was not all about movies. Movies were only a part of his life. He liked other things too, such as music. So I learned a lot of things from him."[2]

————

Honda's two-year absence had stalled his career, while his peers advanced. His first job upon returning to work was on Yamamoto's two-part drama *A Husband's Chastity* (*Otto no teiso*, 1937). Senkichi Taniguchi, Honda's friend since the Friday Party days, was now Yamamoto's chief assistant director (or first assistant director), while Honda remained a second assistant director. Still, Honda accepted his situation and held no resentment toward the studio or his rank-and-file cohorts.

Released in April 1937, *A Husband's Chastity* marked several milestones. It was a big hit, the first PCL film to turn a profit. It did so despite the refusal of Shochiku, Nikkatsu, and other studios to exhibit PCL movies in their theaters, a retaliation against PCL's practice of hiring away its competitors' actors and directors. For Honda, the film had another significance: it marked his meeting with an intensely ambitious new recruit, a man who would become his lifelong best friend.

The job of assistant director in the Japanese studios was not unlike that in Hollywood: keeping the production schedule, preparing call sheets, maintaining order on the set, and so on. Unlike their American counterparts, however, the Japanese were viewed as directors-in-training. At the time Honda joined PCL, trainees were hired strictly through personal connections, and so there were always too few assistant directors on the lot. In 1936, PCL chose ten prospective assistant directors from the general public for the first time to help bolster the ranks. All the new recruits had degrees from top universities except for one. Akira Kurosawa, at twenty-five, had just a junior-high-school education, but his enthusiasm and knowledge of the visual arts impressed the examiners.[3]

"[We] were placed in a sort of cadet system, like at military schools," remembered Kurosawa. "We had to train in every area, even film printing. We rotated through a series of departments."[4] Only after thorough schooling in camera operation, editing, writing, costumes, props, scheduling, budgeting, and other areas could a trainee ascend from the ranks of third and second assistant to earn the coveted title of first assistant director.

PCL's assistant directors put in long, hard days, worked well into the night, longed for sleep, and put saliva into their weary eyes to help them see clearly. Kurosawa quickly noticed Honda's energy and diligence; he nicknamed his new friend "Honda *mokume no kami*"—Honda, keeper of the grain.

"[Honda] was then second assistant director, but when the set designers were overwhelmed with work, he lent a hand. He would always take care to paint following the grain of the wood on the false pillars and wainscoting, and to put in a grain texture where it was lacking . . . His motive in drawing in the grain was to make Yama-*san*'s work look just that much better. Probably he felt that in order to continue to merit Yama-*san*'s confidence, he had to make this extra effort. The confidence Yama-*san* had in us created this attitude. And of course this attitude carried over into our work."[5]

Born on March 23, 1910, in Tokyo and standing five foot eleven and a half, Kurosawa was a year older and several inches taller than Honda and seemed worldly and larger than life. He was introduced to the cinema by his father, "a strict man of military background" who nevertheless loved movies and believed they had edu-

cational value.[6] Growing up, Kurosawa was exposed to many different types of films, from Japanese silents to the *Zigomar* crime serials to Abel Gance's *The Wheel* (*La Roue*, 1923). While Honda's career was interrupted repeatedly by the war, Kurosawa apprenticed under Yamamoto for five straight years, becoming Yama-*san*'s "other self."

Having just returned from China, Honda had no place of his own. He moved in with Kurosawa, who had a one-room apartment on the second floor of PCL's employee dorm, Musashi-so, located near the studio in the Seijo neighborhood of Tokyo's Setagaya Ward. They were opposites: Kurosawa opinionated and driven, Honda quiet and unassuming.

"Kuro-*san* was like a mentor-friend to me," said Honda. "Even though he was the same age, I felt that way towards him because of his great talent." Kurosawa, a gifted painter from a young age, introduced Honda to the work of calligrapher and artist Tessai Tomioka, an originator of the neotraditional Nihonga style, and other painters he was passionate about. The two friends discussed art and film at great length. And as years passed and Honda would go to and from the battlefront, they discussed the war and Japan's escalating militarism.

"Honda and I agreed that it would be a disaster if Japan won, if the incompetents in the military stayed in power," Kurosawa recalled. "Honda said this too. What we'd most hate was to see those military guys have their own way if we won the war, and drive the country into a deeper mess."[7] Thanks to his father's respected name in the military, Kurosawa was exempted from duty. A draft official generously classified him as physically unfit to serve.

————

On the PCL back lot they were known as the Three Crows: Akira Kurosawa, Senkichi

The three crows—Kurosawa, Honda, and Taniguchi—with mentor Kajiro Yamamoto, late 1930s.
Courtesy of Kurosawa Productions

Taniguchi, and Ishiro Honda, three up-and-coming assistant directors who, as Kajiro Yamamoto's top protégés, commanded a bit of respect. No one remembers how the nickname came about, but they seemed significantly taller than everyone else, a trio of "very handsome fellows" who had "a little different vibe," as a friend remembered. They seemed to be together constantly, during the workday and after hours. Theirs was a close-knit and sometimes tumultuous camaraderie based on shared interests and ambitions.

Each crow was a bird of a different feather. Taniguchi was the youngest, born February 12, 1912, in Tokyo. He wore eyeglasses, was perpetually tan, and was known for his ever-running mouth, sense of humor, and sharp tongue. Yamamoto encouraged his assistants to speak freely,

and Taniguchi didn't hesitate. "Taniguchi was merciless," said Kurosawa. "One day he said, 'Yama-*san*, you're a first-rate screenwriter but a second-rate director.' Yama-*san* just laughed."

Taniguchi served in the war, but his stint was shorter than Honda's and didn't stall his career. "[Honda] had really bad luck," Taniguchi said in 1999. "He was drafted when he was young, and just at a time when he could have learned so much about making movies."[8]

Kurosawa was the most volatile among them, complex and opinionated and uncompromising. When he first arrived at PCL, Kurosawa had no place of his own so he'd crashed on Taniguchi's futon, but Taniguchi grew annoyed and kicked him out. Honda was the quiet and contemplative one, not nearly as aggressive. As Kurosawa biographer Stuart Galbraith IV writes: "They called one another by nicknames after the Kanji characters in their family names: 'Kuro-*chan*' ('Blackie'), 'Sen-*chan*' ('Dear Sen,' ironic, given his temperament), and 'Ino-*chan*' ('Piggy')."[9]

They drank, talked, and argued, and in between films they would camp in the mountains for several days. Honda, the Yamagata boy and soldier, was an able hiker, as was Taniguchi. Their trips invariably began peacefully but ended with Kurosawa and Taniguchi arguing incessantly, with Honda playing peacemaker.

Each man took what he learned from Yama-*san* and forged his own path. Kurosawa became a relentless pursuer of perfection. Taniguchi would make a number of notably ambitious early films, including the first adaptation of Yukio Mishima's *The Sound of the Waves* (*Shiosai*, 1954)—a film that created a sensation for hints of erotic nudity[10]—then finished his career with a series of mainstream programmers. Honda most closely emulated his mentor's example by becoming a versatile maker of successful program pictures and putting his heart and soul into those that mattered most to him. The friendships endured long after their early struggles. While Honda went to war, Kurosawa would help his wife care for their children, and much later Kurosawa would make Honda his most trusted adviser. Taniguchi would be like an uncle to Honda's kids; and years later, when Honda later bought a bigger house in Okamoto, a neighborhood in the western part of Tokyo's Setagaya Ward, Taniguchi and his third wife, actress Kaoru Yachigusa, star of Honda's *The Human Vapor*, liked it so much they built a home nearby.

———

In the mid-1930s, with PCL struggling financially, founder Yasuji Uemura had sold a controlling interest in the studio to Ichizo Kobayashi, a railroad executive, real estate tycoon, and the entertainment mogul behind the legendary Takarazuka Grand Theater and its famous all-girl music and dance revue. Kobayashi also owned a chain of cinemas, and acquiring PCL was part of his strategy to supply his movie houses with product. Together with studio chief Iwao Mori, Kobayashi also aimed to shake up the business, building on PCL's innovative model to create Japan's most modern film company.

On August 27, 1937, Kobayashi merged PCL with another small production outfit to form Toho Motion Picture Distribution Company, later the Toho Motion Picture Company.[11] According to film critic Jinshi Fujii, "Toho's entrance into the film business caused the structural reorganization of the Japanese film industry . . . [S]trict budgetary control was put into practice, the producer system was set up, and vertical integration of production, distribution, and exhibition was achieved . . . [T]he Hollywood-style system was transplanted to Japan almost completely." Before long, observers would note that Toho had also "[overwhelmed] other companies in terms of film technology . . . [it] imported new filmmaking equipment from America four or five years [earlier]."[12]

For Honda and Kurosawa, the excitement of working at the upstart new studio was tempered by long hours and a meager salary of ¥28 per month.[13] Assistant directors were paid less than office workers because, with location pay and other incentives, it was possible to earn much more, though it rarely worked out that way. Their social life revolved around drinking, and if Yama-*san* wasn't buying, they drank on credit. Often there was no cash in their pay envelopes, only receipts for vouchers redeemed at the studio commissary and IOUs collected by local bars and clothing stores. On payday, they were already broke.

The dormitory where Honda roomed with Kurosawa had a pool table, an organ, and other diversions. When Honda, Kurosawa, and their friends weren't hitting the bars, they would congregate there, often in Kurosawa's little room, drinking and discussing art and cinema. This group included Sojiro Motoki, a future producer who would play an important part in the careers of both Honda and Kurosawa, and a pretty editor's assistant named Kimi Yamazaki.

Kimi was six years younger than Honda, born January 6, 1917, in Mizukaido, Ibaraki Prefecture, the youngest of eight children. She was different from other women her age; she could hold her own in serious film discussions with the boys and hold her liquor when the beer and sake were poured. Kimi was self-confident and assertive, a modern Japanese woman intent on being more than an office lady or salesclerk, the typical woman's jobs then.

It was *Morocco*, the film that Honda had spent so much time studying, that compelled Kimi to join the industry. She worked briefly for a small newsreel outfit, then passed Toho's entrance exam and became assistant to Koichi Iwashita, one of Japanese cinema's most respected editors. One day, Honda stopped by the editing room to say hello, and Iwashita introduced the young assistant director to his new employee. Sparks didn't fly right away, though. "I still remember how he was wearing this weird looking suit," Kimi recalled. "He was unfashionable, so unpolished, just back from the war. Compared to guys like Kuro-*san* then, he was hardly dashing."

After she was promoted to the position of "script girl," Kimi worked late hours on movie sets. Commuting from her parents' home was impractical, so she moved into the dorm and became Kurosawa and Honda's neighbor. The boys grew so accustomed to her presence that if she didn't show up for their nightly klatch, one of them would rap on her door. One night, Kimi begged off with a severe headache, and Honda went to fetch some medicine. "This was the first time I thought, 'Wow, he is such a nice guy.' But it wasn't like I was head over heels . . . As time passed, I got to know everyone [in the dormitory]. . . . But I think I was most attracted to his warmth, his heart."

Honda immersed himself in his job, working on more than a dozen films between 1937 and 1939 and slowly ascending the ladder. Though Yamamoto was his primary teacher, he also apprenticed under other prominent studio directors, studying their work styles and habits. Honda was an assistant director on *Humanity and Paper Balloons* (*Ninjo kami fusen*, 1937), an acclaimed early *jidai-geki* and the last film by director Sadao Yamanaka, a fellow army recruit who would die as a soldier in China the following year. Honda also worked for the *jidai-geki* specialist Eisuke Takizawa. Sometimes, Honda would visit the set of a Mikio Naruse production to observe the celebrated director at work, which led Naruse to tap Honda as third assistant on two acclaimed early pictures, *Avalanche* (*Nadare*, 1937) and *Tsuruhachi and Tsurujiro* (*Tsuruhachi Tsurujiro*, 1938).

————

Summer 1937: Honda and Senkichi Taniguchi, having been there from the founding days of PCL, were now the two longest tenured assistant directors on the lot. Taniguchi had been Yamamoto's chief assistant for about a year, but he now was transferred to a front office job, using his knowledge of production to help curb expenditures. Needing a new chief assistant, Yamamoto boldly promoted Kurosawa, a third assistant director with only about a year on the job, catapulting him over Honda and others with more experience. Beginning with the drama *The Beautiful Hawk* (*Utsukushiki taka*, 1937), Kurosawa was Yamamoto's right-hand man, a role he would thrive in.[14]

Honda, meanwhile, continued his Sisyphean progress and was finally promoted to first assistant director, a bit ironically, on Takeshi Sato's *Chocolate and Soldiers* (*Chocolate to heitai*, 1938). An early example of the war propaganda films supported by the government, it told the story of a small-town man drafted and sent to China, leaving behind his wife and child.[15]

"[When] I came back from the front, everyone's position had changed," Honda said. "I was the second or third assistant director for the longest time. But after all, I think it worked out better for me." He was now among the most experienced first assistants on the lot. "I just wanted to be by the camera. That is what I liked."[16]

———

As illustrated by his friendships, Honda gravitated toward people much different from himself, and this seems to explain his unusual bond with Kimi. "She was very energetic, and her personality could be completely different from me," he once remarked. "Maybe that is why we got along so well."[17] Friends thought they were mismatched; Kurosawa called them "total opposites."

The two were spending more and more time together. Kimi earned more than Honda did, so when they went out, she would often buy the drinks. Though they didn't work on the same film often and seldom saw one another during the day, they walked to the studio together each morning and joined their regular crowd in the evening. This routine had continued for more than a year when, one morning, Honda and Kimi were standing on the Fujimi Bridge, a small pedestrian overpass in Seijo that, on cloudless days, offered breathtaking views of Mount Fuji and the Tanzawa Mountains to the west. Honda asked, matter-of-factly, "Want to get married with me?"

"Everybody was just friends back then," Kimi said. "I had no idea he viewed me as more than just that. I was so surprised when he asked me. But I recall feeling really warm when I was with him, and I never got sick of being around him. I wondered what he saw in me. I was pretty naïve, simple, and innocent. So I said, 'Sure, OK.' Just like that."

In proposing, Honda was breaking with tradition once again. The great majority of marriages were customarily arranged by a go-between, acting on the parents' behalf, who screened prospective partners for compatibility based on family reputation, income, profession, education, and other factors.[18] Those who deigned to choose a spouse against their parents' wishes might be shunned. Kimi's mother, Kin Yamazaki, supported the couple's engagement but, perhaps unsurprisingly, her father was strongly opposed. Heishichi Yamazaki was a wealthy and conservative landowner in Ibaraki, north of Tokyo; it would be unacceptable for his daughter to marry a country boy with unclear prospects for gainful employment in a new, unproven industry. Kimi stood firm on her wishes, and her father stood equally firm, responding simply, "Suit yourself." With those words, Heishichi denied the couple the financial support they so desperately needed. Once Kimi quit her job, as was customary for new wives, the pair would have to survive on Honda's meager salary. Honda's more unconventional family, by contrast, congratulated the couple. Takamoto wrote to Kimi, "No matter what others say, believe in each other and live with confidence."

Honda was twenty-seven years old, Kimi twenty-two. On their wedding day in March 1939, they filed papers at city hall, paid their respects at Meiji Shrine, and went home. It was so uneventful that, years later, neither one could recall the precise date. There was no ceremony, celebration, or honeymoon. With little money, the pair moved into a tiny, one-room apartment with a shared bathroom.

Before long Kimi was pregnant, complicating the newlyweds' financial struggles. Although Kimi's father would never openly approve of the marriage, the news of a grandchild on the way caused Heishichi to quietly relent; and he sent her a bank book with a ¥1,000 balance, a then sizeable gift. "His head clerk came to give it to me, saying, 'This is from the master,'" Kimi remembered. "My mother expressed her love in a very kind manner, but [my father's] love was more from afar." Each month Heishichi would send money to Kimi, enabling the couple to move into a small rented house on the south side of Seijo, about five minutes from the studio, where they would start their family.

It was a happy time, but short-lived.

6

WAR

I always thought that when this thing is over, I am going to go back to the studio and make movies . . . It helped me not to go insane.

– Ishiro Honda

In mid-December 1939, a week before the baby was due, Honda received a shock: he was recalled to active duty.

In the years since Honda had entered the military, Japan had widened the China conflict on multiple fronts against Chiang Kai-Shek's National Revolutionary Army and Mao-tse Tung's Communists. In July 1937, the Marco Polo Bridge Incident, another staged provocation, became the pretext for a massive troop escalation and the plunge into total war. Then came the occupation of Shanghai, China's largest city; and in December 1937 the Japanese began the six-week-long Nanking Massacre, in which three hundred thousand Chinese soldiers and civilians were slaughtered and raped, one of the most notorious war crime sprees of the twentieth century.

Despite these brutal campaigns, by the end of 1937 there was no end in sight to the conflict. More than six hundred thousand Japanese soldiers were now spread across an area roughly equivalent to the United States west of the Mississippi. The men were weakened by exhaustion and heavy casualties, and many were due to return home. To replace these losses, the army doubled the draft beginning in 1938 and called up tens of thousands of reserves, mostly men in their twenties and thirties with wives, children, and jobs. Some men were so upset that they openly rebelled, only to be severely punished.[1]

Honda, just shy of twenty-nine, shared the resentment but was not one to complain. Protesting would only make his situation worse. "If I were to . . . show my anti-war feelings, then I am sure I would not have survived, not even a day," he would recall.[2]

"My father was the type of person who [thought], 'It is what it is,'" said Honda's son, Ryuji Honda. "'This is my fate. So, what else can I do but to follow orders and do it?' He did, however, have the conviction that he would return alive and make movies."

After Honda's latest draft notice arrived, Kimi's mother congratulated her daughter. It was an honor to have a husband or son at the front, and there was no greater purpose than to fight and die for one's country. Nationalism reigned, and propaganda fueled support for the war. Neighborhood associations and the Special Higher Police kept tabs on the citizenry. The media and schools became indoctrination tools against Western ideals of individuality and materialism. War was a righteous struggle against colonialism; Japan would soon lead a new world order with its superior values, which derived from the cult of the divine emperor as head of the nation-family, the absolute authority.

Kimi gave birth to a daughter on December 23, 1939. Honda had rejoined his regiment for training, but he now had risen in rank and was allowed to visit his wife in the hospital. The baby was premature, tiny and covered with hair; Honda thought she looked like a baby bird. Kimi remembered, "My mother scolded him, saying that he'll be cursed for saying such a thing, and that she will grow up to be a beautiful child." Honda named the girl Takako. He left the hospital and was bound for China.

———

"There were so many [soldiers] who hated war," Honda later wrote. "I was one of them, but I kept my thoughts deep inside my chest, to myself, and every time I received [a draft notice], I [convinced] myself that I was not going to die. Why should that stupid red piece of paper decide the freedom or lives of individuals? Why couldn't I just rip this paper to shreds?"[3]

Honda's belief that he would survive

helped him suppress fear, and it wasn't entirely irrational. When bullets were exchanged, he noticed that few connected. He had become an excellent marksman, and he knew how difficult it was to hit the target in a firefight, with thousands of rounds discharging rapidly and tensions high. The chances of being hit were slim, he told himself. He would listen to the reports of gunfire, and if the bullets whizzed through the air, that meant the enemy didn't have a clear shot; but if he heard the pop of bullets hitting nearby trees, then it was time to move. By keeping vigilant, he could live through this. Most soldiers died, he observed, not from gunshots but from disease.

He would defend himself if threatened, but Honda felt no animus toward the Chinese. "He said, 'Everyone, shoot your guns into the air,'" recalled Koji Kajita, later Honda's longtime assistant and a fellow veteran. "'Why must we kill one another?' he wondered. His long years in the military helped make him the person he was."

With extended periods of inactivity and the doldrums of daily routine, boredom reigned. Soldiers looked forward to the doling out of liquor and cigarette rations, a reprieve from the monotony. Honda developed a taste for sake and became a heavy smoker, a habit he would maintain well into his fifties, though he would eventually quit. By middle age, his fingertips would be brown with permanent tobacco stains.

———

From 1940 to 1941 Honda was assigned to help manage a comfort station, a euphemism for the hundreds of brothels the Imperial Army established in China and the occupied territories. As the Roman Empire had done in its far-flung conquests, Japan provided its soldiers with prostitutes, purportedly to curb sexual assaults on civilians, which were widespread in Shanghai, Nanking, and other places. The first documented comfort stations opened in Manchukuo in 1931–32; and by 1938 an estimated forty thousand *ianfu* ("comfort women") were working and living in often deplorable conditions there, cut off from their families and made to perform sex acts dozens of times per day. The great majority were Korean women, though there were also Chinese, Japanese, and other nationalities, many lured with promises of ordinary jobs and then taken into slavery. One of the darkest aspects of Japan's war legacy, the subject has been dramatized in a few books and movies, notably Seijun Suzuki's *Story of a Prostitute* (*Shunpu den*, 1965) and Kei Kumai's *Sandakan 8* (*Sandakan hachiban-shokan bokyo*, 1974). The comfort women have long been a controversial subject in Japan, where conservative politicians have maintained there is no evidence the women were forcibly enslaved. Relations between Tokyo and Seoul were strained for decades over the issue, and in December 2015 the Japanese government extended a formal apology to South Korea and made an $8.3 million reparations payment.

Honda, then, deserves some credit for writing *Reflections of an Officer in Charge of Comfort Women*, an uncharacteristically candid essay published in *Movie Art* magazine in April 1966, in which he described both his duties at the comfort station and the plight of the women working there.

"[L]istening to their complaints and stories was [part of] my job. Once a week [the prostitutes] had a checkup, and I would sign off on their health documents. At that time, they would tell me things—their complaints, their personal stories. Some girls had been told that they would be doing a kind of consulting job; the reason they accepted was because they [believed] they would be [merely] consoling the soldiers. I couldn't do anything to help them but I told them my story, that being here was also not my choice. Getting the [draft notice] with my name on it, that's the only reason I was there. They [began to understand] they were not the only ones, that the men also were forced to do things. When they would return [to the brothel], they could accept their situation a little better."

Honda recalled tragic stories: a girl who had been sold into prostitution by her parents; a prostitute who had hitchhiked for five days through a war zone in order to find a soldier she'd fallen in love with, only to be rejected; the women's lost dreams of marriage, family, and happiness. And he told of the emotional and physical toll they endured:

"[T]hey sent us a report every day. 'Umeko: 12 soldiers; 2 junior officers; 3 senior officers.' That was the number of men that this one girl serviced in a day . . . Whenever the army would move, whether to the war front or the rear lines, the street with all the [brothels] was like a festival. The next day, my daily report would say that some girls took as many as 30 or 40 men in one night. One girl from Manchuria, a little over 30 years old, told me, 'Back then, I took more than 83 . . . that was the number I could remember up to. After that, I fainted. I don't know how many there were after that.' Whenever a new girl arrived they would come to see us at headquarters. There were some really pretty ones, but after a half year, they all looked like a different person . . . The girls [clung] to their dreams of the future [to survive]. No matter how dirty they felt physically, they tried to stay mentally clean."

Honda recalled one distraught woman who turned to drugs in order to cope and serviced as many soldiers as possible in order to support her habit. "[She] was completely destroyed by this war. War is evil. Once it starts, no one can stop it."

_____

The atrocities in China resulted from the indoctrination and brutal training of Japanese soldiers, which intensified as the country plunged into World War II. The Bushido code, the "way of the warrior" practiced by the chivalrous samurai, was now corrupted into "victory by any means." Honorable rules of war no longer applied. Hatred of the enemy and cruel discipline reigned. Recruits were taught that the Chinese, a people Japan had long revered, were now a nation of subhuman weaklings, easily and justly conquered. War required ruthless killing, and not even civilians were to be spared. Officers became so authoritarian that soldiers learned to hate them. Troops were beaten, cursed, and humiliated at the slightest hint of insubordination. Surrender was not an option. Death was an honor. No less than absolute loyalty to the emperor, commander-in-chief of the military, was expected.[4]

Honda recorded the madness in his journals. "My superior officer killed a young Korean today with his bayonet," he once wrote. Another entry read, "I'm trying to adjust to the environment around me, but if you are a normal person in this place you'd either kill yourself or go crazy."

He hated the way superiors shouted at their subordinates, and especially how they struck them as punishment. "I could not agree with that at all. I tried to avoid getting hit as much as possible . . . I myself never struck anyone."[5] Somehow he salvaged his humanity. He vowed to treat the Chinese, his fellow soldiers, and himself humanely. He was now a low-level officer, participating in the basic training of new arrivals. He taught them the fundamentals: how to line up, how to salute. Most important, he taught them about survival. When you run, run to live. Respect your body; stay healthy. The alternatives were to get shot and die or get sick and die.

He cooked, cleaned, polished shoes, and distributed uniforms and name tags to new recruits, always burying his bitterness, knowing he'd suffer if it showed. He was, he said, "not a professional military person," uninterested in getting promoted through the ranks. He simply worked hard because it was his nature and focused on the task before him rather than dwell on his situation. "I didn't like the war, but that didn't mean you should do a mediocre job," he would say.[6] Kimi wrote daily, and he stayed grounded by reading her letters and writing back. With the exception of one furlough home, this dangerous and dull routine lasted three years. Losing the prime of his life was tortuous, what with a young daughter growing up and a career that might be slipping away.

At the time he was recalled to active duty, Honda had been working on Kajiro Yamamoto's *Horse* (*Uma*), the story of a poor farm girl (Hideko Takamine) and her relationship with a colt she raises from birth. In order to depict the changing seasons, Yamamoto spent two years completing the film, and it was during this time that Akira Kurosawa's stock rose rapidly at Toho. When Yamamoto had to return to Tokyo to begin another project, he left Kurosawa in charge of *Horse*, supervising a lengthy location shoot in northeast Japan.[7] Released in March 1941, *Horse* was a major box-office hit in Japan and the occupied territories—Honda would see it while away at the front—and Toho subsequently made Kurosawa a director, a promotion that followed Satsuo Yamamoto, Tadashi Imai, and a few other assistant directors, all of whom had, like Kurosawa, arrived at the studio after Honda.

In a letter dated August 29, 1942, Kurosawa told Honda the news: "I'm going to direct a film in October. [I'll] write the original story, the screenplay, and direct. Even if things go wrong, there won't be anybody to complain to but myself." Kurosawa expressed sympathy for his friend at the front and wished him well. Honda pressed on, convinced his time would eventually come.

————

Japan's runaway militarism led to a government takeover of the film industry. Censorship was enforced during the invasion of China, but the passage of the Motion Picture Law in 1939, modeled after Nazi policy, brought more severe authoritarian controls. Scripts and films were reviewed to ensure they supported the war effort; filmmakers and studios deemed noncompliant could be punished by firing, harassment, or worse. Under this framework, the government and the army subsidized the industry. Toho was considered the most compliant of the studios—the Information Bureau's offices were located in a theater owned by studio founder Ichizo Kobayashi—and so the company greatly benefited from wartime policies.[8]

Honda returned to Tokyo in December 1942, but now the war was inescapable, even at the studio. Kajiro Yamamoto's latest film, *The War at Sea from Hawaii to Malaya* (*Hawai mare oki kaisen*, 1942), was a big-budget, docudrama-style propaganda piece glorifying the Pearl Harbor attack and commemorating its first anniversary. Made with government support and featuring Japan's most ambitious special-effects work to date, the film was the year's biggest box-office hit, and Toho claimed it was seen by one hundred million people in Japan

and the wartime territories.[9] Its popularity launched a slate of war movies exalting the military. Thus, Honda spent much of 1943 working as first assistant on Yamamoto's follow-up project, *Col. Kato's Flying Falcons* (*Kato hayabusa sento-tai*, 1944), a biopic of World War II ace aviator Tateo Kato (Susumu Fujita). It was a lengthy production, and Honda oversaw major action sequences with two captured US P-40 fighters, shot on location at a military aviation school. More significant, though, was Honda's first meeting with Eiji Tsuburaya, the technician hailed as "the god of special effects" for his convincing re-creation of the Pearl Harbor attack, which was credited with making *The War at Sea from Hawaii to Malaya* such a success.[10]

It was an inauspicious encounter, portending nothing of their eventual partnership. Honda, in his usual hands-on fashion, was prepping a scene wherein a squadron of model fighters would fly over a bank of clouds made of white cotton. When Tsuburaya inspected the shot, he complained to Yamamoto about it. "I could tell Eiji was not happy with the width of the stage, the cloud material, or the method used to operate the model [plane]," Honda wrote in 1983. "I could not help feeling like a failure, but Yamamoto was very reassuring and helped smooth my feelings."[11]

He also settled back into family life. On January 31, 1944, Kimi gave birth to a son, Ryuji. But the war's shadow still loomed. Now Japan was fighting America. Shortages of food and supplies were common. The military was overextended by its conquest of Asia, which now encircled a vast area from the Indian Ocean to the South Pacific. The fighting was bloody; warm bodies were needed. Soldiers in their thirties and forties were pressed into service again.

In March 1944, another draft card

was delivered. Kimi was in the kitchen making doughnuts, a dessert treat recently imported to Japan from the West. The Hondas didn't have a telephone, so she used a neighbor's phone to call her husband at Toho. "He smelled such pleasant sweetness as he came home, that when he found out the news, he thought it was a cruel joke."

This time, the unflappable Honda was rattled. "The third time that I got called up, I felt it really was not fair," he said. "I thought maybe if I just ripped it up, I would not have to go."[12]

His family said good-bye at the train station. It was snowing, but Honda wore short sleeves. His unit was headed for the Philippines.

"Honda-*san* now had small children, so it must have been so hard for him to go," related Koji Kajita. "[But] to not show your emotions on your face was the rule. It was a great national ethos, the good military trait of the time . . . One had to experience it back then in order to understand. You didn't question, you just followed completely what you were directed to do. The times were different, and the education was different."

————

His troop missed the boat. Later, he would learn that it never reached its destination. Somewhere between Taiwan and Manila it was sunk, killing all aboard. Other regiments of the First Division arrived safely in the Philippines, only to die there. In October 1944 many fought in the horrific Battle of Leyte Gulf, the largest naval battle of World War II, by some criteria the largest naval battle in history, which killed more than twelve thousand Japanese soldiers.

Instead, Honda went to China yet again. It was a fortunate break, as the conflict there had reached a stalemate and was now far less intense than in the Pacific and

Southeast Asia. He spent most of the next two years in and around the city of Hankou, which is now part of Wuhan, capital of the central province of Hubei. Situated on the north side of the Yangtze River where it meets the Han River, it was a beautiful place, and Honda's familiarity with Chinese customs and culture made him comfortable dealing with the people there. Honda was now a *gunso* (sergeant), and his job involved communicating and trading with civilians.

Still, even though fighting had subsided in the area, the Chinese continued to live in a state of war, "with a mixture of terror and resignation" and memories of the early days of Japan's occupation, when soldiers might shoot civilians without provocation.[13] Honda would recount that, because the Chinese feared and hated the "oriental devils" occupying their country, he tried to demonstrate that not all Japanese were cruel. When he and his fellow troops entered a village, they would dress in Chinese clothing and be on their best behavior. "We [bought] vegetables and supplies from the Chinese people," he remembered. "We had to interact with them. I never ordered them around as a Japanese soldier . . . I would pay what I was supposed to and I tried to talk to them with the small amount of Chinese that I knew."[14]

Japan launched its final major offensive in China in 1944, conquering parts of Henan and Hunan provinces in the interior. But Chinese forces would not surrender; and with its military resources now heavily overextended on multiple fronts, Japan's presence in China was severely weakened. The Chinese National Revolutionary Army began seizing lands from the Imperial Army and capturing Japanese troops. Honda was relocated to an area between Beijing and Shanghai; and although the exact place is unknown, it was somewhere along the Yangtze River south of Shanghai that Honda was taken prisoner about one year before the war's end.[15]

Imperial soldiers had been taught that being a prisoner of war was "so shameful that it was equivalent to forfeiting one's citizenship," according to historian Ulrich Straus. The Japanese government "had made it absolutely clear that they were to fight to their last breath, and when they could no longer fight, they were to commit suicide."[16] Many prisoners who did not die faced hellish conditions, especially those taken by Russia, which invaded Manchuria in August 1945 and overran weakened Japanese forces in China and northern Korea. More than a half million Japanese soldiers were shipped to work camps in Mongolia and the Soviet tundra, where they endured years of captivity, hard labor, malnutrition, and disease. About sixty thousand prisoners died; many killed themselves, or tried to. Honda was fortunate, for POWs in China fared far better than did those taken by America and Russia. By comparison, the Chinese "treated their 1.2 million Japanese POWs with kid gloves."[17]

Many Japanese soldiers have recounted their experiences as POWs. Honda, in his typical fashion, said little, only that he was treated well. Japan's occupation forces in China formally surrendered on September 9, 1945, one week after Japan had surrendered to Allied forces.[18] That December, the American-led occupation governing postwar Japan began sending ships to retrieve demobilized Japanese troops and POWs from China and South Seas outposts, with priority given to the sick and wounded. Seven months would elapse between the war's end and Honda's release and repatriation; while he waited, he was assigned to help manage the turn-over of Japanese supplies and equipment to Chinese authorities. During this time he was befriended by local officials and temple monks, and posed for pictures with children. As Honda would later tell Kimi, the Chinese came to accept him; and he developed a bond with friends there, a bond strong enough that he was invited to remain permanently, and he gave it serious consideration. He had lost contact with home for more than a year and didn't know if his family had survived, if the studio was still standing, or how he would be treated as an ex-POW. He wondered if there was a life for him in Japan anymore.

"The Chinese told him, 'Don't bother going back to your defeated nation. We will take care of you and your troops, so stay here,'" recalled Kimi. "But he said, 'I have a wife and children, so I will go back just once, to see if they are still there or not. If not, I will return.' Even as a POW, he became friends with the locals."

When Honda left for home, the local villagers gave him several beautiful rubbings of Chinese proverbs, imprinted from stone carvings of sacred temples, as a parting gift. He would cherish them, and when he became a film director, he often wrote the verses on the back of his scripts. His favorite one, roughly translated, was,

Read good books
Say kind words
Do good deeds
Be a good person

Honda would never set foot on Chinese soil again.

————

Honda served three tours of duty totaling more than six years at the front and more than one year stationed in Japan for training. But the record of his service—dates, locations, combat, casualties, captivity—

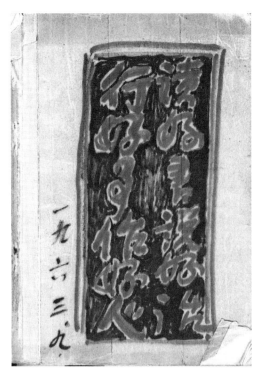

Chinese proverb written on one of Honda's scripts.
Courtesy of Honda Film Inc.

did not detonate; a random misfire spared his life. Later, when the fighting subsided, Honda went back to the site of the skirmish, retrieved the shell, and eventually brought it home to Japan, carrying its more than twenty pounds of iron among his belongings. He would keep it forever; in his later years, the unexploded bomb sat atop his desk in his private study, remaining there until his death.

The images of combat and destruction that would appear in his films were, in a sense, Honda's only real catharsis. Like so many veterans, he took his demons to the grave.

Even as an old man, "He was still awakened by horrible nightmares two or three times each year," Kimi recalled. "He'd see all of his friends in his dreams, all of those who died fighting, all standing in a line.

"The horror of war was with him until he died."

is impossible to reconstruct in precise detail because of the loss and destruction of wartime documents and the unavailability of Honda's war journals. That Honda was reluctant to discuss his war experiences during his lifetime makes the task doubly difficult.

And so it is not known exactly where and when, but during Honda's final tour he escaped certain death in a firefight with Chinese resistance fighters, somewhere near Hankou. In the chaos of soldiers fleeing and bombs hailing, an enemy shell hit the dirt in front of him. At that moment he believed it was all over, but the mortar

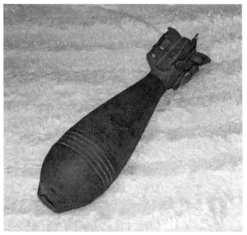

The unexploded shell.
Courtesy of Ed Godziszewski

II
AWAKENINGS
1946–54

There are two types of people in Tohoku [the northeastern region of Honshu, Japan's largest island]. One is like Kurosawa-*kun*. He's the type who challenges the natural order.[1] On the other hand, Honda-*kun* fits himself into the natural order. That's why Kurosawa-*kun*'s films are always about battles, relationships, love, human feelings, and so on, but what Honda-*kun* wants to show in his movies is . . . harmony in the relationship between nature and man.
— Kajiro Yamamoto

7

STARTING OVER

Honda's letters from the front stopped arriving sometime in 1944. Months passed without word of his fate, and Kimi feared the worst. And she feared for her family's safety. In June 1944, American B-29 planes launched from offshore carriers began leveling vast swaths of Tokyo with incendiary bombs, indiscriminately targeting neighborhoods and industrial zones. By 1945 there were hundreds of attacks, almost unceasing.

About half of Tokyo's population fled to the city's outskirts or the countryside to escape the onslaught.[2] Kimi joined the exodus, taking Takako and baby Ryuji to the safety of her parents' home for an extended visit. Before long, though, her father told her: "It would be awful if [Honda] came home and nobody was there. He is not yet dead. Go back to Seijo."

Food, provisions, and money were scarce in the war's waning days, but friends from the studio lent a hand. "Those who were part of Ino-*san*'s group were my friends too; we also worked together," she said. "So if someone got a chicken leg, they would bring some over for me to share. Someone was always looking out for me."

On May 21, 1945, Kimi received a visit from Akira Kurosawa. It wasn't unusual for Kurosawa to stop by—with Honda away for so long, Kurosawa regularly checked in on Kimi and the children—but this was a special occasion, the day of his wedding to the actress Yoko Yaguchi. Kimi regretted she had no wedding gift to offer, but given the dire living conditions of the day, no gift was expected. Instead, Kurosawa asked Kimi if she would make a hot bath for him so he could be presentable for the ceremony. Fire logs for the bath were hard to come by, so Kimi asked Kurosawa not to drain the tub so she could bathe baby Ryuji afterward.

"We were given two bottles of beer a

month as part of our rations," Kimi remembered. "I had one bottle left, so I put it on the table for Kuro-*san*. I told him to please drink it as a token of my congratulations. I left him alone, and took Ryuji into the bath with me. When I came out, I found half a bottle of beer left, with the cap back on, along with a note saying, 'Thank you, Kimi-*san*. Please enjoy the remainder yourself and celebrate for me.'"

————

Though Kimi wasn't alone, it was impossible to forget her husband's absence now that Japan was literally under siege.

"We always carried our babies on our backs because if the sirens went off, we would have to take cover," she said. "In the corner of our backyard was a small hole, which the gardener had dug for us. That was our bomb shelter. Towards the end, it was so bad that we were able to see bombs go off in the air and come falling down from over the Fujimi Bridge."

When air-raid sirens blared, Kimi and the children would hide for fifteen or thirty minutes, until the all clear. After a while, though, Takako could no longer stand the heat and the damp smell of dirt. Kimi remembered, "We had to go in and out of the shelter many times during the middle of the night. Finally, Takako said, 'Mommy, I don't care if we die. Can we please just get out of here? I hate it.' I said to myself, 'This must be destiny.' And from then on, we never went back into the shelter."

In terms of human life and property lost, the devastation wrought upon Tokyo from November 1944 to August 1945 was even greater than what Little Boy did to Hiroshima. Nearly two hundred thousand people were killed or deemed missing, one million injured, and one million homeless, with roughly half of all residential structures destroyed.[3] The suburb of

Seijo, though located miles from the city center, did not go completely unscathed, as some homes were damaged or destroyed by burning debris. Still, most of the area, including Toho Studios and the Honda residence not far away, was spared the sea of flames.

More time passed. News came of defeat at the Battle of Okinawa, of the Russian invasion of Manchuria, and of the destruction at Hiroshima and then Nagasaki. Finally, at noon on August 15, 1945, Emperor Hirohito addressed the nation via radio, announcing Japan's unconditional surrender. Two weeks later, Gen. Douglas MacArthur arrived and quickly established the Occupation government's seat of power, the general headquarters of the Supreme Commander of the Allied Powers, known as GHQ or SCAP. Soon, American officials, businessmen, press, and others connected with the Occupation, along with their families, moved into Tokyo neighborhoods. MacArthur ordered them not to eat the scarce Japanese food. The Japanese, having sacrificed all for the war effort, were now literally starving. Food shortages would last for years.

"After the war ended, I was tending to the field on the side of the road one day and a Black American soldier passed by," Kimi said. "He asked what I was doing. I had baby Ryuji on my back as I was working in the field. With my poor English, I just managed to put a few words together. I said that my husband was still [in China] and has yet to come home, so I am raising vegetables for us to eat.

"He had a [woman] with him. I went home, and that evening the doorbell rang. She said, 'This is from the soldier you saw this afternoon,' and gave me chewing gum and chocolate, wrapped up with a ribbon. At that moment I felt, 'Our countries were at war, but the people are really not.' That visit made me teary."

Kimi still didn't know if Honda had been killed in action, or if he would ever come home. Hundreds of thousands of troops were returning from China and other war fronts, but there was no word of his fate. "Since Allied governments had sent the Japanese [authorities] lists of POWs they held, it would have been possible to assuage the fears of the POWs' relatives," notes historian Ulrich Strauss. However, the authorities "failed to take such action . . . [they] remained under the mistaken impression that notification that their next of kin was a prisoner would not be welcomed, despite the vastly changed circumstances after the war's end."

All Kimi could do was wait, resigned to the likelihood that Honda had died.

"It's unthinkable now. He was like Urashima Taro—no news, no nothing," she remembered.[4] "Not knowing whether someone is alive or dead is really hard for those waiting for their return. Whenever I saw a shooting star, I thought, 'Oh, maybe he just died.' Or when I heard a rooster crow, I'd think, 'Maybe just now.' Frankly, I thought it would be easier if he really had died. I was in my twenties, young enough to start life over and recover emotionally. But to carry this heavy concern with me, every single day, it was unbearable. But once I'd wake up in the morning, the children were there, so we'd try to be upbeat, sing songs, eat sweet potatoes, and carry on.

"One evening, I was washing the dishes in the kitchen and I heard the front door open. Takako ran to see who it was, and didn't come back for a while. I assumed it was the local store guy who always delivered food when the rations came in. I asked, 'Ta-*chan* [Takako], who is it?' But she didn't say a word. Then Ryuji crawled

over to the front door, and I heard him start to cry, really loudly. Surprised, I ran to see what was going on and saw a very gaunt soldier standing there, malnourished. That was Dad.

"To this day, I don't know why I did this. I had waited so long for my husband, wondering where he was and if he was still alive. If I were an American, I guess I would have jumped into his arms with a big hug. But instead, I started stacking logs to prepare a hot bath for him. Thinking back now, I wonder what sort of emotions I was going through. I guess I wanted to clean him up and make him feel comfortable. Along with the smoke from the bath fire came many tears, flowing for the first time. I was then able to finally say to him, 'Welcome home.'"

————

For many Japanese soldiers, the return from the front was the last circle of hell. Demoralized and defeated, some bearing battle wounds or carrying diseases, the men spent weeks or even months at demobilization centers in China and the South Pacific, sleeping in cold, makeshift shelters as they awaited passage home. They were cramped together onto ships, often with insufficient food and drinking water for the journey and poor hygienic facilities. They slept in cramped bunks or on the floor, riding out the hunger and the stench, wondering what fate awaited back home. How would the Americans treat them? Would they be arrested and charged with war crimes? Were their homes still standing? Were their wives and children alive, or had they been killed by the firebombs? Had they been misinformed by the government—as many families of POWs were—that the soldier had died a "glorious death?" After landing in Japan, the men were given money for a train ticket home and rations for a few days' travel. Those who were POWs exchanged their prison garb for old Japanese military uniforms, which many would wear for months because no other clothing was available.[5] Like so much about his war experience, Honda never discussed this chapter of his story in detail.

He arrived home in March 1946. At nearly thirty-five years old, he was eager to start his life over.

————

The most remarkable aspect of the Honda-Kurosawa friendship may have been their diametrically opposed personality types, which would seem utterly incompatible yet proved the opposite. And there was no clearer illustration of their temperamental differences than each man's response to the aftermath of a holocaust.

As a child, Kurosawa walked through the ruins of the Great Kanto Earthquake with his brother, which was "a terrifying experience for me, and also an extremely important one," he recalled. In his auto-biography, Kurosawa wrote viscerally, movingly about the episode: "Amid this expanse of nauseating redness lay every kind of corpse imaginable. I saw corpses charred black, half-burned corpses, corpses in gutters, corpses floating in rivers, corpses piled up on bridges, corpses blocking off a whole street at an intersec-tion, and every manner of death possible to human beings . . . Even if I had tried to close my eyes, that scene had imprinted itself permanently onto the backs of my eyelids."

The stoic, quiet Honda, by contrast, wit-nessed firsthand the damage caused by the atomic bomb at Hiroshima and yet never once described the experience in any detail, though in interviews with writers and journalists he would cite his visit to ground zero as an inspiration for the antiwar

subtext of *Godzilla*. This event, probably the most oft-repeated story about Honda's life, has become something of a minor legend, largely because of Honda's reticence. It's not difficult to imagine a young Honda, rail thin and still wearing a soldier's uniform, wandering the burned-out streets and being deeply moved.

The actual circumstances of Honda's visit to Hiroshima were less dramatic, though equally important. Honda learned of the atomic bombings of Hiroshima and Nagasaki while being held captive in China. About seven months later he was aboard a train streaking home toward Tokyo. It passed through Hiroshima, stopped briefly at the station less than a kilometer from the city center, and then moved on.

Honda observed the city's ruins from the window of a passenger car. That is, he observed what little he could view. He recalled, "They had boarded up the area, put a fence around it, so I really couldn't see much of anything."[6]

Over time, Honda said almost nothing more about the experience, not to his wife, family, or colleagues. One might conclude this silence was the result of emotional trauma, though there is no evidence that glimpsing Hiroshima's ashes was more traumatic than the horrors witnessed during his years in China. The cumulative toll of fighting a war he was not passionate about, being separated from his family, losing prime years of his life and career, and returning to an utterly defeated country had tested Honda's will to survive. Through it all, he was motivated by the desire to work.

"The eight years I spent at war . . . helped me grow as a director," he said.[7] "The war, meeting the people of the continent with whom we were fighting, the relationships

I established with them, their daily lives. I experienced all of that, as a human being . . . These things made me grow tremendously. I lived and survived only by thinking, 'When can I go home? When can I make movies again?'"

———————

Shortly after his arrival, he developed a horrible fever, a symptom of malaria. The military had given soldiers departing from China a supply of Atabrine tablets, a medication to treat the mosquito-borne disease, which was rampant in POW camps and spread rapidly on the overcrowded boats sailing home. Honda was laid up in bed for a short time, but once ambulatory he had only one destination in mind.

To the studio. Back to work.

He was eager to return. He had no bitterness about the years lost, no envy toward fellow rookies who had become directors while he struggled just to maintain a footing in the industry between tours of duty. No regret that he had spent more time on the battlefield than the back lot. All through the war, he was focused on this moment.

When he had returned to Tokyo in between tours, friends and colleagues urged him to quit the film industry, which many considered a frivolous line of work. *Make yourself useful. Do something good for the country. Get a job at a war plant,* they said. *You're getting older. You will probably never get a chance to become a director, so find another career.* But he was resolute. On those lonely nights in China, he chased away doubts by recalling the musical sound of the camera rolling, the intoxicating scent of film stock, and the joy of sitting in a cinema, looking up at the big screen. *This is what I live for.*

At the Toho Studios gate, the guard stopped him: "Who are you?"

It was an abrupt reminder of how much time had passed and how far behind Honda had fallen. He kept his spirits, but others were concerned about him. Kajiro Yamamoto, ever the father figure, made arrangements for Honda to work in Toho's administrative offices. With a university degree, a rare commodity then, the company will give you a secure career, Yamamoto told him. Honda needed a week to mull it over. "He always liked to take a week to think things through," Kimi remembered. "But after much thinking, he said, 'No, I do not want to leave the film studio, even if it means I starve.' From that point, we went through a deep pit of hardship for a while."

The film industry was in disarray. Work was infrequent and pay remained low. Kimi worried that the pressure might be too much, so she decided to put a firewall around her husband as best she could. "I thought, 'This man has lost eight precious years, his peak years. What can I do to help him compensate for this lost time?' He suddenly returned to a country that lost everything, had nothing. I decided to never bother him about materialistic or financial matters. And this lasted until the end of his life." As in most traditional Japanese families, the wife supervised the family budget, but from this point forward Honda would never have to concern himself whatsoever with matters of money—whether or not, as his career ebbed and flowed, he had much of it. Kimi would eventually also serve as Honda's de facto agent and negotiator, handling all contractual matters with his employer.

"Around this time, my motherly instincts towards him grew greater than my feeling for him as a wife, [and] I became focused on trying to care for him," Kimi said, adding with a laugh, "I also thought to myself, 'We shall never fight from this point forward.' But that particular feeling didn't last forever."

————

The "deep pit of hardship" that Kimi remembered affected all Japanese. Many cities and towns were destroyed, including the factories where men and women worked and the neighborhoods where they lived. Roads, buildings, and bridges were demolished, and there was insufficient water and electricity. Shortages of food and commodities were extreme, worsened by a population explosion as soldiers returned home and the birth rate rose. Millions were homeless and jobless, with vagrants and criminals in the streets. The economy was in shambles, inflation was severe and rapid.

In light of the economic and social devastation, Japan's eventual recovery would be remarkably swift, but the first years were painful.

Still, the movie industry was in relatively good shape immediately after the war, with Toho atop the heap. Its production facilities in Setagaya were intact, and though a good number of theaters were shelled, many were open for business even if there were seats missing and holes in the roof. Amid the strife, movies offered a relatively affordable form of escapism, and "Toho was the healthiest of any of the companies and was naturally very pleased with itself," according to historians Joseph Anderson and Donald Richie.[8] "Pride, however, was but a preliminary to the fall."

8

ALLEGIANCES AND ALLIANCES

Toho wasn't the same place that Honda had left behind. The studio was entering a period of transition, and over the next six years it would rapidly fall from first place to last in the industry, nearly self-destructing more than once before finally righting itself. Within this chaotic environment, Honda would attempt to restart his career.

SCAP authorities, as part of their efforts to rehabilitate Japan into a representative democracy, encouraged new labor laws giving trade unions unprecedented power. An unintended result was that communists dominated the unions in many industries, including the film studios. Inside Toho's gates, Honda met not only artists and craftsmen making movies, but also union organizers leading a revolt. In a cruel twist of fate, Toho—after reaping the rewards of making right-wing war films—was now home to ardent leftists. Fights between anticommunists in management and left-wing unionists left directors, actors, and other talent caught in the crossfire, their work increasingly difficult.

Occupation policy shifted from liberalism and economic aid immediately after the war to anticommunism after 1947, and employers began taking back control of the means of production, leading to confrontations with unions. Three film studios remained standing after the war: Toho, Daiei, and Shochiku. All experienced labor unrest, but the three strikes that hit Toho were the most devastating. The first two, in March and October 1946, ended with pay increases for workers and the transfer of production oversight to union bosses, who dictated hiring, firing, wages, and other matters. This, in turn, fomented friction between union leadership and the employees. Splinter factions formed; and in April 1947 most of Toho's top stars and many rank-and-file directors and actors left to form Shin Toho (New Toho), a separate production unit that was semi-independent of the parent company, although continued conflict with Toho management would eventually lead Shin Toho to become a truly independent studio. Toho, meanwhile, would slowly replenish its hemorrhaging talent pool through periodic New Face contests, auditioning would-be actors and actresses from the general public; the great Toshiro Mifune was discovered this way, but it would take years to rebuild the depleted star system.

Under union control, mismanagement reigned and costs soared. Toho made only thirteen films in 1947; the company had originally projected twenty-four. The board of directors appointed a new president, dedicated anticommunist Tetsuzo Watanabe, who summarily purged twelve hundred employees for resisting his cost-cutting measures. In retaliation, in April 1948 the union staged the third Toho strike, one of the biggest work stoppages of Japan's turbulent postwar labor movement. Union members barricaded themselves inside the studio, and management responded by withholding pay. A months-long stalemate culminated in August, when two thousand Tokyo police assembled outside the studio walls, augmented by American soldiers, tanks, and planes circling above; an actress and union activist would famously quip, "The only thing they didn't send were the battleships." The strikers surrendered, but Toho would not fully restart production and repair its shattered reputation until the early 1950s.

———

After reentering Toho's assistant director corps, Honda worked on two pictures in 1946. Honda's longtime friend and fellow Yamamoto protégé Motoyoshi Oda's *Eleven Girl Students* (*Juichinin no jogakusei*),

starring Takashi Shimura, had eleven fifth-grade girls confronting a corrupt school principal. Kunio Watanabe's *Declaration of Love* (*Ai no sengen*), starring Ken Uehara, was a postwar soap opera set in devastated Tokyo, involving three girls laid off from a wartime munitions factory, who pair up with repatriated soldiers.

But as Toho split apart, filmmakers, actors, and other employees were forming alliances and taking sides. Experienced directors leaving the fold encouraged young talent to follow. Kunio Watanabe, who had made his directorial debut during the war years and would go on to become a prolific maker of program pictures in the 1950s and 1960s, was among those departing for Shin Toho; and he strongly urged Honda to do the same, saying he would become a full-fledged director more quickly in the new company. But Honda demurred. He preferred to remain neutral; his commitment was not to a political ideology but to the cause of filmmaking, not to Toho's union or management but to what he felt the company itself represented.

"[Watanabe] told me, 'Honda-*san*, we can't get along with these people who are always trying to push their own agendas and going on strike,'" Honda remembered. "'Why don't you move over to Shin Toho?' I answered, 'Watanabe-*san*, I can't do that. To begin with, I don't think it's right for Toho to separate, and I hope there is a better way to solve this problem without splitting up . . . I just want to stay.'" Others tried and failed to lure Honda away, including the acclaimed director Kon Ichikawa. Despite Honda's resistance, he and his colleagues remained friends. "It wasn't personal or anything. We were still fine with each other."[1]

With production slowing, in 1947 Honda worked on just three Toho films, all of which reflected Japan's postwar malaise, the dominant theme. Though still an assistant director, Honda was now working with producers, actors, and others who would figure prominently in his own directorial career a few years later. The first project was *24 Hours in an Underground Market* (*Chikagai 24-jikan*), jointly directed by Tadashi Imai, Hideo Sekigawa, and Kiyoshi Kusuda, produced by Tomoyuki Tanaka, and starring Takashi Shimura and So Yamamura. The other films were a pair of comedies directed by Kajiro Yamamoto that were big box-office hits: *The New Age of Fools* (*Shin baka jidai*), parts 1 and 2. Set in a Tokyo black market, a hotbed of illegal goods and postwar crime, these films followed a peddler (comedian Kenichi "Enoken" Enomoto) who is comically chased through the streets by a chubby cop (Roppa Furukawa).[2] Still, work was becoming less frequent. If Honda wanted to remain employed and continue pursuing a directing career, he would have to join the exodus from Toho. Fortunately, trusted friends provided a path.

Akira Kurosawa never had a comfortable relationship with the union. When labor had first overtaken the studio, it had pushed him, along with Kajiro Yamamoto and Hideo Sekigawa, to codirect the left-wing propaganda film *Those Who Make Tomorrow* (*Asu o tsukuru hitobito*, 1946), a story of movie studio employees who become labor activists. The union dictated the content, which infuriated everyone; Kurosawa so disliked the picture he later disowned it. The same year, the union forced Kurosawa to rewrite his screenplay for *No Regrets for Our Youth* (*Waga seishun ni kuinashi*, 1946). Kurosawa remained at

Toho as long as he could; but after battling the union again over his *Drunken Angel* script, enough was enough.

Prior to the third Toho strike, Kurosawa defected to the Film Art Association, an independent production company formed by producer Sojiro Motoki and Kajiro Yamamoto. This collective boasted fourteen directors as founding members—including four of Toho's biggest: Kurosawa, Yamamoto, Senkichi Taniguchi, and Mikio Naruse—and six producers, including Tomoyuki Tanaka, later a major figure in the careers of both Honda and Kurosawa. The company's films would be coproduced with the major studios; it aspired to create high-quality work while retaining artistic autonomy.

Honda was first assistant director on a handful of Film Art Association productions over the next few years, while also keeping one foot in the struggling Toho camp. From September to October 1948, Honda was on location in Noto Peninsula on the Sea of Japan, working on Kajiro Yamamoto's *Child of the Wind* (*Kaze no ko*, 1949). The first Film Art Association release, it followed the struggles of a poverty-stricken family, who plant potatoes to survive after the father is drafted into the war. Next, from January to March 1949, Honda worked on Yamamoto's *Flirtation in Spring* (*Haru no tawamure*, 1949), an adaptation of French playwright Marcel Pagnol's *Marius*, about a boy torn between his desire to sail around the world or to stay and marry his sweetheart.

Now one of the most experienced assistant directors in Japan, and with his stature having risen considerably, at last Honda would receive an opportunity to make a film of his own.

9

THE DOCUMENTARIES

Ise-Shima (1949),
Story of a Co-op (1950)

The events leading to Honda's debut as a feature filmmaker in 1951 have previously been difficult to trace because of the lack of official records and the fading memories of those involved. Archival records of the national Film Classification and Rating Committee (Eiga Rinri Kanri Iinkai, or EIRIN), however, provide a clearer timeline of Honda's career progression and help correct long-held assumptions and misinformation regarding the sequence in which certain projects were made, and even the title of one of Honda's earliest films.[1]

Honda's first opportunity to direct came from Toho, though not from the company's near-moribund feature film studio but its Educational Film Division, which produced *bunka eiga* (cultural films). In the 1930s the Toho Educational Film Division and its subsidiary, the Toho National Policy Film Association, had made numerous war propaganda documentaries to stir the nation's fighting spirit, a concept borrowed from the *Kulturfilms* produced by UFA for Nazi Germany. After the war, *bunka eiga* evolved into documentary short subjects about Japanese life, focusing on topics such as agriculture, sports, arts, and tourism. The films were funded by outside backers and shown mainly in schools. Toho sometimes used these productions as proving grounds for assistant directors due for promotion.

In April 1949, Honda began shooting the documentary short film *Ise-Shima*, a highlight reel of the cultural attractions of Ise-Shima National Park in eastern Mie Prefecture. The park is a popular coastal sightseeing destination and home to the Ise Grand Shrine, considered the most sacred Shinto shrine in Japan; the film was commissioned by local officials shortly after the area's designation as a national park, to promote tourism. In a span of twenty minutes, *Ise-Shima* gives a brief history of the shrine, the local people, and the economy. It also looks at the workings of a pearl farm, where gems are harvested from the sea in large quantities.

Honda's *Ise-Shima* is notable for Japan's first successful attempt at underwater motion picture photography, an innovation that was a source of great pride for the new director. The region is well known for the *ama*, female divers who harvest pearls and abalone from the ocean; and from the moment he agreed to make the film, Honda knew he must shoot the divers in their element. Previous attempts at underwater photography were limited to pointing a camera lens into the water from a boat, or other crude methods. Honda wanted to follow the divers into the depths, moving the camera freely beneath the surface; and he spent seven to eight months developing a device to accomplish this feat.[2]

Honda turned to a camera technician colleague, who designed and built an airtight, waterproof, metal-and-glass housing for a compact thirty-five-millimeter camera (possibly an Eyemo or Parvo, portable cameras then popular with newsreel photographers). Two cameramen are credited on the film, Kiyoe Kawamura and Kuniichi Ushiyama, though it is unclear who shot the underwater sequences. As a safety precaution, professional divers assisted the camera crew during the shoot.

Honda's original plan called for a more elaborate apparatus. Blueprints were drawn for a small, submarinelike craft enabling a cameraman to descend underwater, but that project was apparently canceled because of cost and safety concerns. In the end, the available technology was more than adequate for the task, however. An extended sequence shows the grace and beauty of the female divers as they descend, in relatively long takes, into the depths of the bay to collect *noshi awabi* (stretched abalone), the beautiful shells of which, according to local custom, are brought to Ise Grand Shrine each year as an offering.

Honda greatly admired the work of trailblazing documentary filmmaker Robert Flaherty, particularly *Man of Aran* (1934), a beautifully rugged chronicle of the lives of fishermen in the remote, dangerously primitive Aran Islands off the coast of Ireland. Flaherty's views of craggy seaside cliffs and rocky shorelines, and his story of simple people struggling against the elements to survive, evidently influenced not only Honda's approach to *Ise-Shima* but also later works such as *The Blue Pearl* and *The Skin of the South*. (Flaherty's 1922 film *Nanook of the North*, about the indigenous people of northern Quebec, was also among Honda's favorites; its influence is similarly detectable in Honda's *Half Human*.) Even though *Ise-Shima* is a travelogue rather than the work of an embedded documentarian, it bears glimpses of Honda's affinity for a simpler way of life. The centerpiece of *Ise-Shima* is a brief history of the Ise Grand Shrine. According to legend, the great sun goddess Amaterasu chose this shrine as her final resting place. During feudal times, the movements and travel of the common people were severely regulated through a system of travel permits and barriers, called *sekisho*; these are depicted in Kurosawa's *The Men Who Tread on the Tiger's Tail* (*Tora no o wo fumu otokotachi*, 1945; released 1952). People who believed in the shrine's powers would make pilgrimages from all over Japan, defying travel restrictions, just to pray there. Today, about six million Japanese visit the shrine annually. Honda's film illustrates this history through a series of historical woodblock paintings, and also tours the grounds of the shrine, capturing the structure's beauty.

Though not a commercial film, *Ise-Shima* appears to have netted returns for Toho. Honda recalled that a European distributor had come to Japan looking for documentaries, seeking something "extraordinary." Honda showed the man *Ise-Shima*, starting the projector at the scenes of divers plunging underwater. Honda would recall that the distributor was instantly hooked, and *Ise-Shima* was eventually exhibited in multiple European territories, though details of this are lost. The film was rarely seen again until it reappeared on Japanese cable television in 2003, paired with *Japan and Her Imperial Way* (*Kodo Nippon*, 1940), a wartime propaganda documentary glorifying the emperor, directed and shot by Eiji Tsuburaya.

Honda had hoped the technical achievement of *Ise-Shima* would spark interest in underwater photography. "The fact that *Ise-Shima* got sold opened up my way to theatrical features. And, since we made this equipment to shoot underwater, I really wanted to use it again," he said.[3]

———

Honda completed *Ise-Shima* in July 1949, according to EIRIN records. He then pivoted back to the Film Art Association where, for the first time since the war, he would work beside Kurosawa. But if Honda had once had seniority over his good friend, now the roles were reversed. Honda was a fledgling director with one documentary short to his credit; Kurosawa was about to direct his ninth feature, *Stray Dog* (*Nora inu*, 1949), with shooting taking place in Tokyo from July to September 1949. The film was coproduced by the Film Art Association and Shin Toho, and Kurosawa staffed key crew positions with unemployed Toho staffers. He named Honda his chief assistant director.

An early Kurosawa masterpiece, *Stray Dog* follows young police detective Murakami (Toshiro Mifune), whose service revolver is pickpocketed on a crowded bus and used in a series of crimes. The guilt-ridden policeman becomes obsessed with finding the culprit and goes deep into Tokyo's seedy underbelly. As many critics have observed, the film is a near-flawless document of the tension, desperation, poverty, and crime of postwar Japan.

"I had Honda do mainly second-unit shooting," Kurosawa wrote in *Something Like an Autobiography*. "Every day I told him what I wanted and he would go out into the ruins of postwar Tokyo to film it. There are few men as honest and reliable as Honda. He faithfully brought back exactly the footage I requested, so almost everything he shot was used in the final cut of the film. I'm often told that I captured the atmosphere of postwar Japan very well in *Stray Dog*, and if so, I owe a great deal of that success to Honda."

After the war, black-market districts dominated by *yakuza* gangsters, petty criminals, and hardscrabble types had arisen near train stations in Asakusa, Shibuya, Shinjuku, Ueno, and other parts of Tokyo. In search of his gun, Mifune's detective combs these backstreets; but rather than try to re-create the black market on a set, Kurosawa sent Honda and cameraman Kazuo Yamada to Ueno, where they spent about a week filming documentary-style footage of crowd scenes and daily activity, unscripted and without actors.

Honda recalled, "Even newsreel cameramen could not shoot there because of [threats of violence]." In these sequences, Mifune's detective poses as a soldier returning from the front. To blend into the throng, he wears "demobilization fatigues" issued by the military. For shots of Murakami wandering through the black market, viewed from behind or from the waist down, Honda body-doubled for Mifune, wearing an identical wardrobe. As noted in the documentary *Akira Kurosawa: It Is Wonderful to Create* (2002), "Since [Honda] had actually served as a soldier, he was a valuable adviser to Kurosawa, who had never served in the military, and Honda looked the part in a soldier's uniform." Honda and Yamada also went to Ginza to film one of *Stray Dog*'s most recognizable shots, rays of sunlight filtering through a rattan screen, a brilliant visualization of the brutal summer swelter.

Honda and Yamada captured the required footage but not without incident. "Yamada-*kun* put a hand-held camera in a box and followed me around," Honda would recall. "The first five or six shots went fine, but as I was about to enter the side street [of the black market] from Yamashita Park, somebody said, 'Here he comes,' and a man blocked my path. He showed me his [*yakuza*] tattoo. The boy who said, 'Here he comes,' had apparently seen Yamada and me conferring. The man was not frightening at all. He said that he was desperately trying to survive. When I gave him some of my lunch, he seemed impressed. 'White rice!' he said."[4]

Honda had no reservations about taking a secondary position to Kurosawa. "I was Kuro-*san*'s assistant director for *Stray Dog*, but to me it was just two people who were friends, who . . . had the same passion for filmmaking, so the [title] of director or assistant director did not have any meaning to me."[5] Four decades later, Honda would film similar second-unit sequences for Kurosawa's *Rhapsody in August* (1991), capturing a crowded, hot summer in the city of Nagasaki; and he would make essentially the same remarks about their collaborative relationship.

————

Following *Stray Dog*, Honda's stock had risen such that he was subsequently credited as "adviser to the director" on two Film Art Association projects directed by his mentor Kajiro Yamamoto. In early 1950 Honda was busy with *Escape from Prison* (*Datsugoku*, 1950), which starred Toshiro Mifune in a love triangle involving two ne'er-do-wells and the beautiful owner of an *oden* (fish cake stew) stand, played by Mieko Takamine. Later that year, he worked on Yamamoto's *Elegy* (*Aika*, 1951), one of the last Film Art Association projects, featuring Ken Uehara as a classical music composer who falls in with cabaret performers and prostitutes.

In between these films, Honda began preproduction on a drama for Toho titled *Newspaper Kid* (*Shimbun kozo*), which would have marked his feature film directorial debut had it not, for unknown reasons, been canceled. Based on an original story by esteemed novelist Tomoji Abe, whose works often espoused antimilitarist, pro-humanist views, *Newspaper Kid* told the story of Isamu, a sixth-grader living in a provincial town where "the most beautiful castle in Japan" is located. Isamu's family is poor, so he earns money delivering the local paper and doing chores in the newsroom. The editor gives Isamu an assignment to hang out with a group of orphans who shine shoes for money, to collect their stories for an article, and he is immersed in a world of street kids, gangsters, and black market criminals. His friends include a rich boy whose father owns a big factory, and a poor orphan who is cared for by a temple monk. One night, the gangsters break into the factory. The orphan boy is mistakenly accused, and Isamu helps clear his friend's name. The story ends with the kids running a marathon around the castle, and a sentimental theme that resonates with Honda's own outlook in childhood: "[Isamu] felt that it didn't matter if you win or lose. It was important for everyone to come together and run as one."

EIRIN records indicate that Honda spent time working on *Newspaper Kid* in 1950, but no further information about this unmade project is known. Instead, Honda turned his attention to a documentary short about consumer cooperatives. Co-ops had been shut down by the government during World War II, but they reappeared across the country in the late 1940s to distribute affordable food and goods, as a buffer against ongoing shortages, rationing, and starvation. Co-ops remain a major force in the Japanese economy today, comprising large portions of retail and rural trade.

The title of this film is usually given as *Story of a Co-op*, though EIRIN records indicate that its actual title was *Flowers Blooming in the Sand*.[6] It was reportedly made by Toho under the auspices of the government's Ministry of Health and Welfare to educate the public about the advent of co-ops. A Toho newsletter said the film "[introduces] consumer cooperative societies in towns and countrysides, not simply as a documentary but . . . abundantly incorporating theatrical elements." Veteran Toho producer Jin Usami oversaw the production, and Honda wrote the script. The film was shot in docudrama fashion, telling the story of Shozo (Yasuo Hisamatsu), a demobilized soldier searching for work in postwar Tokyo and living with his supportive but impatient girlfriend. Through a newspaper reporter friend, Shozo finds work researching the living conditions of Tokyoites. In meeting the most poverty-stricken citizens, he learns about the existence of consumer cooperatives and pledges to establish one in his neighborhood. Records indicate the film included animated segments and illustrations to explain how co-ops work, though this is unconfirmed. Honda completed the film on October 6, 1950, and it has been seen seldom if at all since then. As of 2015, there were no known extant prints or other film elements. According to Honda's memoirs, it reportedly sold well enough that Toho felt confident in giving him another assignment, his first feature.

———

Honda's transitions from soldier to civilian, and from assistant director to director, both occurred during the Allied Occupation (August 1945 to April 1952), Japan's forced transition from military rule to a Western-style representative government. As part of the effort to demilitarize, democratize, and rehabilitate Japan into a peace-loving nation, MacArthur's SCAP promoted free speech and expression while, conversely, it exerted control over the media and the arts, including cinema. It decided which films could be made, banned hundreds of preexisting films deemed militaristic and feudalistic (prints and negatives were mass-incinerated, a la *Fahrenheit 451*), and imposed a strict censorship program. New films were urged to advocate peace, tolerance, and equal rights; show male-female affection openly; support Japan's new Occupation-mandated constitution; and encourage individualism and other Western ideals. Banned topics included criticism of the atomic bombings; stories portraying the war and militarism favorably; sword fighting; criticism of America and foreigners; suicide and self-sacrifice as an act of fealty; feudalism; and the subjugation of women. References to the war had to acknowledge Japan's guilt for instigating the conflict.

Honda, as an assistant director, did not clash directly with SCAP, but he witnessed the battles fought by friends and colleagues. Iwao Mori, the executive who had brought Honda and many others to Toho, and who was considered the architect of the company's commercial success, was deemed a "war exploiter" and suspended from the industry when SCAP expelled studio executives who had made war propaganda films; he was not allowed to return until 1952. Kurosawa battled Occupation censors over two films. *The Men Who Tread on the Tiger's Tail* was withheld from release for six years because of SCAP's restrictions on *jidai-geki* and kabuki theater (the film was based on a kabuki play). Kurosawa's debut feature, *Sanshiro Sugata* (1943), could not be exhibited during the Occupation because of its samurai story.

Although records are inconclusive, it appears that Honda worked as an assistant director on one of the most heavily scrutinized movies of the Occupation, his old friend Senkichi Taniguchi's antiwar drama *Escape at Dawn* (*Akatsuki no dasso*, 1950).[7] This Film Art Association production, with a script cowritten by Kurosawa and starring Ryo Ikebe and Yoshiko "Shirley" Yamaguchi as a romantically entwined soldier and comfort woman, was based on novelist Taijiro Tamura's *Story of a Prostitute* (*Shunpu den*), a soldier's memoir of life on the front in China. SCAP objected to images of sex and prostitution and ordered Taniguchi to rewrite the script eight times. Among the changes, the prostitute became a singer, and her comfort station a bar. These compromises would be mirrored, four years later, in Honda's *Farewell Rabaul*, a film with similar wartime themes and a female character whose occupation and workplace are similarly veiled. Even after the Occupation's end and the lifting of SCAP censorship in 1952, certain subjects would remain taboo. (*Story of a Prostitute* would be made into a film again in 1965 by Seijun Suzuki, who portrayed the lives of comfort women in stark terms.)

Honda's professional trajectory had been slowed by forces beyond his control, but the timing was fortuitous, as he began his directing career just as Japanese cinema entered a resurgent period. Honda's life experiences—roots in a small mountain village, boyhood interest in science, moving between rural and city life, nontraditional marriage, the hell of war, and his witness to the power of the atom bomb—all these things, coupled with the social and political dynamics of a Japan pressured by Western occupiers, would resonate in his early films. During this pre-*Godzilla* period, Honda would do more writing and exert greater influence over scripts than at any other time in his career; and as a result, he did some of his most challenging work. In an uneasy time when the Japanese worried about the future while still reconciling the recent past, Honda would prove himself an able chronicler of postwar anxiety.

10

SEA, LAND, AND SKY

The Blue Pearl (1951),
The Skin of the South (1952),
The Man Who Came to Port
(1952), *Adolesence Part 2* (1953),
Eagle of the Pacific (1953),
Farewell Rabaul (1954)

The area of Ise Peninsula is land that sunk into ocean and later resurfaced. Because of this, there are mountains that come right up to the shorelines. About 85 percent of the land is mountainous or wasteland, and only the remaining 15 percent or so is suitable for agriculture. This is not nearly enough for the people to maintain economic stability, so the special occupation of the *ama* divers came into being naturally, out of necessity. Most of the workers are female, so the men born on the [peninsula] are sent away, with the exception of first-born sons. The girls start their training in the ocean from about 11 or 12, become fully trained by 16 or 17, and will continue to work in the sea until about 60. They dive into the ocean and harvest abalone, *sazae* (a type of conch) and gelidiaceae (a type of algae). Pearl oysters are harvested for a limited time each year, the best time being usually a week or so in mid-May. Single ladies dive individually and married ladies dive with a lifeline tied to them, which is connected to a pulley and handled by their spouse. The wives dive down to the ocean floor holding a 15-kilogram weight. Their methods are quite primitive, their living standards are quite low, and there are many myths and legends that they believe in. However, all of these things fit their lifestyle well . . . They do not use modernized harvesting methods, diving suits or equipment because this would cause their profession to become obsolete . . . Everything is unwittingly and naturally adapted.

In a poor village with such traditions and culture and an unnatural society where women hold financial power, there is a certain need for traditional conventions to take control and for the people to be content with such ways. These women are born into such dreary living conditions; I wanted to incorporate these elements as the basis of the film and capture their reality.

– From "Ama," an essay by Ishiro Honda (1951)

Japanese culture has clashed with Western values ever since Commodore Matthew Perry made his uninvited visit in 1853 and pried open the nation's ports and markets to the world, a clash intensified by the Occupation's assault on customs and traditions. Honda's romantic tragedy *The Blue Pearl*, at first glance, appears to follow the democratization standards proscribed by the American censors: open criticism of old superstitions, assertive and independent female characters, and affection between the two leads. At the same time, in depicting a traditional way of life suddenly threatened by outside influence, *The Blue Pearl* mirrors the occupied Japan of its day. These themes and ideas reflected Honda's own worldview, and they would recur in his films well after the Occupation. Upon its release, this remarkable little film was praised for its promising director's auspicious debut and for introducing underwater photography to Japanese cinema, but over the decades it has become forgotten, a lost gem.

The Blue Pearl was partly inspired by Honda's experiences filming the documentary *Ise-Shima*. He admired the people he'd met, felt the coastal scenery of Mie Prefecture was an ideal setting for a dramatic film, and wanted to shoot underwater again. The project was suggested by Sojiro Motoki, a close friend of Honda and Kurosawa since the Toho days and a driving force behind the Film Art Association. Motoki was now working for Toho and considered the Japanese film industry's leading producer.[1] Motoki had found an ideal story: *Ruins of the Sea* (*Umi no haien*), a 1949 Naoki Prize–winning novella about pearl divers written by seafaring author Katsuro Yamada. Honda decided to adapt it for the screen, and in 1950 he and Akira Kurosawa

left Tokyo for a writing retreat at an inn in Atami, a popular hot spring resort.[2] While Honda wrote *The Blue Pearl*, Kurosawa adapted Ryunosuke Akutagawa's acclaimed 1922 short story "In a Grove" (*Yabu no Naka*), which became *Rashomon*.

"I wanted to do a film with underwater scenes, and this story just happened to be there," Honda later said. "I wanted to show the relationship between nature and humans through these *ama* [who survive by diving for abalone]. I thought this would lead to a new field of movies that featured undersea scenes."

The two men would begin writing at 9:00 a.m. daily, sitting at adjacent desks. After each had completed about twenty pages, they'd exchange drafts and critique one another's work. Honda would later recall that, within just a few days, Kurosawa disagreed with certain aspects of Honda's script, and "after that he decided not to read mine any more. Of course he still made me read his."[3] Ultimately, though, Kurosawa gave Honda's work a thumbs-up. Honda said, "When I finished writing the screenplay, I could not hold back [the excitement] so I immediately went to see Kurosawa. He was sleeping, but he read through it at once, still lying down. And then he tapped my shoulder. That really moved me. I could not help the tears coming out of me."[4]

After the men had finished writing, producer Motoki pitched *The Blue Pearl* to Toho and received approval right away; it was one of about twenty-seven features produced by the resurgent studio in 1951. Around the same time, Motoki proposed *Rashomon* to Daiei Studios' president Masaichi Nagata, who at first turned that project down, predicting a flop. The irony, of course, is that decades later *The Blue*

Pearl is a footnote in Japanese cinema, while *Rashomon* is indisputably one of the great films of all time.

Honda spent considerable preproduction time hunting locations and conducting research in the Ise-Shima area. "I had written the first draft of the script and the project was officially given the green light," he recalled. "[Toho] gave me about three months to just go around the area [location scouting] from one place to the next. They allowed us to do such things [because of the poststrike slowdown], although in a way, this should be the norm. So once we started filming, there were no moments of hesitation, we were able to just keep moving forward."[5] Honda became a familiar face to the locals, who shared stories and granted him access not usually afforded to outsiders.

———————

This verse appears onscreen after the opening credits of *The Blue Pearl*:

> *Ama* divers and pearls
> Ise-Shima, washed by the Japan Current
> Hidden here are several tragic stories
> About the lives of the *ama* divers and
>   pearls

Set in a rustic, seaside village, *The Blue Pearl* is about a young diver, Noe (Yukiko Shimazaki, later of Kurosawa's *Seven Samurai*), who falls in love with the town's new lighthouse attendant and schoolteacher, Nishida (Ryo Ikebe), freshly transplanted from Tokyo. Nishida's arrival, and his outsider ways—he dresses in city clothes, is a gifted artist, has no patience for superstitions and feudal traditions, and smokes citified cigarettes—stir Noe's desire to leave behind an unwanted arranged marriage and a hard life of diving. The couple is scorned by the locals and split apart by the meddlesome Riu (Yuriko Hamada), a flirtatious ex-*ama* diver. Riu returns from two years in occupied Tokyo as a changed, liberated woman wearing American clothes, sunglasses, a primped face, and painted nails.

The film's second half is both physically and psychologically darker, as rains pelt the coast and Noe's happiness turns to torment. Noe's parents forbid her to see Nishida, and Riu attempts to seduce him in Noe's absence, spreading rumors that she's carrying Nishida's bastard child. The two women settle the score by diving to retrieve the legendary pearl of the *Dai nichi ido* well. Folklore says the pearl brings true love, but the locals fear the gem is cursed and should be left untouched. At the sea bottom, Riu reaches for the pearl, but her hand is caught in the rocks and she drowns, while Noe nearly dies trying to save her. Guilt-ridden, scorned by villagers who believe she killed her nemesis, and haunted by the ghostly cries of Riu calling from the sea, a distraught Noe walks alone on the moonlit sand. The film concludes as Noe wades into the waves, following the disembodied, haunting voice to her death.

Honda's screenplay differed from the original novella in a few significant ways. Honda made the main character, Noe, more sympathetic by omitting an abortion and a scene where she attempts to stab archrival Riu to death underwater. He added the legend of the pearl and the sacred well and other local folklore, much of which he learned during his location-hunting tour of the area.

Honda recalled adapting the story: "Legend has it that whenever an *ama* gets too close to [the *Dai nichi ido* well], she dies. This well is all that remains after an old shrine sank underwater a long time ago.

Directing native *ama* divers as extras in *The Blue Pearl*.
Courtesy of Honda Film Inc.

The *ama* divers fear this legend, and unless there is a significant reward, they will not dare go near it. Also, it is not permitted for them to wed outsiders. This is because the *ama* support the local economy, and the entire village would suffer if they left."[6]

The Blue Pearl introduces themes Honda would revisit often in his non–science fiction films, chiefly that of the outsider who challenges the status quo. Nishida's arrival in the little village triggers conflicts mirroring Japan's universal postwar identity crises: old traditions versus modern thinking; doubts about arranged marriage and feudalistic customs; a generational gulf between conservative adults and liberated youths; the emergence of assertive, independent-minded women; pastoral virtue versus urban decay. Casting its shadow over all is Japan's class structure, officially abolished by the Meiji government in 1873, but still the unspoken rule. Its obligations are understood, its rules unbendable. The *ama* divers are expected to support the village through a lifetime of hard labor. Noe and Riu, who dream of leaving the bubble, both pay with their lives.

————

Since the 1890s, Japan has been harvesting its world-renowned pearls, three-quarters of which are still collected by the women divers of Ise-Shima. Honda provides a window into the daily life and culture of the *ama*: their daily chatter and gossiping, their friendly competition to collect the most oysters, and the rigors and routines of their work. But the most intimate moments of *ama* life are captured during the underwater sequences, when all the chattering stops and the women are truly in their element. Cinematographer Tadashi

The Blue Pearl. © Toho Co., Ltd.

Iimura records the balletic athleticism of the dives, performed by actual divers with the underwater camera system created for *Ise-Shima*, this time with longer takes and more camera agility.

Because *The Blue Pearl* was promoted as Japan's first feature film with underwater photography, journalists were on location to document the logistical challenges. A writer for *Lucky* magazine described the filming of the climactic underwater conflict between the divers:

"[Cameraman] Iimura . . . all dressed up in his diving gear, puts a portable camera into a metallic body that acts as a special waterproofing device. With it under his arms, he dives into the water from the pontoon. [Honda] and his assistant director both watch from the boat using glass scopes. There are two professional divers underwater to assist the cameraman. The battling Riu and Noe are of course real *ama* divers, doubling for the actresses."

Because of a miscommunication between the cameraman and the crew in the boat, Iimura was mistakenly pulled out of the water before the shot was finished.

"[To avoid repeating this mistake] . . . they created 'underwater telegramming.' [Honda] writes on Kent paper in red pencil, 'shoot towards the right,' and an *ama* takes that and dives underwater. Upon receiving the message, the cameraman waves towards the water's surface, signaling, 'Roger.' This is how filming continued smoothly."[7]

The Blue Pearl shows Honda striving for a balance between a documentarian's desire for authenticity and a storyteller's need to connect emotionally. In an early scene, Honda incorporates formal documentary technique as Fujiki (Takashi Shimura), the elder lighthouse man, explains the life and culture of the *ama* for the benefit of newcomer Nishida and, by extension, for the audience. Over a montage of *ama* plunging into the sea, Shimura's narration describes *kachido* style diving, in which young women dive from the shoreline and work in groups, and *funedo* style, wherein more experienced *ama* dive from boats to greater depths, working with a male partner, usually a husband, who pulls them to safety if danger arises. Honda deftly illustrates one fascinating detail of *ama* life without ever mentioning it. When the divers surface, a piercing, high-pitched whistle is heard; though unexplained, this is the sound *ama* make when emptying air from their lungs after a long dive. The documentary approach emphasizes Ise-Shima's natural beauty, and Honda adds another layer of authenticity by casting local children who speak a regional dialect as Nishida's pupils and local adults as background extras, and by including a harvest festival with dancers in indigenous costumes.

Even with all its nonfiction-style trappings, *The Blue Pearl* is a melodrama and Honda does not hesitate to use sound, imagery, and a brilliant score by Tadashi Hattori, one of Japanese cinema's more prolific composers, to punctuate emotion. The director's inexperience is betrayed when Noe and Nishida declare their love during a raging rainstorm, an overused cinematic and literary harbinger of doom. In a moment taken from Yamada's novella, a bird slams into the lighthouse window and dies, telegraphing the lovers' fate.

Other moments are more effective, particularly the race to find the legendary pearl at the sea bottom. Then there is the final, haunting scene, as Noe walks along the beach with the moon and stars illuminating the rocky shore and the water's glistening surface, achieved with effective day-for-night photography. Led by the distant, imagined cry of Riu's voice, Noe sheds her robe and wanders into the surf, surrendering to the god of the ocean as a choral requiem swells and a lighthouse beam scans the night. Several of Honda's early films would reach an emotional climax with a suicide or self-sacrifice, and Noe's tragedy is among the most heartrending. Interestingly, Honda and editor Koichi Iwashita—the man who had introduced Honda to his wife some years earlier—strongly disagreed about the suicide scene, which was longer in Honda's original cut. Iwashita had seniority over the new director and insisted on shortening the ending, despite Honda's objections that the audience would be confused.[8] And in fact, some reviewers complained that Noe's death scene was ambiguous. Honda recalled feeling "upset, frustrated, and bitter resentment."[9]

Even if he was not a demonstrably spiritual man, *The Blue Pearl* reveals Honda's knowledge of Shinto, the indigenous religion with ties to Japanese values and history. A core belief is that all natural phenomena—people, mountains, trees, the ocean, and so on—are inhabited by *kami* (gods), thus deference to nature and the environment are of utmost importance. *The Blue Pearl*'s elder villagers speak of *Ryujin-sama*, their sea god, warning the younger generation to respect the ocean and maintain their traditional way of life. Noe and the other *ama* pay respects and cleanse their spirits in water-purification rituals, a Shinto practice, to appease *Ryujin-sama* and bring a healthy pearl harvest. Still, Honda straddles a delicate line between criticizing and defending feudalistic

Honda (far left) with actresses Yukiko Shimazaki and Yuriko Hamada, and cameraman
Tadashi Iimura, on location for *The Blue Pearl*. Courtesy of Honda Film Inc.

customs. Nishida openly mocks the old
superstitions, saying their true purpose is
to preserve the local way of life by instilling
the *ama* divers with a sense of obligation.
"You shouldn't mock the sea," Noe warns
him. "Leave the ocean alone."

Performances by the cast of veterans and
newcomers are inconsistent, on account of
both Honda's inexperience with actors and
his hands-off approach to directing them.
The standout is Shimazaki, who essentially
gives two performances. In the first half of
the film, Noe is radiant and full of life as she
falls for Nishida; in the second half, she is
distraught and inconsolable as the lovers
are scorned and separated. Shimazaki
was a relative newcomer, while leading
man Ryo Ikebe, in his early thirties, was an

established Toho heartthrob with throngs
of female fans, box-office appeal, and the
ability to play men younger than himself.
Ikebe initially joined Toho as a screenwriter
trainee but switched to acting at age
twenty-three; and during the 1940s and
1950s, he worked with many of Japan's best
directors, such as Naruse, Sugie, Ichikawa,
and Toyoda. Honda would get better results
from Ikebe later in *An Echo Calls You* (1959),
but here the actor lacks charisma, especially compared to the seemingly effortless
performance of Shimura, with whom he
shares several scenes. Shimura was already
a fixture in Akira Kurosawa's company,
playing the woodcutter in *Rashomon* and
the alcoholic doctor in *Drunken Angel*.
He would now also become an occasional

yet supremely important member of the nascent Honda family of actors. Hamada plays Riu without much subtlety, as a cackling, brash femme fatale who chews ample scenery.

Prior to its August 3, 1951, release, *The Blue Pearl* was welcomed by a trio of familiar well-wishers. A Toho Studios newsletter featured testimonials from Honda's mentor Yamamoto, as well as the other two members of the Three Crows, Kurosawa and Taniguchi. All were pleased their friend had persevered. "Some people may have had doubts, saying, 'Honda-*kun* may not be able to return to work in the film world again,'" wrote Yamamoto. "I must say that the arrival of this newcomer, who is an opposite personality to Kurosawa-*kun*, is a great asset to the film industry."

Kurosawa, in his testimonial, said he wasn't sure what to expect from his friend.

"Ino-*san* came up under Yama-*san*, just like Sen-*chan* and I did," Kurosawa wrote. "We were like three brothers. And of these three brothers, Ino-*san* was the quietest. He was always just calmly listening to us debate. That's why, when we heard that Ino-*san* was finally striking out on his own, it made both Sen-*chan* and me a little worried, because we had no idea what Ino-*san* was thinking. We were clueless about what kind of work he was capable of doing.

"But one day, he paid me a visit and said, 'I want to do this.' When he let me read his screenplay, it made me completely happy. We were mere fools for worrying. Ino-*san* had been quietly and steadily building himself in his own way. And Ino-*san*'s world is so fresh, pure and innocent. I was so ecstatic and praised him for his work. But all Ino-*san* said was, 'Stop, you are [embarrassing me].' This is the kind of guy Ishiro Honda is." Taniguchi, meanwhile, took a tongue-in-cheek approach to praising his

friend's debut, likening Honda to an upstart rival who must be eliminated.

The Blue Pearl was one of the first studio feature films shot in the Ise-Shima region, and one of the first to feature actual *ama* divers.[10] Honda would return to the area for the Odo Island sequences in *Godzilla* and parts of the final battle in *Mothra vs. Godzilla*.

Reviews were mostly favorable. Much praise was given to the film's technical merits, not only the breakthroughs in underwater filming but also Iimura's camera work, the extensive location shooting, and strides in sound recording. Like Kurosawa's *Rashomon* (1950), *The Blue Pearl* featured extensive dialogue recording on location, reducing the need for postdubbing; one reviewer called it "a test case for audio recording in film." Many reviewers noted Honda's long journey to the director's chair and gave him high marks for an ambitious, if not completely successful film, while looking forward to his next.

"[Honda] is a person with strong moral fiber and determination," wrote a *Nagoya Times* critic. "His great technique, a fresh and clean sensibility, and attention to detail are refreshing."

————————

There were stretches during the Occupation when work was infrequent. Honda spent time reconnecting with his family and bonding with his children, particularly Ryuji. Having been away at war when his son was born, Honda had trouble relating to the boy at first, but in time they grew closer. On free days, Honda would take the children, and sometimes their friends too, on outings to the Tama River, where they'd play games on the banks. In those days, the neighborhoods of Tokyo's Seijo Ward were home to numerous American families. Many of Ryuji and Takako's friends were American kids, and the Hondas would socialize with their parents. As the family would later recall, there was no talk of the war, no feeling of enemies reconciled—just neighbors.

"There was a family of a high-ranked commissioned officer that lived in Seijo, and I was close friends with their kids," remembered Ryuji. "They spoke English, and I spoke Japanese; when we'd play together the languages would be mixed up, Japanese and English. Once a month, they brought us a big cardboard box full of Levi's jeans and T-shirts and Double Bubble gum and chocolates and things. Those families were there to try to communicate with the Japanese.

"And one day, they disappeared. They had left."

————

When the Occupation officially ended in April 1952, Toho was still recuperating from the devastating effects of the strikes, struggling to regain its footing and produce new films. For this reason, Honda's second film, *The Skin of the South*, originated outside the studio system. The film was produced by Saburo Nosaka, who had previously worked for Toho Educational Film Division but left to form an independent outfit, Thursday Productions. Nosaka bankrolled the project with funds from private investors, primarily Shigeru Mizuno, a wealthy paper company owner and ex-member of Japan's communist party. Nosaka produced the film under his company banner, hired Honda to write and direct it, and struck a distribution agreement with Toho, which desperately needed new product to exhibit in its cinemas. "I accepted this film because the studio was still a mess," Honda later recalled. Shot mostly on location and outdoors, this film finds the young director again treading the line between nonfiction

and fiction, combining documentary elements and a veneration of nature with human drama. *The Skin of the South* was the first true collaboration, on a small scale, between Honda and special-effects man Tsuburaya, who, working uncredited, created a miniature-scale typhoon destruction sequence for the climax.

Later in his career, when making science fiction films, Honda would often visit scientists at universities, querying them about pseudoscientific concepts in the hope of making his films believable, if not always realistic. Honda did this for the first time during preproduction for *The Skin of the South*, a story based on geological fact. Honda was inspired by a news magazine article about disasters in the Satsuma Peninsula area of Kagoshima Prefecture, near the southwestern tip of Kyushu, where farmlands cultivated on unstable soil composed of porous volcanic ash were washing away during heavy rains, leaving behind huge craters and valleys. To learn more about the phenomenon, Honda visited the Institute for Science of Labor, a think tank for industrial and agricultural safety issues, where researchers had been investigating the landslides. Honda also went on a fact-finding trip to the region, where he was shown roads and farm fields that had sunken into the earth.

"There was an elderly man who took us around," Honda remembered. "He said, 'This land had been in our family for generations.' We are talking acres and acres. [During a storm], someone came calling for him yelling, 'Grandpa, it's crumbling!' So he immediately ran out to see. What he found was farmland slipping away right in front of his eyes, making a sound like twenty or thirty army tanks driving by. He was in a pure daze, but then ran straight back to the house, grabbed a bottle of sake, and just drank as he watched his land disappear. What a shocking story . . . I only wished there was something that could have been done to help the situation."[11]

In his initial draft, Honda's geologist hero solved the problem and saved the villagers, a happy ending, but Honda rewrote it after a geologist at Kagoshima University told him no such solution was remotely possible. "We [told] him how we need a happy ending since this is a movie. He made a sad face and said, 'I am very sorry to have to say this, but there really is nothing that can be done to prevent this occurrence . . . Frankly, I am a bit troubled you are going to depict this in a movie.' As a filmmaker, this experience made such a strong impression on me."[12] Honda opted for an ambiguous resolution instead, one showing the area recovering from the tragedy, but offering no assurance that it could not happen again. Indeed, typhoons regularly trigger landsides across Japan; in Kagoshima, a series of typhoons in July and August 1993 caused landslides that killed seventy-one people.

The story follows two university geologists from Tokyo, Kakuzo Ono (Hajime Izu) and Shoichiro Takayama (Shunji Kasuga), researching the soil on a plateau in Kagoshima, where huge swaths of land have been washed away by typhoons, killing two hundred. They are joined by Sadae Miura (Yasuko Fujita), a female doctor conducting a health study on the area's women. A big logging company plans to revive the local economy by cutting down trees, but Ono, the head researcher, warns that deforesting the mountainside will bring massive landslides when it rains, destroying the village. Greedy lumber baron Nonaka (Yoshio Kosugi) convinces everyone that the scientists are meddlesome outsiders, not to be trusted. The feudalistic town elders reject

Ono's plea to relocate the village to a safer area; logging continues, and Ono becomes despondent. Then one night a downpour comes. The villagers run to higher ground, all except the evil Nonaka. Ono risks his life trying to save the villains as a massive landslide wipes out the village. Two years later, Ono and Sadae visit the graves of two friends killed in the disaster. Livestock graze and crops are growing, a ray of hope.

This is the framework of Honda's screenplay, which according to some sources was based on *Blooming Virgin Soil* (*Hana aru shojochi*), an original story by writer Kiyoto Fukuda. But it's really just half of the film. Superimposed onto the researchers' struggle is a soapy love quadrangle involving the three scientists and Keiko (Harue Tone), a mysterious local girl. It is explained that Keiko was sent away to live with a wealthy family as a teenager (a Meiji-era tradition to teach girls manners and etiquette in preparation for marriage) and was sexually assaulted by the family's son, leaving her traumatized. Meanwhile, Ono is so focused on his work that he fails to notice Sadae is falling hard for him. Soon Sadae's uncle tries to convince her to quit her job for an arranged marriage with the wealthy Motomura (Ryuzo Okada), but she rebukes her suitor after learning he is the man who raped Keiko years ago. Then there is Ono's assistant, Takayama, who falls ill halfway through the film, spends much time in bed, and expires while bravely trying to warn others about the impending storm.

With its unusual and beautiful setting and themes of conflict, corruption, love, and destruction, *The Skin of the South* has the makings of a compelling disaster drama. It flirts with numerous interesting ideas: a professional woman rejecting an arranged marriage, the taboo subject

Discussing a scene from *The Skin of the South* with cast and crew on location.
Courtesy of Honda Film Inc.

of rape, and the outmoded custom of enslaving prospective wives. These issues are resolved too easily, leaving Ono's quest to save the villagers from doom as the only plot thread generating conflict and drama. The battle between science and politics, illustrating Honda's concern about the fate of the environment in Japan's then emerging capitalist system, comes to a head in a showdown at city hall, a scene foreshadowing present-day debates over climate change. Ono tries to convince officials of the grave danger ahead, but the conniving Nonaka discredits him. "You people keep saying science this, science that, but when exactly will that mountain crumble?" Nonaka says. "If we cut down the trees, will the mountain slide the very next time it rains? Or will it be ten years from now, or even a hundred years from now? How can we spend tens of millions of yen to relocate the village based on what you say you know, but you're unsure of? Stop with your

dreaming. The village is already worried about the upcoming taxes."

The two halves of *The Skin of the South* unspool as separate stories, unevenly weighted. Honda is most interested in the ethical scientists and their pursuit of truth. Considerable time is spent with the geologists as they mundanely collect and sort soil samples. Copious exposition details the area's history, and Ono repeatedly pleads his case to anyone who will listen. Ono is a precursor to scientists confronting political intransigence in later Honda films, notably Dr. Yamane in *Godzilla*. Honda's favored semidocumentary style is evident during the opening credits and sequences showcasing Kiyoe Kawamura's cinematography of landslide-affected areas, such as a huge crater in the side of a mountain and a field that ends at a sheared cliff. Kawamura, who shot Honda's *Ise-Shima*, renders both the Kagoshima beauty (majestic streams, valleys, and lakes) and the threat to it (newsreel-style shots of trees falling) in stunning black and white.

The three main protagonists are all flawless and therefore rather dull. Izu, the nominal leading man, plays Ono as a single-minded square, passionate about soil and little else. However, Kosugi, a great and prolific character actor for Honda, Kurosawa, and others, steals every scene as the gap-toothed, intimidating thug Nonaka. The only A-lister among the cast is Shimura, making a cameo. "Around this time," Honda remembered, "my films were not so much about the kind of human drama that veteran actors liked to do, so I tended to use new people."[13]

Eiji Tsuburaya had left Toho in 1948, ostensibly because of his involvement in national policy films. According to Tsuburaya biographer August Ragone, Occupation authorities concluded that Tsuburaya's realistic Pearl Harbor miniatures could have been created with only classified information; therefore, they erroneously believed Tsuburaya "must have been part of an espionage ring."[14] Undaunted, Tsuburaya formed an independent company, Tsuburaya Visual Effects Laboratory, and worked for various studios on a freelance basis. He received no screen credit for his work during this period, but several projects are known to bear his handiwork, notably Daiei's *Invisible Man Appears* (*Tomei ningen arawaru*, 1949), one of Japan's first significant science fiction films. *The Skin of the South* was produced in the last days of the Occupation, but before those people banished from the studios were allowed to return openly; Tsuburaya's uncredited involvement has been documented by film historian Hiroshi Takeuchi and others. The landslides during the film's climax are a preview of the more

ambitious disaster scenes Tsuburaya would create in science fiction films years later. There are several brief cutaways to the villagers watching their land wash away, and these appear to be the first-ever scenes combining Tsuburaya's effects and Honda's live-action footage.

————

No one influenced the trajectory of Ishiro Honda's career more than producer Tomoyuki Tanaka. Born into a wealthy Osaka family, Tanaka came from a far different background than Honda; but the two men were close in age and had certain things in common, including the tutelage of studio head Iwao Mori, who had pulled Tanaka from Toho's literature department and groomed him to be a producer. Tanaka produced a handful of Toho movies before the end of World War II; then, during the Occupation he made the controversial *Those Who Make Tomorrow*; Senkichi Taniguchi's debut, *Snow Trail*; and other projects. In 1948 Tanaka left Toho in protest of the communist purge and spent four years working with the Film Art Association, where he produced the aforementioned *Escape at Dawn* and other projects. In 1952 Iwao Mori's banishment by Occupation authorities was over, and Mori returned to Toho, inviting Tanaka to join him. Although in his early forties, Tanaka was still viewed as an up-and-comer. In the years ahead, Tanaka would become one of the studio's most commercially successful producers through a close alliance with Honda and Tsuburaya, the foundation of which was inconspicuously laid in *The Man Who Came to Port* (*Minato e kita otoko*), a film that proved far less than the sum of its substantial parts, including starring turns by Takashi Shimura and Toshiro Mifune.

"This was the film where I met Tomoyuki

Tanaka," Honda later recalled. "We both had the same type of goal . . . At this time [he] was really a beginner; many of the producers were much older then. [Projects with] big stars were done more by the upper echelon, but younger producers had to explore new genres. Because of this, younger producers and directors and staff were all working together [and] people started noticing the kinds of things I wanted to do."[15]

Honda was earning a reputation for his semi-nonfiction style and skill at capturing natural, nonurban settings; so when Tanaka approached the director with a drama about whalers, it seemed an ideal fit. Toho had acquired the book *Dance of the Surging Waves* (*Odore yo Doto*) by Shinzo Kajino, a popular writer of maritime fiction, and it had access to more than twenty thousand feet of documentary footage shot by cameramen Hiromitsu Karasawa and Taichi Kankura on actual Japanese whaling expeditions at sea, including a trip to Antarctica.

At the time, Mori was just beginning to reestablish Toho's special-effects capabilities, and the studio had recently acquired a rear-screen projection system. Shimura and Mifune play captains of competing whaling vessels, and the idea was to use the rear-screen process to combine the documentary footage in the background with shots of the actors firing a harpoon gun on a soundstage, creating the illusion they were on the bow deck of a whaling vessel. Tsuburaya hadn't perfected the process yet, thus the results were unconvincing and used sparingly. Honda liberally incorporates actual footage of whales breaching, harpoon guns firing, whales flailing as they're fatally struck, and cetacean carcasses being towed into harbor; he crosscuts these violent, graphic images

of the animals being hunted with actors matter-of-factly pretending to hunt them. Compared to the reverence for the ocean and the view into the world of the *ama* in *The Blue Pearl*, this film's surface treatment of the dangerous life of whalers, who spend most of their time on land, drinking *sake*, is uninspired. There is no romance of the sea, no worshipping of the mighty, godlike creatures pursued across the hemispheres and, aside from a fleeting reference to a "white whale," no aspirations to Melvillean adventure. *The Man Who Came to Port* is a compact soap opera in which the two main rivals just happen to be whalers.

Set in a small whaling town on Kinkasan Island in Miyagi Prefecture, the story centers on the gruff veteran Capt. Okabe (Shimura). An expert whale gunner and respected seaman, Okabe values tradition and experience above all, but his beliefs are challenged by the arrival of the outsider Ninuma (Mifune), a young, handsome sailor with an urban air, education, and top whale-gunning skills. Sensing his seafaring days waning, Okabe plans to buy the local inn and settle down for retirement, and hopes the innkeeper's daughter, the much younger Sonoko (Asami Kuji), will marry him. Sonoko, however, is attracted to Ninuma, who suppresses his own feelings and, out of respect for his captain, encourages her to marry Okabe, creating a complicated triangle of hurt feelings. Soon Ninuma becomes captain of another whaling ship, infuriating Okabe, who feels pushed aside for the younger generation. Complicating matters is a rocky reconciliation between Okabe and his illegitimate son, Shingo (Hiroshi Koizumi). In the climax, Okabe foolishly tries to prove himself by hunting whales in a typhoon, but he goes adrift and Ninuma must rescue him. Now friends, the two former rivals

The Man Who Came to Port. © Toho Co., Ltd.

leave for a six-month whaling expedition to Antarctica.

Though rarely seen today, *The Man Who Came to Port* was a significant movie for Toho, one of the first projects completed after the studio fully resumed production in 1952 and began to recover from the disastrous effects of the war, the strikes, and the communist purge. This was an A-class picture, evidenced by the personnel in front of and behind the camera. Shimura and Mifune were by now firmly ensconced in Kurosawa's fold and committed to his projects first and foremost, sandwiching other films in between. Shimura had just finished starring in Kurosawa's *Ikiru* (1952), while Mifune was busy working on a number of films after Kurosawa's *The Idiot* (1951) and before *Seven Samurai* (1954), the film that would make both he and Shimura superstars.

Honda's direction of the leads is more nuanced than before, as Shimura and Mifune create believably flawed, yet likeable dueling protagonists. Capt. Okabe feels so threatened by young Ninuma's arrival that he lashes out at his crew when things go wrong, but Shimura also shows the grizzled captain's other side, a lonely and sensitive older man. While best known in the West for his animalistic fury in *Rashomon* and *Seven Samurai*, Mifune in *The Man Who Came to Port* is typical of the stoic, stalwart heroes he played in studio fare outside Kurosawa's oeuvre during this phase of his career. As Ninuma hides his emotions, Mifune layers the character with simmering anger that surfaces in drunken outbursts.

By now Toho had a stable of character actors populating the works of most all the studio's directors. A core group became Honda's favorites, reappearing in numerous films. *The Man Who Came to Port* marks the first appearances of two such actors who became very familiar faces: Ren Yamamoto, who would later stand out as a terrified villager in *Godzilla*, and Senkichi Omura, known for playing excitable working-class types, and later memorable as the goofball interpreter in *King Kong vs. Godzilla*. The cast also features Kurosawa mainstays, including Bokuzen Hidari, known for portraying sad old men, as the glassy-eyed town drunk, and Kamatari Fujiwara, who would go on to play the paranoid peasant Manzo in *The Seven Samurai*. The score was by Ichiro Saito, who had previously worked for Yasujiro Ozu and Mikio Naruse. Honda shared screenplay credit with Masashige Narusawa, who would later write Kenji Mizoguchi's acclaimed *Tales of the Taira Clan* (*Shin heike monogatari*, 1955) and *Street of Shame* (*Akasen chitai*, 1956).

Despite its quality pedigree, *The Man Who Came to Port* was a step backward. Honda had neglected two of his strengths. His previous films showed isolated cultures in their natural surroundings, but remove the documentary stock footage and *The Man Who Came to Port* takes place almost entirely in nondescript interiors. The conflict between man and nature is never contemplated; the whale is little more than a harpooner's target.

Critics assailed the picture. "There are so many spots that just don't make any sense," complained the *Shukan Yomiuri* newspaper. "The script . . . is very poorly done. The direction by Honda is so ama-teurish . . . They inserted actual whaling footage . . . which only adds boredom." A *Kinema Junpo* reviewer actually praised the film's visual style, but added, "What director Honda needs to learn is how to make the drama part better . . . It needs a little more of a climax."

On location for *Adolescence Part 2*.
Courtesy of Honda Film Inc.

————

Honda's next feature revisited ideas explored in *The Blue Pearl*: conflict between traditional and modern values, anxiety about encroaching Western influence, and the impact of these pressures on a small, isolated group of people. The story again concerns a pair of star-crossed lovers subjected to the community's harsh scrutiny, but this time the protagonists are high school students, whose problems are rooted in a generation gap that was widening fast in the years after the war. In *Adolescence Part 2*, Honda created a vivid snapshot of life in a small Japanese village amid the social, political, and economic changes of the Occupation. The film offers an interesting contrast to better-known works covering similar ground, for Honda had a more sympathetic view of Japan's postwar youth than did some of his con-temporaries.

Adolescence Part 2 was a follow-up to Toho's successful coming-of-age drama *Adolescence* (*Shishunki*, 1952), directed by Seiji Maruyama. Set in a small town surrounded by mountains, *Adolescence* focuses on a group of students at a high school located adjacent to a red-light district full of unsavory establishments, and some of the youths are lured down the wrong path. The film ends with a teacher leading a drive to clean up the town.

The public response to *Adolescence* exceeded expectations, and Toho approved a second installment.[16] During preproduction for *Adolescence Part 2*, high school students were asked about their problems and experiences, and their stories were incorporated into the screenplay by Toshiro Ide and Haruo Umeda. The cast includes veteran actors in the adult roles and members of Honda's emerging stock company as the youths, including a young Akira Kubo (also in the original *Adolescence*, playing a different character), Ren Yamamoto, and Toyoaki Suzuki. Two roles were played by actual students after auditions were held across Japan.

Adolescence Part 2, though set in a similar locale and featuring some of the same actors, is not a direct sequel to *Adolescence*. Shot on location during the hot summer months in Kofu City, Yamanashi Prefecture, the story concerns a group of high school friends in a small town located in a mountain basin. The group meets regularly for after-school study sessions, stoking gossip among teachers, parents, and locals. Some don't like boys and girls staying out together at night, others wonder if the kids have left-wing leanings, and still others object to one of the group's meeting locations, a girl's house that doubles as a snack bar owned by her parents and frequented by seedy types.[17] Toho's promotional

materials for *Adolescence Part 2* lay out the film's theme: "Puberty is a time where the young contemplate life and try to face it straight on, with all seriousness. However, the adults view this pubescent period as something dirty." The youths wrestle mightily with pangs of sexual awakening and longing for self-identity, none more so than Keita (Akira Kubo), whose defining character trait is *baka shojiki* (honesty to a fault). This is evident when the boy costs his sumo team a championship trophy by pointing out an illegal move by a teammate.

Keita and his classmate Reiko (Kyoko Aoyama) take a walk in the woods alone and become intimate. Afterward, both are racked with guilt; Reiko, walking in a stupor, is hit by a car. The local press calls it a suicide attempt, the result of teenage *momoiro asobi* (fooling around; literally, "peach-colored play") gone too far; and because both teens' parents are prominent community members, scandal erupts. The parents quell the uproar by pushing Keita and Reiko toward marriage, which further suffocates the youths. Keita goes into the mountains, seemingly intent on suicide, but is saved by a teacher. Cooler heads prevail

Directing actress Kyoko Aoyama in a pivotal scene of *Adolescence Part 2*. Courtesy of Honda Film Inc.

and the two are given a fresh start. Reiko goes to stay with relatives, and Keita transfers to a school in Tokyo.

Having spent his early youth in a small mountain town not entirely unlike the fictional one here, and having been a kid with a zest for reading and the son of a priest, it's possible that Ishiro Honda identified with the youths in *Adolescence Part 2*, and this might explain his exceptional compassion for the plight of his young characters. During the 1950s a good number of Japanese films depicted tensions between the Meiji generation that led Japan to war and the kids who came of age during the Occupation. The most noteworthy of these took a conservative and rather harsh view of youth. An extreme example is Keisuke Kinoshita's *A Japanese Tragedy* (*Nihon no higeki*, 1953), which portrays teens and young adults as flagrantly disloyal and disrespectful toward their parents and elders, and is a classic of the enduring *haha-mono* (mother film) genre.

In *Adolescence Part 2*, the line in the generational sand is clear. An adult looks askance at some teens and notes disapprovingly that there is "a huge difference from when we were young. It was just war, war, war for us." Elsewhere, some parents are reading a newspaper article titled, "Parents are too carefree: a dangerous age for rebellion." Honda's direction evenhandedly illustrates the rift, taking the adults to task for their hypocrisy while not letting the wayward youths off the hook. This isn't a story of teenage delinquency, but of the widening gap between old and young and the upheaval of long-held traditions.

In early scenes, Honda contrasts the earnest teens with the hypocritical, quick-to-judge adults, some of whom gossip about the kids while practicing at an archery range; when they miss the target,

it's a nice visual metaphor for the adults' cluelessness. The students are shown reading the French philosopher Alain and engaging in deep discussion; the teachers are shown reflexively siding with the cops after some of the kids are mistakenly arrested and accused of hanging out in a bar. And while the grown-ups worry about the boys and girls staying out late together, it's the adults who think about sex, as evidenced by a bar patron reading a *kasu tori* magazine (lurid periodicals, popular after the war). Eventually Honda replaces black-and-white absolutes with shades of gray—such as when it is revealed that a female student's sister is actually her mother, posing as the girl's older sister to hide the shame of a teen pregnancy and a fatherless household; the woman's revelation is a warning to the kids not to repeat their elders' mistakes. As for the youths, it turns out that their parents' concerns were not all unfounded. As Keita and Reiko hike into the mountains, the sexual tension builds between them; and when they stop to rest on a rock, Keita makes his move, and the couple kisses off-screen. The camera pans away to the rushing river below.

To the Western viewer, this would seem an unsubtle sexual metaphor—a train speeding into a tunnel—however, it's not made clear whether the kids go as far as intercourse, and this ambiguity is key: Honda is less interested in whether the youths are going too far astray than in the impossibility of breaking free from the traditional values of family, community, and by extension the whole of Japanese society. In 1950s Japan, the mere appearance of such inappropriate behavior could result in unbearable shame and scorn. These two adolescents, seemingly free and independent minded, are instantly changed forever by a simple, universal act that's

Poster for *Adolescence Part 2*, featuring Akira Kubo and Kyoko Aoyama. © Toho Co., Ltd.

confusing, conflicting emotions. Keita suffers quietly, internally, worlds removed from contemporary Hollywood teens, who were shouting "You're tearing me apart" at their own out-of-touch parents. Kubo, just sixteen when this film was made, was beginning a long and fruitful acting career. During the 1950s and 1960s, he mostly played supporting roles as impetuous, hotheaded romantics and heroic types in program pictures ranging from comedies to war dramas. He would appear in numerous other Honda efforts and also play significant parts in Kurosawa's *Throne of Blood* (*Kumonosu-jo*, 1957) and *Sanjuro* (*Tsubaki Sanjuro*, 1962).

Adolescence and *Adolescence Part 2* were part of a wave of high school dramas in the early 1950s, influenced by the increase in coed schools after the war and by the popularity of the Italian drama *Tomorrow Is Too Late* (*Domani e troppo tardi*, 1950), a Romeo and Juliet story with Pier Angeli and Vittorio De Sica.[18] There were trashy Japanese films with titles such as *A Virgin's Sex Manual* and *Bitch*, and classier examples from major directors. The critics seemed to write off Honda's film merely for its subject matter. A *Kinema Junpo* writer said the film was too focused on "the dangers of youth" and "you couldn't feel any of the high schoolers' life or beauty," ignoring its serious themes and the lengths the director goes to, particularly in early scenes, to show that the students are happy and well adjusted.

Adolescence Part 2 is no whitewashed, idyllic portrait of teenage life, and it's to Honda's credit that he rendered the plight of young people with compassion and objectivity, even while showing his own generation's fears and faults. The film begins and ends with announcements over the school loudspeaker chastising students

part of growing up. They are burdened with the guilt of having failed to meet expectations and are duty-bound to suffer the consequences, even if it means a life of unhappiness.

Honda elicits fine performances from the young cast, particularly from Kubo, who plays Keita with the sort of muted angst that is at once completely Japanese but universal in the boy's confused attempts to understand girls, parents, and the looming specter of manhood. There is a powerful sequence in which Keita, beaten and bruised in a fight, is bandaged by a girl who has a not-so-secret crush on him. As Keita lies still, the girl softly kisses him; but rather than accept her affection, the boy walks out and wanders to the school swimming pool and, in a scene breathtakingly shot by cinematographer Tadashi Iimura, swims laps in the moonlight as if to wash off the for violating the dress code and other social rules. These clever bookends show the cycle forever to be repeated: adolescence is a rite of passage all teens must endure en route to accepting society's behavioral boundaries.

I hate war. This film is my tribute, a wish that the Japanese people will never experience this tragedy ever again.
— Ishiro Honda

We cannot bring back the dead, nor can we regain lost time. Still, we can quietly think about the past and learn from our mistakes.
— Narrator, *Eagle of the Pacific*

With the lifting of SCAP censorship, a popular film genre was resurrected: the war epic. Many films would revisit World War II and earlier conflicts, and because they were made by a new generation of filmmakers who had endured or witnessed Japan's defeat, they could be quite different from the propaganda films of a decade or so earlier. As film historian Stuart Galbraith IV writes:

Postwar Japanese movies about World War II generally fall into one of four categories. A tiny number . . . produced by Shin Toho in the late 1950s and into 1960, whitewash Japan's militarists . . . Others, such as Masaki Kobayashi's *The Human Condition* (1959–61) trilogy, uncompromisingly depict the war as it truly was . . . A third type, exemplified by Kihachi Okamoto's *Desperado Outpost* (1959) and *The Human Bullet* (1968), are grimly comical and cynical. Toho specialized in the fourth type, large-scale epics full of romanticized action and spectacle similar to concurrent American-made

war movies like *The Longest Day* (1962) and *Battle of the Bulge* (1965). However, these films temper iconography recognizable to western viewers with equal sobering doses of bitter reality, through protagonists recognizing the great folly that ultimately leaves Japan in ruins and a generation of men wiped out for nothing.[19]

Honda's *Eagle of the Pacific*, the first of Toho's new war movies, cast Adm. Isoroku Yamamoto as the central figure of a drama that methodically and unsentimentally retraces the steps that led Japan into its fateful clash with the United States, largely because of the inability of the Imperial Navy, the "gentlemanly" branch of the Japanese military, to stop the warmongers of the army from getting their way. Yamamoto is portrayed as a man reluctantly yet dutifully carrying out his doomed mission, a characterization that mirrors Honda's own feelings about war. This was Japan's first postwar big-budget, special-effects driven war picture, and the first to exalt Yamamoto's memory.

Sometime in the late 1940s, Toho had asked Honda to develop and direct *Kamikaze Special Attack Troop* (*Kamikaze Tokubetsu Kogekitai*) a proposed film based on the story of the *tokkotai*, student pilots recruited from elite universities during the war to fly suicide missions. The exact dates are elusive, but it appears this project originated before or during Honda's work on his two documentary films, and had it gone forward, it would have been his first dramatic feature. Kimi Honda recalled, "It was after the war and there was a collection of letters written by the suicide squad members to their mothers and such, right before they died. [The producers] had sent these letters, originals mind you, to our house. [Honda] spent days reading each one. And after much thinking he said, 'This is not a film I can make.' At the time, certain things still overlapped with his experiences at war. The story was so raw and real the he couldn't do it." Kimi's account differs slightly from that in Honda's memoirs, in which he recalled interviewing pilots' family members and writing a screenplay, which "[openly] criticized the commanders who issued those orders, but the story was too real and we were told by the company that it was too soon [after the war], and now that script is lost."[20] The pilots' letters were subsequently compiled in *Listen to the Voices of the Sea* (*Kike Wadatsumi no Koe*), a best-selling, antiwar book published in 1949, which was adapted into a film directed by Hideo Sekigawa for Toei Studios in 1950.

According to Kimi, after this experience Honda decided he would not make war movies, but changed his mind when Toho offered him the story of Yamamoto. "He had read Yamamoto's biography, which contained his thoughts towards the war," she said. "[Yamamoto] was very against it. This is something which resonated within Honda and he decided, 'I am going to do this.' He was quite enthusiastic."

Explaining his desire to make the film, Honda wrote:

There were high-ranking people back then who opposed the war. Isoroku Yamamoto was one of them. He knew that he was a target of assassins, but he still opposed the idea of the Tripartite Treaty among Japan, Germany, and Italy. He spoke out, saying there was no way to win once war started between Japan and America. But the public was never told that there was any such voice within the military. When he learned

Honda behind the camera while shooting *Eagle of the Pacific*. Courtesy of Honda Film Inc.

Eagle of the Pacific.
© Toho Co., Ltd.

the war had started, he was thoroughly depressed . . . He wrote a letter to his best friend about his feelings, saying something like, "It wasn't my idea, but once it was decided, I had to go along. My position is to lead the people towards something I am against. This is my fate." . . . During the war, he held out hope for a treaty between Japan and America. Until his end, when he died in the skies above Rabaul, he hoped that the war would end soon, with Japan still in good shape.[21]

————

After four films of limited commercial and critical success, Honda's stature at Toho rose with *Eagle of the Pacific*, which placed fourth at the box office in 1953 and was, according to some sources, the first Toho postwar film to gross more than ¥100 million (about $278,000). This was Honda's biggest production yet. A full-scale set of an aircraft carrier deck was ordered, so big that it had to be constructed at a nearby horse racing track, and the special-effects sequences, though somewhat limited, were the most ambitious since the war days. A massive publicity campaign claimed the film was budgeted at ¥170 million, likely a gross exaggeration, and with its increased use of miniatures and pyrotechnics, this marked the first true special-effects film on which Honda and Eiji Tsuburaya collaborated. Honda, as well as the studio brass, was worried that, eight years after Japan's defeat, it might still be too early to make a film questioning the war effort, but their fears were allayed by the public's response.

Even as *Eagle of the Pacific* relaunched Toho's war genre, and even as it glorifies the bravery of military men and the excitement of battle, Honda's film is weighted by postwar feelings of regret and does not glorify the war itself. The script was by Shinobu Hashimoto, who had penned the original draft of *Rashomon*, had written Kurosawa's *Ikiru*, and would soon add *Seven Samurai* to his credits. Hashimoto's script begins in 1940, with militant and moderate factions of the Japanese government and military bickering over the direction of the war in Asia. Vice Adm. Isoroku Yamamoto of the Imperial Japanese Navy has received assassination threats for his opposition to the proposed Tripartite Pact. Yamamoto fears being drawn into war with America, while the militants increasingly support it. The moderates prevail briefly, but eventually the navy accedes in the name of national unity; and the Axis treaty is signed amid much national celebration. Yamamoto, now faced with the grim likelihood of war with the United States, dutifully begins planning an attack on Pearl Harbor. With Japan militarily outmatched, his strategy is to strike first, secure an advantageous position, and then hope to negotiate a settlement with America. In one of several interior monologues, a solitary Yamamoto ponders his fate: "I acknowledge that the situation has reached the absolute worst. This is very shameful, but nothing good will come from pointing fingers now, arguing over who's wrong and who's right. Following orders that are the total opposite of my personal feelings is strange . . . [But] the only choice left for us is to take our military power and go straight to the enemy."

As efforts to negotiate with America fail, the most hawkish factions overtake military leadership, and the attack is authorized. Japanese warplanes take off from carriers on December 8, 1941, and destroy Pearl Harbor. Over the next months Japan's war campaign achieves a series of successes. Seeking a decisive victory over the United States, Yamamoto's fleet destroys the US

Honda (center), surrounded by extras and crew on *Eagle of the Pacific*.
Courtesy of Honda Film Inc.

base at Midway Island, but retaliation from the Americans is overwhelming; a series of US victories in the South Pacific follows, yet Japan blindly fights on despite diminishing resources. Yamamoto moves the fleet's base to the island of Rabaul, but casualties mount and military hardware dwindles; defeat is near. As Rabaul is abandoned, Yamamoto's plane is shot down over Bougainville Island in the Solomon Sea on the morning of April 18, 1943.

More a dispassionate reenactment than entertainment, *Eagle of the Pacific* is a mea culpa, an admission of a collective mistake, though it stops short of examining the depths of and reasons for it. Honda's direction is deliberate, unfolding the story in conversations and strategy sessions, with cinematographer Kazuo Yamada's camera framing military officers and government officials in formal, portraitlike angles that seem to acknowledge strength and weakness, seniority and rank. As in most Japanese war films, the story is told entirely from Japan's point of view; the enemy is an unseen force. Thus, during the Midway battle, the documented fact that the Americans had cracked the Japanese military's radio codes is not mentioned, and the viewer is just as confused as Yamamoto and his men about the enemy's whereabouts, creating real tension and suspense. The characters have no personal stories, only their duty to the war effort. This detachment and the ample use of wartime newsreels give *Eagle of the Pacific* the most documentarian feel of all Honda's dramatic films.

Even so, there are modest directorial flourishes. Honda none-too-subtly creates tension during static dialogue scenes with a recurring motif of clocks ticking loudly and hours elapsing, a harbinger of fate. The movement of the clock hands is most effective in Honda's handling of the frantic Battle of Midway as Yamamoto and his officers, unable to gauge the enemy's counterattack, waste valuable time deciding whether to arm their warplanes with bombs or torpedoes, indecision that leaves the imperial fleet helpless at the moment the Americans strike with a vengeance. Earlier, Honda contrasts the beauty of nature and the ugliness of war, transitioning from cherry blossom trees to newsreel footage of American aircraft carriers and B-29 planes bombing Japan in April 1942.

Eagle of the Pacific marked Tsuburaya's official return from exile to the studio and the flashpoint of Toho's second special-effects boom. It also marked the unofficial adoption of the two-staff system employed by Toho on nearly all its effects films ever since, with separate crews concurrently shooting the dramatic and effects scenes. To help create a seamless final product,

With actor Denjiro Okochi (as Admiral Yamamoto). Courtesy of Honda Film Inc.

studio chief Iwao Mori used *Eagle of the Pacific* as a test case for storyboarding, using *e conte* (continuity drawings), a practice that Mori had learned about during fact-finding trips to Hollywood. This process would become essential to Honda and Tsuburaya's collaborative process in the years ahead. Not only did it maintain continuity between the drama and effects scenes, but Mori and his producers liked that it kept budgets in check by identifying shots that could be eliminated or replaced with stock footage.

Stock footage was used amply in *Eagle of the Pacific*, and some sources indicate that producer Sojiro Motoki secured approval for the project by promising to curtail costs by reusing action sequences from *The War at Sea from Hawaii to Malaya*. Thus, Tsuburaya's return to Toho was not a lavish homecoming. He had only a small crew, and much of his contribution to this film consists of rehashed footage augmented by a limited number of impressive new effects. Some newspaper critics weren't fooled, citing the stock footage as evidence that Toho's trick photography hadn't advanced.

Veteran star Denjiro Okochi, who a few years earlier had led the exodus from Toho to form Shin Toho, has the distinction of being the first actor to play Isoroku Yamamoto on film and does so with steadfast reserve. Okochi's task is a difficult one; the script is based almost entirely on strategy and politics, and there is little evidence of Yamamoto's real-life character. An inveterate gambler and womanizer, a tough military leader with a sentimental side—he was known to cry at the funerals of fallen comrades—and possessing a playful, child-ish streak in private life, Yamamoto was complex, sympathetic, and contradictory. The film shows none of this, nor does it mention his time spent studying abroad in the United States, a major reason for his reluctance to go to war with America. The focus is on the strain of command, the weight of decision, and the bond of duty.

Though he doesn't get inside his subject's head, Honda gives Yamamoto two brief, personal scenes: a solitary interior monologue while standing on his ship's deck, set against a surreal backdrop of ocean and night sky, and pondering fears about the coming war (Honda would later claim this scene was one of the first in Japanese cinema to significantly utilize rear-screen projection); and an emotional moment after the defeat at Midway. Honda was drawn to Yamamoto's story partly because the admiral didn't seek military glory; he wanted only to complete his service with honor and then retire to private life, not unlike how young Honda spent his years at the front wanting only to make movies. When Yamamoto's plane is shot down, Honda lingers on Yamamoto's pained face, and the moment is less about the martyrdom of a hero than the tragedy of a man who sacrificed all for a war he did not believe in.

Toshiro Mifune is excellent in an extended cameo as a self-sacrificing pilot. Mifune was concurrently shooting Kurosawa's *Seven Samurai*; this was his only screen appearance in the year prior to the release of that film.[22] Mifune's swagger brings the movie suddenly to life, and one can only wonder what Honda might have accomplished had he and Mifune worked together more than just a handful of times.

————

Whenever Honda was assigned a new project, he would bring the screenplay home and, before going out of the house, leave it on the dining room table. This was an unspoken request for his wife—a former script supervisor, whose opinion he valued highly—to read it. When he returned home, they would discuss it at length. Kimi was young and opinionated; so if she thought the story was poor, or if a character—especially female—wasn't believable, she spoke right up. "If I said, 'I don't think you should do this one,' he would say, 'I was thinking the same thing.' We were, after all, [both from the film world], so he would consult me," she said.

Toho was eager to capitalize on the success of *Eagle of the Pacific*, and so Honda was assigned to make another war picture, *Farewell Rabaul*. But when Honda brought home the script, his wife became concerned the subject matter could prove too stressful. "I told him and Yuko-*san* [Tomoyuki Tanaka's nickname], 'Please don't do it. Doing two war films back-to-back would not be good.'[23] However, Ino-*san* and Yuko-*san* said, 'We're going ahead with this.' So then it was like, 'OK, do your best, then.' And this one was a big success too. So from that point forward, I did not read another one of his scripts . . . I felt that as I raised children, my senses had started to shift and that I shouldn't hold him back, be his dead weight."

By 1954, Toho was fully recovered from the effects of the strikes. Film output had increased dramatically, and its stages were humming with factory-line efficiency. *Farewell Rabaul* was released on February 20, 1954, almost exactly four months to the day after *Eagle of the Pacific*. The middle chapter in what can be viewed as Honda's antiwar trilogy, this film is a 180-degree pivot from *Eagle*, a historical dramatization told from the viewpoint of the upper military echelons. The wholly fictional *Farewell Rabaul* is an entertainment picture, a melodrama set at a remote air base. Honda draws on his own war experience and focuses on the dangers of blind nationalism and the strain endured by the rank and file who fought to the war's bitter end.

The port town of Rabaul, situated in a corner of New Britain Island in Papua New Guinea just north of Australia, was home to a major Japanese air base from February 1942, when Japanese forces trounced the Australian forces defending it, until the end of World War II.[24] The film depicts the months after December 1943, when US Marines seized surrounding islands, isolating the Japanese at Rabaul and choking off their military capability. *Farewell Rabaul* is part melodrama, with the air corpsmen seeking connections in their lonely, isolated lives, living under a cloud of certain doom and defeat. It is also part action movie, with exciting aerial dogfights rendered via Eiji Tsuburaya's special effects. The film is similar in content, if not in tone, to Hollywood fare such as Nicholas Ray's *Flying Leathernecks* (1951), starring John Wayne as a gruff, by-the-book commander leading a squadron of ne'er-do-well pilots against Japan at Guadalcanal and to Fred Zinnemann's *From Here to Eternity* (1953), with soldiers stationed in Hawaii, drinking and romancing under the specter of war.

The screenplay was cocredited to Shinobu Hashimoto and two other writers, both of whom would pen numerous Honda films in coming years, Dai Nishijima and Takeshi Kimura. By now, however, Honda was routinely polishing the screenplay himself, even on projects in which he did not take a writing credit. "Kajiro Yamamoto told me, 'The director is supposed to write the screenplay.' So in my case, whenever I made a film, even if it was someone else's story, I always took a week or so and fixed

it, made it into more of my vision," Honda said.[25]

Though it's obvious the film was shot mostly on studio sets, even without his customary views of natural surroundings Honda still finds an oasis in hell, under a beautiful, starlit sky. And there are several you-are-there details that reinforce the life of the islanders (natives enjoying fresh water on a blazing day) and the plight of the soldiers (bowing to urns, placing ribbons on photos of recent KIAs).[26] The film was publicized as a romantic melodrama, but it is only partly concerned with its characters' love lives. The real focus is on Japan's single-minded drive to win the war at any cost and on a military culture that honored fighting to the death even in the face of certain defeat. It was packaged as light entertainment—posters emphasized the romance between Ryo Ikebe and Mariko Okada—and not considered controversial upon its release. Even so, Honda raises serious questions about the war.

According to Honda, the inspiration for the movie was the "Ballad of Rabaul," a *gunka* (war anthem) popular during the later years of World War II, with lyrics that speak of "sadness, sunsets, waves" and describe the island's tropical paradise.[27] In the waning days of the Pacific War, Japanese airmen stationed at Rabaul are fighting a lost cause against the superior American forces. Their leader is Lt. "Daredevil" Wakabayashi (Ikebe), a top-gun pilot with a record number of kills, a steadfast dedication to the war, and no patience for those bitten by the "defeat bug." He believes victory can be achieved only through strict discipline. Wakabayashi is so mean and heartless that he earns the sobriquet *oni* (demon) from a local girl. Death is part of duty; Wakabayashi feels nothing when

Farewell Rabaul. © Toho Co., Ltd.

a pilot dies and no compulsion to rescue flyers who crash-land in enemy territory. But slowly Wakabayashi's ice begins to melt after his adversary, ace American pilot Thomas Hain (Bob Booth), code-named Yellow Snake, is shot down and captured. The POW says he can't believe Japanese pilots don't carry parachutes. "Japanese tactics, military thinking, and even equipment [are] all based on the principle of making light of human life," Hain says. "A nation that doesn't consider the importance of human life cannot hope to win."

This truth shakes Wakabayashi to the core. Soon he refuses to send his pilots on a suicide bombing run; and when his close friend Noguchi crashes his plane, Wakabayashi flies to the rescue, suffering bullet wounds. Noguchi, badly injured in the crash, soon dies; and his lover, the island

girl Kim, throws herself into a volcano (off-screen) in grief. Another close friend, pilot Katase, is killed during an American air raid. Rabaul is evacuated, but not before Wakabayashi takes to the air one last time to battle Yellow Snake, who has escaped and returned to the air. Wakabayashi shoots down his foe, but his own plane sustains damage and he, too, crashes to his death. The movie ends with the first example of what would become a Honda signature, particularly in his monster films: a group shot of the survivors of a tragedy bidding farewell to the hero or fallen warrior. Here it is the women, departing the island aboard a ship, singing the "Ballad of Rabaul" as a requiem.

Farewell Rabaul shows Honda directing his cast with growing assurance. Ikebe is twice the actor he was in *The Blue Pearl*, delivering a forceful performance with gravitas. Ikebe was a bona fide movie star by now; and though he'd begun receiving better critical reviews for his acting, his handsome face was still his biggest asset, and Honda and cinematographer Kazuo Yamada provide several flattering close-ups. During a strategy session, Ikebe is the only officer without a hat, highlighting the star even in the obligatory group shot. This film marks Honda's first work with Akihiko Hirata, a recent graduate of Toho's New Face system soon to become an important member of Honda's fluctuating troupe. For Honda, Hirata would usually play a sober scientist or authority figure, so his turn here as the emotionally wrought Noguchi, torn between the duty to die and the will to survive, is a bit of a revelation. Handsome, with hints of mystery and sophistication, Hirata never became a big star, but he was a fine character player and would hold key roles in many Honda films, notably the upcoming *Godzilla*.

Nineteen-year-old Akemi Negishi, a revue dancer from the Toho-owned Nichigeki Dance Team, had made her film debut as the island girl in Josef von Sternberg's Japan-lensed *Anatahan* (1953). For Honda, Negishi would have notable roles in *Half Human* and *King Kong vs. Godzilla*, playing primitive women; here she is the exotic dancer Kim, whose romance with Lt. Noguchi is the film's only full-blown love affair. Like the dancer in Senkichi Taniguchi's aforementioned, controversial *Escape at Dawn*, Kim appears to be a thinly disguised comfort woman. Even after the end of SCAP censorship, the subject is handled in the same vague way, with the local bar standing in for a comfort station. As many as twenty brothels may have been at Rabaul, with up to three thousand Japanese and Korean prostitutes serving

the soldiers and officers, and possibly some native New Guineans. Kim—scantily clad, gyrating erotically onstage, alluding to affairs with the many officers whose photos decorate her wall—is in complete contrast to the demure Japanese women, all nurses and kimono-wearing hostesses. (The name "Kim" and the character's broken Japanese likely indicate she is Korean, another clue to Honda's intent.)

Given the suppression of the comfort women issue, Honda deserves some credit for hinting at this taboo subject through Negishi's tragic character. Also noteworthy is Honda's humanizing of the enemy. The dreaded Yellow Snake is revealed to be a plainspoken, if poorly acted, patriotic refrigerator salesman who volunteered for the military after Pearl Harbor. This is in major contrast to typical Japanese war films, *Eagle of the Pacific* included, which portrayed American and Allied forces as faceless and unseen, represented by war machines rather than soldiers. (It's also a fairer depiction of the enemy than the many Hollywood films that made Japanese soldiers into bucktoothed savages.) Bob Booth, who played the POW, was a Tokyo-based American magazine publisher moonlighting as an actor, a member of a small contingent of foreigners who played diplomats and soldiers in Japanese films in the 1950s and 1960s.

Despite his wife's concerns about making two war pictures back to back, Honda considered *Farewell Rabaul* one of his favorite films. He often told a story about shooting the rescue scene on location at Enoshima, an island not far from Tokyo. A full-size prop of a crashed Zero fighter was placed on the beach for filming. Honda recalled, "Two US Army helicopters hovered nearby and opened their side doors, and they started watching us with binoculars.

No doubt they wondered what we were doing there with a fighter plane, so I waved and pointed to the camera. They seemed to understand and waved back, then they left. The fighter was so well made that the US military had gotten suspicious."[28]

The collaboration between Honda and Eiji Tsuburaya took a step forward here. *Farewell Rabaul* includes a considerable amount of special-effects work, all new. No stock footage from earlier war films was used to keep costs down, though some air battles are augmented with newsreel footage of actual planes and bombs. Tsuburaya's miniature planes are unconvincing at times; but overall the dogfights are well staged, and the effects sequences are integrated with the drama more effectively than before. Though this film was only a moderate box-office success, it was a fine debut for the creative nucleus of Honda, Tsuburaya, and Tanaka, who were about to embark upon a project that would define each man's career—a project inspired by a tragedy stirring Honda's darkest memories of war.

III

SCIENCE FICTION
1954–64

[What was] special about the production of *Godzilla* . . . was the great care, the close attention to detail. That's especially true of Godzilla's movement. Godzilla's trying as hard as it can to assert itself and suffering for it. I wonder if that wasn't a reflection of Honda himself. Among the many monster films that have been produced, Honda's work in particular features this quality. . . . [T]he fact that you felt more sympathy for the monsters in these films . . . kept audiences coming back for a long time.
— Tadao Sato, film critic

Whether for good or bad, *Godzilla* decided the course of my life.
— Ishiro Honda

11

NO LAUGHING MATTER

Godzilla (1954)

Everyone was miserable. Honda and his team were roughly four hundred kilometers southwest of Tokyo, on a remote peninsula along the coast of Mie Prefecture, so remote that it was inaccessible by car. Every morning the cast and crew commuted by boat from their base in the small city of Toba, then spent the day shooting in sweltering temperatures. There were daily snafus: equipment malfunctions, misplaced gear, rough terrain. Honda was so focused that he forgot about the heat. Working shirtless, he suffered a blistering sunburn on his back and neck. It would leave permanent scars.

The soldier was at war again. This time, he was fighting the elements, fighting the doubts, fighting the naysayers who said a monster movie could sink his career. Perhaps that's why the sight of a dandelion blooming brought back an old battlefield memory. Honda stopped what he was doing and turned to his assistant director, Koji Kajita, and recalled seeing such a flower on the Chinese plains. Like the butterfly in *All Quiet on the Western Front*, it was a reminder of the beauty of life amid the horror of war. As bullets hailed, Honda had paused. "Why must we kill one another in such a peaceful place like this?" he wondered.

Koji Kajita tells this story more than fifty years later, while sitting at the dining table in the Honda family house, recalling the years he spent working beside his *senpai* (mentor, or senior), who was twelve years older. Kajita is small in stature, but his abiding admiration and respect for Ishiro Honda are beyond measure.

Kajita was Honda's chief assistant director for ten years and seventeen films. Their partnership provided a foundation for the second phase of Honda's career, an alternating mix of dramas about the struggles of young adults in rapidly growing postwar

Japan and outsized spectacles of science fiction and monsters. Kajita always refers to his mentor in respectful, formal terms, never using familiar endearments such as *-kun* or *-chan*.

Honda and Kajita first met in March of 1954 to begin work on *Sanshiro the Priest* (*Bokushi Sanshiro*). Details about the project are scarce now, and Kajita remembers only that it was the story of a priest and judo expert; it likely had some connection to Kurosawa's *Sanshiro Sugata*, but no one can recall for certain. The screenplay was to be written by frequent Kurosawa collaborator Hideo Oguni, it was to star Toshiro Mifune, and the producer was Sojiro Motoki. Honda and Kajita went location hunting and preproduction was under way, but after several rewrites Honda and the strong-willed Oguni couldn't see eye to eye about the screenplay. The project was canceled, but Honda and Kajita pledged to work together again. *Godzilla* began their partnership.

"I had always heard he was a very quiet gentleman, and that was exactly right. Never once did I see Honda-*san* get upset. All the other directors like Kurosawa, they would get mad and yell on the set, but Honda-*san* was never that way. He always kept his cool. No yelling, no sarcasm. So I have nothing negative to say about him, just like everyone else. Everyone knew he was a gentleman who had something [special] in him. I was surprised to find a director of such manner."

A pilot in the South Pacific, Kajita also knew the horror of battle. The war was part of their bond, though they seldom spoke of it. The story triggered by the dandelion was one of few such moments. Kajita said, "It was just the two of us, and Honda-*san* told me, 'People who have no use for war are made to kill each other. I think of this

whenever I see dandelions.' And I told him I felt the same way, looking down from the sky as I flew."

———

Unexplained shipping disasters plague Japan's coastal waters. During a typhoon, a fishing village on Odo Island is flattened by a mysterious, unseen force. Soon the culprit is revealed, a fifty-meter-tall prehistoric creature, revived and mutated by hydrogen bomb tests. Godzilla lands in Tokyo and exhales radioactive fire, setting all ablaze. The reclusive chemist Dr. Serizawa holds the only hope for mankind's survival, but his Oxygen Destroyer may be more dangerous than Godzilla itself . . .

Honda stood before the crew of roughly thirty men and issued an ultimatum. He was about to take a monumental career risk, and they must be willing to do the same. "He told them on the very first day, 'Read the script. If you are not convinced, please let me know immediately and leave the project,'" recalled Kimi Honda. "I remember him saying this very firmly. He only wanted those who had the absolute confidence to work with him on this film."

Godzilla first appeared in America in 1956 during a spate of popular science fiction and monster movies; but when the film was originally made in Japan two years earlier, it was an outlier, the first of its kind. This was a significant gamble for Toho Studios, with a production budget of approximately ¥60 million, three times that of the average Japanese feature, plus prints and advertising costs pushing the figure to about ¥100 million, or roughly $275,000.[1] Skeptics said it was the stuff of B movies and predicted a flop, but Honda, Tanaka, and Tsuburaya were determined not to become a laughingstock. On a spring day in 1954, they sealed their commitment to each other while standing at the front gates of

Godzilla. © Toho Co., Ltd.

Toho. This movie, the men pledged, must depict the attack of a giant monster as if it were a real event, with the seriousness of a documentary. Never mind that the very idea was absurd. There would be no trace of humor, no self-conscious joking.

Honda said, "[If] our hearts were not in it 100 percent it would not have worked. We wanted [the monster] to possess the terrifying characteristics of an atomic bomb. This was our approach, without any reservations."[2]

Added Kajita: "We knew the critics had no respect for science fiction films. So we said, 'Let's play this completely straight.' That was our motto. At first, everyone was anxious and felt uneasy. Even the staff was worried, asking, 'What the heck is Godzilla?' But our attitude trickled down, and once we began filming everyone started to feel the potential."

———

Godzilla wasn't Honda's idea, and he wasn't Toho's first choice to direct it. Even the concept of Godzilla's baptism by an H-bomb preceded him. Honda took this premise and the basic trappings of a monster melodrama and produced a plea for sanity amid the madness of the nuclear arms race. *Godzilla* is his darkest work, a window to his fears.

In early 1954, producer Tomoyuki Tanaka was prepping *In the Shadow of Glory*, a big-budget drama to be directed by Senkichi Taniguchi, coproduced with Indonesian film company Perfini, and shot on location in Jakarta. This was to be a major project, the first Toho color production and an attempt to open markets for Japanese films in Southeast Asia; it would star Ryo Ikebe as a Japanese soldier and Yoshiko "Shirley" Yamaguchi as his half-Indonesian love interest in a story about Indonesia's postwar independence struggle.[3] However, likely because of political tensions between Tokyo and Jakarta, the Indonesians backed out and the project was canceled on April 5, 1954, just before shooting was to start.

Suddenly, Tanaka needed a replacement project with blockbuster potential, or he'd lose face with studio chief Iwao Mori. In Tanaka's oft-repeated anecdote, the producer was flying home from Indonesia, "sweating" the situation, when he looked down at the sea below and wondered, so the story goes, what if a nuclear test in the Pacific awakened a giant monster from the depths?

Tanaka was a shrewd producer with a finger on the national pulse and an eye on movie trends. Japanese anxiety about the bomb had persisted since the war's end, thanks to atomic testing by the United States in the South Pacific and by the Soviets in Central Asia. Fears of nuclear fallout raining over the region were raised again during the Korean War (1950–53), and then a tragedy confirming Japan's paranoia grabbed headlines. On March 1, 1954, a tuna trawler ironically called *Dai-go fukuryu maru* (Lucky Dragon No. 5) sailed dangerously close to an American hydrogen bomb test at the Marshall Islands (formerly a Japanese territory, and still a prime fishing area for Japanese vessels) and was showered with radioactive fallout. When the contaminated boat and its sickened crew returned home, the Lucky Dragon incident created a "sense of emergency," recalls film historian Inuhiko Yomota, for "this was the third time that Japanese citizens had been killed and maimed from nuclear exposure." Fears of radioactive fish spurred a tuna boycott, and activists launched an antinuclear movement that was still in evidence following the 2011 Fukushima disaster, nearly sixty years later. Tanaka's new log line tied together these real-life postwar anxieties with a story line borrowed directly from Eugène Lourié's *The Beast from 20,000 Fathoms*, which Warner Bros. had, just a few months earlier,

purchased from independent producers for $450,000 and then released to great success in the United States.[4] *Beast*, the story of a rampaging dinosaur revived by an atomic blast, had followed in the wake of RKO's 1952 international reissue of *King Kong*, which netted more money than all previous releases of that film combined; both *Kong* and *Beast* had cost their respective companies relatively little and earned a fortune. With monsters making box office and nuclear fears making news, Tanaka's new proposal was savvy, timely, and relevant.

Senkichi Taniguchi and his crew were expected to jump from the aborted *In the Shadow of Glory* to this new project. But Taniguchi begged off; instead, he moved on to *The Sound of Waves* (*Shiosai*, 1954), an adaptation of Yukio Mishima's novel, and there may have been other directors who passed.[5] Honda was available; *Sanshiro the Priest* had been canceled on April 3. He might have declined, too—he was not above rejecting a project if the material wasn't right—but he accepted readily, confident that his background in documentaries and his interest in science were well suited. Still, the only prototypes were imports such as *King Kong* and *Mighty Joe Young*. Honda was more qualified than most directors, having made several pictures using special effects by Eiji Tsuburaya, who would be tasked with creating the monster, but this was unmapped terrain.

"When the plan for *Godzilla* came up," Honda said, "people had no clue about what it was, so everyone looked at it as if it was funny. 'What, some big thing shows up in Tokyo? That's stupid!' But because of my background as a kid, when I liked [science and] unusual things, I had no problem taking it seriously."[6]

Even so, Honda worried that he'd accepted an impossible task. Kimi knew the stakes were high, so she gave her husband space. She didn't ask questions when he came home from the studio, though she saw the concern on his face. "I wondered, 'Is this going to end his career as a director?'" she said. "And he, too, must have thought, 'God forbid if this fails.' This was considered such a bizarre idea back then."

————

Eiji Tsuburaya was not easy to work with. Though the director was in charge of any given production, Tsuburaya refused to cede control of his own domain. He protested when his scenes were reedited and would refuse to let principal-photography directors peer into the viewfinder lest they critique the camera angle, set, or other details. But studio head Iwao Mori had good reason for tolerating Tsuburaya's ways. It was Mori who in the 1930s had recognized Tsuburaya's talent for cinematic tricks and hired him away from the Nikkatsu studio in Kyoto. In 1942, Tsuburaya's acclaimed special effects had helped make *The War at Sea from Hawaii to Malaya* the most financially successful Japanese feature film to date and winner of *Kinema Junpo*'s best picture award. Prior to the war's end, Tsuburaya and his special arts department had achieved a certain level of clout; now, with Tsuburaya having returned from his forced hiatus and the studio back on its feet, Mori was intent on restoring that clout. Hollywood films such as *Mighty Joe Young*, *Destination Moon*, and *When Worlds Collide* had recently received Academy Awards for their special effects. A science fiction movie presented an opportunity to use Tsuburaya's talents in new and bigger ways, and thus to position Toho as the leading Japanese film studio in the growing field of special-effects filmmaking.

Beginning with *Godzilla*, Honda and Tsuburaya forged a partnership that was as mysterious as it was successful. They were totally different. Tsuburaya could be gruff and demanding, a perfectionist who wielded a level of power that only Akira Kurosawa and few others in the Japanese film industry did; Honda, by contrast, was quiet and polite, seldom expressing his feelings outwardly. Tsuburaya was a dreamer, interested in using film technology to create fantastic images; Honda was rooted in science, facts, and reality. They were not personal friends and rarely socialized outside the studio. Tsuburaya was ten years older. Yet, though it was all business between them, the two men developed a *tsu-ka* relationship—a perfect partnership, able to read one another's minds, finish the other's sentences.[7] They were equals: Honda, unlike his peers, regarded special effects not as a cheap gimmick but a legitimate craft. Tsuburaya, in turn, would make an extra effort to seamlessly mesh his work with Honda's, often shooting his effects from multiple camera angles to provide more options in the editing room, something Tsuburaya rarely did for anyone.

"Other directors such as Hiroshi Inagaki, Jun Fukuda, and Shue Matsubayashi also worked with Mr. Tsuburaya, but they were all the 'me-first' type and they really didn't work well together," said Kajita. "Directors tend to think they are number one, and the effects team should just follow behind. Mr. Tsuburaya didn't appreciate that. Honda-san and Mr. Tsuburaya got along so well because they were both very mature men."

Toho's two-director system, in which the live-action drama and special-effects sequences were shot by different crews, was rooted in war films such as *The War at Sea from Hawaii to Malaya* and resurrected with *Eagle of the Pacific*. In effect, two halves of a movie were shot separately and later combined into one; careful planning and clear communication were required to ensure the footage would sync. When one of Honda's actors looked up at a giant monster, the height of Tsuburaya's creature had to match the performer's eyeline. Honda and Tsuburaya would map out details during the early planning stages, and then meet briefly at the start of each day's shooting. As Honda's chief assistant, Kajita made sure each team knew what the other was doing. He would shuttle Tsuburaya to Honda's set to watch how the actors were positioned for a shot; he would usher Honda to the effects stage to see how Tsuburaya was filming a miniature city or other illusion. As Honda edited his live-action footage together, he would leave blank leader where Tsuburaya would later insert his effects sequences.

"No matter how much we thought things through, we couldn't see the finished result until it was done—editing, dubbing, etc.," Honda said. "When that time came, sometimes I had to tell him that we had to cut out something he may have really wanted. That was really hard. Of course, sometimes Tsuburaya didn't want to use some of my cuts because they didn't match his footage. But in the end, we always went with my idea. . . . These decisions belong to the director."[8]

———

Tsuburaya had wanted to make a monster movie ever since he saw *King Kong* two decades earlier, and he had once proposed a story about a giant octopus. That idea was briefly considered in early discussions, but Tanaka soon hired Shigeru Kayama, a popular writer of detective mysteries and speculative adventures in the vein of English author H. Rider Haggard, to pen an original scenario instead. Kayama created the entire foundation for the film; in broad terms, the plot, characters, themes, and

structure of his writing would remain intact in the final cut. Kayama apparently culled ideas from his 1952 short story "Jira Monster," in which a giant, bullet-repelling lizard that walks on its hind legs terrorizes primitive people.[9] Still, Kayama's draft was really a reworking of *The Beast from 20,000 Fathoms*. Numerous ideas were nearly identical: a dinosaur reawakened by an atomic test, shipping disasters, an undersea confrontation with the monster. Other ideas traced back to *King Kong* (an island culture that makes sacrificial offerings to the monster) and even to the 1925 silent film adaptation of Sir Arthur Conan Doyle's *The Lost World* (the creature's climactic urban rampage, the juxtaposing of primitive and modern worlds).

Tanaka's proposal was titled *The Giant Monster from 20,000 Miles under the Sea*, echoing its primary inspiration. But when Kayama turned in his scenario on May 25, 1954, it was titled *G-Project*. "G" reportedly stood for "Giant," though there is evidence that Kayama was already referring to "Gojira" in his diaries by this time, indicating that the monster's name was decided early on.[10] However, Kimi Honda recalled that her husband was quite concerned that the production team was unable to come up with a satisfactory name for the creature, and weeks passed before he and other members of the production team jointly agreed on "Gojira." Either way, the name's origins remain mysterious. Over the years, Honda, Tsuburaya, and Tanaka would often recount how they borrowed it from a big, burly Toho employee known on the lot as Gojira, a hybrid of "gorilla" and *kujira* (whale), because of his girth. However, this bit of studio folklore has never been satisfactorily corroborated.

"I suspect the name was thought up after very careful discussions between Mr.

Tanaka, Mr. Tsuburaya, and my husband," Kimi Honda said. As for the burly man called Gojira, she said, "The backstage boys at Toho loved to joke around with tall stories, but I don't believe that one."[11]

"Those of us who were closest to them don't even know how and why they came up with Gojira," added Kajita. Toho would later transliterate the monster's name as "Godzilla" to sell the film overseas.

Takeo Murata, a seasoned scriptwriter and assistant director, teamed with Honda to cowrite the adapted screenplay. After Murata completed the first draft, the pair sequestered themselves at a Shibuya inn for intensive writing and rewriting. "For three weeks, we racked our brains and collaborated to turn Kayama's story into a workable screenplay," Murata said. "Honda told me that he would write first, so I gave the whole thing to him. Then I polished what he wrote."[12]

The men were visited often by Tanaka, who preached budget restraint, and by Tsuburaya, who described the methods he was developing to bring the monster to life. Though Tsuburaya admired the stop-motion animation with which Willis O'Brien had created *King Kong*, that painstaking and time-intensive process was impractical because of cost and schedule constraints. Thus, Tsuburaya devised a brilliantly simple alternative. He would use his expertise in miniature design to erect scale models of Tokyo, which would be crumbled by a man in a monster costume. Taken alone, these techniques were nothing new—miniature effects dated back to French director Georges Méliès's *A Trip to the Moon* (*Le Voyage dans la Lune*, 1902), and Charles Gemora, Hollywood's "King of the Gorilla men," had been wearing ape suits in movies since the 1920s—but never before had they been combined to create

the illusion of a giant creature trampling a city. Born of necessity, Tsuburaya's innovative hybrid method would make possible an unprecedented scope of destruction and enable Honda to transform Kayama's monster-on-the-loose yarn into a nuclear-age cautionary tale.

Honda and Murata finished writing on June 10, 1954. The studio's artists then began drawing over three hundred storyboards. This process, which originated with *Eagle of the Pacific*, was considered crucial to ensuring that Honda and Tsuburaya's teams, working independently, created a seamless film. At an all-hands meeting in the Toho commissary, Murata walked everyone through the drawings and screenplay, describing each shot and whether it would be done by principal photography, special effects, or a combination of both.

Meanwhile, Teizo Toshimitsu, a designer who'd created miniatures for Tsuburaya's war movies a decade earlier, was sculpting a clay model of the creature. Many design concepts had been discarded; some of the earliest resembled a strange primate, but eventually Toshimitsu and Tsuburaya turned to dinosaur books for inspiration. Still, Kajita remembered, "It was just a reptile, not a bit scary. Tanaka, Mori, Honda, and Tsuburaya all put their minds together and had it redone. How about making the scales more prominent? How about making the face a bit more ferocious?" Eventually they chose a design loosely inspired by the T. rex and other prehistoric animals. It was a fantasy creature, scientifically inaccurate, standing upright and dragging its tail behind it (a few years later, paleontologists would conclude that dinosaurs such as the Tyrannosaurus stood instead with their bodies parallel to the ground). It had bulky thighs, long arms, and opposable thumbs. Concessions to human anatomy were necessary. This was the template for the first Godzilla suit.

————

After a long hike, Honda and Kajita paused atop a low mountain in Mie Prefecture. On one side were the swells of the Pacific below; on the other, a dirt path descending toward the run-down, lonely little fishing village of Ijika. An old watchtower stood atop the hill, a lookout for American ships during the war. On the horizon was the pearl island of Mikimoto. Honda remembered this place from shooting *Ise-Shima* and *The Blue Pearl* in this region a few years before. It was perfect for the big reveal in *Godzilla*, when the monster pokes its head over the ridgeline, an image that would become one of the most recognized in science fiction and horror movie history.

It was mid-July and the men were scouting locations for the fictional Odo Island. There is no actual island here, but instead a long, unspoiled coastline with rocky peninsulas jutting out. "Honda-*san* wanted to create a strong visual of this beautiful, serene place being absolutely destroyed by Godzilla," said Kajita.

Tanaka formally announced the launch of *Godzilla* on July 5, 1954. The studio's publicity strategy was to pique public interest while shrouding the creation of the monster in secrecy. The press was invited to observe Honda's live-action shooting, but Tsuburaya's special effects were off-limits. A half-hour radio drama, *The Monster Godzilla*, aired for eleven weeks beginning in July; and photos of the monster would begin appearing in newspapers prior to the film's November release date.

Shooting began in early August. There were three photography teams. Team A, under Honda's direction, handled the live-action dramatic portions of the film. Team B, under Tsuburaya, shot the monster and other practical effects. Team C, led by Hiroshi Mukoyama, created the many composite shots combining live-action and effects. Mukoyama's men were the unsung heroes. They simulated Godzilla's atomic breath using primitive optical animation; and with crude techniques such as in-camera mattes, glass paintings, and paper-cutout traveling mattes, they created giant footprints on a beach and other illusions that sold the monster's size.

Toho supported Honda with some of its elite technicians. This would be Honda's only collaboration with the excellent cinematographer Masao Tamai, who shot all of Mikio Naruse's 1950s masterpieces. Tamai agreed to shoot *Godzilla* only if other members of Naruse's staff also were hired. They included lighting director Choshiro Ishii, sound recordist Hisashi Shimonaga, and art director Satoru Chuko. "This was the best filming crew we could have had," Kajita said. Tamai also demanded that he, as cinematographer, have authority on the film's overall look, "in order to avoid confrontations with Eiji Tsuburaya," according to historian Nobutaka Suzuki.[13]

Samuel Fuller's *House of Bamboo* (1955), shot in Japan, opens with a glorious color widescreen vista of Mount Fuji. Ironically, such an image wasn't yet attainable in Japanese films, which were still mostly made with 1930s vintage cameras and equipment, shot on monochrome and nitrate film stock in the Academy ratio. Tamai used this aging technology to give *Godzilla* a moody, noirish look, unique among Honda's works. Many scenes take place at night or indoors, with low-key lighting from a bonfire, searchlight, or streetlamp. Light streams in through windows, and high-contrast shadows angle across walls and faces. Smoke fills the night air. Tamai coordinated with Tsuburaya's crew to sustain this darkness throughout the picture, and during Godzilla's nocturnal raids, the eerie black makes the monster's enormity all the more believable. Art director Chuko was known as "the great dirtier" because his sets looked lived-in and worn. Chuko's interiors contribute to this dominant feeling of tension; a dim laboratory filled with mad-scientist props transcends old clichés to become the cramped, claustrophobic hiding place of a troubled man.

Honda assembled his cast, crew, and equipment and headed back to the rustic coast of Mie for what would be an arduous location shoot beginning August 7, 1954. This area, "way out in the sticks" and possessing "old-time customs," as a news reporter observed, would lend the Odo Island sequences a documentary-like realism. However, filming here presented many challenges. Honda struggled to direct dozens of local extras, many of whom knew nothing of movies. "How can you make the film when Godzilla isn't even here?" they'd ask. Never mind, just run away, they were told. Those are actual villagers chasing after Godzilla with sticks; and when a shipwrecked sailor is pulled from the surf, several real *ama* divers, topless as per local custom, are seen in the background. The ritual dance to appease Godzilla was actually part of a local *kagura* festival at a shrine in Toba, the same troupe that appeared in *The Blue Pearl*, though here their music is overdubbed by composer Akira Ifukube, using Western instruments to imitate traditional Japanese folk music. Honda's first and second units would spend a combined total of twenty days here before returning to Tokyo to shoot on city locations, open sets, and sound stages. Toho was so busy, it didn't have enough space to accommodate all of Honda's filming, so stages were also rented at five other Tokyo studios.

Directing Akira Takarada and Momoko Kochi in *Godzilla*. Courtesy of Honda Film Inc.

Takashi Shimura, wizened beyond his forty-nine years, had played Kambei, leader of Kurosawa's *Seven Samurai* just a few months earlier, and had appeared in more than two hundred movies to date. Shimura's turn as the stoic Dr. Yamane gave Honda's film credibility, and his veteran presence on set provided mentorship for the young protagonists. Newcomers Momoko Kochi, twenty-two, and Akira Takarada, twenty, starred as lovers Emiko and Ogata, while the slightly more seasoned Akihiko Hirata, twenty-six, was the reclusive Serizawa. In Kayama's original draft, both Ogata and Serizawa were about forty; but with monster movies appealing to youth, the studio chose to promote fresh talent and the characters were aged down. Honda had directed Hirata in *Farewell Rabaul*, but Kochi and Takarada were recent graduates from Toho's acting school, the New Face program, and had only a few minor credits. Honda met with the pair beforehand to be sure they could handle their roles. During shooting, however, their inexperience became apparent.

Takarada recalled, "I went to the set on my first day of work. Trying to be proper, I went to [Honda] and greeted him. 'Hello, I am here to play the lead character. I am very pleased to work with you!' Then, I think it was Choshiro Ishii, the lighting guy, who yelled, 'Idiot! You're not the lead, Godzilla is!' I was immediately put into place. All I could say was, 'You are absolutely correct.' [Laughs.]"

Honda took a more hands-on approach than usual with Takarada, who could appear wooden, and Kochi, whose ingénue role required some key dialogue in addition to the usual screaming and crying. "At the time, there were things I had no idea about, like how the scene would turn out after it was composited with the effects shots," Takarada remembered. "We were like schoolchildren, asking questions about everything. 'Teacher, what should we do here? How do we do this?' Because [Honda] was such a decent man, he would try to answer each question as best he could. His patience made such a strong impression."

The pivotal scene on the mountaintop begins with a village alarm clanging. A horde of locals rushes up the hill with swords, sticks, and farming implements to confront the danger, but then Godzilla appears, huge beyond belief, and everyone turns and flees in terror. In the chaos, Emiko stumbles and Godzilla bellows a mighty roar at her. Kochi belts a Fay Wray scream, then Ogata grabs the girl and helps her escape. "Both of the main actors were . . . clueless about what to do," said Kajita. "Honda-*san* got up in the extreme heat, held up Kochi and said, 'This is how you save someone!' And he ran down the hill, dripping with sweat. Then he made Takarada do it. As for the scared face [Kochi]

was supposed to make, we went, 'No, not like that,' and [Honda] just showed her himself. He had to show them every step. They were nothing like the other young actors, like Yukiko Shimazaki, with whom he had worked before. It was a lot of work for him."

———

The heat was brutal. Temperatures topped one hundred degrees, and the humidity soared. When Dr. Yamane reaches the top of the hill and snaps a photo of Godzilla, actor Shimura's shirt is soaked with sweat. Shimura told a journalist that filming there was hell: "It takes an hour and a half from Toba every day. A coast guard ship is transporting us, so the motion is not as bad as on a fishing ship, but still, by the time we reach Ijika, four or five actors or actresses are down because of motion sickness and heat. Then from the port to the top of the mountain, a really steep hill, it takes another hour. When we get to the top, there isn't a single bit of shade there. So when we get there, filming is not even a concern. We are most worried about how to prevent getting sick from the heat."[14]

The mountain scenes were a logistical nightmare. The hilltop was so high that it was nearly impossible to direct the long line of extras along the trail. There were no walkie-talkies to communicate with the assistant directors below, so a white flag was waved at the summit when it was time for everyone to run. Once, the camera magazine was left at the hotel, and an assistant director had to walk all the way back to retrieve it.

Serizawa and Ogata's diving scene was perhaps the biggest challenge. The location was farther east, in Gokasho Bay, a spot Honda chose for its clear waters. The cast and crew spent several days floating aboard a coast guard ship, and again the sun pounded them. Actors Hirata and Takarada waited hours between takes wearing twenty-five-pound diving suits, sweat pooling at their feet. Momoko Kochi poured buckets of water over their heads to keep them from passing out. "I wanted to just throw the Oxygen Destroyer on the deck and put us all out of our misery," Hirata joked.[15]

When it was time to film at the bottom of the bay, a pair of divers from a marine salvage company, like the one that employs Ogata in the film, doubled for the actors. The task of shooting underwater footage fell to assistant cinematographer Yuzuru Aizawa, a man completely inexperienced at diving. Honda called "Action!" but someone forgot to turn on Aizawa's air pump; suffocating, the cameraman tugged his lifeline, but nobody noticed. Aizawa blacked out; when he came to, he was floating at the surface. "I was thinking, 'Goddamn it! I'm going to tell them I quit!'" Aizawa recalled. "But when they pulled me out of the water, everyone was kneeling on the ground, prostrating themselves. I couldn't say anything, and even though I hated the very idea of it, there I was the next day, back in the water."[16] This would be Honda's final opportunity to use the waterproof camera developed for *Ise-Shima* and *The Blue Pearl*, and "It was almost a tragedy," Honda said.[17]

———————

Sometimes when Honda told them to act terrified, the cast members would laugh. He described Godzilla as taller than the Marunouchi Building, a Tokyo office tower erected after the war, but they couldn't imagine an animal so big. They tried fixing their eyes on a cloud, but the cloud would move. It was a difficult task to get all of them to look in the same direction, at the same imaginary monster.

Others sensed when Honda was frus-trated, even if he never said so. "I was in charge of picking him up in the morning to go to the location," Kajita recalled. "When [we] would greet him at his front door, he would sometimes look very contemplative. Then we would think, 'Oh, he's in deep thought. I wonder if today will go well.' When he was faced with a big problem, it showed on his face. I could tell right away. 'Today's filming will be challenging,' I would think to myself."

When shooting, Honda rarely expressed his satisfaction or dissatisfaction with a shot. Still, the crew sensed how he felt. Kajita said, "We would think, 'That was a good take,' but Honda-*san* would not say anything. He just nodded and that meant 'good.' Sometimes he might say, 'Perhaps I should have shot that from afar,' or, 'Maybe I should have zoomed in more.' In that way, he taught the cameraman how he wanted things."

———————

The studio had greenlit *Godzilla* because Eiji Tsuburaya assured the brass that he could successfully create a monster. However, the creature had made an inauspicious debut. The first Godzilla suit, constructed of latex rubber over a wire mesh and bamboo structure, was built in secret and then unveiled at a demonstration for Honda, Tsuburaya, Tanaka, and members of the effects team. The costume was so stiff and heavy that the stuntman wearing it could barely move. After ten paces, Godzilla collapsed. Another, somewhat lighter suit was made.

The secrecy surrounding the special effects concealed the fact that Godzilla was played by an actor. Indeed, Toho would not publicly acknowledge this fact until more than a decade later, though it was already well known. And there was another, internal layer of secrecy. Tsuburaya refused to show rushes of his work to anyone other than Honda, Kajita, and members of Mukoyama's compositing team. Cast members especially wanted to see their monster costar, but it was not allowed. The concern, again, was that people might laugh. "Mr. Tsuburaya was hesitant," Kajita said. "He always had short rolls of footage in his pocket and he would take them out to show us. It was before the special effects had been combined with other footage, so the monster still looked like a toy puppet. It would be meaningless to show everyone footage that looked like toys . . . It was just the five or six of us that saw the special effects parts. That is how much he was worried."

Tsuburaya's work was just as problematic as Honda's. The finished film would contain 868 cuts, of which 263 were special-effects shots. (By way of comparison, Stanley Kubrick's *2001: A Space Odyssey* [1968], which later revolutionized visual effects, would have 205 such shots.) To complete this workload Tsuburaya assembled a core crew of trusted colleagues and protégés, some of whom he'd known since *The War at Sea from Hawaii to Malaya*, augmented by a large group of craftsmen and laborers with little or no experience, who found it difficult to meet Tsuburaya's expectations. The men spent thirty days constructing a detailed, 1:25 scale miniature set of Tokyo's tony Ginza Ward for Godzilla's attack, but Tsuburaya deemed it unsatisfactory and had it torn down and rebuilt. And there were mishaps. On the first day of shooting, the actor playing Godzilla was supposed to smash the National Diet Building; but when his foot caught in the set, he fell and injured his jaw. More than five hundred miniature buildings would be constructed; sets were made in precise detail, right down to the wires strung between telephone

poles. Often it took all day to prepare, then shooting took place from 5:00 p.m. until dawn. Sometimes just a few seconds of usable footage was captured per day. Many crew members slept and ate at the studio for about two months.

Honda and Tsuburaya began each day with a brief meeting, then went to their respective corners of the lot. "For a director, the number one problem is vision: how to capture a desired atmosphere and relate it visually," said Honda. "So, Tsuburaya's plans were always known to me. When my work wrapped early, I would go down to check on the special effects set. Or I would tell him, 'We've shot this scene from the script today.' He would reply, 'Well, what about the scene's transition to special effects?' This way, our two staffs kept in close contact."[18]

The weight of the monster literally rested on the shoulders of Haruo Nakajima, a young stunt actor who'd been looking forward to a career in period action films. He had recently played one of the bandits dispatched by Toshiro Mifune in *Seven Samurai*, and in Honda's *Eagle of the Pacific*, he had performed what was reportedly the first fire stunt in Japanese cinema, as a pilot set ablaze when his plane is hit by enemy fire. Nakajima was known for his physical strength and endurance, and he so relished the role of Godzilla that he would don the costume twelve times over a span of eighteen years, while also playing many other monsters. Nakajima was one of two actors cast as Godzilla, but wound up performing the majority of stunts. He studied the movements of bears and other zoo animals for inspiration, but the stiffness and bulk of the 220-pound suit limited Nakajima's flexibility. The resulting performance is slow, methodical, and menacing.

Upon being cast in the unusual role,

Nakajima sought guidance from the filmmakers, but he was left to his own devices. "They told me to go see director Honda about it so I went over, not knowing anything," Nakajima said. "I saw him and greeted him. He replied, 'Just do it well.' Even Honda-*sensei* didn't know what to expect because I was the very first person to ever do this. So then I went to get briefed by Tsuburaya-*san*, but he said, 'Well, I really don't know either.' He told me . . . to make it look like there was a machine inside—meaning, they didn't want it to look like there was a person inside the suit."

Nakajima could remain inside the costume for just a few minutes under the hot studio lights. He passed out several times. When filming Godzilla's rise from the ocean, he nearly drowned. Honda rewarded his beleaguered monster with small on-camera roles in this and many future films. "Honda-*san* would often come to the special effects studio when he had to discuss with Mr. Tsuburaya matters of continuity, camera angles, lighting, or matching sets. If there was an interval, or I was waiting for the next take, sometimes Honda-*san* or the assistant director would ask, 'Haru-*bo*, do you have some free time?' I would go over to the live-action sequence and get dressed as a soldier or put on a tie, or something." In *Godzilla*, Nakajima briefly plays a reporter.

Honda's friends and colleagues would snoop around the set, trying to get a glimpse of the creature. "Akira Kurosawa sometimes came to the studio to watch the shooting," recalled Nakajima. "There was a booth for the recording engineer in the soundstage, and he watched from behind the booth." Senkichi Taniguchi stopped by too, his facial expression betraying a deep skepticism. Meanwhile, producer Tanaka and studio chief Mori were growing con-cerned. They saw the monster in the dailies and asked Honda, "Do you really think this is going to work?"

"We couldn't reassure them," Kajita remembered. "There was still no sound-track, and without it, the film looked stupid."

Confidence rose when the film was finally paired with the brash, beautiful, deceptively simple melodies of composer Akira Ifukube. Like Max Steiner's *King Kong* score, Ifukube's music is the pulse of the film, punctuating every emotion from the fearsome power of the monster to the tragedy of the finale. And like Steiner, Ifukube built his score upon Wagnerian leitmotivs, with stirring martial music to propel the military scenes; a slow, guttural horror theme for Godzilla's assault; and a mournful requiem for the denouement. Ifukube's music would become strongly identified with *Godzilla* in much the same way that John Williams's themes would later be associated with *Jaws* and *Star Wars*.

Ifukube was a product of the explosion of Western classical music in Japan that began during the Meiji era in the late 1800s, but his primary influences were not the German masters. Raised in Hokkaido, it was his exposure to the folk music of the ethnic minorities of northern Japan, including the indigenous Ainu tribes, coupled with his admiration of the musical patriarchs of Stalinist Russia, that produced Ifukube's distinctive style. From the work of Igor Stravinsky, Ifukube adopted a driving sense of rhythm and extended musical ideas constructed from two- and three-note phrases. Another major influence was Sergei Prokofiev, composer of such widely heard works as the ballet *Romeo and Juliet* and the children's symphony *Peter and the Wolf*, and who scored Sergei Eisen-stein's epic films. Prokofiev's alternately militant and lyrical passages, frequent use of blurred tonalities and chromaticism (utilizing not just the basic seven scale steps but all twelve chromatic tones, resulting in harmonic ambiguity), and his other techniques for creating discord and tension—including *col pugno* ("with fist"), literally banging the piano keys for a cacophony of adjacent notes—are echoed often in Ifukube's music. Other major influences included the nineteenth-century Russian composer Modest Mussorgsky, the early twentieth-century Spanish composer Manuel de Falla, and the modernist French composers Maurice Ravel, Claude Debussy, and Erik Satie.

Ifukube was one of Japan's most internationally acclaimed composers for the concert hall, with symphonic works performed worldwide, and simultaneously among the country's most respected composers of film music, scoring more than two hundred movies from the 1940s to the 1990s. His works outside the science fiction realm include Kurosawa's *The Quiet Duel* (*Shizukanaru ketto*, 1949), Kon Ichikawa's *The Burmese Harp* (*Biruma no tategoto*, 1956), Hiroshi Inagaki's historical epic *Chushingura* (1962), Kenji Misumi's *Buddha* (*Shaka*, 1961), Kei Kumai's acclaimed *Sandakan 8* (*Sandakan hachibanshokan bohkyo*, 1974), and numerous *Zatoichi* films. Ifukube's driving, repeating motifs would help define the Japanese giant-monster genre that emerged in the wake of *Godzilla*.

"Mr. Ifukube's style was very classical . . . but it was also very bold and direct," Honda said. "That's why we picked him. Mr. Ifukube and I also shared very similar ideas about nuclear weapons." Before *Godzilla*, Ifukube had scored *Children of the Atom Bomb* and *Hiroshima* (both 1953). He understood the subject matter. While serving in the Imperial Army, Ifukube was forced to work with X-ray technology and suffered radiation poisoning.

"What made me realize what an incredible composer he was is this," said Honda. "Here is this story about a creature totally out of control, destroying everything in its path. It is completely brutal and violent. What kind of sound and music is most suited to this living thing [born] of nuclear power? Can we actually come up with such a sound? When I saw him in deep thought saying, 'What have I gotten myself into? What to do, what to do?' I thought, 'This will be a success.'

"I do not know how he worked with other directors, but when it comes to something like *Godzilla* it is not as simple as 'put a loud noise here' or 'play happy music here.' We thoroughly discuss what sort of sound effects will be used for various scenes with the sound effects engineer. There are cases where the sound effects and the music clash with one another and it does not work. When you watch the visuals, there are places where you hear things falling down or cannons going off. And we try to insert music into places where you hear nothing. There are places where music may not be needed. Ifukube-*san*'s music . . . comes together with the sound effects and increases the volume and depth of the [film]."[19]

Godzilla begins with the boom of gigantic footfalls, then an earthshaking roar. Ifukube, an expert in acoustics, devised these sound effects after the audio crew had run out of ideas. He bowed the detuned strings of a contrabass with a leather glove to create the monster's voice, and simulated the footsteps by banging on a primitive electronic amplifier. Because of the compressed schedule, Ifukube had only about a week after the filming wrapped to finalize and record his score.

Honda and Ifukube mapped out the cues, scene by scene, and the composer noted where the roars and steps would sound. These noises so effectively reinforced the illusion of Godzilla's size and power that Ifukube was concerned they would drown out Toho's orchestra, which according to various sources consisted of only twenty to twenty-five musicians. He told Honda, "The music mustn't lose to the monster's roar." Sometimes they solved this problem with strategic passages of silence: When Godzilla first appears on the mountaintop, the absence of music makes the monster more dangerous and the chaos more realistic. Later, when Godzilla confronts the army at the Tokyo shoreline, the orchestra goes mute while a cacophony of cannons, explosions, and monster roars fills the void.

Ifukube's score and sound effects so elevated the visuals that some felt he had saved the project. "When it all got put together, the music expressed the grandness of Godzilla," Kajita said.

Atomic bomb versus atomic bomb. Hydrogen bomb versus hydrogen bomb. And to introduce this new terrifying weapon to humankind on top of that? I cannot allow it as a scientist. No, as a human being.
— Dr. Serizawa

When it was completed, Honda's film bore only superficial similarities to *The Beast from 20,000 Fathoms* and its other Hollywood cousins. *Godzilla* was an epic disaster drama of postwar Japan, a snapshot of a resurgent nation haunted by old fears and regrets of war, of a once-mighty country paralyzed by political and military impotence. Though Honda does not put forth a specific political viewpoint, the film is highly politicized nonetheless. Its chilling visual analogies to nuclear destruction, and the questions it poses about the human and global costs of reckless scientific inquiry, still resonate.

This is not a pristine masterwork. There are scattered flaws in the acting, special effects, editing, and scripting, perhaps the most egregious being Yamane badly misdating the Jurassic Period and a splash on the lens during Godzilla's death throes, piercing the fourth wall. There is a bit of superfluous product placement for motorcycles. Yet *Godzilla* is greater than the sum of its parts, and these things do not negate Honda's achievement.

Godzilla is bookended by shots of the ocean's surface. The sea is a recurring visual motif, a classical symbol of nature's vastness and the unknown it harbors. The first act unfolds as a mystery. Honda creates tension and dread immediately, with the fiery sinking of a salvage ship and a frantic distress signal. An ensemble of characters, some of whom are strictly expository in nature and will disappear for long stretches, is gradually introduced. Panicked families crowd the coast guard offices, but officials have no answers. Journalist Hagiwara (Sachio Sakai) follows the disasters to Odo Island, where a village elder (Kokuten Kodo, who played a similar role in *Seven Samurai*) says the accidents are an omen of the legendary sea monster Godzilla. Kayama's original story revealed Godzilla's full visage and its atomic breath on Odo, but Honda changed the scenario and delayed the inevitable, prolonging suspense. The audience can't see what terrifies the sailors as their boat sinks, or what makes fisherman Masaji (Ren Yamamoto) scream in fear as his house is crushed. Even when Godzilla first appears, only its head and arm are visible; its full size and power are withheld until later. In a lengthy, exposition-heavy lecture before the Diet, Yamane solves the mystery and drops a bombshell: He believes Godzilla is a prehistoric holdover, dislodged from an undersea habitat by a nuclear test, which exposed the creature to massive levels of radiation. Members of parliament want to conceal his theory from the press. "The government, the economy, and international relations would plunge into total chaos," insists one official. The Japan Maritime Self-Defense Forces attack the creature with depth charges, but succeed only in driving it out of hiding, with brutal consequences.

In a long second act, *Godzilla* assumes war footing. The monster strikes back, efforts to stop it fail, and the military suffers catastrophic defeat. Honda introduces scenes and sights that would become genre standards: army rollouts, crowds fleeing, a conference, war rooms, blackouts, evacuations, and the construction of a big defense system or weapon to repel the monster. The human drama shifts to a latent love triangle. Emiko and boyfriend Ogata try to move forward with plans to marry despite the chaos all around. Emiko wants to break the news to the scientist Serizawa, her childhood companion and onetime fiancé in an arranged marriage, but she never gets a chance. Instead, Serizawa shows Emiko a secret experiment that shakes her to the core, and he extracts from her a solemn promise not to tell anyone about it.

Eiji Tsuburaya's special effects take the spotlight in act 2. Godzilla's fast-paced first rampage is one of the finest action set pieces that Honda and Tsuburaya would ever produce, showcasing the effects man's virtuosity and revealing the director's attitude toward the monster. It begins with Godzilla's pounding footsteps interrupting an ordinary, quiet moment in the Yamane living room. In an iconic scene, Godzilla tramples through the Shinagawa rail hub. Passengers flee the ghostlike giant, and a train collides with its enormous foot, the cars careening into a deadly pileup. Children cower under the wreckage. Ogata and Yamane watch the attack from a hilltop, far removed from the action, a type of scene that would repeat again and again in Honda's later monster films. Unlike *King Kong*, there is no interaction between the protagonists and the monster. Shigeru Kayama's early drafts had Godzilla behaving as a hungry beast that chased after Emiko, but Honda saw the creature as impersonal, a force of nature. Godzilla occasionally behaves like an animal, annoyed by a chiming clock or flashbulb, but otherwise it hardly notices human beings.

Godzilla's final assault is fourteen minutes of merciless carnage and crumbling landmarks accompanied by Ifukube's eerie dirges. Exhaling its radioactive breath for the first time, Godzilla melts the city's last line of defense, a giant electrical barrier. Then, in the third act, the unfathomable human suffering compels Emiko and Serizawa to make pivotal reversals. Even with some overacting and heavy-handed dialogue, Honda finds emotion in these scenes. Emiko tearfully betrays the scientist, who must now face an agonizing dilemma: kill Godzilla with the Oxygen Destroyer but risk it becoming a weapon of war, or watch Japan be destroyed. Strident Ogata makes an impassioned plea for help, but Serizawa refuses: "Until I die, how can I be sure I won't be forced by someone to make the device again?"

Serizawa's prophetic question seals his own fate and points to one of Honda's main themes: the human responsibility borne by scientists, and a concern that science could run amok or be misused in dangerous ways. If Yamane represents the prestige and influence that scientists such as Albert Einstein had attained, then Serizawa symbolizes a dangerous trade-off of scientific advancement: the specter of brilliant men, working in secrecy—like those involved in the Manhattan Project—opening a Pandora's box.

"I wanted to express my views about scientists," Honda said. "They might invent something wonderful, but they also must be responsible for how it is used. A good example is Alfred Nobel, for whom the Nobel Peace Prize is named. He invented dynamite for mining purposes, but in the end it was also used to kill people. That's why he created the award. It was his wish that [science] benefit and bring peace to humanity. Similarly, I wanted to warn people about what happens if we put our faith in science without considering the consequences."[20]

Honda empathized with Serizawa, who emerges as the latent hero, the lone character to undergo a personal catharsis and the only man to confront the monster. There are stereotypes—the smock, eye patch, and rubber gloves; the creepy, test-tube-filled basement laboratory—but Serizawa is different from the mad scientist characters that proliferated in sci-fi literature and film; he is no Victor Frankenstein, and has no God complex. He is shrouded in mystery, disfigured by war, and tormented by the implications of his discovery. Serizawa lives and works alone, and it's unclear who underwrites his research. A reporter presses him about a German connection, perhaps implying Serizawa's involvement in wartime weapons research, though nothing more is made of it.[21] Yet, despite all this darkness, Serizawa is inherently good. He

fears his invention could destroy the world, yet hopes to find a peaceful use for it. And he can barely hide his feelings for Emiko. The scientist-gone-too-far character would return in future Honda films, but never with such emotional and ethical weight. Serizawa has been likened to physicist J. Robert Oppenheimer, father of the atomic bomb, who came to fear that the forces he helped unleash might bring about the end of the world. The similarities are coincidental, but strong.

————

Over TV news footage of Godzilla's aftermath, a choir of young girls sings "Prayer for Peace," a haunting Ifukube melody with lyrics from Shigeru Kayama, which translate into English as:

> Oh peace, oh light
> May you return
> To those of us who pray for our lives
> Regard this passage of misery
> Oh peace, oh light
> May you return

Hundreds of students from a Tokyo girls music school participated in filming the scene. As the camera dollies past row after row of singing children, the sadness of this vigil becomes overpowering. Watching the broadcast, Serizawa is moved. His resistance crumbles.

In the denouement, Serizawa and Ogata dive into Tokyo Bay. The heavy atmosphere remains. This is the antithesis of a typical monster-movie climax. There is no exciting showdown, only anxiety about whether the plan will succeed. In its natural habitat, Godzilla is peaceful and vulnerable, an innocent displaced in time by man's nuclear hubris. Honda paces these moments deliberately until Serizawa, now alone at the sea bottom, detonates the Oxygen Destroyer. Then, in an unexpected twist, he bids "sayonara" to his friends, cuts his lifeline, and takes the secret with him to the grave. Serizawa's suicide saves the world from a new doomsday weapon and ends his personal hell of regret and heartbreak, while allowing Emiko and Ogata to marry without any trace of dishonor. And Godzilla, the indestructible menace born of the bomb, now dies a pitiable, agonizing death in a bubbling liquid mushroom cloud. Ifukube's requiem wells up; a coast guard officer salutes the lost man, and Honda seems to be offering a prayer for Godzilla as well. There is no rejoicing, only a profound sense of loss.

————

Godzilla was made at a time of rising anti-American sentiment. A flood of popular novels and magazines critical of American policy, as well as radio programs and newsreels, had appeared after the Occupation.[22] There were 210,000 US troops stationed in Japan, and accounts of GIs and ex-servicemen committing rape, murder, and other crimes with impunity fanned the flames of resentment; anti-US views were espoused by college students and conservative politicians alike. Several Japanese movies exposed the ugly American and his arrogance; even Honda's *Young Tree* and *Inao* would make brief asides on the subject a few years later. Simultaneously, the Americanization of Japanese popular culture that began in the 1920s continued, as youths embraced American fashion, jazz music, and movies. And the surging economic recovery was dependent on America, which was Japan's primary trade partner and also using its influence to help Japan enter European markets.

Yet, despite the tremendous shadow it cast, America is conspicuously absent from *Godzilla*. International advisers arrive in Tokyo; but except for several Caucasian faces in the back of the room, the West is invisible throughout the film. The American military's complete uninvolvement in the crisis might be interpreted as a reflection of national anxiety over the Treaty of Mutual Cooperation and Security, which was signed by Japan and Washington in September 1951. Known by the acronym AMPO in Japanese, the lopsided pact allowed the United States to keep military bases in Japan as an Asian bulwark against Soviet communism and required Japan to defray part of the cost. America was permitted to defend Japan against external threats and to suppress internal ones, yet the treaty did not explicitly guarantee protection by the US military, an omission that would make AMPO a political lightning rod for years. The treaty also remilitarized Japan by authorizing the Japan Self-Defense Forces (JSDF), a contingent of 150,000 ground, sea, and air troops established in March 1954. Yet under Article 9 of Japan's US-written 1947 constitution, Japan had renounced "war as a sovereign right of the nation." There were concerns that the constitution prohibited Japan from defending itself, worries that the JSDF was too small and underequipped, and fears that America would not honor its role as Japan's primary defender. Notably, in the film Japan battles Godzilla without American help.

"The story proceeds as a purely domestic affair," notes historian Yoshikuni Igarashi. "Godzilla . . . is subsequently killed by Japanese without external assistance . . . In 1954, the concerted attack that the film portrays would have been possible only with the help of American forces. Nevertheless, the [Self-Defense Forces] . . . are solely responsible for the attacks against Godzilla. If the [monster] indeed embodied American nuclear threats, it is only logical that the Japanese forces alone should attack. The

American forces by definition could not."[23] Anxieties about national security are mirrored: Japan's fledgling military cannot halt the monster's massive onslaught, though fighter planes eventually succeed in driving it back to the sea, to the cheers of civilians. The EIRIN ratings board, in approving the screenplay on July 8, 1954, included a requirement that the film portray Japan's new military "with the utmost care and respect."[24]

As Igarashi points out, "There is not even a hint of [American] responsibility in the . . . destruction of Tokyo by the monster." Godzilla's ties to the atomic bomb have nevertheless led some Western critics to mischaracterize Honda's film as anti-American. Several contemporary Japanese scholars, meanwhile, have interpreted Japan's military self-reliance and the monster's reenactment of wartime destruction as "ambivalent notions of nationalism and anti-nuclear ideology," writes critic Inuhiko Yomota. In recent decades, influential film scholars have reinterpreted *Godzilla* as evoking a powerful national trauma, with the monster symbolizing the restless ghosts of Japanese soldiers lost in the Pacific War, a concept inspired by the postwar essays of folklorist Kunio Yanagita. Among those popularizing this view is prominent critic Saburo Kawamoto, whose 1994 book *Revisiting Postwar Japanese Film* theorized that these souls had taken the form of Godzilla and returned; as evidence, Kawamoto offers the monster's deference to the prewar order. "Those who died in the war are still under the spell of Japan's emperor," Kawamoto writes, therefore "Godzilla cannot destroy the Imperial Palace."[25]

However, Honda's own attitudes toward Godzilla, the bomb, America, and his own country are more nuanced and complex; the film is not an anti-US polemic but an even-handed treatment of the tenuous and asymmetrical Japan-US relationship, casting light on both the invisible hand of American hegemony and the spineless politicians who are more concerned about safeguarding Japan's client-state relationship with Washington than about the welfare of the nation. Just as some real-life leaders tried to downplay the Lucky Dragon incident, legislators move to suppress information about Godzilla's ties to the H-bomb, wary of antagonizing Uncle Sam. As Godzilla approaches Tokyo, one politician frets not about the threat to public safety, but to international shipping. Godzilla doesn't think much of the national leadership. It demolishes the Diet building, Japan's equivalent of Capitol Hill.

Honda does not depict all Western influence, Occupation reforms, and new attitudes negatively. Women's suffrage was enacted in 1945, and the first female member of the Imperial Diet was elected in 1946, changes mirrored by the fiery women's caucus that insists Godzilla's radioactivity be revealed. Emiko's decisive role in the drama and her rejection of arranged marriage also point to the changing times. Emiko is openly dating Ogata, with no fear that her father will forbid their relationship.[26] Issues of class status, and clashes between old and new values, create less conflict than in Honda's other works. Yamane is respected and well off, evidenced by his large home and television set (broadcasting began in 1953, and only the affluent could afford a TV as yet); but he allows his daughter to date a working-class sailor, and he adopts the poor island orphan Shinkichi (Toyoaki Suzuki) into his family.[27] The Odo people are backwater folk—there is a funny moment when their mayor awkwardly tells the senate about cows and pigs eaten by Godzilla—yet the Tokyoites don't ridicule their superstitions, as Ryo Ikebe did in *The Blue Pearl*. Yamane names the monster after an Odo Island legend, simultaneously linking Godzilla to modern science and old mythology, and to America's atomic bomb and indigenous Japanese folklore and culture. In this way, Honda shrouds the monster's origin in mystery. It's not perfectly clear whether Yamane's theory is correct, or if the creature is a god, or both.

An early draft of Kayama's story began with the Lucky Dragon No. 5 returning to Japan, directly linking Godzilla's birth to America's hydrogen bomb. Honda saw his monster not as an indictment of America but a symbol of a global threat, so he rewrote the scene. The vessel destroyed in the opening scene is a fictional one, though a lifebuoy on deck is labeled "No. 5."

"I did not want to [reference] the Lucky Dragon," Honda said. "If I did, I would have to [show how the] creature was born from that explosion. The screenplay is written with the 'speculation' that this creature was a result of a nuclear test, you see. I think that if I visually showed that [the bomb created the monster], that would have gone too far and I would not be surprised if people came out to protest such a film."[28]

"Putting a real-life accident into a fictional story with a monster would not be appropriate. Instead, it became a matter of . . . the feeling that I was trying to create as a director. Namely, an invisible fear . . . the creation of the atomic bomb had become a universal problem. I felt this atomic fear would hang around our necks for eternity."[29]

————————

Though a handful of films about the atomic bombings were produced during the Occupation, film critic Tadao Sato notes that, "Only very sentimental treatments of the subject were allowed, such as *Eternal Song of Nagasaki* (*Nagasaki no kuta wa wasureji*, d. Tomotaka Tanaka, 1952) or *The Bells of Nagasaki* (*Nagasaki no kane*, d. Hideo Oba, 1950)," the latter a true-life story about a physician who contracted leukemia while treating irradiated patients.[30] *Godzilla* is now understood to be among a small but important number of movies about the bomb that appeared after the Occupation ended and its censorship policies ceased. These films were far different from Hollywood's version of nuclear armageddon, as seen in films such as *The World, the Flesh, and the Devil* (1959) and *On the Beach* (1959), which follow the plight of isolated survivors. Japanese filmmakers knew of the death and destruction wrought by the bomb, and its physical and psychological effects.

In terms of tone and content, *Godzilla* closely follows two films that immediately preceded it, both commissioned by the Japan Teachers Union (JTU) to educate the public about the atomic bomb's horrors. The first, Kaneto Shindo's *Children of the Atom Bomb* (*Genbaku no ko*, 1952, aka *Children of Hiroshima*), about a schoolteacher who returns home to find Hiroshima still in ruins, included a limited yet terrifying flashback reenactment of the bombing; even so, it was dismissed by critics as a "tearjerker" and a self-indulgent art film, and so the JTU immediately commissioned another production to illustrate the tragedy more straightforwardly.[31] Directed by Hideo Sekigawa, *Hiroshima* (1953) had a harrowing, graphic, and lengthy explosion sequence, with scorched victims fleeing through a burning city littered with dead bodies. Both *Children of the Atom Bomb* and *Hiroshima* showed survivors crammed into makeshift shelters and wailing children watching their parents die of burns and radiation sickness, presaging similar scenes in *Godzilla*. Together, these three films form a de facto trilogy of early atomic-bomb cinema. Not only do they dramatize the catastrophe in similar ways, each one has a haunting, elegiac score by composer Akira Ifukube, bridging the films musically and thematically. They expressed what historian Donald Richie called Japan's "sympathetic sadness" and foreshadowed later Hiroshima-themed works such as Kurosawa's brilliant *I Live in Fear* (1955), the manga *Barefoot Gen* (published 1972), and Shohei Imamura's film *Black Rain* (1989).

————

In *Godzilla*, Honda alludes directly and repeatedly to the war, the bomb, and the *hibakusha*, the survivors of Hiroshima and Nagasaki. Warplanes, tanks, and convoys are deployed. Artillery units shoot and depth bombs explode, depicted with real military stock film. The monster's onslaught is a slow-moving shockwave, its radioactive breath incinerating people, cars, and buildings. Mass evacuation is ordered; people huddle in shelters. A mother comforts her terrified kids as Godzilla nears, saying they'll soon be in heaven with their father. Tokyo's ruins unmistakably resemble photographs of Hiroshima's aftermath. A final plea for disarmament comes via the beleaguered Dr. Yamane: "If we keep on conducting nuclear tests, it's possible another Godzilla might appear, somewhere in the world, again."

Over the years, Honda would repeatedly cite the metaphorical connection between the monster and the bomb. He told Kimi, "Having seen the terror of the atomic bomb in real life, it is most important to weave this element into the film well, so that everyone will understand." He also told journalists that Godzilla's destruction of Tokyo was meant to resemble the American firebombing of Tokyo.[32]

Even so, assistant director Kajita said Honda never discussed the matter with his *Godzilla* crew. Kajita believed the film was not political.

"Honda-*san* didn't incorporate such a message into the film," he said. "He directed *Godzilla* purely as an entertainment work, and I do not feel it was his intention to advocate the abolition of the atomic bomb. The scene where a group of students sing the "Prayer for Peace"— I think *that* is Honda-*san*'s theme.

"The film is made from the viewpoint that Godzilla itself is the victim."

————

The completed film was screened privately for Honda, Tsuburaya, Tanaka, and their assistants for the first time on October 23, 1954. It was also viewed and approved by the EIRIN ratings board on that date. Two days later, the cast and crew were joined by other Toho stars and staff, including Toshiro Mifune, for a big celebration, a traditional well-wishing Shinto ceremony and the first screening before an audience. Lead actor Akira Takarada wept when Godzilla died; writer Shigeru Kayama was also moved to tears. Everyone seemed pleased and confident, but Honda was worried. The publicity campaign had built tremendous anticipation, and the press appeared eager to tear the film down. Already some journalists were casting doubt. Weeks before *Godzilla* opened, a critic for the *Shin Kyushu* newspaper predicted it was the type of film whose "only purpose is to shock us with weird things . . . It's just a stupid trick for little kids."

Kimi recalled, "After the company screening, everyone wondered, 'Now, how will the public react?' This was a very scary feeling for [Honda], a sense of not knowing . . . Toho was worried too."

Godzilla was released in Nagoya on

October 27, 1954, a Wednesday; its official release date in the history books is one week later, November 3, when it premiered in Tokyo and at theaters nationwide.[33] It sold out the Nichigeki Theater, Toho's cake-shaped, high-end flagship venue in the Ginza District, where huge "Godzilla" banners hung over theater facades and people waited in line for hours to buy tickets. The film set a new opening-day record for a Toho feature, selling about 33,000 tickets at the company's Tokyo cinemas. "The line went around the Nichigeki three times," Kimi said. "The CEO of Toho personally called [Honda], thanking and congratulating him on a superb job. That sort of thing didn't usually happen."

Honda was so excited, he went to the Nichigeki and walked around the building, wanting to see the crowd with his own eyes. His son Ryuji, now aged ten, bought a ticket and went inside. It was standing room only, and the boy could barely see over the patrons' heads. "It was like a rush hour train . . . So quiet, everybody watching," Ryuji recalled. "Everybody said they were scared, and couldn't sleep for a couple of days."

In later years, Honda tended to recall only the sting of negative press. He would repeatedly tell interviewers that critics had savaged the film. "Critics said the special effects were very good, but overall the film was just weird," he said. "I felt really defeated, because we worked so hard . . . I didn't even want to go to work anymore. If it was that bad, why even bother to write so harshly? But it was a huge hit and made a lot of money. The people who went to see it, they all told me it was really good."[34]

However, a survey of notices published in November and December 1954 shows that opinions varied widely. Interestingly, many critics compared *Godzilla* favorably to *The Beast from 20,000 Fathoms*, which opened in Japan just a few weeks later. The following excerpts are taken from published reviews:

"They tried to make it realistic . . . but it just doesn't work. The dark imagery is just plain unenjoyable. I understand that they are trying to make a statement against the atomic bomb, but this is just asking too much." (*Kinema Junpo*)

"It looks like it was the wrong subject for [Honda]. The drama had too strong of a social commentary and not enough imagination . . . It is too serious, too heavy, there's no enjoyment. They should realize that when one swing of Godzilla's tail destroys the Nichigeki theater, that's humorous . . . They should have [made a] comedy . . . instead of a mediocre psychology story." (*Chugoku Shimbun*)

"It's a lot more complicated than *The Beast from 20,000 Fathoms*, and a lot more interesting . . . As the first of this type of movie in Japan, it's very successful. Toho's effects group should get credit for that. As for the drama, Takashi Shimura was the only one who stood out. All the rest, their immature acting skill was very noticeable . . . But after all, the main character was Godzilla, so it should be good enough to draw the kids, as a spectacle movie." (*Osaka Daily Shimbun*)

"The *Beast* is simply a monster that comes ashore in New York and destroys things, whereas Godzilla is actually described as a nuclear bomb. Its message is against the bomb, and for peace in the world . . . When Godzilla lands in Tokyo . . . think of what would happen if it were a real nuclear weapon. Nothing would help. That's what makes it particularly effective and scary." (*Mainichi Shimbun*)

"Ishiro Honda says he wants a lot of people to watch and enjoy it, but to also get his message against nuclear weapons. His effort was successful. However, when Godzilla shows up from the sea, it's . . . obviously a water tank in the studio. That was a disappointment." (*Tokai Evening Issue*)

———

Godzilla earned ¥183 million (just under $510,000) during its theatrical run. According to *Kinema Junpo*, it was the eighth-highest grossing Japanese film of 1954.[35] Of the sixty-eight features released by Toho that year, it was the studio's third-biggest hit behind *Seven Samurai* and Hiroshi Inagaki's *Samurai I: Musashi Miyamoto*. All three had been big financial risks for Toho, and their success affirmed the studio's resurgence as an industry leader. *Seven Samurai* had the highest budget (¥210 million, about $580,000) of any domestic film to date; *Musashi Miyamoto* (about $500,000) and *Godzilla* were second and third highest. All three films would become internationally renowned, but only *Godzilla* would quickly net substantial foreign money. It would also be the first Japanese film to achieve a wide US theatrical release, though under unusual and somewhat unfortunate circumstances.

Honda recalled learning that *Godzilla* had been sold to America. "When Mr. Ichizo Kobayashi [founder of PCL] was still alive, they would hold these artists' meetings every year at the Tokyo assembly hall, composed of directors, screenwriters, and producers. They would go over the previous year's works and discuss how to make better films next year. At this meeting, the president of the company at the time, Fusao Kobayashi [first son of Ichizo] announced that *Godzilla* had been sold.

"[Ichizo's] facial expression suddenly changed. He turned around in awe and said, 'What? Is that true? Don't you lie to me now, you hear?' But it was true. We told him, 'I think we got more than $20,000, may have even gone up to $25,000 for it.' He then said to me, 'Kid, this is a huge deal!' It was during a time where everyone wanted to obtain US dollars. Some people were seeking just a buck or two, and here we got over 20 grand . . . This was a wonderful thing for all of us on the staff."[36] Though Japan's economy began to revive in the early 1950s, the poverty and devastation of the postwar years were still recent memories. Personal incomes remained very low, and the country suffered massive trade deficits; therefore, $25,000 in highly coveted American currency was indeed a huge deal. But while the money was a boon to Toho, the amount was an absolute steal for the film's American distributors, a tiny fraction of the bargain price that Warners had paid for *The Beast from 20,000 Fathoms*.

Following the success of *Rashomon* at Venice, several acclaimed Japanese films had played in American art-house cinemas in the early 1950s, including Kenji Mizoguchi's *Ugetsu* (*Ugetsu monogatari*, 1953) and Teinosuke Kinugasa's *Gate of Hell* (*Jigokumon*, 1953), which won the Oscar for best foreign film. In response, Toho and other studios began actively marketing films for overseas distribution. *Godzilla*, however, was not acquired by art-house types, but by a group of exploitation-film producers led by Joseph E. Levine, founder of Embassy

Pictures Corp. and a master of massive advertising campaigns. What happened next is something of a minor Hollywood legend. *Godzilla* was extensively recut, with new scenes featuring actor Raymond Burr, playing a journalist, spliced into Honda's footage. Waylaid in Tokyo during Godzilla's attack, Burr is conveniently acquainted with Dr. Yamane, daughter Emiko, and Dr. Serizawa, and so he steps right into the action and covers the story with the aid of an interpreter. The new footage was shot by journeyman director and editor Terry Morse, who chopped everything down to about eighty minutes, retaining Tsuburaya's effects while gutting Honda's work. A moody flashback motif was added that, coupled with Burr's Western point of view, effectively disguised this as a monster B movie from second-tier Hollywood. Burr's scenes were filmed on cheaply made sets, with body doubles, over-the-shoulder shots, and clever editing to create the illusion that he was interacting with Honda's Japanese cast. The American distributors misleadingly claimed the film was entirely shot on location in Japan. Much of Honda's footage was trimmed or deleted, including a darkly humorous discussion between subway passengers directly referencing both the Lucky Dragon incident and the bombing of Nagasaki. These changes, and the elimination of a native Japanese context, had the effect—intentional or not—of depoliticizing the film and muting any perceived anti-Americanisms.

From a commercial standpoint, the revamped *Godzilla* provided a path for the many *kaiju eiga* that would eventually follow it across the ocean. *Godzilla, King of the Monsters!* opened in Times Square in April 1956 and subsequently played across the country. According to *Variety*, it earned about $2 million in its US theatrical run, a sizeable sum for a low-budget, black-and-white horror programmer (and nearly four times what the Japanese release had netted). Though this was for all intents and purposes an American product, the release appeared to far surpass previous foreign-made films in terms of theatrical bookings and box-office receipts. For decades, this truncated version was how *Godzilla* was known throughout much of the world. Most Western film critics and scholars had no access to or knowledge of Honda's original cut until 2004, when it received a fiftieth anniversary release in American art-house cinemas. As a result, Honda's achievement was obscured, and the film was thought to be a typical exploitation movie.

Honda was unaware that *Godzilla* had been reedited overseas until Toho, adding insult to injury, brought *Godzilla, King of the Monsters!* to Japan in May 1957 and released it in cinemas as *Monster King Godzilla* (*Kaiju o Gojira*). To capitalize on emerging interest in widescreen movies, Toho converted the entire film from its original format to 2.35:1 anamorphic scope, causing some scenes to appear severely and awkwardly cropped. Japanese subtitles appeared for Honda's actors, now speaking entirely different English dialogue. Advertisements said this version was "100 times more interesting" than the original.

———

The success of *Godzilla* had an immediate impact for Eiji Tsuburaya. He and his staff would receive several awards for their work, and special effects would begin to earn the legitimacy Tsuburaya had long sought. Producer Tanaka rushed a sequel into production, *Godzilla Raids Again* (*Gojira no gyakushu*), released on April 24, 1955. Whereas Tsuburaya held no formal title in the *Godzilla* credits, he was now officially the special effects director and would wield increasing power on the lot.

Honda had proven the doubters wrong; nobody laughed at his monster. But the film's success did not immediately change his career, and he would not direct the sequel. Iwao Mori felt Honda's sensitive nature was well suited to stories about the plight of women, and so Honda's next two pictures would feature female-centered dramas. *Godzilla Raids Again* was instead made by the prolific Motoyoshi Oda, who brought a more action-oriented approach. The sequel featured a new Godzilla fighting the four-legged monster Anguirus in Osaka, and also a *King Kong*-style battle between Godzilla and fighter pilots.

"They had to start filming right away," Honda said. "Since I was already working on something else and the company had not yet determined that I was a monster-movie guy, they decided it did not matter who worked on it. Or maybe for them it was not important to wait until I was free."

According to Honda's recollection, the reviews for Oda's sequel were more positive. "Back then, the media thought that it was stupid for a director to put his ideas or themes into a movie. They may have treated auteur types differently, but for something like a science fiction movie, putting thoughts or ideas into your movie was considered plain stupid. That's why I think that the first *Godzilla* was only considered a 'weird' movie. That's probably why they liked the second movie much better."[37]

12

OBLIGATIONS

Love Makeup (1955), *Mother and Son* (1955), *Half Human* (1955)

Honda followed *Godzilla* three months later with *Love Makeup* (1955), a romantic drama about the trials and tribulations of postwar Tokyoites, focusing on two lovers (Ryo Ikebe and Mariko Okada), who reunite after being separated by the war and its brutal aftermath. While the middle and upper classes are enjoying the fruits of Japan's nascent economic boom, these sons and daughters of laborers live on the fringes, the women employed as bar hostesses or geishas and the men working blue-collar jobs or resorting to crime.

Love Makeup is the first Honda film made specifically for a female audience. Studio publicity called it "a gorgeous love melodrama with Toho's best cast, meant for all the women fans." It was based on *Blow, River Wind*, a story by author Hidemi Kon and adapted by screenwriter Dai Nishijima (*Farewell Rabaul*). Though Ikebe is the protagonist, *Love Makeup* is largely told from the female point of view.

The story is part love triangle, part crime caper. Rikiya (Ikebe) spends his days captaining a tugboat up and down the Sumida River. He rooms with the beautiful singing geisha Hatsuko (Fubuki Koshiji), his platonic friend since childhood. Hatsuko is the type of long-suffering woman seen in Honda's *The Skin of the South*, *The Man Who Came to Port*, and *Farewell Rabaul*, deeply in love with an oblivious man. Rikiya, meanwhile, pines for Sonoko (Okada), whom he hasn't seen since leaving for the war front. One morning, Rikiya witnesses a car theft and agrees to help police solve the crime. While searching local taverns for the suspect, Rikiya finds his old flame working as a bar hostess. Their reunion is uneasy: Sonoko fell upon hard times after her parents were killed in the Tokyo fire raids; she is engaged to a man she doesn't love, but to whom she feels

Walking the postwar Tokyo streets during the making of *Love Makeup*.
Courtesy of Honda Film Inc.

indebted for rescuing her. Her fiancé turns out to be the scar-faced car thief, Ishijima (Hiroshi Koizumi).

This time, the young characters are shackled not by the usual constraints of arranged marriage and parental meddling, but by another bedrock of Japanese life: *giri*, the deep-rooted obligation to repay social debts in equal or greater amounts, even when it hurts. With typical restraint, Honda questions this custom even while reinforcing it. Rikiya tells Sonoko, "I hope you're not too bound by silly obligatory *giri* feelings," but in the end *giri* trumps all. Sonoko stays with Ishijima even though it likely means an unhappy life, while Rikiya finally accepts Hatsuko even if he doesn't exactly fall for her. Hatsuko is repaid for her faith and patience, the only person who finds true love. It's a sliver of a happy ending, indicative of Honda's romantic, optimistic nature.

Actresses Mariko Okada and Chieko Nakakita (wife of producer Tomoyuki

Tanaka) also appeared in Mikio Naruse's *Floating Clouds*, released roughly a week after *Love Makeup*. Naruse's film is based on a similar story, written by a female author, of lovers who reunite after the war and struggle to get by in Tokyo. While Tanaka said that if he hadn't steered Honda in the direction of science fiction, Honda would have become "a director like Mikio Naruse," these two films highlight the gulf between Naruse's pessimism and Honda's tendency to look on the bright side. Set immediately after the war's end, *Floating Clouds* depicts the exploitation of women by selfish, compassionless men. It's a bleak world where women die of tuberculosis or are murdered by their husbands. Honda, by comparison, sets his story in the present day, when things are improving, and he gives all of his characters a chance at happiness even if it's not everything they want. Honda's men are not the callous leeches of Naruse's world, and he colors the drama with touches of humor. The entourage includes a sumo wrestler (Nobuo Chiba), the butt of fat jokes. Even the criminals are funny: One man (Senkichi Omura) develops the hiccups under interrogation, and the thugs cower or mug for the camera during fight scenes. Honda's first seven features had few laughs, but humor would now become a prominent part of his style.

Bridges are a recurring visual motif, a link between past dreams and future hopes. Two flashbacks atop bridges, in particular, bear mentioning for their seemingly auto-biographical content. The first depicts the initial meeting between Rikiya and Sonoko, love at first sight, and it's not difficult to imagine Honda thinking of his sheepish proposal to Kimi on another Tokyo bridge years before. The second flashback mirrors, poignantly, the numerous times Kimi said good-bye as Honda departed yet again for the front. A sign hangs on a bridge by the river, bearing a military slogan: "Pray for long-lasting luck to our soldiers in battle." Rikiya wears military garb, and Sonoko bids him farewell as he departs for the front. Rikiya has much to say, but doesn't know where to begin; Sonoko understands—no words are necessary. She promises to wait for him. "Don't die, come back alive!" She hands him a thousand-stitch belt, a traditional good luck charm given to soldiers.

The film opens with a happy Rikiya chugging his tugboat up the Sumida River, his friends waving hello from the arc-shaped bridge above. Later, at his lowest ebb, Rikiya passes under the bridge again, but this time no one's there. Finally, when all is well again, Honda ends on a long shot of the same bridge as Yoshio Nikita's sentimental music swells, indicating a bright future ahead. Honda and cameraman Tadashi Iimura capture the flavor of the neighborhoods flanking the river, from the gritty red-light district where Sonoko works to the historic Asakusa Shrine, where she prays in times of trouble.

Love Makeup was an A-level picture, evidenced by the casting of Mariko Okada, a top Toho star, and by the appearance of two prominent singers. Fubuki Koshiji was primarily known not as an actress but as a chanteuse; her hits included a cover of "Save the Last Dance for Me." Pop star Takashi Nakajima performs the film's pivotal musical number, "The Earth Quietly Turns" (*Chikyu wa damatte mawatteru*). The lyrics strike a nerve with the heart-broken Sonoko, driving her to tears:

Once it's passed, forget about it.
After all, everything's just memories.
But this is life. So don't cry, don't cry.
The Earth quietly turns.

Working with more experienced actors than in *Godzilla*, Honda gets effective, restrained performances. Koizumi is especially good as the troubled young villain, despite obvious scar makeup on his cheek. In later years, Koizumi would be repeatedly cast as a conservative, bland scientist for Honda; but before that he excelled in interesting parts, some of them scoundrels. (A year earlier he had costarred in Naruse's *Late Chrysanthemums* [*Bangiku*, 1954] as a selfish son exploiting his good-hearted, ex-geisha mother.) Okada is fine if unremarkable as the weepy Sonoko; she was near the beginning of a long acting career that included work for Ozu, Naruse, and other masters. The second-tier cast has Yoshio Kosugi as the tough-and-rough head of the car thieves, speaking in an intimidating Kansai gangster dialect. Bokuzen Hidari, the town drunk in *The Man Who Came to Port* and frequent Kurosawa actor, cameos as the retired owner of the auto garage; the thugs include Senkichi Omura and Yutaka Nakayama, regulars in Honda's forthcoming science fiction films. Also emerging as one of Honda's important actresses of this period is Kyoko Aoyama as a young geisha. Not yet twenty, Aoyama had already played a major part in Honda's *Adolescence Part 2* and would star later in his teen drama *Young Tree*.

————

Six months after *Love Makeup*, Toho released Honda's *Mother and Son* (1955), one of Honda's best-directed films, with exceptional performances and a story that trades the conventional portrait of saintly Japanese mothers for one more complex and confounding. It tells the story of a middle-aged, meddlesome mother, her loyal adult son, and his long-suffering fiancée within the familiar setting of post-war working-class Tokyo. Dai Nishijima's screenplay is adapted from a *Shinpa* stage play, a type of old-school melodrama about women enduring class and social prejudice.

Once again, Iwao Mori urged Honda to make a film for female moviegoers. "Mori [said], 'Ino-*san*, you should make films in the direction of *Shinpa* thinking, with the new-school views on women,'" Kimi Honda recalled. "There are emotions which can only be expressed in *Shinpa*, [and] basically, Mori wished for Honda to become a director who depicted women in these ways. You know, Mori was a great mentor to him . . . As a director, Honda felt *Mother and Son* was the perfect material. And still being young, he put a lot of effort and passion into this particular film."

Motherhood is traditionally the most important social role for Japanese women. Unlike the Western family structure based on husband and wife, the principal relationship in the Japanese home is that

Mother and Son. © Toho Co., Ltd.

between mother and children; and the bond between mother and the eldest son is strongest and closest. Traditionally, the eldest son continued living with his parents even after marrying, moving his wife into the home, where she would be tutored in family customs by an often domineering mother-in-law.

Mother and Son is about the inevitable breaking of that bond and the hurt feelings and resentment that result. Oen (Yaeko Mizutani) is a widowed fishwife working out of Tokyo's famous Tsukiji Fish Market, assisted by her son Hiroshi (Hiroshi Koizumi). Hiroshi is engaged to his sweetheart Tamako (Yoko Tsukasa), and everyone seems happy about it except Oen, distraught at the prospect of giving up her only son. She becomes so engrossed in meddling—thwarting Hiroshi's plans to build a house and, finally, canceling the wedding outright—that she misses her own chance for happiness when an old flame, Tani (Masao Shimizu), returns from Brazil in the hope of rekindling their relationship. Seeing how upset his mother is, dutiful son Hiroshi resigns himself to a life of ennui.

Honda (far right) watches *Mother and Son* stars Yaeko Mizutani and Hiroshi Koizumi in rehearsal. Courtesy of Honda Film Inc.

After Tamako reluctantly becomes engaged to another man, Hiroshi sinks into depression. In a drunken, rain-soaked street brawl with Tamako's new fiancé and his gang, Hiroshi is badly beaten. While he's recuperating, the lovers reconcile.

This is not a *haha-mono*, a type of postwar film about maternal suffering and self-sacrifice, often depicting mothers as saints and their children as ungrateful sorts. A well-known example is Naruse's *Mother* (*Okasan*, 1952), with Kinuyo Tanaka as a widow abandoned by her kids. By contrast, the roles in *Mother and Son* are reversed. Oen is one of Honda's most contradictory characters, selfish and irrational and yet sympathetic. She is what Japan scholar Ian Buruma calls the "eternal mother," who raises her children to foster near-total dependence. "The mother needs the child's dependence to satisfy her own emotional needs," Buruma writes. "[She] tries to hang on as long as she can."[1]

Similarly, Hiroshi is hardly the usual *haha-mono* ingrate son. He is loyal to a fault, forgiving Oen's transgressions out of guilt and obligation. Hiroshi's wish to move out and live independently represents the postwar generation's desire to rebuild Japan in its image; his plans for a Western-style house with the toilet and bathtub in the same room (very modern for the time) symbolize the ongoing tension between traditional and new values.[2]

As Oen, Mizutani gives the most interesting female performance in a Honda film thus far. Mizutani began acting in the 1920s in *Shinpa* theater and silent films. It's fitting, then, that one of the most powerful scenes in *Mother and Son* has little dialogue and succeeds because of Mizutani's subtle gestures. When Hiroshi and Tamako go shopping at one of the new, American-style department stores in Ginza, Oen tags along; she's always picked out her son's clothes and has no intention of giving up this right. Wandering through the displays and surrounded by mannequins in Western suits, Oen is a solitary figure in her *komon* (fine pattern kimono), a traditional mother watching her son drift away in a sea of change; and composer Ichiro Sato's music-box tones underscore her feelings of childlike helplessness. This early moment establishes Oen's deep sadness. Not even the reappearance of her old suitor, showering her with gifts, can lift Oen's spirits. Hiroshi is her entire world; losing him is too much to bear.

In his first leading man role for Honda, Koizumi gives a spirited performance. Koizumi worked repeatedly for the studio's top golden-age directors, but was probably best known for playing the husband in the film and TV adaptations of *Sazae-san*, a popular comic strip and roughly the cultural equivalent of *I Love Lucy*. Koizumi and the far more experienced Mizutani are surprisingly well paired, depicting the tension and love between son and mother believably, sometimes without dialogue. As Oen begins unraveling, Hiroshi tries boosting her spirits by taking her to a performance by Hikoroku Hayashia, a famous *rakugo* (traditional comic monologue) entertainer. Oen is enraptured by this outdated act, while Hiroshi is bored out of his mind.

Honda's direction continues to evolve away from documentary-style realism and toward a formalist depiction of the reality of everyday people. He employs mostly close-ups and medium shots focused on individuals and pairs. The melodramatic tone is again broken up by occasional comic relief, though more sparingly than in *Love Makeup*. Honda was never particularly comfortable with physical violence, so he takes a detached approach to Hiroshi's climactic fistfight with the thugs, which is shot from high above a bar-lined street. The bad guys include Godzilla-suit actor Haruo Nakajima and burly Shoichi Hirose, who would later play King Kong and other monsters.

Honda's documentary touch reappears briefly in opening and closing bookends depicting the bustle of the Tsukiji Fish Market, the world's largest fish wholesale marketplace, founded after the Great Kanto Earthquake.[3] With fishmongers sampling the wares and three-wheeled trolleys hauling fish through the narrow backstreets, the oily surfaces and fishy odors almost permeate the black-and-white film. Despite all that's changed, Tsukiji has survived the war and remains a symbol of stability; likewise, the characters' world doesn't appear to have changed all that much when the film closes, despite the ostensibly happy denouement. The lovers are back together; but Oen, waving good-bye to Tani's plane

passing above, seems melancholy still. It's a bittersweet ending, hopeful yet mindful of the delicate cultural balance of life in 1950s Japan.

First the abominable snowman, now these mysterious *buraku*. What have we gotten ourselves into?
— Prof. Koizumi

Worldwide interest in the legendary abominable snowman of the Himalayas spiked after British explorer Eric Shipton photographed large footprints in the snow on Mount Everest in 1951. An internationally publicized expedition to find the creature in 1954 produced more purported evidence. The movie world took notice; and Honda's second monster movie, *Half Human* (1955), fell within a mini-cycle of topical films bookended by United Artists' low-budget *The Snow Creature* (1954) and Hammer's suspenseful *The Abominable Snowman of the Himalayas* (1957). Over time, *Half Human* has become nearly as mysterious and elusive as the abominable snowman, withheld from distribution for decades because of concerns about its grotesque depiction of a fictional mountain clan. Though not Honda's best work, the original Japanese version is far superior to the more widely seen US cut, which unmercifully edits Honda's drama, replacing huge chunks with shoddily filmed expository inserts starring John Carradine as a scientist.

Even before *Godzilla* was released and proved a great success, Toho had already set its next monster film in motion and attached Honda to direct it. Writer Shigeru Kayama was again hired to pen an original

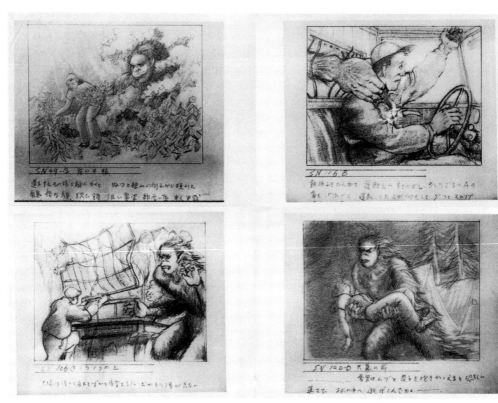

Storyboards from *Half Human*. © Toho Co., Ltd.

story; he completed his treatment on October 16, 1954, with the working title *S-Project*, and the production was officially announced in November with the revised title *Snowman of the Alps*. Screenwriter Takeo Murata worked on this project and Oda's *Godzilla Raids Again* simultaneously, and both scripts were submitted within days of each other to EIRIN, the national ratings board, for approval in January 1955. It appears that Honda's commitment to *Half Human* is what really prevented him from directing the *Godzilla* sequel; for just as *Godzilla Raids Again* was being hurried into production for an April release, Honda had to depart Tokyo for the mountains to shoot *Half Human's* snowy winter scenes. When Honda returned, Tsuburaya was busy with *Godzilla Raids Again*, so the abominable snowman film was put on hold while

Honda moved on to *Mother and Son*. The shooting of *Half Human* resumed and was completed in June and July, for an August 14 release.[4]

Kayama's scenario appears to have been loosely based on a pair of award-winning supernatural stories he published in 1947–48, *Revenge of Orang Pendek* and *Fate of Orang Pendek*, in which a Japanese anthropologist discovers a race of mysterious ape-men in the Sumatran rainforests. Folk talks of the Hibagon, a primitive creature purportedly haunting the mountains of Japan's Chugoku region, were another inspiration. *Half Human* is essentially a horror-mystery, incorporating elements of film noir and classical horror tropes (the false scare, the screaming woman in peril). With ample location shooting in the Japanese Alps, it also showcases Honda's customary semidocumentary lensing of beautiful natural environs.

Half Human begins ominously, with composer Masaru Sato's stirring title theme backed by howling winds and the opening credits supered over snow-blanketed mountains. The narrative utilizes a noir-style framing device: on a rain-soaked night, a trench-coated reporter visits a train depot to interview an expedition team that has experienced a harrowing ordeal. An urn of human remains sits atop a table, a foreboding omen. Ijima (Akira Takarada) shows the reporter a ragged, handwritten note from someone who witnessed "the most terrifying thing in the world," then he launches into a flashback recalling the group's fateful adventure. Ijima, his girl-friend Michiko (Momoko Kochi), Michiko's brother, and other college friends hit the ski slopes for New Year's vacation, and two men vanish in a blizzard. At a ransacked lodge, a search party finds two dead bodies, including one of the missing skiers, and discovers large footprints in the snow and strange hair fibers. Heavy snowfall forces authorities to postpone the rescue until spring.

Then, inexplicably, Ijima's flashback concludes and, after a brief return to the interview, the story resumes in a second, longer flashback told by Prof. Koizumi (the great character actor Nobuo Nakamura), a zoologist, who accompanies the searchers back to the mountains after the snowmelt. Koizumi believes the footprints and hair belong to a creature related to the abomi-nable snowman, and so the search becomes a quest to find both the other missing skier and the creature. Shadowing the group is the villain Oba (Yoshio Kosugi), who plans to kidnap the snowman and exploit it around the world like a circus animal. Along the way, the searchers encounter an indigenous, primitive mountain tribe that worships the snowman as a god. Outsiders are distrusted and rejected by all the tribe members except Chika (Akemi Negishi, the exotic dancer of *Farewell Rabaul*), a beautiful and innocent native girl, and the only human being that the snowman appears to trust. Chika becomes attracted to Ijima, but ends up as the third wheel in a love triangle; and she gullibly discloses the location of the snowman's cave to Oba and his gang, a naïve betrayal that sets off a series of tragic events. Oba captures the snowman, and when the creature's child tries to save its father, Oba shoots the youngling. Enraged, the snowman takes revenge on all humans. It kills Oba and sets the tribal village ablaze, then kidnaps Michiko and, when the heroes give chase, threatens to hurl her into a boiling pit. The native girl Chika intervenes and Michiko is saved, but the snowman is shot during a struggle. The creature falls into the pit, pulling Chika with it.

There are parallels to *Godzilla* (mys-terious disappearances, a scientific

Honda (center) and cameraman Tadashi Iimura (left) shooting *Half Human* on location in the Japan Alps. Courtesy of Honda Film Inc.

investigation, an isolated clan worshipping a monster-god, a latent love triangle that resolves with a tragic death) and also to *King Kong* (a would-be Carl Denham), but *Half Human* suffers from weak plotting, thin characters, and distracting humor. Honda creates tension and suspense in the early scenes—the eerie snowstorm, the waylaid skiers desperately trying to telephone their lost friends, their futile search with flares lighting the night and calls echoing in the canyons—yet this tension deflates during the second act, with long mountain climbs and talks at the campsite. The flashback motif does not enhance the narrative, and the switching of storytellers is peculiar, with no apparent change in point of view. The protagonists are bland: Takarada's ineffectual leading man, Kochi's weeping and screaming girlfriend, Naka-mura's expository scientist. The tone shifts wildly whenever the villain Kosugi chews the scenery, ably assisted by his dimwitted, toothbrush-mustached henchman (Akira Tani) and a stuttering lackey. The most interesting person is the compassionate and lovelorn mountain girl Chika, whose special relationship with the monster enables her to save the others, only to lose her own life. The character played a bigger part in early story drafts, and in a scene that was scripted but not filmed, the snowman secretly watched Chika bathing nude in a river.[5]

At its core, *Half Human* is another Honda story of a clash between the modern world and traditional culture with disastrous results, but what exactly it says about this clash remains ambiguous. Honda sympathetically portrays the snowman, the "most terrifying thing in the world," as a peaceful father that attacks only when provoked, saves two men's lives, and is lonely because its entire clan died after feeding on poisoned mushrooms. As the story ends, the protagonists have indirectly caused the deaths of the creature, its offspring, Chika, and the mountain tribe; but in their silence it's unclear whether they feel remorse, grief, fear, shock, or some other emotion. Dr. Yamane's final lament in *Godzilla* puts that film's tragedy into perspective, but *Half Human* offers no such resolution. The interview concludes, the train arrives, and everyone quietly files out.

————

The mountain tribe, which Prof. Koizumi calls "mysterious *buraku*," is overtly analogous to Japan's largest minority group, *burakumin* (hamlet people). *Burakumin* are descendants of feudal outcasts who worked in slaughterhouses, cemeteries, garbage dumps, and other jobs considered unclean and taboo. To this day, *burakumin* occupy a uniquely complex place in Japanese society. Despite official decrees of equality, they still face discrimination, yet they also benefit disproportionately from generous government assistance and protections. However, the very subject of their existence remains taboo, and the word *burakumin* is rarely spoken out loud.

Though *burakumin* are ethnically undistinguishable from other Japanese, the mountain tribe of *Half Human* is a gross exaggeration, an uncivilized, primitive colony of subhuman freaks. Nearly all suffer missing eyes or limbs, lesions, and gross disfigurements that hint at inbreeding. They wear animal skins, have cockeyed heads, are filthy, and live in a place that appears on no map. The notable exception is Chika, who is inexplicably beautiful, clean, and well spoken. Honda's works generally reflect a nonjudgmental worldview, but in this and subsequent monster films he would render indigenous peoples as clichéd stereotypes. *Half Human* is the most extreme example, with the caveat that it reflects prevailing attitudes of its time and caused no controversy when released. Nevertheless, these unflattering images would eventually prove problematic.

Half Human has rarely been seen in Japan over the past forty years. Some sources indicate it last aired on television during the 1960s or early 1970s, and it was screened at a film retrospective in Kyoto as recently as 2001, but the complete film has not been released in any home video format. Though Toho has not acknowledged the matter, the film is embargoed to avoid a backlash from pressure groups, such as the Buraku Liberation League. The image of *burakumin* in movies and TV became an especially thorny issue after a 1973 scandal in which a broadcast of Ozu's *Floating Weeds* (*Ukikusa*, 1959), which depicts a forbidden marriage between a girl and a *buraku* boy, brought a fierce response that publicly humiliated the responsible TV network. Since then, offensive references to *burakumin* have been avoided as part of a larger self-censorship effort by studios, networks, publishers, and the news media to purge discriminatory language and images. Material considered insensitive to victims of the atomic bombings led to the embargo of Teruo Ishii's notorious *Horrors of Malformed Men* (*Kyofu kikei ningen: Edogawa Rampo zenshu*, 1969), Toho's disaster film *Prophecies of Nostradamus* (*Nosutoradamusu no daiyogen*, 1974), and an episode of Tsuburaya Productions' *Ultra Seven* (1967–68). Other works have been shelved or censored for offending the disabled, the mentally ill, women, gays, foreigners, the Ainu, and other minorities. *Half Human* is just one of numerous suppressed works,

and it is unlikely to be officially released soon given the country's climate of political correctness and aversion to corporate embarrassment.[6]

And that's regrettable because, despite its shortcomings, *Half Human* is unique among Honda's monster films, with a sympathetic, humanlike creature that exhibits compassion, love, sadness, and anger. Giving an expressive performance inside the snowman costume is a man who helped create it, Fuminori Ohashi, an actor and pioneer in Japan's special-effects field. Ohashi reportedly had worked on the lost film *King Kong Appears in Edo* (*Edo ni arawareta Kingu Kongu*, 1938), which may have been Japan's first true giant-monster movie, though little is known about it. *Half Human* also shows the early evolution of the Honda-Tsuburaya tandem, this being just their second monster film. Honda was already using motifs that would recur for the next twenty years: ensemble casting, mountain-climbing sequences, a love triangle, but he also was still experimenting. There is more camera movement than in later films; darkness, shadow, and forced perspective contribute to atypically eerie shot compositions inside the snowman's stalactite-filled cave. Tsuburaya seems to pay homage to *King Kong* with a brief stop-motion animated snowman scaling the cave wall, girl under arm. Some effects reveal budget and technical limits: unconvincing rear projection, a floppy dummy hurtling to its death.

Half Human was radically altered, a la *Godzilla*, though with less care, for its 1958 release by a low-budget American distributor. Most of Honda's footage was deleted, as was Sato's score and all Japanese dialogue, overdubbed with narration by John Carradine. The rewrites and inserts turned the snowman into a typical, murderous, B-movie monster; and the running time was cut to about sixty-three minutes. The only notable scene is the ending, when Carradine unveils the snow child's carcass on a morgue slab, the actual costume, sent by Toho to Hollywood for filming. This version is, unfortunately, the only legitimate means of viewing *Half Human* until the unlikely event that Toho's embargo on Honda's cut is lifted.

Ready to return to military service.
Courtesy of Honda Film Inc.

The three crows: Senkichi Taniguchi, Akira Kurosawa, and Ishiro Honda, late 1930s.
Courtesy of Kurosawa Productions

Peering over cameraman Tadashi Iimura's shoulder while filming *The Blue Pearl*.
Star Yukiko Shimazaki looks on. Courtesy of Honda Film Inc.

Directing Toshiro Mifune in *The Man Who Came to Port*.
Courtesy of Honda Film Inc.

Honda observing Dr. Serizawa (Akihiko Hirata) in his laboratory on the set of *Godzilla*.
Courtesy of Honda Film Inc.

Honda and cameraman Tadashi Iimura prepare a scene with the snowman
(Fuminori Ohashi) on the set of *Half Human*. © Toho Co., Ltd.

Farewell to the Woman I Called My Sister: on location in the Shizuoka tea fields with
stars Hiroshi Koizumi and Chikage Ogi. Courtesy of Honda Film Inc.

Showing an extra how to load a mortar shell in *Varan the Unbelievable*.
Courtesy of Honda Film Inc.

Inao, Story of an Iron Arm: coaching baseball star Kazuhisa Inao in his biopic.
Courtesy of Honda Film Inc.

Honda (right) directing stars Kyoko Anzai (left) and Ryo Ikebe (center) in *Battle in Outer Space*.
Courtesy of Honda Film Inc.

Effects director Eiji Tsuburaya (center) and Honda (right) on the Faro Island set of *King Kong vs. Godzilla*. Courtesy of Honda Film Inc.

Directing the mutated mushroom man (Eisei Amamoto) in *Matango*.
© Toho Co., Ltd.

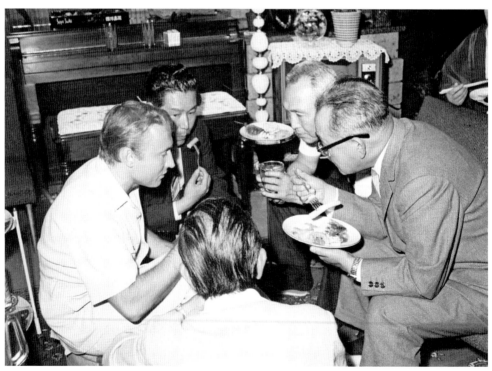

Producer Tomoyuki Tanaka, Honda, and Eiji Tsuburaya share a meal with Nick Adams
while making *Frankenstein Conquers the World*. Courtesy of Honda Film Inc.

Honda at the National Museum of Nature and Science during the filming
of *Frankenstein Conquers the World*.
Courtesy of Honda Film Inc.

Fun with the full-sized prop of Gailah's hand, from *War of the Gargantuas*.
© Toho Co., Ltd.

With the villainess Lady Piranha (Mie Hama) on the set of *King Kong Escapes*.
Courtesy of Honda Film Inc.

The creatures of *Destroy All Monsters* pose with (left to right) effects director Sadamasa Arikawa, Honda, Eiji Tsuburaya, and Tomoyuki Tanaka. © Toho Co., Ltd.

All Monsters Attack: Honda directs Tomonori Yazaki (left) and Hidemi Ito (center). Assistant effects director Teruyoshi Nakano (right) looks on. Courtesy of Honda Film Inc.

Directing Godzilla (Haruo Nakajima) in *All Monsters Attack*.
© Toho Co., Ltd.

Examining a huge prop claw on the island set of *Space Amoeba*.
Courtesy of Honda Film Inc.

Directing a battalion of warriors for a scene in *Kagemusha*.
Courtesy of Kurosawa Productions

Kurosawa reads a eulogy at Honda's funeral, flanked by Honda's son Ryuji (with memorial photo), wife Kimi, granddaughter Yuuko, and daughter-in-law Kuniko Honda. Courtesy of Honda Film Inc.

With Godzilla, c. 1991.
© Toho Co., Ltd.

13

YOUTH MOVEMENT

Young Tree (1956),
Night School (1956),
People of Tokyo, Goodbye (1956),
Rodan (1956)

From the symbolic clash of primitive and modern cultures in *Half Human*, Honda moves on to the very real clash between country and city, and between high school girls who harass one another with ridicule, jealousy, rumors, and gossip. Released on January 22, 1956, Honda's *Young Tree* (1956) is about a backwoods girl who moves to Tokyo and endures harsh trials before winning everybody over with her impossibly good nature. This is Honda's second youth drama, but where *Adolescence Part 2* looks at the generation gap and teenage sexual awakening, *Young Tree* is more idealistic. Honda focuses on the customary rivalries at an all-girl high school, relegating adults to the background while the students, from a variety of cultural and economic backgrounds, eventually resolve differences on their own. Strong-willed and full of potential, not yet saddled by the obligations of marriage or the limits of society, these "young trees," as a teacher calls them, show the growing independence of a new generation of Japanese women.

When Hiroko (Kyoko Aoyama of *Adolescence Part 2* and *Love Makeup*) enrolls at Tokyo's Kiyoka Girls High School, she's good-naturedly teased about her rural Kumamoto dialect and earns the nickname *batten-san* (*batten*, her frequent refrain, is Kumamoto for "however"). Hiroko joins the school ping-pong team and impresses with her excellent play, but Hanako (Keiko Mori), the popular girl, views Hiroko as a romantic rival for the team's coach, a handsome college student and ping-pong champion, Takuo Hotta (Shinji Yamada), affectionately nicknamed *Pin-chan* (i.e., ping-*chan*). In a plot with many twists and turns, Hiroko is falsely accused of writing a love letter to *Pin-chan*, a disgraceful offense in a school environment where boy-girl relationships are off-limits. A seemingly

Filming *Young Tree* before a crowd of curious onlookers. Courtesy of Honda Film Inc.

flawless character, Hiroko quietly does numerous good deeds for her classmates even while they continue to accuse her. Eventually the stress of school, work, and ping-pong are too much, and Hiroko almost quits the team. The finale takes place at the All Kanto High School Ping-Pong Tournament. In the title match, Hiroko faints from exhaustion and her team must forfeit. There is consternation and blame until everyone realizes her collapse was caused by her unselfish dedication to others. Tears are shed as the girls unite around Hiroko and resolve to win the tournament next year.

In Honda's early films it was the city folk who disrupted the pastoral status quo; here, the situation is reversed. A pure-hearted, orphaned country girl moves to the city and lives with her aunt, who runs a noodle shop. Even before she arrives in Tokyo, Hiroko is introduced to its corruption via lecherous, drunken city men (Honda regulars Senkichi Omura and Yoshio Kosugi among them) who taunt and ogle her on a train. Hiroko's new classmates mock her boondocks dialect; even the teacher can't help laughing. Her only real friend is

Kuniko, a no-nonsense, straight-A student who speaks and conducts herself with a dignified air, concealing the fact her family has lost its upper-class status. Unknown to her classmates, Kuniko and her ill mother live next to a cemetery, on the cheapest land in town.

Though *Young Tree* appears a rather innocent little story, nearly everybody is indicted for the problems in the school's microcosm of society. Kuniko blames all men for the evils of the world because her sister abandoned her family for a lover. "It is most important to remember not to trust any man, even if they shower you with kind words," she tells Hiroko. When the love-letter scandal blows up, a teacher blames the "malicious jealousy of an ugly female's heart . . . The most unattractive nature of women." The authority figures take their lumps too, expressing guilt for failing to notice that the girls have been quite literally working themselves sick. The Japanese education system is known to be exhausting, and *Young Tree*'s heroines endure its demands unquestioningly, while also working to support their families and friends. The film doesn't seem to challenge the system; instead it holds up Hiroko as its model citizen. "We're still very young and we'll mature and grow much, much more," she says. "That's why all we should concentrate on now is to work on ourselves to become better adults."

Physical action and suspense were not always Honda's directorial strong suits, and while a boating accident scene is executed rather poorly, it should be noted that Honda stages the final ping-pong tournament skillfully, from the excitement in the packed gymnasium to the rapid cutting between the players and the ball jumping across the table. It all builds nicely to the anticlimax, when because of extreme exhaustion, Hiroko's vision goes blurry, blood streams from her nose, and she's dragged off, barely standing. Though defeated, the team members are united as one—city and country, poor and not-so-poor. This theme of unity and mutual cooperation despite overwhelming differences would become a constant in Honda's works, from science fiction films with global implications to another little film, this one nearly forgotten, about students from the right and wrong side of the tracks.

————

Honda's dedication to the studio system was not absolute. During a brief respite between Toho projects, he collaborated with a handful of colleagues and fellow Nichidai graduates on *Night School* (1956), a forty-four-minute independent featurette. It was the only film Honda ever directed entirely outside Toho, and among his most elusive. After it was acquired by Daiei Studios and distributed as a secondary feature in April 1956, *Night School* essentially vanished for more than fifty years. It was among the first movies about night schools, which were considered refuges for troublemakers and poor students, preceding Yoji Yamada's popular *A Class to Remember* (*Gakko*, 1994) and others.

The idea for the project came from Kanesaku Toda, a staffer in Toho's cultural film division, who approached Honda and other ex-Nichidai men. The group acquired the short story "Mail Desk" (*Yubin zukue*), which had appeared in the children's magazine *Boys and Girls*. The story was written by Teiji Seta, a popular children's writer who later translated *The Lord of the Rings* and *The Chronicles of Narnia* into Japanese. Loosely based on Seta's experiences teaching at a public night school after the war, *Night School* follows the pen-pal relationship between two middle school pupils sharing the same desk, one attending classes during the day and the other by night. The screenwriter was Yoko Mizuki, whose stellar credits include several films by Mikio Naruse and Masaki Kobayashi's horror masterpiece *Kwaidan* (*Kaidan*, 1964), while famous Nichidai grads Keiju Kobayashi and Jukichi Uno starred as a teacher and a student's father. Teiji Takahashi, a young Shochiku actor who had worked for Ozu, was the night school teacher, while frequent Honda actors Yoshibumi Tajima and Yutaka Nakayama had small parts. The credentials of the cast and crew belied the fact that the film, produced under the auspices of the Nihon University College of Art, was made for almost no money and everyone worked without pay.

Honda and the producers submitted *Night School* to the Japanese government's education department, hoping to secure an official seal of approval certifying the film's appropriateness for families and students. The government advised Honda and the others to change the title because of the stigma around night schools, but they declined and their request was denied.

A dozen or so Nihon University students worked as gofers on the set. One of them was Teruyoshi Nakano, who later would become one of Eiji Tsuburaya's assistants. At the time, Nakano was a first-year film major, and he jumped at the chance to work on a professional shoot. "We were just students, not knowing a single thing about the film world," Nakano said. "I participated as an observer, a trainee. Honda-*san* was such a cool guy!"

Night School is a story of class conflict set against Japan's stark postwar struggles, told in a style befitting a young audience and ending on a hopeful note of friendship. The film opens at sunset, as poor children employed by day in factories and other jobs

Directing students in a scene from *Night School*.
Courtesy of Honda Film Inc.

end their workday and head off to night
school. Senta (Okinari Yoshioka) lives with
his mother and little brother in a shelter for
fatherless families. To support his family, he
works at the post office by day and attends
eighth grade in the evenings. One day,
Senta finds a letter in his desk from Ryohei
(Takeshi Ando), a student who uses the
same desk by day. Ryohei has lost his pencil
case and asks his night-school counterpart
to return it, if it has been found. The letter
implies that other items left behind by day
students were stolen in the past. The night
school students are offended, and Senta
writes an angry reply: "We work during the
day, waiting on people or doing office work,
and are fatigued as we arrive to school. Why
do you, who have the luxury of studying
carefree, assume that we poor students
have poor hearts as well?" Tensions flare.
Eventually the pencil box is found, and
Ryohei writes a letter of apology, leaving a
gift of two apples for Senta. Thus begins a
correspondence between the boys, using
the desk as a mailbox. Even though they
never truly meet, the boys become friends
and learn life lessons from each other.

Several scenes exemplify Honda's
ideal of mutual aid and cooperation. On a
crowded train, a girl loses her ball and calls
out for help. A passenger finds the ball, and
the camera follows as it gets passed from
hand to hand, back to its owner. In the
climax, the night school loses power during
one of Tokyo's frequent 1950s blackouts. It
is final exam time, and the students have all
brought candles just in case. A fire is passed
around and the candles on the desks are lit,
all filmed in one long tracking shot. Honda
then cuts to a wide view of the classroom,
forty flames flickering in the dark. In the
empty classroom the next morning, wax
marks remain on the students' desks.

Unseen for decades, *Night School*
resurfaced in 2009 as part of the Yamagata
International Documentary Film Festival's
retrospective, "The Man Who Shot *Godzilla*." In attendance was film director Shusuke Kaneko, a longtime Honda admirer
who helped revive the *kaiju eiga* genre
with a trilogy of Gamera films in the 1990s.
Kaneko first learned about the existence of
Night School in his youth from a monster-
movie magazine article and had wanted to
see the film ever since. After the Yamagata
screening, Kaneko participated in a panel
discussion with Honda's son, Ryuji.

Kaneko contrasted the authenticity of
Night School with more recent films such as
Takashi Yamazaki's popular *Always: Sunset
on Third Street* (*Always san-chome no yuhi*,
2005), which paints postwar Tokyo as an
idyllic, charming place. "When I see a film
like *Night School*, I notice . . . a very deep
yet kind perspective," he said. "In Japan,
there were many people who worked but
were still very poor back then. The landscape looked like that of China or Taiwan or
other Asian countries, nothing like what it
is today. There's a sense today of nostalgia
about the fact that Japan also once looked

like that and society was like that back then. A nostalgia for poverty.

"It feels like the changes in the social sensitivity of Japan that occurred from the Meiji era to prewar and then postwar times are packed into this [short] film. [It's] very substantial."

Reviewing *Night School* in the June 1956 *Kinema Junpo*, critic Hajime Takizawa wrote, "This was done by Nichidai as an experimental film, so it should be viewed as semi-amateur rather than an independent production. One can see that the filming circumstances were rather insufficient, but one can also sense fresh feelings."

Honda apparently neglected to tell his Toho bosses he was freelancing. When Toho executive Sanezumi Fujimoto asked Honda about the project, the director sheepishly replied that he and the others just sort of got together and made it, collaborating with whoever was available. There were no repercussions for straying from the fold. Quite the opposite: the studio was about to launch Honda into the busiest period of his career.

———

Because of the chaste relationships between men and women in most of his genre films, those who know Honda only through *Godzilla* and its offshoots might never guess he was, in his own modest way, a romantic.

On matters of love and marriage, Honda was a nontraditionalist, uncomfortable with arranged marriage and the way young people's feelings are ignored as parents and go-betweens force strangers into unions for reasons of economics, class status, and the continuity of bloodlines. Honda's views must have been influenced by his own marriage to Kimi and the ripple effect of her father's disapproval. The couple had no ceremony, no money, and began life together with none of the support afforded a wedding blessed by family and friends. For Ishiro and Kimi Honda, marriage was a matter of love and friendship, not something decided according to the needs and wishes of family or community. They chose the freedom to love, despite the consequences.

On-screen, Honda's characters usually do the same. Not one of his female protagonists willfully submits to an arranged marriage. Instead, she ignores the arrangement or openly breaks it, as in *The Blue Pearl*, *The Skin of the South*, and *Godzilla*. With the rare caveat, Honda's women choose true love, even if it means hardship and heartbreak.

People of Tokyo, Goodbye (1956) is the first of three short features starring teenage *enka* singing sensation Chiyoko Shimakura that were made in conjunction with independent producer Ryo Takei's company, Sogei Pro, and distributed by Toho. Shimakura, who won a talent contest sponsored by the Nippon Columbia record label in 1954, makes her acting debut.[1] The screen-

Directing stars Chiyoko Shimakura and Shinji Yamada in *People of Tokyo, Goodbye*. Courtesy of Honda Film Inc.

play, credited to Honda alone, showcases Shimakura's vocal talents by weaving several songs into a simple plot about young lovers trying to follow their hearts in spite of parental meddling. Honda leaves the city and returns to lush natural surroundings, a farming commune on Izu Oshima, a volcanic island with beautiful black-sand beaches, jagged coasts, plunging cliffs, and forests scarred by lava flow.[2] There, a group of families and their laborers cohabit a vast plot of land beneath mighty Mount Mihara, one of the last active volcanoes in Japan, harvesting indigenous camellia flowers and living in *bunka* (communal housing). Working for the first time with cinematographer Isamu Ashida, who would later shoot *Rodan* and *An Echo Calls You*, Honda films the outdoors in familiar splendor, but interior scenes look quite different from his previous films. Ashida's camera gives its subjects breathing room, taking in entire roomfuls of detail: furnishings, wall hangings, background activity. Conversations between pairs of characters are filmed in Hollywood-style foreground-background two-shots. Ashida gives a new look to Honda's constant pursuit of authenticity in everyday things; his style appears to have been influenced by Atsuta Yuharu's camera work on Ozu's home dramas of the same period.

In a familiar setup, a handsome young man from Tokyo arrives on the island. Shinichi (Shinji Yamada, the ping-pong coach from *Young Tree*) is taking time to recover from an unnamed illness before starting college. Shinichi reunites with Chiyo (Shimakura), a farm girl he befriended as a child. The son of a wealthy businessman, Shinichi is well known to the islanders; he and his parents used to summer there when he was a youth, and his dad is the community's philanthropist, bankrolling a big,

new fishing boat to be captained by Chiyo's father. Shinichi and Chiyo fall in love, but it appears doomed: Chiyo's parents have promised her to a local sailor, Jintaro (Kenji Sahara); Shinichi's parents have set him up with a Tokyo girl.

At the village festival, Chiyo's performance is the main attraction. Distraught, she manages to sing the film's title song, the lyrics of which compare a brokenhearted girl to the island's native flower.

> Sunset-lit sea, sunset-lit harbor
> The steam whistle echoes as tears form
> Love flower of *Anko Tsubaki* blossoms[3]
> Her petals fall even if there's no wind
> blowing
> The one from Tokyo, good-bye
> If I'm a flower that blooms for your
> compassion,
> Then once we split, I'll be just a flower
> of tears
> The black hair of the island beauty
> Please don't forget me, please come visit
> again
> The one from Tokyo, good-bye[4]

Shinichi and Chiyo declare their love, though it's too early for marriage. The boy heads back to Tokyo, vowing to return after college, she vowing to wait for him.

Despite the short running time, Honda's script is noticeably padded with workers singing in the field and a few unnecessary scenes. During the first ten minutes, Shinichi arrives on the island and immediately goes missing. Everyone worriedly searches the slope of the volcano crater, known for "lovers' suicides." This implies that sickly Shinichi may have come here to kill himself, but moments later he appears—he'd simply gone hiking—and the entire episode is quickly forgotten. Later on, Chiyo inexplicably leaves the farm to work in her uncle's camellia oil factory in town. Lovelorn

Shinichi follows, and they take a tour of the plant, the purpose of which seems to be an advertisement for Oshima Camellia Oil Corporation.[5]

Shimakura was only about eighteen when the film was made, and she looks even younger. She gives a fine performance as a typical Honda heroine, strong-willed and quietly defiant of the clueless adults, mostly men, around her. In a powerful scene, Chiyoko is forced to participate in a Shinto ceremony to bring good luck to the new fishing boat, a rite in which a lock of hair from the captain's daughter is offered to the vessel's guardian deity. The ceremony is also meant to seal her betrothal to Jintaro, who performs the hair-cutting ritual. Chiyoko bravely endures, wordlessly fighting back angry tears. They can take her hair, but not her heart.

It's when Chiyoko expresses her feelings to Shinichi that Honda reveals a bit of his own romantic side. She quotes from *The Tsugaru Fields* (*Tsugaru no nozura*), a 1935 novel by author and mountaineer Kyuya Fukada, in which the heroine offers, in veiled language, to surrender her virginity to her sweetheart. Honda's use of *The Tsugaru Fields* is evidence of the types of stories that inspired him. The novel is similar to many Honda films, a story of ordinary people surviving in the harsh natural surroundings of Aomori Prefecture in northeast Japan, not far from Honda's birthplace in Yamagata. Its heroine is like many of Honda's women: strong-willed and stubborn, working among men, unreluctant to assert herself.

According to Honda, *People of Tokyo, Goodbye* was made at a time when Toho was "trying everything out," and thus came the idea to build a film around Shimakura, a burgeoning pop star. Even though the script was his own, Honda wasn't immedi-ately comfortable in the song-heavy format. Still, during this period, "[I] tried my best at whatever kind of thing would come my way instead of rejecting something that might not have been for me," he said.[6]

————

Kenji Sahara embraced the world of science fiction more than any of Honda's actors. Sahara was still a greenhorn when he made his starring debut as Shigeru Kawamura in Honda's *Rodan* (1956), and he credited Honda with helping him hone his craft and establish his career:

> Director Honda always told me, "Don't overreact, just try to act natural . . . Just think of any old regular day. If something like this happened for real, how would you react to it? That's how you do it."
>
> During the first half of filming [*Rodan*], all I could do was play my part exactly as director Honda told me to. He was very gentle and nice and clear, and he told me what was good about my acting when I did well. But when I wasn't very good, "Cut! Sahara-*kun*, you're try-ing too hard." Or, "Cut! One more time." He very clearly pointed out what was wrong, but he spent more time giving me positive comments than criticizing. I got more and more relaxed as shooting went on, and midway through filming I was getting into my role and starting to create the character by myself.
>
> There's a concept in school that one should not criticize a bad student, but praise them when they do well. Director Honda was exactly that type. But his charm wasn't only that. Something about his way of direction always surprised actors. He could have been a really good actor himself.

Honda (far right) readies the *Rodan* cast for a scene in the coal mine set.
Courtesy of Honda Film Inc.

Two honeymooners drive to a scenic volcano to take honeymoon snaps. As the beautiful bride poses on a rock, an ominous roar fills the air. The husband tries to save his wife, but an enormous shadow swoops out of the sky, snatching both away. Authorities find only a camera and a high-heeled shoe. A double suicide? No, this is the work of Rodan, one of the Honda-Tsuburaya tandem's most inspired achievements.

With the success of *Godzilla* and *Godzilla Raids Again*, Tomoyuki Tanaka was eager to make more monster films. After discussions with Honda and Tsuburaya yielded the idea of a giant flying creature based on the Archaeopteryx, a birdlike dinosaur, Tanaka hired a popular writer of science fiction. Takeshi "Ken" Kuronuma (who had been considered for the *Godzilla* assignment before Shigeru Kayama was

chosen) penned an original treatment in which a supersonic flying monster appears over Japan and is chased by fighter planes, evoking the much-reported Mantell UFO incident of 1948, wherein a military pilot was killed while pursuing a supposed flying saucer.[7] Honda and screenwriters Takeo Murata and Takeshi Kimura expanded the idea into a hybrid horror–giant monster story with deadly, man-sized bugs, pseudo-science, and spectacular urban devastation rendered with innovative Tsuburaya effects. Honda rightly considered *Rodan*, his first color film, one of his best genre efforts.[8] It is among the most entertaining atomic-monster rampages of the 1950s and, while not as politicized as *Godzilla*, offers a battle against monsters as another analogue for war's horrors.

Like Honda's first two monster films, *Rodan* opens with mysterious disappearances and deaths. The dark, dank tunnels of a coal mine are infested with huge, prehistoric dragonfly larvae, called Meganurons. These man-in-suit insects are as realistic as a pantomime horse, but grating sound effects make for good scares as they prey on miners and terrorize the town. Admirers of Gordon Douglas's *Them!* (1954) will recognize similarities to that sci-fi classic: the military's confrontation with the insects in a mineshaft mirrors Douglas's extermination of giant ants in the Los Angeles sewers. Rodan's nest is a cavern inside Mount Aso, site of the largest volcanic crater in the world, fifty miles around, while the people live and work in a mining town at the foot of the mountain. (This is a bit of creative geography, as there was no coal mine located there.) Honda and crew shot on location both at Mount Aso and in Shikamachi, a coal-mining town in Nagasaki Prefecture. The setting is timely and prescient. This fictional mine is modeled after the Mitsui Miike coal mine in western Kyushu, which was Japan's biggest mining complex. Coal was a major force in Japan's postwar economic growth, and the infighting among Honda's miners reflects real-life tensions between labor and management. In 1952, 282,000 miners went on strike over wage limits, and a 1953 protest against layoffs at the Miike mine drew 25,000 people.[9] Meanwhile, the cave-in that traps Shigeru underground foreshadows a deadly accident that would occur at the Miike mine in 1963.[10]

The first half of *Rodan* is insular and claustrophobic. Honda shows the shock and grief inflicted on the community by a string of brutal killings, and the guilt and shame suffered by poor Kiyo (Yumi Shirakawa), whose brother Goro is suspected. Honda goes deep into the hot, oppressive coal mine shafts and galleries that seem to drive men mad, and into the miners' village, a string of row houses along a common path, where wives remain by day while their husbands toil underground. He goes into hospital corridors, where women and babies wail, and into the coroner's lab, where bloodied bodies are washed and examined. Finally, he goes into Shigeru's mind, traumatized and rendered amnesiac by horrors witnessed below the surface. The second half, conversely, is an entirely impersonal action movie in which Honda focuses on scientific plausibility. Akihiko Hirata plays an exposition-spouting scientist who believes shifting plates and global warming caused by nuclear tests awakened Rodan after two hundred million years. The film ends with everyone reduced to spectators, watching the final showdown from a safe distance, now a recurring Honda motif.

Rodan succeeds largely because of its sober detachment. Honda again treats impossible events as if they're really happening, with little emotional hyperbole. "My intention was to give [Rodan] a sense of authenticity and credibility, and not to make it a mere fairy tale . . . I wanted to create something that has ample scientific factual background and support, something that is not false."[11] Tsuburaya ultimately based the monster on the Pteranodon, a flying dinosaur, and it is arguably a bigger threat than Godzilla, seemingly impervious to weapons, outrunning jet fighters, and creating typhoon-force gusts with its massive wings. It eats Meganurons and livestock, and human remains are found outside its nest. Rodan comes to life through several different techniques, including a costume again worn by Godzilla stuntman Haruo Nakajima and several puppets.

Rodan's windblown assault mimics scenes from *Godzilla*—tanks attacking the monster, a ring of fire around the city—but now Tsuburaya's work benefits from the move to color stock. The damage is staggering: buildings blow apart, vehicles sail through the air, and pedestrians futilely grasp trees for safety. Images of roof tiles flying off were inspired by a crewman's memories of 1934's disastrous Typhoon Muroto. Sometimes Rodan's wings resemble plastic sheets, and Nakajima visibly stumbles when stomping the miniatures; but Tsuburaya's work is convincing overall. Akira Ifukube's stirring music paces the action, and his title theme is particularly dark and haunting. Honda frames Tsuburaya's effects between documentary-style shots of merchants boarding up stores, people searching the skies from rooftops, and mass evacuations.

"If you look at the scene where Rodan destroys the area around the . . . department store," Honda said, "the quality of the miniatures is something else. You can just feel the creators' passion in the details. In special effects films like this, it is all about destruction, how beautifully it all crumbles."[12]

With *Rodan*, Kenji Sahara became the anchor of the "Honda family" of actors. In the throes of amnesia, and especially in the cave flashback, Sahara sweats through trauma and raw emotion. As Shigeru watches the monster hatchling feasting on insects, the camera zooms into Sahara's horrified face—a favored Honda technique to punctuate emotion—and the symbiosis between actor and director is cemented. This was the start of a fruitful partnership that would span two decades and many memorable characters.

Still a rookie, Sahara wanted to prove himself. He studied the causes of memory loss and engaged in a sort of method acting. Between takes, he practiced unfocusing his

vision and whipped himself into a paranoid state. Unaware of his surroundings, he kicked a table, suffered bumps and bruises, and ripped his pants, causing a stir when Honda had to have them mended. Sahara recalled, "If I focused my eyes, it looked like I was sane and serious. So I avoided focusing on anything. [Honda] would watch me and say, 'Yeah, that's good.'" Later in the shoot, Honda took the kid out for drinks, a rite of passage. Honda began calling his protégé Ken-*bo*, an affectionate nickname that stuck.[13]

Yumi Shirakawa was nineteen and inexperienced when tapped to play the weepy, embattled girlfriend. Sahara recalled Shirakawa's shyness when filming Shigeru and Kiyo's embrace. "Shirakawa-*kun* was crowned Miss Morinaga and had just started [at Toho], so she never had done such a scene and got really embarrassed.[14] [Honda] told me, 'Stand over here, okay?' and then he ran over and hugged me. Seeing this, Shirakawa-*kun* started giggling. 'Why are you laughing?' Honda said. '*You're* the one who has to do this.'"

A second Rodan suddenly appears during the city rampage, a surprise development that sets up a tragic climax synthesizing Tsuburaya's spectacle and Honda's heart. The army bombards the volcano crater, triggering an eruption; and as the Rodans flee, one of them falls into the flowing lava, mortally wounded. Its mate circles helplessly above, then with a wailing cry it joins the other in a Shakespearean death. This hint of a relationship between the creatures gives Rodan, as opposed to the dead-eyed Godzilla, a modicum of personality, the shape of monsters to come.

It's an emotional ending, but it wasn't planned quite that way. Because of the intense heat on the set—the hot lava was reportedly molten steel—a wire broke while

Observing the interaction between amnesia-stricken Shigeru (Kenji Sahara) and his sweetheart Kiyo (Yumi Shirakawa) in *Rodan*. Courtesy of Honda Film Inc.

filming the first Rodan's death; as a result, the monster puppet jerks unnaturally. Tsuburaya thought the scene was ruined, but Honda salvaged it by increasing the intensity of Rodan's mourning. "At first, there was just the regular sound of the monster, but we modified it to make it sound as if it were crying out for something," Honda said. "Without that sound, it just looks like Rodan is flapping around . . . Sound effects made the difference."[15] Other changes arose during script revisions. There was just one Rodan in the first draft, and the creature

was seriously wounded by American fighter planes over Okinawa, giving the story a whiff of postwar tension; and as originally written, Sahara's character led the effort to kill Rodan by dynamiting the volcano.[16]

Though not as big a hit as *Godzilla*, *Rodan* earned a respectable ¥143 million (roughly $397,000) and ranked twenty-fourth among the year's domestic films. Upon its December 26, 1956, release, *Kinema Junpo* reviewer Masahito Ara wrote, "The overall color hue in *Forbidden Planet* [released in Japan three months earlier] is cheerful . . . whereas [*Rodan*'s] strong use of blues and blacks lends the impression that the creators are trying to give off a more gruesome feel." Ara praised the film's synthesis of horror and war imagery and felt its setting in a coal mine was effective; however, he believed Honda had failed to attach a strong subtext. "[Perhaps] there is no need to make such a criticism because this is an entertainment film. But is it not a characteristic of fantasy film to go beyond spectacle and comment on society? In this light, *Rodan* is [lacking]."

Nevertheless, Honda's growing mastery of the giant-monster format foretold the road ahead. "I think it was *Rodan*," Honda said, "that put me on my path."[17]

14

LOVERS AND ALIENS

Good Luck to These Two (1957),
A Teapicker's Song of Goodbye
(1957), *A Rainbow Plays in My
Heart* (1957), *A Farewell to the
Woman I Called My Sister* (1957),
The Mysterians (1957)

Japan's most well-known film genre is the
samurai picture. Many of his contemporaries staked their careers on stories of
feudal warriors, but Honda showed no
interest; his milieu was modern Japan. If
Akira Kurosawa had prevailed, however,
Honda might have made one samurai film,
a quite significant one. It has long been
known that Kurosawa developed *Throne of
Blood*, his Noh-inspired *jidai-geki* adaptation of Shakespeare's *Macbeth*, to be made
by another director, someone "younger"
as Kurosawa once told Donald Richie.
However, recently discovered information
reveals that Kurosawa's first choice to direct
Throne of Blood was Honda.

Kurosawa aspired to gain more
autonomy over his work, and the success
of *Seven Samurai* opened the door. In
May 1956, Kurosawa announced he would
fulfill his contractual commitment to
Toho by producing three samurai films by
other directors, each to be quickly filmed
back-to-back from September 1956 to early
1957. *Throne of Blood* would be directed
by Honda, *The Hidden Fortress* by Hideo
Suzuki, and *Revenge* by Hiromichi Hori-
kawa.[1] The plan was scuttled after the Toho
brass read the *Throne of Blood* script and,
realizing a big budget was required, insisted
Kurosawa direct it himself. Eventually,
Kurosawa would direct all three pictures
(*Revenge* became *Yojimbo*), but he would
attain a degree of independence by forming
his own production company.

By now both Honda and Kurosawa were
thriving, but this story shows how their
paths had diverged. Honda found his niche
using the system to communicate themes
he cared about, while Kurosawa sought
escape from the constraints of the studio.
There's no telling if a Honda-directed
Throne of Blood would have resembled the
stylized, visually rich, and idiosyncratic

film Kurosawa made, but the fact that Kurosawa intended to tap Honda says much about their relationship: opposites, but with deep mutual respect. When actor Yoshio Tsuchiya, the terrorized farmer in *Seven Samurai*, told Kurosawa he wanted to appear in one of Honda's sci-fi productions: "[Kurosawa] said, 'If Honda-*san* is making it, then it must be good.'"

———————

Japan experienced surging economic growth in the 1950s thanks to domestic rebuilding efforts and the procurement of materials for the Korean Conflict. In the big cities, corporate offices were staffed by a rising class of white-collar worker, the salaryman, who existed in a highly structured bubble of managers and subordinates, vying for upward mobility. He dressed in suit and tie with briefcase and commuted by train into the city. Survival required knowing one's place in the hierarchy and obeying the unwritten rules of conduct. From the mid-1950s through the mid-1960s, Toho produced many films about these men, from dramas to comedies satirizing the life of the Tokyo office worker, not unlike how Billy Wilder's *The Apartment* (1960) poked fun at his New York counterparts.

   Good Luck to These Two, set in the salaryman's world, is another soap opera about two young lovers swimming against the tide of parents and go-betweens who want them to marry other people. Wakao (Hiroshi Koizumi) is a young pencil pusher who rejects an offer to marry his branch manager's daughter despite the promise of a promotion and job security. His mother wants him to marry an heiress, but he declines that arrangement, too. He proposes instead to his true love, coworker Masako (Yumi Shirakawa), but she has her own obstacles. Her stern father is still upset

Good Luck to These Two. © Toho Co., Ltd.

that his oldest daughter ran off with a musician, and with no sons of his own, he insists Masako marry an acceptable husband who can take over the family business. Wakao and Masako marry in a tiny ceremony shunned by their parents. They begin life together, but after intervening in a drunken fight between two superiors, Wakao loses his job; and with no luck finding work, he becomes irritable. Masako takes a job to help make ends meet, which only makes Wakao feel worse. In an argument, Wakao strikes Masako and she runs away. The couple reunite in the end, a tender moment during one of Tokyo's then frequent power outages. In their tiny, shabby apartment they pledge to be happy together just as the lights come back on, a ray of hope.

   This early script by Zenzo Matsuyama, whose credits include Masaki Kobayashi's superlative antiwar trilogy *The Human Condition* (*Ningen no joken*, 1959–61), delves a little deeper into Honda's recurrent theme of love versus tradition. For instance, in marriage there are practical matters of finance: when the couple first decides to marry, the first thing they discuss is Wakao's paltry salary and tally how much alcohol and tobacco he can afford on their meager budget. Mundane details, but they're overjoyed to be discussing them; it's practically romantic. There are matters of marital due diligence: Masako's stubborn father does not simply reject Wakao out of hand; he first goes to Wakao's company and conducts a background check, a not uncommon practice. In the workplace, Matsuyama and Honda show the politics, rivalries, and gossip, and the humiliation men endure. Wakao's supervisor, shipped out of town to make way for an ambitious junior exec, is resigned to his fate: "This is what it means to be a salaryman." Finally, this is the first Honda film to show what really happens when couples marry against the wishes of others. Instead of a big, traditional ceremony and reception, with dozens of family and friends bearing gifts and money, Wakao and Masako's little wedding is attended by no one but her sister and brother-in-law, plus Wakao's busybody landlords acting as go-betweens, a formality. The couple are truly on their own in 1950s Tokyo, an unforgiving place. Economic growth was rising, but there still weren't enough jobs for everyone and the couple is soon *lumpen* (down on their luck), Wakao spending his days sitting in the park or scouring the help-wanted ads.

Koizumi again proves a capable leading man, going full circle from nervous suitor to angry, unemployed husband, and finally back to the nice guy he is at heart. Shirakawa, after playing the weepy girlfriend in *Rodan*, released just two months before, is something of a revelation. Returning home after the couple's first date, Shirakawa stops at the gate to do a little hop of joy, a positively charming moment. Still, the highlights belong to two supporting players: Takashi Shimura, who gives the stern, old father a warm and sympathetic side, and an energetic Toshiro Mifune as Maruyama, the free-spirited brother-in-law and French horn player. In a touching moment, Shimura and Masako's mother (Shizue Natsukawa) watch the little wedding ceremony discreetly, from across the street; and as the newlyweds drive away, Maruyama salutes them, tooting an impromptu wedding march on his horn. It's bittersweet: the poor but happy bride and groom setting sail while the parents hide in the shadows, hopeful for the couple but weeping because they cannot support the union and won't be part of their lives.

————

Good Luck to These Two marks a significant turning point, the first Honda film shot by cinematographer Hajime Koizumi (no relation to actor Hiroshi), who is perhaps single-handedly responsible for the signature visual style of Honda's post-*Godzilla* work. Over the next decade Hajime Koizumi would shoot twenty-one Honda films, including seventeen science fiction and fantasy pictures. Koizumi's camera work was the perfect complement to Honda's conservative, risk-averse style of composition. Beginning with *The Mysterians*, Honda's first film in color and scope, Honda and Koizumi would always frame the actors in familiar ways, using wide-angle group shots and medium-length two-shots to emphasize the ensemble format, which rarely featured a singular hero. Honda and Koizumi's use of color, light, and shade was consistent, and when expertly combined with the special effects sequences shot by Eiji Tsuburaya and his crew, formed the basis of an alternate reality, a uniquely recognizable world of monsters and aliens. Koizumi also enlivened Honda's static images with movement, sometimes via background activity, sometimes with a strategic zoom-in or zoom-out, quick or slow, emphasizing a face or object during a crucial moment. It's a trademark move that Koizumi employs more than once in *Good Luck to These Two*.

"Koizumi was Honda-*san*'s favorite," said Koji Kajita. "He was sharp. He was a cameraman with a keen sense, and the no. 1 disciple of a cameraman named Mitsuo Miura, who worked with the masters at Toho: [directors] Heinosuke Gosho, Shige-yoshi Suzuki, Mikio Naruse, Kajiro Yama-moto. Koizumi's footage was so beautiful, thanks to the teachings of Miura. He would use a filter for shooting, but would never show it to anyone. He would take it out, use it, and put it right back into his pocket so nobody could see which one he used. He would not let his assistants touch the camera settings, either. He would say, 'OK, it's all set up,' but after that, the camera could not be touched. That is the type of man he was. He was a very interesting person, a great cameraman. His footage always came out so nicely, with excellent composition as well. His framework was pristine.

"He understood what Honda-*san* wanted, so there was no need to tell him each time in terms of the frame sizes and whatnot. He'd be called by the director, 'Komi-*chan*!' and he knew exactly what to do, what the director wanted. No words were needed, a *tsu-ka* relationship."

Born in 1926, Hajime Koizumi was fifteen years younger than Honda. He graduated from the Japan Film School, a two-year program established by the government

Honda and cameraman Hajime Koizumi.
Courtesy of Honda Film Inc.

during the war, and joined Toho as an apprentice in 1945. *Good Luck to These Two* was Koizumi's debut as cameraman; he would work for other directors including Kajiro Yamamoto, but was known mainly as Honda's cinematographer.

Kaijta said, "The cameraman is like the wife to the director. A poor cameraman is very troublesome when trying to capture a scene. It would be so tiring and tedious if the director had to instruct the cameraman where to go, or how to film every single shot. So Honda-*san* left it all up to Koizumi, and he had no complaints. He got the sizes correct each time, and by looking at the storyboards he knew where to position the camera for the scenes . . . He was a trusted cameraman. No wonder Honda-*san* never let go of him."

———————

While Japanese cinema is not famous for musicals, a great many were made. A popular film genre dating back to the 1930s is *kayo eiga* (pop song movies), which use *enka* or *kayokyoku* (traditional pop) hits as their titles and motifs, and star or guest star the singers of those hits, capitalizing on their popularity. In *kayo eiga*, songs are sung incidentally while people are at work, taking a walk, and so forth; there are no big, Hollywood-style production numbers that halt everything while the cast breaks into song and dance (although Japan has produced those films, too). In the fifties, *enka* superstar Hibari Misora crossed over into movies this way, and many pop idols followed suit, from Yujiro Ishihara and Kenji Sawada in the 1960s to members of the modern pop group SMAP.

A Teapicker's Song of Goodbye and *Farewell to the Woman I Called My Sister* (both 1957) are the second and third films in Honda's trilogy featuring Chiyoko Shimakura, and as with *People of Tokyo, Goodbye*, both were based upon hit songs recorded by Shimakura. Released less than two months apart in July and August 1957, the films were shot back-to-back by the identical production team and feature interconnecting stories set in the tea-growing business. All three pictures in the trilogy were short program or "SP" films, running about one hour long. These were popular during the film industry's mass-production phase of the 1950s and 1960s, when double and triple features in the cities and outskirts were the norm. Some were vehicles for the debuts of directors such as Nagisa Oshima and Yoji Yamada, while others were directed by veterans such as Honda and his mentor Kajiro Yamamoto, who helmed Toho's *Diamond* series of SP features, based on literary works.

Both films were shot on location in and around Shizuoka, one of Japan's primary tea-growing regions, and feature travelogue-like shots of the lush fields and hillsides covered with neatly organized rows of tea bushes, flanked by Mount Fuji on one side and the Pacific on the other. *A Teapicker's Song of Goodbye* is a simple

story of a young romance between Chiyo (Shimakura), who works on her father's tea farm, and Hideo (Kunio Otsuka), a young naval cadet preparing for his first deployment. Chiyo's father is losing business as new varieties of tea, grown by rival farms, become more popular. The stubborn old man refuses to replant, insisting he can succeed with the same old teas, despite mounting debt. Finally, dad falls ill and, aided by a family of local tea barons, Chiyo and her mother save the business. The film ends with Chiyo singing to Hideo from a hilltop as his ship sails off.

This breezy little film features a half-dozen songs, from the *enka* main title theme sung by Shimakura to a *shin minyo* (new folk) tune sung by popular recording artists Kikue Hanamura and Masao Kato, who guest star as tea pickers. The sweethearts Chiyo and Hideo are quite nostalgic for their age, spontaneously breaking into several songs including *Autumn in the Home Country* (Sato no aki), about a child saying good-bye to his father at the start of the Pacific War. Contemplating their future together, sitting on the beach, they sing "I Am a Child of the Sea" (*Ware wa umi no ko*), an elementary school song about the life of ocean villagers and fishermen. The film also acts as a sort of travel brochure for the city of Shizuoka and its surroundings, with nice views of an amusement park on a department store rooftop, a popular attraction in Japan from the 1940s to the 1960s, and a ropeway tram carrying tourists over the glorious mountains and tea fields.

The companion film, *Farewell to the Woman I Called My Sister*, showcases more sites and rituals of Shizuoka and features many of the same characters, but focuses on Chiyoko's best friend Michiko (Chikage Ogi) and her tragic love story, unspooling in one long flashback. Honda makes major shifts in tone and style—this is not a true *kayo eiga*, though Chiyo reappears for a few incidental songs. It's an old-fashioned tear-jerker, narrated by Michiko and expressing her innermost thoughts. Michiko falls for Masao (Hiroshi Koizumi), an agricultural engineer from Tokyo, but her older brother Tatsuo (Akihiko Hirata) wants her to accept an arranged marriage with a client. Michiko follows Masao to Tokyo against the wishes of her rich family, who disown her and cut off financial support. The straightlaced, well-to-do country girl finds it hard adjusting to near-poverty life in Masao's tiny, drab *danchi* (public housing) apartment. Michiko is forced to work in a seedy bar when her husband becomes seriously ill, and after he dies, she tearfully reunites with her family and lives quietly as a kindergarten teacher. She concludes, "All I have to live on are the memories, although brief, of my life with the man I loved, and the relationship with these pure and innocent children. Perhaps these are all I will have, forever and ever."

The film lacks Honda's usual optimism. Arranged marriage is depicted as a trap, but the alternative is struggle and suffering. Michiko's brother selects a husband for her in the same way that he would hire an employee, collecting resumes and head-shots; and when she refuses to cooperate, he predictably accuses her of selfish behavior. The optimism of love soon yields to the realities of life and death, as those who flee to the promised land of Tokyo find it harsh and unforgiving. Unaccustomed to working-class city life, Michiko commits one faux pas after another and incurs the wrath of busybody neighbors and lecherous drunks.

All three of the "good-bye and farewell"

films were successful, but Honda would not work again with Ryo Takei, an older-generation producer who had started in the silent era as a screenwriter. It was also the last time Honda would work with either Shimakura, who would endure as "the goddess of *enka*," though her film career was short, and Chikage Ogi, who would leave acting to become one of Japan's most prominent female politicians. It was an extremely busy period for Honda, however, and in between *Teapicker's Song* and *Farewell* he completed another unusual project.

————————

Radio was still a dominant form of entertainment in Japan during the 1950s, even with the growth of film and the rise of television. Among the biggest radio programs were soap operas, dramas luring listeners into a tawdry, passionate world of forbidden love and sins of the flesh. The most popular shows aired a new episode every weeknight, about fifteen minutes long, and many remained on the air for months or even years. Some of them were turned into films: the success of Shochiku's three-part adaptation of the soap *What Is Your Name?* (*Kimi no na wa*, 1953–54), set during the Pacific War and featuring effects by Eiji Tsuburaya, helped start the trend.

A Rainbow Plays in My Heart was a radio drama that ran for more than two hundred episodes, its popularity leading Toho to create a film version consisting of two parts, released simultaneously as a short-program double bill on July 9, 1957. This all-star film marks the third and final time *Godzilla* stars Momoko Kochi and Akira Takarada were paired as romantic leads; it was intended as a star-making vehicle for the beautiful, doe-eyed Kochi, who had mostly played supporting and ensemble roles until now. Here she is the nominal protagonist,

A Rainbow Plays in My Heart: Honda (left, by camera) with actresses Akemi Negishi and Momoko Kochi. Courtesy of Honda Film Inc.

daughter of the wealthy executive of a shipbuilding company and the only well-adjusted member of a family wrought with secrets, lies, and assorted melodrama. The story concludes abruptly, cliff-hanger style; Toho's intent was to continue the saga as a series, but these first two installments were a commercial disappointment and no more were made.

The messy plot is a series of coincidences and missed connections, devoid of Honda's usual charm, humor, and optimism. Ikuko (Kochi) rejects a blind arranged marriage to an employee at her father Shuji's (Ken Uehara) company. She randomly meets the handsome Ito (Takarada) and falls for him; it turns out Ito is the guy she was supposed to marry, but now her father forbids them from dating because he's lost face at work for declining

the arrangement. Ikuko's sister Atsuko (Akemi Negishi) is insanely jealous of her jockey husband's (Yoshio Tsuchiya) doting on his horse. Ikuko's teen half-brother Jun (Tatsuyoshi Ehara), like Sal Mineo's troubled teen in *Rebel Without a Cause*, hates his distant father and drinks too much. Shuji's wife has been dead for years, but he still won't marry his long-suffering mistress Yoshie (veteran actress and singer Mieko Takamine), a bar hostess and Jun's mother. The rest of this unsavory cast of characters includes Akihiko Hirata as a racehorse owner who coerces Atsuko into sleeping with him; Fuyuki Murakami, the stolid assistant scientist from *Godzilla*, as a pushy barfly; Yoko Sugi, a young actress seen in some of Mikio Naruse's best films, as a lovelorn secretary who has a suggestively creepy relationship with Jun, the teenager; and Hisaya Ito, emerging as one of Honda's most reliable villains, as a sleazy doctor with the hots for Ikuko.

After showing so many well-intentioned young people struggling to get by and be happy in post-Occupation Japan, Honda enters new territory: the sufferings of the privileged class. This combination of director and material seems an awkward match from the first scene, with teenage Jun recklessly speeding through the city in his convertible, oblivious to the bicyclist he nearly mows down, all courtesy of a rear-projection effect that's so unconvincing it's almost surreal. Then there is the final act of part 2, a bloodletting of pent-up lies, sexual tension, and hostility that is the antithesis of Honda's milieu. The patriarch Shuji is blinded in an industrial accident; laying in hospital, his eyes bandaged, he reveals to Ikuko that she is not his biological daughter, but the illicit child of her dead mother's infidelity. Shocked, Ikuko stumbles out into the street and is accosted by the lecherous stalker-doctor, whose idea of comforting her is to grope and kiss her. Her little brother witnesses the assault and stabs the doctor to death. Ikuko breaks up with her boyfriend; she's now unmarriageable. "There is tainted blood running through me," she says. "I am a child of sin."

Still, Honda's direction of the actors is quite good, as they play their alternately arch and self-pitying characters believably. Working with cinematographer Minoru Kuribayashi (a silent-era veteran, who also had shot Honda's two recent *kayo eiga*), Honda renders Shuji's enormous house, with its big rooms and Western-style kitchen and furnishings, as a prison of upper-upper-class petty problems and grievances. The film also deals in some detail with the concept of *ie* (the Japanese family system) and the importance of

bloodlines. Shuji refuses to list his illegitimate son on the official family registry, causing shame and hardship for the boy. These themes give the film hints of substance, but it's not much of a commentary on the spoils of the moneyed class.

The problem is lack of conviction. *A Rainbow Plays in My Heart* is like a Japanese version of *Peyton Place*, the 1956 novel by Grace Metalious, adapted into a film in 1957. It's populated by flawed, cynical, amoral types who are simply not Honda's crowd. There are also structural issues. The screenplay by Tokuhei Wakao (Hiroshi Inagaki's *Samurai* trilogy; Honda's *Song for a Bride*) plays more like a radio drama than a film. The frequent histrionics and long, expository dialogue sequences in which relationships and hurt feelings are explained and expressed, again and again, feel lifted from the original fifteen-minute radio format, which relied on emotional spikes and repetition to keep listeners hooked.

The Mysterians is a project several times larger in scale compared to *Godzilla* or *Rodan* and is aimed to be more of a true science fiction film . . . I would like to wipe away the [Cold War–era] notion of East versus West and convey a simple, universal aspiration for peace, the coming together of all humankind as one to create a peaceful society.
– Ishiro Honda[2]

At the foot of Mount Fuji, villagers are enjoying a traditional *bon* dance festival when a mysterious forest fire erupts. Huge landslides decimate the area, a giant robot trashes a village, and flying saucers flit across the sky. A technologically advanced race of aliens from planet Mysteroid has arrived. They claim to be peaceful, but they're constructing a huge underground fortress from which to launch their conquest of Earth . . .

As *Godzilla* shows, Honda had little faith in politicians to resolve a crisis. When disaster looms, the world looks to rational men of science for answers and to the Japanese military for protection. The apex of this alter-reality is *The Mysterians*, Toho's whiz-bang answer to *War of the Worlds* (1953), *Earth vs. the Flying Saucers* (1956), and the wave of 1950s movies inspired by interest in UFOs. While it's loaded with typical genre trappings, and to Western eyes it may appear to be a juvenile picture, *The Mysterians* is an atypical alien-invasion film. Honda is uninterested in the veiled anticommunist allusions of Hollywood sci-fi and instead offers something quite the opposite, an idealistic plea for international cooperation. Honda's concerns about the corruption of science and the nuclear threat are revisited, but *The Mysterians* is optimistic, depicting a world where archrival superpowers unite for the common good.

The Mysterians was released roughly one year after Japan became a member of the United Nations on December 18, 1956, and some events in the film reflect the country's real-life return to world politics. Japanese leaders had coveted a UN seat since signing the 1951 San Francisco Peace Treaty, which restored Japan's independence but left it politically isolated. Japan joined the UN with a pledge to become a force for world peace; to that end, it would spend a decade trying to convince the US and USSR to end nuclear testing. Those efforts failed, but *The Mysterians* idealizes this newfound geopolitical influence. Japan leads the effort against the alien threat, bringing the Americans (who provide the heroic military assist) and the Soviets (with whom Japan had just normalized relations) to the table. In Hollywood prototypes such as *When Worlds Collide* (1951), only Washington's allies are invited to international meetings. Honda's worldview is egalitarian.

Honda said, "In every single international conference or meeting scene, I have everyone from all countries there, such as Russia, every time. And they all put their heads together with the scientists. This

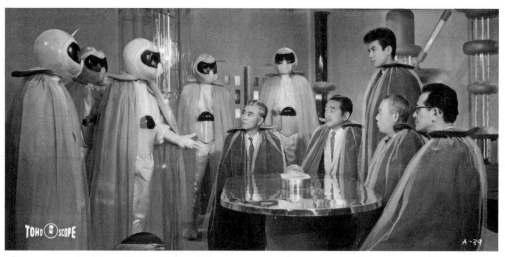

The Mysterians. © Toho Co., Ltd.

sort of thing is my theme, the basis of my work."[3]

The handiwork of three writers is evident. Producer Tanaka recruited Jojiro Okami, an aeronautical engineer and military test pilot who became a sci-fi writer and was adept at dreaming up spacecraft, future weapons, and other speculative technology. Shigeru Kayama's familiar structure brings suspense to the first act, a series of mysterious disasters culminating when the Mogera robot, looking a bit like an iron armadillo, bores out of a mountainside.[4] The human drama is very thin, with an ensemble of one-dimensional characters, but screenwriter Takeshi Kimura darkens the light story with a struggle between good and evil that anticipates his later work on Honda's *The Human Vapor* and *Matango*.

The struggle occurs in the heart and mind of Ryoichi Shiraishi (Akihiko Hirata), a young astronomer with radical theories and a thirst for knowledge blinding him to the aliens' dastardly plot. Honda clearly places scientists and their work on a pedestal: When the aliens do the "take me to your leader" routine, it's the scientists they want to meet, not politicians; and when Shiraishi delivers his long-awaited report on the Mysterians, the camera regards the document as if photographing a holy scroll. Still, Shiraishi's alliance with the nuclear-armed Mysterians alludes to the scientists who devoted their skills to the Cold War arms race; Honda respected scientists, but he was concerned about their egos and ethics. "At that time I feared the danger of science, that whoever controlled it could take over the entire Earth," he said. "If a scientist possessed that kind of knowledge and was left to his own devices, it could be the end of the world."[5]

Unlike Honda's dramatic films of this time, women are merely a plot point here.

Their planet destroyed by nuclear war, the aliens face extinction from birth defects related to fallout poisoning. They want to breed with Earth women, and female leads Momoko Kochi and Yumi Shirakawa are on the shortlist. The Mysterians kidnap the ladies, setting the stage for third-act heroics when well-dressed scientist Joji Atsumi (Kenji Sahara) penetrates the alien fortress to rescue them. It's tempting to believe this subplot is a comment on the status of women, but in published interviews Honda said it was intended to inject a little human drama into the long final battle between the alien base and the Markalite ray cannons, a mechanical war of stationary objects exchanging beams.

This is the first Honda-Tsuburaya collaboration shot in anamorphic Tohoscope, which the studio had recently introduced, and both directors make a smooth transition to the wider canvas. Honda and live-action cameraman Hajime Koizumi use gleaming futuristic sets, concave walls, and forced-perspective matte paintings to create the high-tech interior of the clearly *Forbidden Planet*–inspired alien base. They also use the new format to establish several standard shots that would define the visual style of their work together and emphasize the group ethic of Honda's sci-fi films. These include side-by-side medium shots of two or three characters for dialogue scenes and symmetrically diagrammed conferences where scientists, generals, and politicians are arranged democratically, surrounded by a formation of subordinates and press. In contrast, the despotic Mysterian leader is flanked by flunkies, their hierarchy indicated by uniform color.

Tsuburaya exploits the scope dimensions throughout, from the eerie opening of the Mysterians' space station orbiting Earth to the final conflagration, a nonstop barrage of wire-controlled flying miniatures and optically animated rays moving laterally across the screen. Big improvements in live-action and effects compositing are apparent in several scenes, notably Mogera's attack on a village near Mount Fuji, and a formation of saucers flying over Tokyo by night as people watch from rooftops; the nimble saucers with lighted undercarriages and slick design make this one of the most memorable scenes of its kind in any 1950s science fiction film.[6] The widescreen image and the glut of effects also means some shortcomings are more noticeable. Scratches and negative debris are visible in optically processed shots of ray beams, but this problem would be corrected in subsequent films.

Reliable budget figures for *The Mysterians* are elusive, but Honda's claim that it surpassed *Godzilla* and *Rodan* appears true, what with all the eye candy. This was the introduction of the futurized military weaponry and aerospace tech that would become standards of Toho's special effects films. The Mysterian base, the cigar-shaped Alpha-1 and Beta-1 flying warships, and the Markalite FARP cannons, a radar dish that can return incoming ray beams with amplified force, were based on ideas by Shigeru Komatsuzaki, a designer hired by producer Tanaka for his interest in aeronautics. Komatsuzaki would have substantial influence on the visual design of certain Honda-Tsuburaya productions in the coming years. The studio's in-house technical research department, which investigated then emerging technologies such as color film and 3-D, suggested using plastic—then newly available—to construct the alien base, including the miniature dome and the tubes, spheres, lights, and gizmos inside.

"Around that time, a lot of plastic containers started being manufactured, so we used those for . . . the Mysterians' machinery and the dome," said Honda. "We couldn't really make it with glass. . . . Our challenge was, 'What materials can we use to represent something that does not exist on Earth?' . . . Cost-wise, [plastic] was not so cheap, but we could work more quickly than with glass, and it was also safer."[7]

The military deployment scenes are bigger than before, with six hundred soldiers from a Japan Self-Defense Forces base at Gotenba appearing on camera, driving tanks, shooting weapons, and firing real flamethrowers shooting flames fifty meters long, an impressive sight. In later films, the JSDF reduced its involvement; soldiers would be mostly played by extras who, Honda lamented, didn't walk like military men.

Yoshio Tsuchiya, a costar of Kurosawa's *Seven Samurai*, deserves special mention for playing the Mysterian leader. Tsuchiya relished the opportunity to play a spaceman, unconcerned that he'd be covered head to toe in helmet, glasses, and a skin-chafing costume made from flameproof fiberglass fabric. Tsuchiya compensated with staccato gestures—"space acting"—of his own design. His dialogue was also obscured: Tsuchiya spoke a nonsensical "alien language" decoded by the aliens' translation machine, which was voiced by another actor, but Tsuchiya didn't mind.

"Toho said no [to casting me in this role], because my face would be covered. I disagreed, saying that being an actor isn't all about just showing our faces. This impressed Honda-*san* very much, and we formed a relationship, both at work and outside of work," Tsuchiya said.

"It was [Tsuchiya's] wish [to play the role], but I also knew him very well, so I thought he would be well cast," said Honda.

"When someone willing to do it gets the part, that feeling actually shows up on screen. . . . Especially in this type of movie, each person really has to be interested in the theme or their acting won't be [believable]."[8]

Caucasian faces are highly visible, evidence of Toho's overseas ambitions for the Honda-Tsuburaya films. George Furness, a British lawyer who had represented former Empire of Japan defendants in the Tokyo War Crimes Tribunal, and Harold S. Conway, a businessman working in Tokyo, play UN scientists. Both were among a clique of Tokyo-based Westerners moonlighting as actors despite their limited talents. Their interpreter is Heihachiro "Henry" Okawa, a gruff actor with an eclectic career in Japan and overseas. Okawa was a stunt pilot in Howard Hawks's World War I film *The Dawn Patrol* (1930), attended Paramount Studios' acting school, and was in David Lean's *Bridge on the River Kwai* (1957). Okawa also often played an important behind-the-scenes role in Honda's films as the on-set translator for English-speaking actors and extras.

A short but notable scene shows the parallel between Honda's monsters—here, the Mogera robot—and the sudden onset of natural disasters. Etsuko (Yumi Shirakawa) is bathing when she is startled by Mogera outside her window. The scene adds nothing to plot or character, but it puts the monster in the real world of daily life. "I filmed that scene on purpose, trying to create a natural atmosphere," Honda said. "When something like a monster attack happens, not everyone in town notices right away

and panics. Some people are not aware of it and continue their regular daily activity."

The Mysterians ends like *Godzilla*, but on a somewhat more hopeful note that reaffirms both Honda's concern about the corruption of science and his commitment to humanism. Shiraishi sacrifices himself to save the world, leaving with a warning: "The tragedy of the Mysterians is an example for us. Don't use science in the wrong way. Don't repeat the tragedy." But the remorseful scientist also seems to realize that mutual destruction is not the answer; in his final moments, he allows a handful of aliens to escape, then pauses to regard the dead and dying Mysterians scattered about, just before the alien base is destroyed. "If I were in [Shiraishi's] position, what would I do?" Honda said of these scenes. "If my sacrifice saves a lot of people, then I would be happy to do it. I think it's the kind of humanism that . . . [when] seeing people are in danger, I might do the same."

Order returns to the cosmos; Honda succeeds in rendering his "universal aspiration for peace," but at the same time, *The Mysterians* sees Honda's themes and ideas beginning to lose ground to Tsuburaya's special effects. The film was a significant hit, earning ¥193 million at the box office. It was Toho's second-biggest release of 1957, trailing only Hiroshi Inagaki's *Rickshaw Man*, and the tenth-highest-grossing domestic film of the year overall. Spectacle was triumphing over substance, and over time the resulting constraints would become increasingly frustrating for Honda.

15

BRIDES, BLOBS, AND A BOMB

Song for a Bride (1958),
The H-Man (1958),
Varan the Unbelievable (1958)

Starting roughly in the mid-fifties, Iwao Mori and his producers rebuilt Toho's brand with a highly successful slate of film series, each with its own ensemble of popular stars and, in most cases, a primary director. There were the *Three Dolls* musical comedies by Toshio Sugie, starring a trio of starlets. There were white-collar comedies: the *Salaryman* series directed by Masanori Kakei, starring Keiju Kobayashi; the *Company President* (*Shacho*) films usually directed by Shue Matsubayashi; and the *Station Front* (*Ekimae*) movies starring Frankie Sakai and Hisaya Morishige. Eventually came the *Young Guy* (*Wakadaisho*) series starring heartthrob Yuzo Kayama, and other franchises. The emerging *Godzilla* series and its science fiction offshoots were part of this strategy to appeal to all audiences, from housewives to children. At the same time, these bread-and-butter films helped bankroll pictures by Kurosawa, Naruse, and other prestigious directors.

Honda's focus began to narrow in 1958, when Tomoyuki Tanaka attached him to both *The H-Man* and *Varan*, the first time Honda made two special-effects pictures in one year. But the transition was gradual, and Honda made the most of what would be his final opportunities to direct the kind of warmhearted comedy-dramas he favored. *Song for a Bride*, released February 11, 1958, is one of his best films of this period, a charming ensemble romp with familiar themes, familiar faces, affable characters, and a good dose of witty banter. Honda's direction expertly trades off between comedy and sentiment, and the screenplay by Tokuhei Wakao ties together five storylines with a feel-good effortlessness. Shot by Hajime Koizumi in Tohoscope, this film has an energetic look and feel despite the black-and-white photography, and showcases Honda's flair for comedy in ways similar to *Mothra* and *King Kong vs. Godzilla*, made a few years later.

There are no monsters, but what *Song for a Bride* has in common with those two films is a great comic actor at the forefront. This story is about young people, but it is the eccentric father played by fifty-seven-year-old Kingoro Yanagiya who steals scenes and sets the tone. Yanagiya was a famous *rakugo* comic monologist who rose to popularity in the 1930s with his routine "Comedian soldier," which inspired a new *rakugo* style during Japan's military buildup and the occupation of China, when the drudgery of military service became fodder for comedy. In the late 1930s he was part of a comic troupe that entertained imperial troops stationed in China, and by the 1950s he was making frequent film appearances for Toho.[1]

Yanagiya plays the widower Heikichi, owner of a grocery store and father of three young, marriage-eligible girls. Heikichi is what Donald Richie labeled the "funny father," a comedic stereotype in Japanese films during this period. Usually played by a popular comedian such as Frankie Sakai or Hisaya Morishige, the funny father satirized patriarchy and was given to ridiculous antics; he was, according to Richie, often "more childish than any of the children."[2] Heikichi fits the bill: he is a wannabe first responder who awakens at the sound of sirens in the middle of the night and chases after fire engines on foot, wearing a bizarre flame-retardant suit that draws stares from puzzled passersby; he looks like a rubberized samurai firefighter. The overarching plot concerns Heikichi's ambition to run for a local political office, though it's only a setup for various missed connections and misunderstandings. What really holds the film together is the relationship between

Heikichi and Otoyo (veteran actress Nijiko Kiyokawa, previously in *Young Tree*), the madam of a bar across the street and known as "auntie" to Heikichi's daughters. Heikichi and Otoyo bicker like an old married couple, but they grow closer as they realize their meddling in the girls' romantic affairs does more harm than good. The film ends with all three daughters happily married and Otoyo sweetly helping Heikichi don his ridiculous gear as he rushes off to chase another fire.

The rest of the cast is young and attractive. Mitsuko Kusabue, as the sensible older sister Teruko, and Akemi Negishi, as the cabaret dancing, ditzy middle sister Nobuko, were popular working actresses. Reiko Dan, just twenty-two years old, had been in only a handful of films; and the studio viewed her turn as Taeko, the sassy youngest daughter and ambitious fashionista, as a star-making role. Their male counterparts are frequent Honda actors, all playing against type. Hiroshi Koizumi is a poor, nerdy inventor who's determined to prove his husband worthiness, a precursor

Song for a Bride: attending to details on star Reiko Dan's fashion show costume. Courtesy of Honda Film Inc.

to Akira Kubo's character in *Invasion of Astro-Monster* a few years later. Yoshio Tsuchiya, sans his *Mysterians* alien mask or *Seven Samurai* angst, plays a good-hearted painter. And Kenji Sahara, more youthful than ever, plays Shinichi, a pampered and pompadoured mama's boy who secretly quits college to become a rock star. Sahara provides the film's only real lowlight, crooning in a weak, nasally voice. Sachio Sakai, the reporter from *Godzilla*, is the comic foil. The prospective groom in Nobuko's arranged marriage, he's a rich kid with a pervy fetish for filming women's legs and busts with his eight-millimeter camera.

Wakao's screenplay succeeds in all the ways his work on *A Rainbow Plays in My Heart* did not. Again he employs long, play-like dialogue scenes, but here the back and forth has rhythm and byplay, delineating a big cast of characters in a short span of time. The script is also packed with cultural tics, behaviors, and superstitions. There are references to *butsumetsu*, the unluckiest day on the Japanese calendar; a comic gag in which Shinichi cuts the straps on his mother's *geta* sandals to keep her from leaving the house (a broken strap signifying a bad omen); various hand gestures, word-play, and old sayings; and sexual innuendo. In a sign of the times, Heikichi and his political adviser hold a meeting at a Turkish bathhouse, a notorious type of establishment that arose in the 1950s to skirt antiprostitution laws. In real life, women bathed the male customers and offered sexual favors. Here the old men merely leer at the female employees in swimsuits.

Song for a Bride works on multiple levels and is one of Honda's most thoroughly entertaining films. It is worth noting that, unlike his previous dramas and comedies, there is no equivocation, as the film sides squarely with the younger generation in the

ever-present conflict between tradition and new values. "People like you and us youth think differently," Taeko tells her elders. "What you think is stupid may be important to us, and vice versa." The story concludes with a lighthearted, idealized view of the modern Japanese family, a stark contrast to the films of Ozu and other directors who depicted its disintegration: the young people have all gotten what they wanted, the parental figures are satisfied, and the family unit remains intact.

————

A sexy, exotic dancer slinks across the stage, showered in flickering lights. A bebop combo wails, sax and drums riffing like Charlie Parker and Max Roach. Square-jawed gangsters with slick hair and flashy vines smoke, drink, and watch, doted on by giggling bar hostesses. A few tables over, undercover cops keep an eye on the bad guys. Just another night at Cabaret Homura, but the heat's about to come down on these mobsters. That is, until an even more dangerous villain appears . . .

The H-Man is a unique, genre-blending gem that finds Honda leaving his comfort zone for a violent underworld of criminals, cops, narcotics, divas, strippers, and deviants. Grafted onto the lurid backdrop

The H-Man: Honda directing Yumi Shirakawa, with cameraman Hajime Koizumi (far right) and Kenji Sahara looking on. Courtesy of Honda Film Inc.

is an eerie tale of jellylike atomic goblins haunting the rainy Tokyo streets and alleys, and an equally creepy subplot about an irradiated ghost ship, a proxy Lucky Dragon. Dark, mysterious, and a tad risqué, this noir hybrid takes its grit from the burgeoning *yakuza* movies out of rival Nikkatsu Studios, and its pathos from Cold War sci-horror films, with clicking Geiger counters exploiting fears of radioactive fallout.

Takeshi Kimura's screenplay opens like *Godzilla*, though nothing is left to metaphor.[3] A hydrogen bomb test in the Pacific, shown via documentary footage, exposes fishing trawler *Dai-ni ryujin maru* (Dragon God No. 2) to massive fallout. Then begins a police procedural: the gangster Misaki (Hisaya Ito) literally vanishes during a drug heist, leaving empty clothes in the street. Chief Det. Tominaga (Akihiko Hirata) thinks he's got a naked crook on the run, but nerdy biochemist Masada (Kenji Sahara) is working on a wild theory: what if radiation turned the crew of the *Ryujin-maru* into radioactive liquid creatures that dissolve human flesh? The police dismiss this as nonsense until a detective meets the same fate. Caught between the cop and the scientist, and harassed by the mob, is Misaki's long-suffering girlfriend, beautiful songbird Chikako (Yumi Shirakawa), who endures interrogations, beatings, kidnapping, stripping, ogling, and other humiliations.

This isn't a full-blown film noir, but it captures the feel, thanks to lighting and art direction stressing darkness and color. The setting is mostly nocturnal, and Honda builds suspense by hiding what lurks in the shadows. This is especially effective during a flashback aboard the ghost ship, where a rescue party meets a grisly fate. Actors are bathed in near-total darkness, illuminated only by a lantern, flashlight, or candle and some strategic lighting; sometimes the film speed was accelerated during processing, emphasizing extreme contrasts. This creatively creepy use of darkness and shadow recurs throughout the film: in the rainy streets, in a dark apartment, and finally in the Tokyo sewers, filmed on sets left over from Kurosawa's *Drunken Angel*. This is the first and only time Honda worked with Tsuruzo Nishikawa, who was considered one of Toho's two top lighting technicians along with Choshiro Ishii (*Godzilla*).

"Nishikawa taught us how to use lighting effects in a very realistic way," said lighting technician Isao Hara. "The inside of the sewers is pitch black, and we needed to show the absence of light. Back in those days, we used very large lighting equipment [but] we couldn't use any of the large ones, [so] we had to use smaller 'catch lights' in various places . . . The lights could not be shown on the water surface; it had to look very natural . . . If we could accomplish that, we would be able to maintain the realism."

"Nishikawa-*san* was particularly great at low-key, dark scenes. He could make them very bold and dramatic," recalled assistant director Kunihiko Watanabe.[4] Conversely, the cabaret scenes mix bold colors and moody shadows against Takeo Kita's hip set, highlighted by mod-art paintings and a provocative octogram dance floor.

Honda asked professors at the University of Tokyo's biology department for reassurance that the film's pseudoscience held at least an iota of realism. "He wanted some confirmation before filming began about whether life in liquid form could really be possible," Koji Kajita said. "He always wanted to have some sort of factual proof behind everything." Realistic or not, the gelatinous H-men are actually a dense, blue-green seaweed concoction used for making cosmetic lotions. The stuff was purchased in bulk, chopped into pieces, and soaked overnight in lukewarm water, then stirred up each morning to the right consistency. The illusion of the goo crawling along walls and corners was achieved with a partial set and fixed-position camera that could be flipped sideways, an effect akin to Fred Astaire's ceiling dance in *Royal Wedding* (1951). Other times, the film was simply printed in reverse, and the liquid appeared to climb upward.

With a human-sized monster, Honda's live action and Tsuburaya's effects intersect more seamlessly. The actors felled by the H-man endure grotesque deaths as goop pours down on heads or crawls up pant legs; then at the moment of meltdown, they trade places with Tsuburaya's inflated dummy hanging on piano wires, which deflates into a bubbling heap of clothes. Yoshio Tsuchiya teased fellow actor Yoshibumi Tajima when it came time to film Tajima's death. "[Tajima] went like this [feigning horror] and started to do the scene. I knew we shouldn't laugh at him, but it was so funny."

The characters are one-dimensional, but the actors perform admirably. Hirata makes a fine no-nonsense lawman, far removed from the tragic Dr. Serizawa; and Sahara plays another boyish hero, a socially awkward junior scientist with the latent hots for the leading lady. Shirakawa, a statuesque Julie London type crooning English-language torch songs, seems terribly underused; her performance hints at a femme fatale, but she turns out to be a mere damsel in distress.[5] Honda surrounds this youthful trio with more mature actors, most notably Koreya Senda, esteemed thespian from the influential Haiyuza theater acting company. Senda plays the elder

biologist Dr. Maki, who proves Masada's theory by zapping a frog with radiation and turning it into a deadly liquid H-frog.

Once the mystery is solved, the story loses steam and resorts to formulaic stuff after Chikako is kidnapped by the sneering, leering gangster Uchida (a young Makoto Sato). First comes a slow-speed car chase—tires screeching even when pedestrians outpace the automobiles—that lacks the requisite tension but possesses a time-capsule quality, with big American cars pushing through tiny streets and evidence of postwar Tokyo construction clearly visible. Uchida drags Chikako into the sewers and sadistically forces her to strip, professing his affections while waving a pistol in her face. Then it's a race against time as Masada rushes underground to save the girl before authorities ignite a river of gasoline to burn up the H-men. Giant firestorms engulf a near-undetectable Tsuburaya miniature of Tokyo in a visually impressive but emotionless climax. Because the H-men are faceless killing apparitions rather than tragic victims a la Godzilla, their extermination is a remorseless exercise; Koreya Senda's parting warning about the dangers of radioactive fallout seems perfunctory. Early script drafts were somewhat different, with both Sahara's and Shirakawa's characters submitting themselves to scientific experimentation to help solve the mystery, and the story was to end on an upbeat note with the pair united as a happy couple. As originally written, the H-men were exterminated by charging the river with electricity.[6]

While *The H-Man* reprises many Honda-isms, it's a departure from his modest sensibilities, visually bolder and heavier on shock value. It's also his most sexually suggestive genre film. Shirakawa is alternately a glamorous beauty or a suspicious

Poster for *The H-Man*. © Toho Co., Ltd.

The H-Man debuted in Japan on June 24, 1958. By this time, movie critics were developing a patronizing, dismissive view of Toho's science fiction films, typified by Masami Ogura's review in the March 1958 *Movie Arts*. "The Tsuburaya part is overcoming Honda's drama part," Ogura wrote. "That's because the drama part is so boring . . . All the humans are stupid. They are all like dolls, no personality or anything . . . I wish they'd make a scientist character who can do something more than just [say], 'Oh, we're in trouble.'"

This was the first of three Honda films to be distributed in the United States by Columbia, which cut out several minutes and released it in May 1959. American critics wrongly assumed *The H-Man* was a rip-off of Irvin Yeaworth's hoodlum-horror hit *The Blob* (1958), even though Honda's film came out earlier in Japan and the two have little in common beyond amorphous monsters.

————

gangster's girl, lusted after and forced out of her clothes by cops and crooks alike. Scantily clad dancer Emi (Ayumi Sonoda) is killed by an H-man crawling up her bare legs, symbolically violating her body and leaving behind only a bikini. What's more, the film alludes to real-life criminal activity in Tokyo. The gangster Mr. Gold (Tetsu Nakamura) is a *sangokujin* (third-country person), a derogatory label for Koreans, Chinese, and other ex-colonial nationals involved in the drug and black-market trades after the war. (A telling detail: during Gold's interrogation, the cops throw a Chinese-language newspaper at him.) Even Masaru Sato's score is atypical, with American-style jazz and weird electronic themes for the jelly monsters. Strangely, when discussing this film years later, Honda didn't mention these detours, saying only that he wanted to address the social problem of drugs, a minor plot point.

The success of *Godzilla, King of the Monsters!* created an American market for Honda's genre films in the late 1950s, drawing interest from both small distributors and Hollywood majors. Arriving amid the golden age of atomic science fiction movies, Toho's highly exploitable pictures now appeared on marquees across the United States.

The seeds of this development were sewn during the Occupation, when Hollywood studios opened offices in Tokyo to import American movies (which provided entertainment from home for the occupying Americans, and helped offset decreased Japanese domestic film production after the war), and business ties developed between Japanese and US film professionals. After Kurosawa's *Rashomon* won the grand prize at the 1951 Venice International Film Festival, Japanese studios saw opportunities to export product overseas. By May 1953 Toho had established a subsidiary in Los Angeles, Toho International, targeting North and South America; among the first major films it offered for foreign sale were *Seven Samurai*, which was acquired quickly by Columbia and released to art-house cinemas in November 1956, and *Godzilla*, which proved a harder sell but ultimately would be released in the United States earlier.

In February 1955, an English-subtitled print of *Godzilla* was showcased in a small Los Angeles cinema to attract interest from US distributors, but no immediate offers came. "The Japanese films that were popular overseas were *jidai-geki* films [such as] *Rashomon*, notable for their displays of exoticism," writes film historian Nobutaka Suzuki. "This . . . made it difficult to sell *Godzilla*." Goro Uzaki, the head of Toho International, had worked in Twentieth Century-Fox's Tokyo office after the war. He reached out for help to an old friend, Edmund Goldman, a former agent for Columbia in Japan and now a film importer, who brokered the sale of *Godzilla* to Joseph E. Levine's group. The buyers received the express right to make "revisions, additions, and deletions" for the American release.[7] The die was cast: As Toho sought more foreign sales and distributors competed for inexpensive Japanese sci-fi imports, Honda's work would be altered in similar ways, again and again.

Beginning in August 1957, Honda's *Rodan* was distributed across the United States by exploitation mavens Frank and Maurice King, retitled *Rodan, the Flying Monster*. Like *Godzilla* and *Half Human* it was heavily reedited, with narration by actor Keye Luke and a tacked-on prologue of grainy stock atomic-test footage. Much of Akira Ifukube's excellent score was replaced with library music, some scenes were reordered, some effects shots deleted (including Rodan's shadow flying over two doomed lovers, one of the best moments), while others were "flipped" and reused, and so on. Some changes were, arguably, improvements. Via clever reediting, the second Rodan enters the film earlier, though this spoils the reveal that there are two creatures, not one. The film reportedly earned $500,000 (a sizeable sum at the time) during its opening weekend in California, and an engagement at theaters in the New York area in March 1958 netted $375,000 in two days. Police were reportedly summoned to contain the enthusiastic crowds at some venues.[8]

Metro-Goldwyn-Mayer's summer 1959 release of *The Mysterians* also contained significant edits. Many scenes and shots were rearranged or deleted, including the third-act appearance of a second Mogera robot. On the positive side, Akira Ifukube's masterful score was mixed more audibly in MGM's cut than in Toho's. Its box-office return was estimated at $975,000. Though these robust figures didn't enrich Toho directly, company officials considered them good advertising for future foreign sales.[9]

————

It was Toho's desire to further its Hollywood ties that apparently led to the making of *Varan the Unbelievable* (1958), a poorly conceived film and arguably Honda's weakest effort.

Though surviving details of the project's history are sometimes contradictory, it appears to have begun at the urging of an American producer or distributor. "*Rodan* had arrived in the US, and a request for another came from [America] to Toho," said writer Ken Kuronuma. "[Producer Tomoyuki Tanaka] approached me, asking me to come up with something, anything."[10]

Kuronuma penned a familiar storyline in which scientists from Tokyo visit the remote forests of Tohoku searching for a rare butterfly species and accidentally awaken the malevolent monster Varan, known to a superstitious local tribe as the god Baradagi. The monster rises from a lake, tramples a village, and swims to Tokyo, where the military kills the beast with relative ease.

Rather than in color and widescreen, in July 1958 Honda started shooting *Varan* in black and white, in the standard 1.33:1 aspect ratio. Honda and others would later recall that Toho intended this from the start as a made-for-television film to be broadcast in three parts, each thirty minutes long, with fade-ins and fade-outs for commercial breaks. It was an unusual decision, as made-for-TV movies were still uncommon in the United States, and almost unheard of in Japan.

As Honda later recalled, "It was requested by an American television studio . . . They wanted us to make a made-for-TV movie for America. Television back then was still not in color so we filmed it in black and white. And in the midst of the production, all of a sudden [Toho said] they want it to be a [theatrical] movie . . . If this were in America . . . the filming [would] be done all over again from scratch. But since we could not do that, we had to resort to 'blowing up' [the film] . . . to turn it into [widescreen format]."[11] The awkward result is noticeable in close-ups of the monster's face, so severely cropped that its eyes or chin are outside the frame. This was apparently the same, unconventional method used when *Godzilla, King of the Monsters!* was brought to Japan and converted from standard size to widescreen. *Varan* was likewise marketed as a 2.35:1 Toho Pan Scope release, but it remains unclear whether any scenes were actually shot in scope, even after the made-for-TV project was scuttled.

"This change was forced on us," said Honda. "We were shooting things so that they looked big and powerful on the small screen, but suddenly we had to take the same footage and try to make the same impression for the big screen. It just doesn't work that way. And on top of that, we had been shooting based on the premise of making it in three episodes. Now we had to . . . somehow combine it all into one continuous story. Of course it did not work. We had a very hard time adjusting it. The desk-side planners just did not understand how the filming side worked."[12]

Even more curious, sources indicate that Toho completed both a domestic *Varan* for theaters *and* a made-for-TV export version, or at least part of it. After Honda finished shooting in mid-August, Toho management slated the Japanese theatrical release for October, but work on the three-part telefilm continued as well. Sources show that composer Akira Ifukube recorded a separate music soundtrack specifically for the TV version on August 27 and 29, and a test print consisting of three reels (totaling about thirty minutes, perhaps the first of three parts) was then shipped to Toho International in Los Angeles.[13]

Varan marks Honda's first collaboration with screenwriter Shinichi Sekizawa, whose early drafts bore the subtitle "Monster of the East." The characters occasionally engage in the type of witty banter that would become part and parcel of Sekizawa's later science fiction scripts, but overall it was an inauspicious debut for a partnership that would produce many lively movies during the next decade.

"We told Sekizawa to keep it basic and simple," assistant director Kajita said. "It was fun. It was such a short period of time.

Usually, a theatrical film takes about 40 days to shoot; special effects take about 45 days. That was the norm. But Honda-*san* and I [finished] this film in 28 days. It had a very small budget." Some scenes could not be filmed at Toho, so the production rented a cheap soundstage and an "open set" (back-lot space) nearby. Some of the customary evacuations were filmed on the Toho lot, and extras can be seen running between the soundstages and offices.

The film vaguely revisits the conflict between modern and traditional Japan, and it has a couple of documentary-style moments; but what gives *Varan* the usual Honda feel are the music and the cast. Akira Ifukube's score transcends the material and features a haunting monster motif that would later be reworked and used more effectively in *Ghidorah, the Three-Headed Monster*. The actors are a mix of regulars in smaller roles and two notable newcomers. Character actor Kozo Nomura is the reporter Kenji, the ostensible hero. Nomura returned in numerous later Honda films, almost always as a journalist. For the second film in a row, Koreya Senda plays a respected biology professor, lending the production a little star power. Ayumi Sonoda, slinky dancer of *The H-Man*, is a cub reporter.

Tsuburaya's effects don't fare much better than the live action. The spiky Varan is a satisfactory monster, but it adds nothing new to the formula; and it looks silly when crawling on all fours because the stunt actor (Haruo Nakajima) must walk on his knees. At one point the monster sprouts a parachute-like membrane from wrist to ankle, then alights like a giant flying squirrel.

Cost-curbing measures are apparent. The battle between Varan and the navy is a long, repetitive ordeal to pad the run time, and there is no extended destruction sequence. Stock film from *Godzilla*, *Godzilla Raids Again*, and other sources appears during the military battles. Several scenes written by Sekizawa were not filmed, including one with children pretending to be Varan—an early acknowledgment of the genre's appeal to kids.[14] Remaining from the original TV-movie version are a narrated prologue, which promises "the most mysterious story ever told," and a brief narrated coda.

"This is not a work I am happy with," Honda later said. "If we could have restarted from the beginning, scenes such as those with the Self-Defense Forces might have been more grand. Everything was pretty much shot on [a small] set, with maybe a tiny bit of location filming . . . The entire film would have turned out a little [better]."[15]

Varan briefly alludes to the delicate *burakumin* issue. Early on, two researchers arrive in a remote area and are met by villagers, some of whom bear visible deformities (as in *Half Human*, possibly indicating inbreeding). Possibly because of potential controversy, the film was withheld from the home video market for some time; in the 1980s it became one of Toho's last sci-fi films released on VHS videotape. Scenes referring to the village's location as "unexplored and secluded"—code words for a *buraku* enclave—were initially omitted. This content was later restored when the film was reissued on DVD.

Released on October 14, 1958, *Varan* made little impact. A reviewer for *Tokyo Weekly* felt the giant monster genre was already stale. "Varan attacks Haneda Airport, but it reminds me of the conclusion of any other old Godzilla. There's nothing new. It's really about all they can do with a monster movie."

Though there are no known records to confirm it, *Varan* likely originated at the behest of AB-PT Pictures, an outfit created by ABC-TV and Paramount Theaters to make low-budget genre films for theatrical release and subsequent TV syndication.[16] However, AB-PT Pictures ceased production sometime in 1958 or 1959, which would have left Toho without a buyer.[17] The made-for-TV version of *Varan*, if it indeed existed, has not surfaced.

Instead, the film was released theatrically in the United States in 1962 by a small distributor, extensively and poorly revamped. In cheaply filmed new footage, actor Myron Healey (known for playing heavies in Westerns) starred as a scientist conducting experiments at a Japanese lake. Much of Eiji Tsuburaya's effects remained, but Honda's footage was mostly replaced and he received no on-screen credit. Honda was unaware of this as late as the 1980s, when he claimed to have "no clue" if *Varan* had been released overseas.

16

MARRIAGE, MONEY, AND THE MOON

An Echo Calls You (1959),
Inao, Story of an Iron Arm (1959),
Seniors, Juniors, Co-workers (1959),
Battle in Outer Space (1959)

Traditionally, marriage in Japan is a union of two families rather than of individuals. In years past, a prospective wife might receive prewedding *hanayome shugyo* (bridal training) in homemaking, cooking, cleaning, flower arranging, tea ceremony, and other matters. As part of this, she might temporarily move into the home of the groom and his parents, a trial period in which she was tutored by her often domineering future mother-in-law in family customs and domestic affairs. Honda's twenty-third feature, *An Echo Calls You* (1959), is about a young woman who undergoes these now somewhat antiquated rituals as she faces the usual crossroads: true love and its uncertainties, or an offer of marriage that promises wealth and comfort. It's a sweet, romantic, funny movie with a slightly serious edge, and with a superior cast starring twenty-one-year-old pop singer Izumi Yukimura at the height of her popularity. Of all Honda's "women's films," this one is aimed most squarely at a female audience.

The screenplay by Goro Tanada—likely inspired by Mikio Naruse's popular *Hideko the Bus Conductor* (*Hideko no Shasho-san*, 1941) starring Hideko Takamine—has the familiar Honda touchstones. The story takes places in the beautiful Kofu basin of Yamanashi Prefecture, a mountainous region known for Chichibu Tama Kai National Park. Tamako Miyoshi (Yukimura) is a conductor for the local bus line. Every day she rides a twenty-five-kilometer route from Kofu city up into the mountains, stopping at little villages along the treacherous, winding roads. Tamako's sunny disposition is contrasted with that of her bus driver, Seizo Nabeyama (Ryo Ikebe), a gruff widower and ex-soldier. The pair has worked together for years and obviously care for one another, but Nabeyama is the

An Echo Calls You: a poignant moment with stars Izumi Yukimura (left) and Ryo Ikebe (right). © Toho Co., Ltd.

all-business Japanese man, incapable of expressing his feelings.

Tamako is uneducated and poor; she lives with her parents (Ikio Sawamura and Noriko Sengoku), who own a barbershop. One day her parents receive a surprise marriage proposal from the Hirasawas, the richest family in the city. Kenichi Hirasawa (Yu Fujiki), an archetypal mama's boy, works in the family's bookstore and has the hots for Tamako. Frustrated with Nabeyama's coldness and longing for a better life, Tamako quits her job and moves into the posh Hirasawa home for a trial period, where she is lorded over by Kenichi's mother. Suffocating, Tamako hops a bus home to visit her family and ends up helping Nabeyama in an emergency, navigating his bus back down the mountain in a raging storm to deliver a pregnant woman to the hospital. Realizing where she truly belongs, Tamako rejoins Nabeyama for a simpler life and the promise of real love.

An Echo Calls You is propelled by the charisma of Yukimura, who plays Tamako as a blissful but not ignorant everywoman. She knows her prospects are limited because of gender and class. She dreams of Tokyo, but knows her roots are planted on the outskirts. She learns to embrace her working-class roots rather than change her ways for wealth and status. In the climactic scene, the evil mother-in-law rebukes Tamako for declining the marriage, saying, "You're just a mere bus conductor." To which Tamako responds: "And what is wrong with that! I can tell anybody with pride that I am a bus conductor! It is a fine occupation where we help so many people! Those who are mean and look down on others are much more vulgar beings!"

Yukimura was the "Barbara Streisand of Japan," her popularity rivaling that of superstar Hibari Misora and Chiemi Eri, with whom Yukimura costarred in several musical-comedy films. In the early 1960s Yukimura played the Latin Quarter club in New York, appeared on "The Ed Sullivan Show," and was profiled in *Life* magazine. This is not a *kayo eiga*—Yukimura never sings on camera—but as the bus wends its way uphill, she is heard on the soundtrack, singing about the beauty of traversing the green mountains with the refrain *yaho* (i.e., "Hello there"), a call that echoes across the canyons.

Ikebe was nearly forty-one when the film was released, though he appears younger; and the chemistry between the by-the-book driver and free-spirited conductor twenty years his junior is the story's heart. This is Ikebe's fourth leading role for Honda, each character quite different from the last. Though Nabeyama is stern, Ikebe brings humor to the man, sometimes subtly and sometimes in an over-the-top manner typical of Japanese comedy. It's fun to watch Ikebe get flustered by his busybody landlady (Choko Ida), constantly prying into his nonexistent love life, against the wishes of her equally flustered husband (Bokuzen Hidari).

The mood darkens when Tamako enters the house of her fiancé. Honda fans know actor Yu Fujiki as the goofy sidekick in *King Kong vs. Godzilla* and the egg-eating reporter in *Mothra vs. Godzilla*, but he also did fine work in dramatic films by Kurosawa, Naruse, Ozu, and Hiroshi Inagaki. Fujiki plays the milquetoast Kenichi with a stereotypical *maza-con* (mother complex), tiptoeing through the house to avoid upsetting "mommy." The stereotypical, dictatorial mother is played with ice in her veins by Sadako Sawamura, an iconic stage and film actress who was jailed for her communist leanings during the war, and sister of Daisuke Kato, who would star in Honda's *Seniors, Juniors, Co-workers* later that year.

There are several of Honda's customary scenes and the usual second-tier characters whose banter and gossip keep the atmosphere light. Like Honda's previous films set in pastoral locations, *Echo* opens with a wide, long-distance pan of the Kofu basin, capturing the natural beauty. Then there is the local village festival, in which *Ryujin-sama* (dragon-lion god), a man in costume, "bites" villagers on the head, a promise of luck in love and marriage. Nabeyama awkwardly gets chomped, then dismisses the ritual as poppycock. The scene recalls the water-splashing rite in *The Blue Pearl*, but it's played for laughs here, a taste of local color. Cinematographer Isamu Ashida previously shot *People of Tokyo, Goodbye* and *Rodan* for Honda, and his work here in black and white and scope is similar to Honda's recent collaborations with Hajime Koizumi, nicely photographing idle moments (bus workers playing *shogi* [Japanese chess] during downtime) and scenery (snowy Japan Alps in the distance, sunset in the little town).

An *Entertainment Yomiuri* critic was generally positive, while equivocating: "Up through the first half, it was a very light comedy style, but then . . . it gets a little too serious . . . The ending became light and happy again, so that was better. But this seriousness seems like a bit of a miscalculation by director Ishiro Honda . . . Overall it was a very entertaining film."

In 1960, *New York Times*' critic Bosley Crowther said Takashi Shimura "measures up with the top film actors anywhere." In his roughly two decades as a Kurosawa mainstay, Shimura transformed into numerous memorable characters with precision, layering humanity and emotion with an economy of words. He wasn't handsome, but his face was a great asset, as were his receding hairline and deeply penetrating eyes. Outside Japan, Shimura is most famous for starring in the Kurosawa trifecta of *Ikiru*, *Seven Samurai*, and *Rashomon*. With Ishiro Honda, the actor had big and small parts in *Godzilla* and other sci-fi movies, but there were also dramatic roles in overlooked titles such as *The Blue Pearl* and *Skin of the South*. Among the best of these is *Inao: Story of an Iron Arm* (1959), with Shimura as the father of a real-life baseball hero.

Released on March 21, 1959, three weeks before the start of baseball season, *Inao* is a biopic of Kazuhisa Inao, one of the greatest pitchers in the history of Nippon Pro Baseball. The film was rushed into production amid the hysteria over Inao's heroics in the 1958 Japan Series, held the prior October. Inao brought the Fukuoka Nishitetsu Lions back from the brink of elimination against the famed Tokyo Yomiuri Giants, pitching his team to victory in each of the final four games and hitting a "sayonara home run" to finish one game in dramatic fashion. The film charts Inao's rise from humble beginnings in postwar Japan as the seventh son of a poor fisherman, a last-in-line runt who accidentally discovers a love for baseball. It is the father-son relationship and Shimura's portrayal of the outwardly stern but privately proud papa that make *Inao* more than run-of-the-mill hagiography. (Baseball pictures were popular in the 1950s; Shimura previously starred as a coach in *There Was a Man* [*Otoko arite*, 1955].)

The first half is the story of this relationship. From the moment his son is born, Kyusaku "Kyu-*san*" Inao is already teaching him pride and perseverance. The boy—small for his age, prone to nodding off asleep—endures a childhood of long days fishing with his dad, teasing from bigger kids, and the sudden death of his oldest brother. Father endlessly spouts old sayings and Chinese proverbs about devotion to duty that make his older sons laugh, but Kazuhisa takes it all to heart. He becomes a high school baseball star and signs a pro contract to play in nearby Fukuoka, declining bigger offers in Tokyo. His first two seasons are phenomenal, but after Kyusaku dies of stomach cancer, Inao endures a tough 1958 season, inspired by his father's teachings. The film's second half is all baseball, a mix of newsreel footage, reenactment, and family and friends tuning in via radio and TV as the Lions ride Inao's arm and bat to a championship. It is perhaps the most purely documentary-like sequence of all Honda's feature films.

Inao was a high-profile project from Sadao Sugihara, producer of the highly popular *Sazae-san* family comedies, who attended the Japan Series and made the deal for Inao to star in the film, telling the press, "Baseball players should now start contributing more to cultural enterprises." The script, a soft paean to the old patriarchal order and a tribute to the sacrifices of fathers, was cowritten by frequent

Deep in thought while making *Inao, Story of an Iron Arm*. Courtesy of Honda Film Inc.

Kurosawa collaborator Ryuzo Kikushima. Though a lesser film, *Inao* has much in common with Ozu's poignant *There Was a Father* (*Chichi ariki*, 1942). It was an unusual assignment for a director carving dual niches in science fiction and women's subjects, but Honda was by now a reliable, versatile craftsman of contemporary commercial films.

The casting of Kazuhisa Inao as himself attracted publicity, and several of his Lions teammates, coaches, and even radio announcers also played themselves. Inao's acting is passable during sports sequences and scenes with minimal dialogue, but the experiment fails in the emotional final meeting with his dying father. Inao's wooden line readings are on par with attempts by Babe Ruth, Jackie Robinson, and Muhammad Ali to play themselves on film, and he appears to wear a nervous smirk. "[Honda] said to me, 'Inao-*san*, you can't be smiling here because your father is gravely ill.' But I had no intentions of smiling. 'This is the natural face I was born with,' I said. We must have reshot the scene about 10 times."[1] Inao's misfortune is to appear onscreen opposite the great Shimura, who lets the father's steely façade crack just a little, a tear falling from one eye.

"He was good, old Shimura," said assistant director Seiji Tani, working with Honda for the first time. "It was a shame for him to be used . . . in minor parts [in Honda's sci-fi films] . . . He was great in *Inao* . . . because he held his acting back a little . . . That man could speak no words and just moan, and he was great."

Secondary roles went to some of Honda's favorite actors, including *Godzilla* alums Ren Yamamoto and Sachio Sakai as Inao's older brothers, and Fuyuki Murakami as a high school coach. Even sometime monster stuntman Katsumi Tezuka appears briefly as an athletic trainer. Curiously, Yumi Shirakawa is billed prominently in the credits but appears only briefly as a love interest, with no lines. Honda filmed additional scenes with Inao and Shirakawa, but these were apparently cut to keep the 106-minute running time from getting longer. Also deleted was the film debut of actress Yuriko Hoshi, who is credited though she does not appear. Hoshi would later star in Honda's *Mothra vs. Godzilla* and *Ghidorah* and become one of Toho's most popular actresses.

Inao also features a contribution from Eiji Tsuburaya. Early on, young Inao goes sailing alone and gets trapped in a raging storm. His father rows out to help, but rather than rescue the struggling lad, he gives him a pep talk, coaxing him to save himself. The storm was created on a soundstage, and Inao's rowboat tossing in the surf was a miniature built by Tsuburaya himself.

A *Shukan Tokyo* reviewer excoriated Inao's nonacting. "In the second half . . . Inao plays himself, and the film is a mixture of actual footage from last year's victory and the acting parts. The acting and actual footage really don't match, and Inao himself is so arrogant, but I guess that is pretty much the way those big stars are." After Inao's death at age seventy on November 13, 2007, a memorial screening of this rarely seen film was held at Fukuoka City Public Library.

There's this very natural warmth in the way [Honda] observes people . . . There are others who film comedy with very cold eyes.
— Seiji Tani, assistant director

In 1958–59, Honda made a de facto trilogy about fathers and children. *Song for a Bride* offered the loveable, eccentric father as comic relief, while the by-the-bootstraps dad in *Inao* aimed to inspire and tug the heartstrings. The third film, *Seniors, Juniors, Co-workers* (1959), is almost Ozu-like in its worldview, a hybrid salaryman film and home drama peppered with Honda's familiar light comedy and starring moon-faced Daisuke Kato as a middle-aged, white-collar widower trying to manage career, family, and love in a fast-paced, fast-changing Tokyo. Kato plays a typical Meiji man who believes in hard work above all, but everywhere are signs that his old-school way of life is under threat. Scandals at the office, disrespectful youth, America's cultural fingerprints all over the place, television, career women, materialism, weird modern art, and so on. Though the kids make fun of their stodgy old man, they grow closer and learn to appreciate his old-fashioned values, and he their free-spirited ways. Worlds removed from Honda's previous look at the generation gap in *Adolescence Part 2*, this is the director at the height of his power to entertain, to find humor and commonality in everyday things, to underline his story with ideas about class, wealth, age, gender, and love. When it screened at the 2009 Yamagata International Documentary Film Festival, fifty years after its release, the festival's curators rightly called this forgotten gem a masterpiece.

Curiously, the screenplay for this mildly conservative but essentially apolitical story was by Tsutomu Sawamura, whom critic Tadao Sato called "an ultra-right scriptwriter . . . who had promoted militarism and praised the war effort in prewar and war-time scripts."[2] *Seniors, Juniors, Co-workers* was loosely adapted from an essay about corporate culture by Yuzo Yamato, a management consultant, but the business world is only half the story. The flip side is the growing popularity of television and imported rock and roll, and the accompanying allure of celebrity, fame, and wealth.

By 1959 television was already the ultimate symbol of adopted Western consumerism and a powerful tool of the advertising age. TV sets remained beyond the reach of the average Japanese household, making them all the more coveted. Ozu covered this territory brilliantly in his comedy *Good Morning* (*Ohayo*, 1959). *Seniors, Juniors, Co-workers* looks at the upper-middle-class world of big houses with backyards, housekeepers, and prominently placed TVs tuned to the latest nightly drivel, such as "The International Glamour Stars Show." The plot is simple and familiar: Shuhei is a middle manager at Sakura Rayon, a big textile company. One of his colleagues, the good-natured Satake (Yoshibumi Tajima) fixes him up with the widow Michiyo (Mitsuko Kusabue, *Farewell to the Woman I Called Sister*) and the two take a genuine liking to each other, though their courtship is slow and awkward. The requisite high jinks ensue when Shuhei's nephew Yoichi (Shunichi Segi), an ambitious, would-be promoter with a pre-Beatles moptop, convinces Shuhei's company to hire his girlfriend, the sexy nightclub singer Domon (Machiko Sakura), as a spokes-celebrity, and her popularity skyrockets. These developments lure Shuhei across the generational divide, to where money and youth are misspent on freewheeling dance parties, drinking, and flirting.

Both *Seniors, Juniors, Co-workers* and *Good Morning* bemoan the erosion of traditional Japanese ideals and rising materialism. Neither film is a harsh criticism of this change, but simply an objective view of a society in flux. And in both films an irreversible Occupation holdover, the English language, symbolizes American cultural hegemony. In Honda's film, the faddish use of "Japanese English" phrases, such as "I'm sorry" and "just a moment" and "thank you," are second nature. Even stodgy Shuhei incorporates English into the very Japanese motto by which he lives: "Work *speedy*, fall in love *slowly*." The film also reflects the *rokabiri* (rockabilly) craze that spread from US military bases across Japan, with teens donning rebellious American-style leather jackets and pompadours, much to their parents' horror. Japanese-Canadian *rokabiri* legend Mickey Curtis appears, as does Kyu Sakamoto, whose 1963 hit "Sukiyaki" would reach no. 1 on the US Billboard charts. English is sung and spoken throughout the film; at the Crazy Crazy Club, where everybody hangs out, the lyrics to Elvis Presley's "Love Me Tender" are emblazoned on a wall. Banal, parroted American pop is contrasted with the sweet Japanese children's song *Hana* ("Flower"), about cherry blossoms along the Sumida River, sung by Shuhei's daughter.

Americanisms are everywhere. Kids decorate their rooms with US car license plates; teens dress in cowboy hats and drink Coca-Cola. Holding the center of this collapsing moral universe is actor Daisuke Kato as the chubby everyman with an unwavering sense of right and wrong. Kato was a versatile character actor, probably best known as the policeman in *Rashomon*, one of the *Seven Samurai*, and the grotesque comic villain of *Yojimbo*.[3] The supporting players include Akira Kubo as Taro, an aspiring young salaryman whom Shuhei takes under his wing, and who falls victim to a ¥100,000 embezzlement frame-up orchestrated by a jealous coworker. Shuhei's oldest daughter Yoshiko is played by newcomer Kumi Mizuno, displaying more than a hint of the sex appeal that would become her trademark in later Honda films. The usual romantic conflict arises when the company president tries to fix up his son, abstract sculptor Yasuhiko (Hisao Katamochi), with Yoshiko, who's in love with the upstart Taro. In a fresh twist, here the father sides with the kids and rejects his boss's offer out of principle, unwilling to give away his daughter to benefit his own career. And instead of reprisals for this risky move, Shuhei's superiors admire him for it. "This is what's good about him," one man says. The greedy Yoichi and the jealous coworker get their just desserts, but there are no serious villains. In the tidy ending, the honest and upstanding folks find love and happiness, and traditional virtues are vindicated.

Honda's post-*Godzilla* period began with stories about working people of the city and country, many on the postwar poverty line. *Seniors, Juniors, Co-workers* arrived in the midst of Japan's economic rebound, spurred by massive increases in exports to the West in the second half of the 1950s. The textile industry, where Shuhei makes his living, was a major source of those exports. Much of this film's dialogue and action concern Japan's new prosperity and the ways it complicates life and corrupts individuals. Honda uses the characters' attitudes toward money to assess their moral fiber. At one extreme are greedy Yoichi and his celebrity girlfriend, who extort the company to feed their frivolous lifestyle; at the other is virtuous Taro and his mother, who offers to sell her house to pay back the embezzled funds, even though her son's not to blame. In between are the executives and their wives, who bitch about the high cost of handing out *ochugen* (*bon* festival gifts), entertaining, and keeping up appearances for the job's sake. Even Shuhei's kids are money-minded: daughter Yoshiko gets promoted for targeting wasteful spending at the office, while young son Kenta (Ken Kubo, Akira's younger brother) is obsessed with a new wristwatch, a status symbol at school. The offices, homes, and nightclubs of this newly moneyed Tokyo are rendered in finely detailed sets by Yoshiro Muraki, Kurosawa's regular art director during this period.

In *Song for a Bride*, the comedy was situation- and character-based, but here Honda uses humor to poke fun at the trivialities of the new Japan. Both films share Honda's fondness for his characters; his humor is never cynical or cold. *Seniors, Juniors, Co-workers* would be the last of Honda's home comedy-dramas, and also his last film to indulge in extended dialogue about everyday things, scenes that do not necessarily propel the plot but give the characters room to talk and come alive.

There are several long, warm conversations between Shuhei and his children about college, his retirement, their inheritance (or lack of it), marriage, and other mundanities. Honda also bookends the movie with job interviews, Taro's at the beginning and youngest daughter Sachiko's (Ryoko Koda) at the end. Sachiko confirms what is by now apparent: that Shuhei's kids are all right, straight shooters and hard workers just like him. Sachiko chooses to forego college, spare her father the expense, and become an office lady instead—and eventually, marry a company man. "It's not too bad," she says, "to be a salaryman."

———

Even as they vied for nuclear supremacy, the Cold War's archenemies were engaged in another rivalry: the space race.

In 1957 and 1958, the Soviets and the Americans launched their first satellites into orbit. The following year, the United States took the first picture of Earth from space, countered by a Soviet rocket snapping the first photos of the far side of the moon. Eiji Tsuburaya urged Toho to make a film about a lunar voyage, knowing it was only a matter of time before it somehow became reality.

Battle in Outer Space (*Uchu daisenso*) is another alien invasion epic, lighter on plot and heavier on action than *The Mysterians*. Honda's two-track career was coming to an end; he would hereon direct genre projects almost exclusively, and the transition is abrupt. His fourth movie of 1959 shares none of the warmth and humor of the previous three, and it looks like the work of a different director. And in one sense it is, for Tsuburaya dominates with special effects set pieces linked together by Honda's exposition and action. The film opens with flying saucers attacking a satellite, Akira Ifukube's horns blaring and timpani thundering, and

concludes with the coup de grace of a giant spaceship sucking Tokyo skyscrapers off the ground. It's popcorn stuff, and though not one of Honda's strongest efforts, it was nonetheless among his personal favorite works. As in *The Mysterians*, Honda creates an idealized world of international solidarity with Japan and the United States leading the way, though this idea is secondary to the spectacle of war, demonstrations of military-aerospace hardware, and the future-tech production design.

"We tried making this film different in several ways," recalled Koji Kajita. "*The Mysterians* was a bit more fantastic in concept, so rather than filming with attention to realism, we made a lot of things with bright colors . . . In [*Battle*], our big point was to realistically portray how people would respond to an alien invasion. We simulated a real invasion."

Battle in Outer Space is often mistaken for a *Mysterians* sequel. It may have began as one—two characters reappear, though in name only and played by different actors—but this is a new story with no reference to earlier events. Writer Jojiro Okami provided another tech-heavy treatment, which was expanded by Shinichi Sekizawa into something akin to a Japanese version of Fred F. Sears's similarly themed *Earth vs. The Flying Saucers* (1956). The film also includes what would appear to be Tsuburaya and Honda's nod to George Pal's *Destination Moon*, a lunar landing by twin rockets, called SPIPS ("speeps"), gracefully descending.

Ray guns blasting as he rescues the girl from aliens, the astronaut Katsumiya (Ryo Ikebe) is a bit more of an alpha male than Honda's usual sci-fi hero. Honda gives Ikebe star treatment: he's the only astronaut without headgear, so as not to muss his handsome mane. But the movie isn't about Katsumiya, or about anyone really,

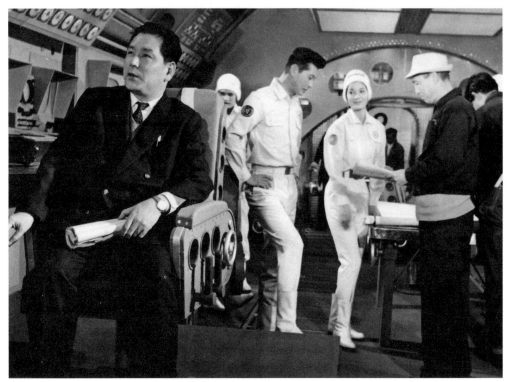

Honda with *Battle in Outer Space* stars Ryo Ikebe (center left) and Kyoko Anzai (center right); producer Tomoyuki Tanaka (left) examines the spaceship set. Courtesy of Honda Film Inc.

and other than a romantic moment under the stars, the characters have no lives. The most interesting person is Iwamura (Yoshio Tsuchiya), an astronaut who succumbs to alien mind control and nearly sabotages the moon mission. Realizing his misdeeds, Iwamura sacrifices himself, fending off the aliens to enable his comrades to escape back to Earth. His valiant death offers a brief moment of emotion. "We will be back again one day," astronaut Kogure (Hisaya Ito) says to his fallen friend as the moon recedes in the distance. "You'll be waiting, right?"

With a stronger script, Honda might have had an antiwar film. The astronaut-soldiers are sent off with a real-life military band saluting them, a color guard presenting arms, and cheers of "Banzai!" Their reconnaissance mission quickly becomes

a series of skirmishes in space and on the moon's surface, where they climb craggy rocks (filmed on the black ash slopes of Mount Mihara) in search of the enemy. Girlfriends, wives, and children are left behind as men rush into battle. Allusions to the bomb recur: a man burned by the aliens' freeze ray, missiles launching, the symbolic nuking of New York and San Francisco. Mankind wins the battle, but there are no heavy hearts for the millions apparently killed. Everyone rejoices and shakes hands.

Honda's antiwar feeling briefly resonates when the astronauts discover the body of a colleague killed by the aliens floating in space. There is a solemn moment of multidenominational prayer. "That was Honda-*san*," Kajita said. "It was from his war experience. He wanted to express the sadness of war and offer prayer for its victims." Then again, the film is hardly pacifist. Once the aliens' evil intent is apparent, there is drumbeating for war around the globe, and a massive drive—illustrated with factory footage resembling wartime propaganda—to weaponize surveillance rockets into combat ships. An official declares, "There is no being diplomatic with our war against Natal!" As the Earth offensive is launched from air bases in Japan, the United States, and the USSR, Honda has Dr. Adachi (Koreya Senda) lamenting the war. "I never thought we'd have to put a person in one of those rockets," says the Japanese scientist, but the American Dr. Richardson (Len Stanford) is resigned: "It's what we have to do to protect peace on Earth."

Battle was released on December 26, 1959, about three weeks before the controversial Treaty of Mutual Cooperation and Security (AMPO in its Japanese abbreviation) was updated, strengthening ties between Washington and Tokyo. Reflecting these developments, the film puts the Japan-US alliance front and center, symbolized by twin astronaut crews—one led by an American, the other by Ikebe. In Honda's idealized reality Japan is a major international player, thus the global science meeting and the aerospace project are based near Tokyo. Again, the international coalition is broad, including former wartime enemies and allies as well as smaller powers such as India and the Philippines. Moreover, the film doesn't share the Cold War paranoia of the American sci-fi films it emulates; Russia is shown fighting on the side of the angels. This was just months before Soviet Premier Nikita Khrushchev's fabled shoe-banging declaration of "We will bury you!" at the United Nations. With

Battle in Outer Space: the international conference, a staple of Honda's sci-fi films.
© Toho Co., Ltd.

worldwide political tensions high, Honda's simple message of unity was timely.

The production design is again based on Okami's sci-tech concepts and sketches by Shigeru Komatsuzaki. There are some real-life influences too, space suits modeled after those of Russian cosmonauts and rocket fighter jets after the experimental X-15 aircraft, which the United States unveiled in June 1959. The aliens' antigravity beam is yet another example of real-world science tweaked to suit the plot. According to Kajita, a science journal had recently postulated that if an object were to reach the theoretical temperature of absolute zero, its gravitational pull might be negated. The theory never gained traction, but no matter; it provided a timely and interesting rationale for the enemy's superweapon.

It was the ever-curious actor Yoshio Tsuchiya who suggested stepping lightly on the moon to illustrate its low gravity. "[The other actors] didn't want to do it," Tsuchiya said. "They were embarrassed. I was adamant. Honda-*san* was smiling nearby. I turned to him and said, 'You're the director. What do you say?' He said I was right. So, I came out from the spacecraft real slowly, floating. I showed them how to walk on the moon." Years later, watching Neil Armstrong's historic step on TV, Tsuchiya felt vindicated.

There are few noteworthy performances. Ikebe is wooden compared to his feisty personality in *An Echo Calls You*. The tone veers wildly when the aliens invade the minds of Tsuchiya and Dr. Ahmed (Malcolm Pearce), an Iranian scientist, with each man clutching his skull in agony before exploding in violence and hammy acting. There are unintentional laughs: Ahmed's bizarre death scene, Tsuchiya stretching his cheeks to simulate the g-force of a rocket launch, the inept alien

invasion, and the tittering, munchkin-sized Natalians. (Early screenplay drafts indicate the aliens were originally to be depicted as plantlike monsters.)[4]

As the 1950s ended, the Japanese film industry was at its economic zenith. In 1960 the studios would release a total of 547 domestic feature films, an all-time high and an amazing turnaround; in 1946, the first year after the war, the studios had put out only sixty-seven films. The total number of cinemas in Japan would peak in 1960 at 7,457, and more than one billion tickets would be sold for the fourth year in a row.[5] The 1959–60 season was a banner year, with Toei's *jidai-geki* hit *Lord Mito: The Nation's Vice Shogun* (*Mito komon tenka no fuku shogun*) topping the heap at ¥390 million; major directors such as Kurosawa (*The Bad Sleep Well*), Yasujiro Ozu (*Late Autumn*), Mikio Naruse (*Daughters, Wives, and a Mother* and *When a Woman Ascends the Stairs*), Kon Ichikawa, Keisuke Kinoshita, and others also had significant hits. *Battle in Outer Space* held its own, earning an estimated ¥123 million (about $342,000), ranking no. 25 at the box office.

Yet, Honda remembered this not as a time of success, but the moment when the Toho bean counters began tightening the reins to squeeze out more profits. "It was around this time that we had to start simplifying things. It was not the idea of our side, but the company . . . talking all the time about the budget and saying, 'We can't afford that.' When the desk people start acting big, it ruins the movie.

"We would try to negotiate with them on the budget," Honda said. "But they would not budge. The audience will respond by coming in bigger numbers and paying more to see it if it is made better, but they just did not understand this."[6] Honda and Tsuburaya cut a few corners. The alien attacks on

Venice and the Panama Canal were illustrated with unconvincing paintings; Sekizawa intended the latter to be a full-blown effects sequence. Conversely, certain scenes were made bigger. A spectacular flying saucer attack on the moon—a fast-moving sequence presaging *Star Wars* by almost twenty years—was a less ambitious ground skirmish in early drafts.[7]

Battle has an unprecedented number of non-Japanese faces, though most of the foreign cast members were expat businesspeople, military personnel, and others who moonlighted in films; and their lack of professional acting chops is sometimes apparent. Casting foreigners was part of a strategy to create an international flavor and increase overseas commercial appeal. "We also avoided filming [in] ordinary Japanese housing, like tatami rooms," said assistant director Kajita. "We stuck to the science center, the moon, and regular places to set a more international mood. The foreign audiences could relate easier this way." The strategy apparently worked: Columbia Pictures sent reps to Tokyo to acquire the US rights soon after the film's release, and a moderately edited and rather poorly dubbed English-language version was distributed stateside in 1960.

As Toho's genre films grew in popularity abroad, Eiji Tsuburaya attracted international attention for his special-effects work. A Hearst newsreel crew filmed Tsuburaya shooting his special effects on the *Battle in Outer Space* set, while taking only a glimpse of Honda. In the next year or so, Tsuburaya would be profiled by the Associated Press and *American Cinematographer*. Honda, meanwhile, would receive no attention from the foreign press, even as his films continued to draw increasing interest, and dollars, from Hollywood.

17

ACCIDENTAL MONSTERS

The Human Vapor (1960),
Mothra (1961),
A Man in Red (1961)

Toho required assistant directors to successfully complete three films before officially promoting them to the position of director, and with this promotion came a significant change in job status. Whereas an assistant director was a studio employee with a guaranteed salary, directors worked under one-year contracts that were renewed at the studio's discretion.[1] Honda was one of Toho's more profitable and prolific filmmakers during the industry's boom decade, and he was rewarded with earnings northward of ¥2 million (about $5,550), well above the average Tokyo per-capita income of about ¥274,000 as of 1961.[2] In addition, Honda might receive a bonus of ¥200,000 after completing a successful picture.

Ever since they were married, Honda and Kimi had lived in Seijo, a quiet residential neighborhood in Setagaya, the most populous of Tokyo's twenty-three municipal wards, located on the southwest tip of the city. Today, Seijo is less than twenty minutes by express train from Shinjuku, but it's far removed from the bustle of central Tokyo. Its epicenter is Seijogakuen-Mae Station, a major hub on the Odakyu railway line. To the north of the station is Seijo University, a private college, and some of the most desirable homes in all of Tokyo; to the south are somewhat more modest neighborhoods and, nestled among them, a large parcel of land upon which Toho Studios resides. In the fifties and sixties, the majority of Toho's actors, directors, crew members, and other employees lived in Seijo, walking to work on streets lined with cherry blossom and gingko trees and enjoying the ample open space. After Honda's return from the war, the family had moved into a small rented house on the south side of the station; but when his fortunes improved in the late 1950s, they purchased a plot of land spanning three hundred *tsubo* (more than

10,500 square feet, enough space for "about three fairly large houses with attached gardens"[3]), located at the first major intersection north of the train station. Its large size was not unusual. In those days, the area was sparsely developed, and residential lots averaged three hundred to five hundred *tsubo*. There the Hondas constructed a roomy house measuring about one hundred *tsubo* (about 3,500 square feet).

The "Honda mansion," as family and friends called it, was a one-story Japanese-style dwelling with a huge backyard. By today's standards it was an enormous Tokyo house, and Honda's cast and crew would fondly recall the big parties held there, when dozens and dozens of friends met for eats, drinks, singing, and socializing. "We weren't rich, but we needed a house large enough to fit everyone who came over," said Kimi.

Depending on how much Honda was working, he and Kimi might host up to eight parties a year. There was one before crank-in (the start of film production), another after wrap-up, one at the end of the year, and every January 2 or 3 there was a big New Year's bash. Akira Takarada recalled, "Everybody loved [Honda], so all of the staff and cast would gather. When we arrived at his house and he opened the door, greeting, 'Happy New Year,' you'd see rows and rows of shoes in the entrance. They were stacked on top of each other; we just stepped over them to go inside. That's how big the turnout was."

There were no announcements or invitations; everyone just knew when to show up. Big stars such as Takarada and Toshiro Mifune were there, and Honda regulars such as Kenji Sahara and Jun Tazaki might help out as party coordinators. Supporting players such as Ikio Sawamura came, and there were even some extras or stand-ins

Wrap party for *Dogora* at Honda's home (from left to right): Ishiro Honda, Kimi Honda, Kenji Sahara, Hiroshi Koizumi. Courtesy of Honda Film Inc.

Camaraderie at the *Dogora* wrap party (from left to right): Yosuke Natsuki, Ishiro Honda, Nadao Kirino, and Yoko Fujiyama. Courtesy of Honda Film Inc.

whose names Honda didn't always know. All were welcome, regardless of status. Kimi would prepare a feast, and Honda's ritual was to sit at a table with glasses in front of him: one for beer, one for whiskey, one for sake, and one for a cocktail. Friends would stop to refill his glass and chat. He never got hung over, and as years went by he developed the "hiccup method" to avoid overdoing it. He would party until he began to hiccup, then tell his guests, "Thank you, I am going to bed." The party would carry on into the night. Sometimes there were arguments or fights, but everyone remained friends.

The "mansion" was practically an open house. Even without a party, people came and went freely. Actor Yoshio Tsuchiya and a gang of friends once dropped in unannounced, and while limbo dancing to music out back, they tore the lawn to shreds. Most nights after work, Honda was accompanied home by actors or staff, and Kimi served a meal, snacks, or drinks. "Even while he was filming, [Honda] would ask everyone, 'Want to come over?' And they would all come along. I remember telling him more than once, 'I am not a magician, you know.'"

Honda's hospitality was not limited to colleagues. Once, a young fan of Honda's movies ran away from home and showed up at the director's doorstep. The Hondas took the boy inside and fed him, then notified police and bought him a train ticket home. Other times, young fans came seeking autographs, and he would make time for them.

————

During the second half of the 1950s, Honda grew closer with Ryuji and exposed the young man to cinema and art. But the quiet father was not one to explain or discuss things, leaving the son often bewildered.

"My father would suddenly say, 'Let's go,'" Ryuji recalled. "That meant it was time to go see a movie with him. We had very few conversations together. We'd get on the train and I would stare out the window, then jump off and follow my father. He was very big for the time, and very quick because he had been a soldier. So quick. I was always running behind him."

They would catch an early train to the museums and galleries in Ueno. "My father went into this one building, and I had no idea what was inside. There were lots of paintings on the walls, and my father explained absolutely nothing. He pointed to a big clock and said, 'Let's meet back here in an hour.' Then he went into the museum by himself. I was scared to be alone, so I just followed him and looked at the paintings. [Laughs.] And after that, we'd go back to Ginza and go to the cinema."

Sometimes father and son took in three movies in one long day. The films were always European and American, never Japanese. There were Mervyn LeRoy's war drama *Waterloo Bridge* (1940), Fellini's *La Strada* (1954), and De Sica's *Indiscretion of an American Wife* (1953), among many more.

When Honda did speak, he talked about composition within the frame. "It was about the screen: how to cut, how people are moving within it," Ryuji said. "He'd say, 'It's an interesting point. You have to think about that.' Maybe that's what he was trying to teach me, but he never talked about it in detail."

Other times, Honda went by himself and watched new films by his contemporaries. And when his own movies were released, he would slip into the audience. Theater managers would offer to comp him, but Honda preferred to pay his admission and sit alone, quietly and anonymously observing the crowd's response. "It's different from a screening, the [public] reaction," Kimi said. "And he never ever used his professional status for personal gain."

————

Toho would send a driver to pick Honda up each morning. Often he was deep in thought about that day's shooting and preferred to walk. The driver couldn't return alone; it was his responsibility to get the director to work, so the car—a big, 1950s-era Ford or Chevrolet—would creep slowly behind as Honda paced the streets. Honda was oblivious; he sometimes wondered why the big automobile was shadowing him.

As Honda walked southward from Seijogakuen-Mae Station, he passed the commuters on foot and bicycle heading in the opposite direction, to their jobs in the city. His path took him through the narrow streets lined with gardens and houses clustered around the perimeter of Toho Studios. He walked past the palm trees and guard stand at Toho's front gates, and the first things he saw upon entering the studio grounds were Stage No. 1 and Stage No. 2, two big, tan structures located side by side. Behind the front gate was a large courtyard with a circular stone fountain surrounded by a green lawn; workshops and sound-stages stood along a grid of streets that extended toward the rear of the lot. Back in the 1930s and 1940s, the fountain was where major directors such as Kajiro Yamamoto, Mikio Naruse, and Sadao Yamanaka would sit and chat. These days, it was where actors and actresses posed for publicity photos and a yearly calendar featuring Toho's "Cinderellas," as the resident starlets were called.

"The entire place was filled with energy," remembered Ryuji, who would drop by after school or during vacation to watch his father work. "People were all around, working or preparing for the next film shoot.

"To the left of the front entrance was a building composed of rows of staff rooms, divided by ongoing projects. Each room had [a name], such as Honda-*gumi* [team], Kurosawa-*gumi*, and Taniguchi-*gumi*, posted on the entrances. Various movie posters and flyers were on the walls.

"To the right of the front entrance were the administrative offices, and to the right of that was the studio commissary, which was called 'the salon.' This cafeteria was always filled with directors, staff members, and actors all mingling and chatting. Even directors who didn't have a project going at the time would still drop in if they had a moment of free time."

The decade of the Showa 30s (1955–64) was the most productive and commercially successful period in Japanese film history. Toho routinely put out two new films per week. Top stars made up to ten films per year, while workhorse minor players—called *obeya* (big room) actors because they literally waited for work in a big room—appeared in dozens more. As historian Stuart Galbraith IV writes: "The 1950s has widely come to be regarded as the 'Golden Period' of Japanese filmmaking. Indeed, by the late 1950s Japan was producing more features than anywhere else in the world, including the prolific India. Though Japan could not compete with the lavishness afforded the very biggest Hollywood films, by the end of the decade Toho's films had a slickness rivaled only by the biggest American studios, and were virtually unrecognizable from the films Toho made earlier in the decade."

"It was so much fun back then," said Koji Kajita. "The filmmaking business was driven by young people. Everyone wanted to make something new. The studios and staff were all in full rotation. There were four main times of year for which we needed to produce hit films. We had the Golden Week holiday in May, Silver Week in November, New Year's, and Bon Festival.[4] We had no time to take a break."

The Golden Period, as it turned out, was short-lived.

———

Around the time of *Godzilla*, the Honda family had acquired its first television. Initially, only three hours of news and sports programming were broadcast daily, and every evening neighbors congregated in the

Hondas' living room to watch sumo wrestling. They posted a chart on the wall, tracking each wrestler's won-lost record. But by decade's end, many families had their own TVs, and the days were now filled with soap operas, quiz shows, and children's programs; even American shows such as the TV Western *Laramie*, starring Robert Fuller, were immensely popular. Television symbolized Japan's new, consumer-driven prosperity of the 1960s, and it was slowly supplanting movies as the primary entertainment medium. By 1960 televisions would be in 28 percent of Japanese homes; by 1962 the figure was almost 60 percent, and it would continue climbing as people acquired TVs in anticipation of the 1964 Tokyo Olympics.[5] Programming diversified and color broadcasting was introduced. During roughly the same period, movie ticket sales dropped about 50 percent, from 1.1 billion annually in 1958 to five hundred million in 1965.[6]

By now, each of Japan's film studios had developed a trademark style targeting certain sectors of the moviegoing public, and each would begin changing its approach in response to the rising dominance of television and evolving social trends. Toei Studios had been the dominant mass producer of popular *jidai-geki* film series during the 1950s; but when the samurai genre began migrating to TV, Toei shifted to more violent "cruel *jidai-geki*" and *yakuza* pictures.[7] Shochiku, one of Japan's original film companies, was known in the 1950s as the home studio of the great Yasujiro Ozu, and for its "Ofuna flavor," a bittersweet brand of women's melodrama. But when its formula fell out of favor in the 1960s, Shochiku would survive on the success of its *Tora-san* films, warmhearted comedies about an itinerant peddler. Nikkatsu, Japan's oldest studio, resumed production

in 1954 after a wartime layoff and survived the 1960s with big-budget action movies for the youth market, toplined by stars such as Yujiro Ishihara and Akira Kobayashi. The Daiei studio, founded during the war, excelled at classic and contemporary literature adaptations, focusing on female protagonists. It had launched the exporting of Japanese cinema with *Rashomon* and produced works of prestigious directors such as Kenji Mizoguchi and Kon Ichikawa; but by the 1960s it would be churning out *Gamera* monster movies and *Zatoichi* swordfight action comedies. Then there was Shin Toho, the studio spawned by Toho's labor strife, which was known for cheap thrillers, ghost stories, and nationalistic war films before it went bankrupt in 1961.

Toho, too, altered its business strategy, and this change was partly responsible for Honda's career shift toward science fiction movies and his decline in output, as he would never again direct more than three films per year. After the death of Toho founder Ichizo Kobayashi in 1957, the studio came under increasing influence from the Hankyu Corporation, the parent stockholding conglomerate that controlled numerous businesses—railroads, department stores, real estate, travel, freight, and so on—which Kobayashi had founded or acquired. Although box-office numbers were slipping, Toho's management doubled down on movies. The company bought about one hundred cinemas in prime real estate areas, and it tried to stem the industry's decline by dropping smaller-scale films and focusing on bigger-budgeted productions in color. In 1959 Toho made thirty-six A-class productions; the following year, that number increased to forty-eight, and the company stopped making B-class and C-class pictures almost entirely.[8] The belt-tightening that Honda felt during *Battle in*

Outer Space was real: there was more focus on the bottom line, and producers and directors were under pressure to make big hits. The Toho brand became a narrowing mix of mass-market genres: war films, salaryman comedies, science fiction, and action pictures. In this new climate, Honda would leave behind the heartwarming little dramas and family comedies he'd enjoyed making for the past half-decade.

I am no longer a human being. Therefore I am no longer subject to human law.
– Mizuno, the Human Vapor

The new decade began mired in unrest. In June 1960 hundreds of thousands surrounded the National Diet Building for the biggest political demonstration in Japan's history. The protesters were angry about major changes to the AMPO Treaty that were rammed through the Diet without public debate, changes widely perceived as enslaving Japan to America's Cold War strategic interests while compromising the country's political neutrality and democratic reforms. A state visit by President Dwight D. Eisenhower was abruptly canceled for fear of a hostile reception. Prime Minister Nobosuke Kishi soon resigned in disgrace.

Elsewhere, politicians tried unsuccessfully to restore the wartime powers of search and seizure for police. A 312-day miners' strike ended in bloody riots. A string of Tokyo bank heists, inspired by a famously bizarre 1948 bank robbery in which twelve people were poisoned to death, made the papers.

The Human Vapor, Honda's first film in almost exactly one year, reflects this backdrop of rebellion against authority. Mizuno (Yoshio Tsuchiya) is a disgruntled

ex-pilot, expelled from the air force for medical reasons and now working in a mundane job. He is infatuated with beautiful Kasuga Fujichiyo (Kaoru Yachigusa), a once-famous performer of traditional Japanese *buyo* dance. A shady scientist enlists Mizuno as an unwitting human guinea pig in a genetic experiment, purportedly for Japan's nascent space program. Instead of becoming a superastronaut, however, Mizuno acquires the ability to transform into a living mist. Freed of human and societal constraints, the vapor man goes on a crime rampage, robbing banks with impunity and mocking the police. He uses the funds to bankroll Fujichiyo's comeback performance and kills anyone standing in his way.

Honda begins with opening credits supered over a stylized bank holdup, sans dialogue, shot from the perpetrator's point of view and backed by composer Kunio Miyauchi's Bernard Herrmann-esque title theme. Takeshi Kimura's cynical script is a hybrid of crime caper and sci-fi/horror in the vein of H. G. Wells's *The Invisible Man*.[9] Honda's ever-present concerns about mis-

Yoshio Tsuchiya (center) confers with Honda (right) on *The Human Vapor*. Costar Kaoru Yachigusa looks on. Courtesy of Honda Film Inc.

appropriated science are embodied by Dr. Sano (Fuyuki Murakami), who works in a creepy lab filmed in canted angles, and who cruelly uses Mizuno to test his theories. But this film is less interested in the ethics of Sano's quackery than in the antiestablishment threat it unleashes. Mizuno becomes a celebrity outlaw, "society's problem" as a newspaper editor says, and must be disposed of. Still, Honda portrays the villain as a tragic if remorseless figure; though his deeds are evil and he relishes the power he wields, Mizuno did not choose to be a monster. In his twisted logic, he kills and robs for love, and his victims resemble the authority figures who have tormented him; an early screenplay draft had Mizuno murdering the wife and child of a policeman, but Honda omitted the scene.[10] There are no heroes, and arguably no true antihero. Kimura's script takes a dim view of the police, showing morally bankrupt detectives giving no thought to sacrificing Fujichiyo and her servant in order to kill the villain.

Above all else, Honda saw *The Human Vapor* as part of a long Japanese literary tradition dating to the works of the Edo period dramatist Chikamatsu Monzaemon: the romantic tragedy ending in *shinju* (double suicide).

"My view of life is about purity, and that includes the relationship between a man and woman," Honda said. "In my films, this theme is always there. When I was young, I thought the most extreme expression of pure love between a man and a woman was double suicide . . . Not because someone doesn't allow them to be together or because they don't have money—not that kind of thing. But when their love is pure, and they are in the happiest time of life, they would kill themselves just to preserve

that love . . . Of course, this kind of thing really does not exist."[11]

Mizuno and Fujichiyo are unlikely lovers. He is a lowly librarian; she is the *iemoto* (grand mistress) of a respected lineage that preserves the secrets and traditions of Japanese dance. Fujichiyo is a mystery; for unknown reasons, her wealth has run out and she now lives modestly in a big, dim, Japanese-style house on the city's wooded outskirts, accompanied by her elderly attendant, Jiya (Bokuzen Hidari). She spends her days studying ancient art prints by Utamaro and her nights preparing to return to the stage.[12] Fujichiyo is distinguished, evidenced by her diction, her upright posture, her beautiful kimonos (a different one in each scene); but when Honda frames her face next to a devilish *hannya* mask, it suggests another side to her personality. Later, Fujichiyo unashamedly bribes reluctant musicians, and openly but quietly shows disdain for the cops. Fujichiyo wants nothing more than a return to the stage, and it's impossible to know whether she accepts the vapor man's help, even after learning of his crimes, out of love or selfishness, or both. This moral ambiguity creates one of Honda's most interesting and complex, if somewhat unsympathetic, female characters.

Yachigusa, one of the Toho Cinderellas, began as a dancer in the Takarazuka review and had already appeared in more than thirty films, starring in Hiroshi Inagaki's *Samurai* trilogy (1954–56) and *Madame Butterfly* (1954). Yachigusa married Honda's close friend from the early Toho days, director Senkichi Taniguchi, in 1957, and this was one of her comeback films. She usually played idealized, traditional young women, and so she found Fujichiyo to be a challenging departure. Each day after shooting,

Yachigusa practiced Fujichiyo's lengthy recital piece, entitled *Passion* (Joki), which she performed in its entirety before the cameras. "And the role was such that I had to look dignified and proper at all times, which was quite tiring," Yachigusa recalled. "Having been on break [from acting] for a bit, I was just so nervous and each day after work, I was completely drained."[13]

Honda and cameraman Hajime Koizumi capture a deep sadness about Fujichiyo in the emptiness of her house, in the isolation of a jail cell, and finally on the big proscenium stage of the Azabu Futaba Hall. Her gloom may help explain why Fujichiyo accepts such an unsuitable suitor, but her final motivation is, again, ambiguous. Does she choose to die with Mizuno out of love, guilt, or because there's no other way to stop him? Is it because she realizes her dance career, reduced to performing in a near-empty hall, is over? Pumped full of flammable gas, the theater explodes and the vapor man dies trying to escape, his smoldering form collapsing and disappearing on the front steps as the building burns. A congratulatory flower bouquet crashes down, a symbolic funeral wreath.

Tsuchiya gives a breakout performance as Mizuno, whose powers unleash the impulses of the id. Tsuchiya repeatedly looks at his hands, checking whether they're still there; it's the body language, the darting eyes, and the cackle that make Mizuno unpredictable and scary, more so than his crimes. Even Fujichiyo is afraid at first—she recoils slightly when he touches her shoulder—but the vapor man's grandiose declarations of love convince her that his acts, however heinous, are noble and chivalrous. As the doomed pair finally unite, a foreboding thunderclap fills the night.

Honda and Tsuchiya came up with a nifty tic for Mizuno's transformations. "I asked [Honda], 'How should I disappear?'" Tsuchiya recalled. The actor placed his right hand inside his coat, over the heart. "'Should I do something like this?' Honda-*san* said, 'Oh, that is really great!' and we ended up going with it." Tsuburaya devised simple yet effective visuals combining smoke, optical animation, and other tricks—witness Mizuno slipping through the jailhouse bars—but there are no big set pieces. This is all Honda's film; the effects support the drama, giving the characters some room to breathe. And because a human monster demands less suspension of disbelief, it is arguably more threatening than a gigantic, impersonal Godzilla destroying a city.

Actors unfamiliar to the Honda brand give this film a different feel. Tatsuya Mihashi, a big star of Toho's actioners of the 1960s (and husband of *Battle in Outer Space* star Kyoko Anzai) is the glib Det. Okamoto, while neophyte Keiko Sata plays ambitious reporter Kyoko, holding her own in a male-dominated world. The flirty, Hepburn-and-Tracy banter between these two Tokyoites contrasts sharply with the formal, arm's-length courtship of Mizuno and Fujichiyo.

Critics were now dismissing special-effects films as *okosama ranchi* (children's lunch), but *The Human Vapor* received excellent notices from the *Asahi Shimbun*, Japan's second-largest newspaper, and other outlets. Its reputation has grown over the years, and in 2009 it ranked no. 65 in the *Kinema Junpo* list of the two hundred best Japanese films of all time, a survey of critics conducted every decade. In the late 2000s, the film was adapted into a Tokyo stage play.

This was yet another Honda title extensively altered for US release. It was acquired by producer Edward Alperson, veteran purveyor of B movies, who would also have a hand in releasing Honda's *Gorath* and Toho's nuclear disaster epic *The Last War* (*Sekai daisenso*, 1961) in America. Alperson recut *The Human Vapor* into a series of flashbacks, linked by narration. According to both Honda and Tsuchiya, Alperson had hoped to finance a sequel, *Frankenstein vs. The Human Vapor*, in which the gas man has survived the fire and seeks help from Dr. Frankenstein to revive Fujichiyo from the dead. That production, penned by future *Star Trek* writer John Meredyth Lucas, was announced by Toho in May 1963, but the project never went forward.[14]

————

Screenwriter Takeshi Kimura took a dim view of postwar Japan. Born in 1912, he was only a year younger than Honda and had also served in the war, though the experience fomented a strong leftist streak. He'd concealed his membership in Japan's communist party when joining Toho in the early 1950s, but his screenplays sometimes betrayed his antiestablishment politics and reflected his rumored run-ins with the law.

Screenwriter Shinichi Sekizawa, conversely, was an eccentric. Born in 1921, he was younger than many of his contemporaries but would dress like an old man, wearing a formal kimono to work instead of a shirt and tie. Model railroads chugged through his house. He was multitalented, dabbling as a manga cartoonist and writing songs for the wildly popular Hibari Misora, a "Japanese Judy Garland."[15] He reluctantly served in the South Pacific and endured the dark days of the war's end, when defeat was imminent and rations scarce. Later, Sekizawa became a ghostwriter and assistant director for acclaimed director Hiroshi

Shimizu, whose documentary-like works focused on the downtrodden outcasts and children of wartime and postwar Japan; Sekizawa was credited as coproducer of Shimizu's *Children of the Beehive* (*Hachi no su no kodomotachi*, 1948). Sekizawa directed the obscure Shin Toho sci-fi film *Fearful Attack of the Flying Saucer* (*Soratobu enban kyofu no shugeki*, 1956) before joining Toho, then brazenly breached his Toho contract by writing animated films for rival Toei Studios. He could have been fired, but he was too valuable. Sekizawa became Toho's primary scripter of breezy, comedic, entertainment actioners.

"I like movies that are on the light side, or action movies," Sekizawa once told an interviewer. "There are a lot of European films that I like, such as the French movie *Pepe Le Moko* (1937) with Jean Gabin. Then there are things like [John Ford's] *Fort Apache* (1948), *Rio Grande* (1950), and *Stagecoach* (1939), and Kurosawa's *Yojimbo* (1961) and *Sanjuro*." Though he had no background in science, Sekizawa considered himself a sci-fi specialist. "When I was writing these movies, there weren't any new people trying to do this yet. And whenever we did try using new guys, it took a lot of work to fix their stuff up . . . No one else was really interested in doing this kind of thing."[16]

Polar opposites, either Sekizawa or Kimura scripted all of Honda's 1960s genre output, creating abrupt tonal shifts between films. The transition from Kimura's dark, tragic *The Human Vapor* to Sekizawa's lighthearted *Mothra* was the most abrupt of all.

Honda said, "If the story were very positive or even childlike, it would go to Sekizawa. If it were negative or involved politics, it would go to Kimura. I really can't compare the two styles because they're so different . . . Sekizawa-*kun* had more of a humanistic touch . . . He has a very joyous and at times very humorous sensibility. That was his world, completely. On the other hand, Kimura-*kun* . . . was very good at writing about social and political problems. When it came to stories about human traits in particular situations, it had to be Kimura-*kun*. I felt that the two were [equally talented] and depending on the topic, each had his strength and weakness."[17]

Koji Kajita said, "Kimura was a serious writer with a very interesting style, excellent with dialogue. In films like *The Human Vapor*, the dialogue was so perfectly calculated that you couldn't change things, or the entire script would fall apart. Each and every word had its place and meaning. That's why, when working with Mr. Kimura, we met often about the script and, since he was a pro, he would immediately go back and fix things" as Honda requested. "The final decisions were made by the director."

"Mr. Sekizawa was a fun guy, and his writing tended to be more rough . . . But his scripts were very good, filled with humor. Honda-*san* was very good at speaking to each of them in such a way as to pull out the best qualities of the writer."

———————

An unscrupulous promoter from the Western nation of Rolisica kidnaps tiny twin singing fairy girls from Infant Island in the South Pacific and forces them to perform as a sister act in Tokyo. The show is a hit, but the girls' telepathic voices travel back to their island, beckoning the insect-god Mothra to rescue them. The giant caterpillar swims to Japan and, when attacked by the military, cocoons itself on the Tokyo Tower. The Rolisican military comes to Japan's aid, roasting the chrysalis with an atomic heat ray; presumed dead, the monster instead reemerges as a huge, beautiful moth. The kidnapper flees back to the Rolisican metropolis of New Kirk City with the girls, but Mothra follows and causes great damage before the fairies are rescued.

Mothra (1961) is a resplendent mix of science fiction and fantasy, bigger and more audacious than anything Honda and Tsuburaya achieved before or after. Produced just as the Japanese film industry was cresting commercially, it had a relatively enormous budget of ¥200 million (about $560,000) and a star-studded cast. This film marks a major departure, with a sympathetic monster triumphing over man's arrogance and a happy ending in which the creature survives. Heavy ideas are handled lightly; where *Godzilla* was dark and joyless, *Mothra* charms with color, humor, and humanity. There are admirable heroes and despicable villains, big musical numbers, mass destruction, and fairy tale trappings.

"We wanted to do something that was new, for the whole family, like a Disney or Hollywood type of picture," said Honda. "We wanted it to be brighter, nicer."[18]

Tomoyuki Tanaka was looking to change things up. In summer 1960 he hired novelist Shinichiro Nakamura to write an original story for a new monster movie. Nakamura was at the height of his popularity as a scripter of radio dramas; he was a scholar of Henry Miller and French literature, he had adapted Yukio Mishima's *The Sound of Waves* for the screen, and several of his own books were made into films. Nakamura discussed the job with two fellow scribes: Takehiko Fukunaga, a William Faulkner scholar, and Zenei (aka Yoshie) Hotta, whose novel *Judgment* examined American guilt over the atomic bombings, and who'd written an influential book about his travels to India. The trio decided to collaborate, each writing one part of the story.

The Glowing Fairies and Mothra was serialized in January 1961 in *Weekly Asahi Extra* magazine. It was a meandering yarn, with a lengthy mythology of the lost civilization of Infant Island, and ended with the fairies and Mothra flying into space and settling on a "negative Earth." There were major political tensions between Japan and Roshirica (an amalgam of "Russia" and "America" in Japanese, later changed to Rolisica), and unsubtle nods to the recent AMPO treaty furor. From the serialized story, screenwriter Sekizawa cherry-picked what he liked and changed everything else, patterning his script after the original *Godzilla* and *King Kong*. He downplayed the politics, cut the number of fairies from four to two, made them smaller (they were supposed to be twice as tall), and omitted a romance between one of the fairies and a male protagonist. "What's most important is entertainment," Sekizawa said. "If there's too much detail . . . the audience won't be interested. So my philosophy is [to] just add enough to tell the story and keep it moving along."

Honda said the fantasy aspects of *Mothra* were "more Sekizawa's idea than mine," while the director was very interested in "the bomb, and how [the Infant Islanders] survived radiation."

"The setting was an adventure . . . on a South Seas island, where a mysterious giant creature is worshipped as a god," Honda said. "There is also a showman, and beauty . . . causes a city to be rampaged. So . . . this is a Japanese version of *King Kong*. However, I wanted to make our final act a happy ending, and not like the denouement of *Kong*, which ended in tragedy."[19]

The Small Beauties, or *shobijin*, give *Mothra* its magic realism. An inspired bit of cinematic trickery, the fairies are played by The Peanuts, an immensely popular pop singing duo consisting of identical twin sisters Emi and Yumi Ito. The ladies' elegant beauty and mesmerizing harmonies perfectly suited the characters.

Honda directing Frankie Sakai on the Infant Island jungle set from *Mothra*.
Courtesy of Honda Film Inc.

"The studio had the toughest time clearing The Peanuts' schedule to make them available for the shoot," remembered Hiroshi Koizumi, who plays affable Prof. Chujo, an expert in ancient languages who deciphers the Infant Islanders' writings. "It was the height of their popularity." Honda directed the Ito sisters' synchronized acting and dialogue in front of a blue screen or on oversized sets, then the girls were composited or edited into the film. They did not interact with the full-size cast. "When I had a scene with them, there were dolls to help set my eyeline instead of the actual Peanuts," said Koizumi. "The Peanuts' lines were played on a tape recorder and I pretended to talk to them."

The Peanuts' "Song of Mothra" is the movie's centerpiece. This catchy pop tune—with tribal polyrhythms and lyrics written in a hybrid of Japanese and Bahasa (the national language of Indonesia) for an exotic flavor—was a radio hit, and the verse "Mosura ya mosura" remains a global pop culture tidbit. Composer Yuji Koseki was a former in-house writer for Columbia Japan, and his music has a more Western sensibility than that of Akira Ifukube, who declined to score *Mothra*. "[Ifukube] said that he couldn't do those kinds of songs for us," Honda said.[20] Koseki's music contributes to the fantasy atmosphere, both in Infant Island rituals and staged production numbers. One of Honda's best sequences has the fairies singing the haunting "Daughters of Infant Island," with lyrics by assistant director Koji Kajita, on a surreal cherry blossom backdrop, dissolving to a dreamlike view of the Mothra caterpillar sinking an ocean liner by night.

Three major roles are played by actors outside Honda's usual circle. Fukuda, a reporter nicknamed "Snapping Turtle" for his journalistic tenacity, is played by

Honda (center left) with *Mothra* stars Frankie Sakai (left), Kyoko Kagawa (center right), and Takashi Shimura (right). Courtesy of Honda Film Inc.

Frankie Sakai, a chubby, thirty-two-year-old funnyman and star of Toho's *Company President* and *Station Front* white-collar comedies. Sakai's physical antics provide the comic relief—wriggling a mouse out of his clothes, fending off thugs with a newspaper swat. Honda plays everything else straight, and Sakai proves a clever, compassionate hero in contrast to the pushy throng of journalists in the background. Kyoko Kagawa, respected film actress and a fixture of Kurosawa's films from *The Lower Depths* (1957) onward, and who had also worked with Ozu, Naruse, and Ichikawa, makes her only appearance for Honda as photographer Michi. She's likeable and clever too—snapping pictures on the sly with a spy camera—though this sidekick role doesn't showcase Kagawa's considerable acting talent enough.

Japanese-American Jerry Ito gives a bravado performance as Clark Nelson, a kidnapper, murderer, slave master, and Honda's most vile villain yet. Ito, who began acting on Broadway and live television in New York, is more charismatic than the Japanese cast, playing the greedy foreign exploiter with an exaggerated flourish. Honda's moral dichotomy pits evil Nelson against an ensemble of goodhearted heroes: the journalists, the fairies (always cheerful no matter how badly they're abused), and Mothra, instinctively compelled to protect its people. Regrettably, the conflict is not resolved in an emotionally satisfying way. The heroes and villain never face off, and Nelson is killed in an uninspired shootout with police. Rotten to the end, Nelson's final crime is to steal an old man's cane!

Rolisica may have Russian-looking military uniforms and a star-and-crescent flag, but its capital city is a hybrid of Manhattan, Los Angeles, and San Francisco. Rolisica is clearly an American stand-in, yet Honda treats two regular themes, nuclear anxiety and the (proxy) Japan-US relationship, differently than before. The movie opens with another Lucky Dragon nod, a shipwreck near Infant Island, site of atomic testing. As doctors examine survivors for radiation poisoning, Frankie Sakai fumbles with a surgical mask, lightening up a serious scene. The Japan-America alliance of *Battle in Outer Space* is gone: Rolisica is a pushy capitalist superpower, enamored of Nelson's money and enabling his crimes. The expedition to Infant Island, inexplicably headed by Nelson, seems more like a cover-up than an effort to aid the irradiated natives. Rolisica's deployment of the atomic ray gun seems to violate Japan's three nonnuclear principles, which ban atomic weapons from its territory.[21] Sakai again injects comic relief, fumbling with his Manhattan Project sunglasses; the political satire never gets too serious. Ultimately, Honda's ideal of understanding and cooperation prevails again, not through science this time, but through religion. Catholic prayer, church bells, and Infant Island iconography briefly meld into a vague universal spiritualism that helps restore peace.

Eiji Tsuburaya's set pieces enhance Honda's live action and showcase an improved sense of movement and composition. Jet fighters encircle Mothra in a sea of fire; Mothra impressively destroys Okutama Dam, and Honda stages an exciting rescue scene; and there are aerial views of the caterpillar destroying a large, detailed miniature Tokyo set. Tokyo Tower, then just three years old and a landmark of Japan's postwar revival, is toppled over and then set ablaze with colorful ray-beam and fire effects. In an interesting change, Mothra wrecks a Western metropolis, soaring over the Manhattan-like skyscrapers of New Kirk City, blowing away cars like little toys. People and miniatures occupy the same frame; and even if the models don't always look realistic, they are visually appealing and acceptable within this alternative reality. Tsuburaya takes a different approach to designing Mothra itself: the creature is smoother, softer, and more feminine compared to the roughness of Godzilla.

As the movie ends, Mothra lands at the airport to take the fairies home, and everyone waves good-bye. This moment is a turning point for *kaiju eiga*: Honda has now created a world where not-so-scary monsters simply exist, without scientific rationalization. Eugène Lourié's *Gorgo* (1961), with a story similar to *Mothra* (and *Godzilla*-style special effects) and released just a few months earlier, marked the end of the Western giant-monster cycle. The Japanese *kaiju* films would continue for more than a decade.

Having distributed both *Battle in Outer Space* and *The H-Man* in America, Columbia Pictures acquired the rights to *Mothra* while the film was in preproduc-

Directing the alternate, unused ending of *Mothra*.
Courtesy of Honda Film Inc.

tion. Shortly thereafter, a disagreement emerged over the movie's final act. Toho had deemed the special effects for Mothra's attack on New Kirk City too expensive, so Honda and Sekizawa wrote a new, more cost-conscious ending. This revised version had Nelson fleeing into the mountains with his hostages aboard a Cessna, with Mothra giving chase. In the final showdown, Mothra's wing-flapping gusts caused the villain to fall into a volcano, and the fairies were saved. Because the contract with Columbia stipulated that the climax would take place in an American-looking city, Toho sent a letter requesting approval of the script change from the US side. But rather than wait for a reply and risk delaying the start of production, Toho instructed Honda to commence principal photography as planned. The revised ending was first on

the schedule, and Honda took his cast and crew to a remote location on the island of Kyushu. The scenes were shot near Mount Kirishima, an active volcano in Kagoshima Prefecture, the most southwesterly part of Japan. Things went smoothly, though a careless mistake caused some embarrassment. A dummy that was used in the filming of Nelson's deadly plunge was left at the bottom of a ravine; a hiker spotted the "body" and authorities, beliving it was a suicide, sent a team down to retrieve it. Honda and his team were "roundly scolded," he recalled.

"When we returned to the studio after getting everything safely in the can, Toho received a 'no' answer from [Columbia], so we had to [shoot the original] ending after all," Honda later told writer Hajime Ishida.[22] Images from the unused alternative ending appeared in publicity stills, but none of the footage was ever developed, Honda said.[23] In summer 1962, Columbia released an edited, English-dubbed version of *Mothra* in the United States, about ten minutes shorter than Honda's 101-minute cut.

Mothra ranked no. 10 in *Kinema Junpo*'s annual box-office tally; but despite its relatively big budget and apparent success, Honda would lament that, "Unfortunately the budget was stretched in creating the New Kirk City sets," and other scenes suffered from apparent cost cutting as a result. Honda had intended to shoot second-unit footage in America, but had to use grainy library film of Los Angeles freeways and beachfronts instead. The scenes on Infant Island—a mash-up of monolithic statues, Greek columns, cave writings, lush forests, and deadly vampire vines, populated by a dark-skinned tribe that performs choreographed dances—were also scaled back. Honda had wanted to show how its inhabitants had survived a nuclear blast, but he was limited to a short scene in which Chujo probes an unimpressive cave overgrown with mossy, moldy plants, the source of the islanders' antiatomic elixir.

"How could they have survived?" Honda said. "[There was a mysterious] drink, made from something naturally occurring on the island. When Koizumi goes into the cave, the important thing is the image of the mold. I got a microscopic photo of mold and asked our art department to reproduce it. There were all those mysterious ferns, with seven different colors, the big forest . . . But we couldn't create the atmosphere of the mold forest so well. That was disappointing, but it probably would have cost too much. I really wanted to . . . create this mysterious scene on an island that had been bombed. I actually wrote that scene."

The energy and spirit behind *Mothra* belied that Honda was growing weary of these flights of fancy. "I asked him why he was directing these monster movies," actor Jerry Ito said in a 2004 interview. "He told me he didn't have a choice, but he really wanted to make something like *The Red Shoes*."

Later in life, Honda had hoped *Mothra* might be remade or rebooted as a Disney-style animated feature. That never happened, though Toho eventually produced the live-action children's fantasy *Rebirth of Mothra* (Mosura, 1996) and two sequels, films that lacked the charm of the original.

———

Minor title similarity aside, Honda's next film would bear no resemblance to Powell and Pressburger's 1948 balletic fairy tale. *A Man in Red* is a violent, humorless *yakuza* (gangster) thriller set in a jazzy, seedy underworld of murder, revenge, drug addiction, and sex. As Japanese gangster pictures go this is routine stuff; for Honda, it's a major departure, a testosterone-powered detour down the road of crime and redemption directed with uncharacteristic style, action, and energy.

Still, Honda did not recall this film fondly. In memoirs he referred to it as filler, a contractual obligation. Honda wasn't certain why the studio offered him a gangster picture, speculating only that the decision came from "headquarters." Honda had apparently declined several other projects during this period, but he did not reveal why he accepted this particular assignment, saying only that once the job was given to him, he devoted himself to making a successful picture. *A Man in Red* was made quickly, hitting theaters just one and a half months after *Mothra*.

This film, also known as *The Scarlet*

Man, is based on a book by novelist Shinya Fujiwara, many of whose works became films, notably *The Den of Beasts* (*Kedamono no yado*, 1951), coscripted by Kurosawa and starring Takashi Shimura. *A Man in Red* was put together by Reiji Miwa, who produced numerous Toho crime films in the early 1960s, thrillers with great titles such as *Brand of Evil, The Merciless Trap, Big Shots Die at Dawn, Structure of Hate,* and *Get 'em All.* For this project, Miwa enlisted one of his favorite leading men, square-jawed tough guy Makoto Sato, as the eponymous, red-shirted, lone-wolf antihero. It's the usual good *yakuza* versus bad *yakuza* scenario, but without the moral ambiguity that often colors these pictures. As in *Mothra*, Honda paints evil and good in black and white. In his idealistic gangland, crime doesn't pay and the good guys win—even if more than a few people get killed in the process.

Four years after taking a murder rap for his crime-boss father, reluctant mafia scion Takashi (Sato) is released from prison and returns to Yokohama looking for his girlfriend, Tomiko (Chisako Hara). Instead he finds his dad's gang, the once-respected Katsuta family, now working in the drug trade. To rout the dope-dealing scumbags, Takashi joins forces with high school chum Det. Makikawa (Akira Kubo) and Ikuko (Yumi Shirakawa), who's investigating the murder of her brother, a narcotics officer. Takashi learns that his father Iwago (Gen Shimizu) is being blackmailed by the evil, scar-faced heroin kingpin Misumi (Hisaya Ito). What's worse, Takashi's girlfriend has turned to drugs and is now Misumi's junkie mistress. After his father and best friend are killed by the bad guys, Takashi engages in a revenge-fueled showdown with Misumi in an empty nightclub.

In the early 1960s Japan was suffering

A Man in Red. © Toho Co., Ltd.

A Man in Red: Honda (left) with drug dealer Misumi (Hisaya Ito, center) and his girlfriend Tomiko (Chisako Hara, right). Courtesy of Honda Film Inc.

from a heroin epidemic, with an estimated forty thousand addicts.[24] The epicenter was Yokohama's Gold Town District (the sleazy neighborhood depicted in Kurosawa's *High and Low*), where dope fiends were shooting up on street corners. *A Man in Red* reflects this troubling reality, and its depictions of drug abuse and paraphernalia, while not unusual for a Japanese gangster movie, are more graphic than most anything Hollywood dared to show under the Motion Picture Production Code. Honda holds nothing back: the strung-out Tomiko is ashen, emaciated, groveling for a fix, and suffering sweaty withdrawal throes. Misumi torments the girl, withholding drugs and then injecting her, the needle just outside camera range, into a narcotic stupor when it suits him. Honda avoids the socio-psychological causes of the drug problem, painting it in simple terms of perpetrators and victims. Still, considering his most recent villain was the cartoony Nelson, it's an unexpected change to find the director confronting the ugly side of modern life in this unflinching way.

Equally unexpected is the level of violence, particularly against women. Twice, Misumi nearly commits rape before somebody interrupts him; women are psychologically abused, beaten, and killed. Not counting the destruction wrought by monsters and the military, *A Man in Red* is Honda's most violent movie, with more punching, kicking, and shooting than all his others combined, though it isn't terribly graphic. Yakuza pictures were the bread and butter of Nikkatsu and Toei studios, which rendered violence in more gritty, realistic ways, while Toho's gang-sters tended to shoot and punch wildly, missing their targets more often than not; and *A Man in Red* follows this formula. Still, Honda's fistfights and gunfights are fast-paced and fluid, and very different from his previous direction of violent scenes. He showcases the bulging biceps and street-brawl skills of leading-man Sato, a predecessor of the Japanese martial arts star Sonny Chiba.

Honda's staging of the final gun battle at Club Azami, a modern nightspot, is straight out of an old Western. Like Shane walking into the saloon, Takashi arrives alone, challenging his foe to drop his gun and fight like a man, to which the gutless gangster replies, "That's so old-school.

That's not how people roll these days." A fierce duel erupts and glasses shatter in a hail of gunfire; bodies are used as shields, bottles are broken on heads. Tomiko, hiding in the wings, fires the fatal bullet at Misumi. The villain does a classic slow fall off the balcony, reeling off one last shot that kills Tomiko. She dies in Takashi's arms.

An atypical Honda protagonist, Makoto Sato started out playing villains in *The H-Man* and other films, then became a star with Kihachi Okamoto's antiwar masterpiece *Desperado Outpost* (*Dokuritsu gurentai*, 1959). Sato shouts and growls his way through *A Man in Red*, an unsubtle performance accompanied by an unsubtle, mismatched metaphor. Takashi seems to own only one shirt, a bright-red number that illuminates every scene, yet he isn't really a scarlet man at all. He is flawless, the epitome of the mythical good *yakuza*. As the movie ends, he adds a tan blazer over the red shirt, a new look symbolizing his rehabilitation.

Hisaya Ito relishes the role of Misumi, the most unsavory character in all Honda's films, a man who nonchalantly files his nails while his goons carry out a hit. Tall and handsome in a sinister way, Ito began in films while still a teen, joined Toho in 1957, and made a career as a durable char-acter actor. He was a favorite of Honda's, as were two other cast members who rate a mention. Hideyo Amamoto, a bony, creepy character actor who later played big parts in *King Kong Escapes* and *All Monsters Attack*, works with Honda for the first time here as a drug runner. Then there's the scene-stealing, impish character actor Ikio Sawamura, who was favored repeatedly by Honda and Kurosawa throughout the 1950s and 1960s. Dressed as Charlie Chaplin's tramp, the diminutive Sawamura walks the local bazaar, twirling a cane. He's the eyes and ears of the Katsuta gang and mob boss Iwago's confidant. As the tide of public opinion turns against the *yakuza*, Sawamura has a rare, lengthy dialogue scene imploring his boss to give up the life. "No matter how much you do things for the better of the town and your men, those who get attracted to this world are no-good losers. In the end, we're all just like a car with crippled suspension. As time passes, we ultimately derail and flip."

There are a few Hondaisms. Pop singer Kenji Kitahara sings the theme song, "A Man in Red," and *enka* star Sakae Mori appears as a nightclub singer. The happy ending bears Honda's characteristic optimism, with Takashi and Ikuko leaving for a new life in far-off Hokkaido. Honda obviously didn't buy into the ambiguous moral code of the *yakuza eiga*, so it's not surprising he never made another. Gangster-like characters turn up in later films such as *Ghidorah* and *Dogora*, but they would be more exaggerated and satirical.

18

GOING GLOBAL

Gorath (1962),
King Kong vs. Godzilla (1962)

Japan's Interstellar Exploration Agency launches rocket JX-1 on a mission to Saturn. Shortly after takeoff, the astronauts' assignment is changed: instead of visiting the ringed planet, they will gather data on Gorath, a mysterious, massive comet hurtling through the cosmos. But something is wrong—Gorath seems to have vanished from space. The runaway star is much smaller than astronomers believed, though its density is six thousand times that of Earth, creating an inescapable gravitational pull that quickly ensnares the rocket. The doomed astronauts use their final moments to transmit information about Gorath back home. Reading the data, scientists reach a deadly conclusion: Gorath is on a collision course with Earth.

In March 1962, less than one year after cosmonaut Yuri Gagarin became the first man in space, Toho released *Gorath*, an epic-scale science fiction and doomsday disaster drama that is arguably Ishiro Honda's most ambitious project. Set in the 1980s, the film envisions a future in which the United Nations is a forum for solving global problems, and a world that embraces Honda's twin ideals of international cooperation and the elevation of science above politics. The tautly paced, eighty-eight-minute film is no-nonsense in tone, and its only major blemish is a giant walrus that makes a brief, unnecessary appearance. Honda would later say *Gorath* was "My top favorite film, except for that monster."[1]

It was the height of the space race. Later that year, President Kennedy would pledge to put a man on the moon by decade's end, and America's Mariner 2 probe would reach Venus. The notion of a Japanese space program was not entirely far-fetched; in 1960 the government had created the National Space Activities Council, advocating for peaceful space exploration.[2] Japanese scientists began experimenting with solid-fuel rockets in 1955, and the National Space Development Agency (Uchu kaihatsu jigyodan) would be founded in 1964. Jojiro Okami's original story reflects these developments while borrowing the plot of George Pal's *When Worlds Collide*, and Honda uses the framework to show science being pursued ethically and positively, as opposed to *Godzilla*, *The Mysterians*, or *The Human Vapor*.

"Originally, the idea was to pick just the Japanese elite and evacuate them, letting the planet be destroyed," Honda said.[3] Honda and screenwriter Takeshi Kimura refashioned the story, bringing the nations together to save the world by constructing massive rocket thrusters at the South Pole to move Earth out of harm's way. Astronaut Endo (Akihiko Hirata) seems to take an unintentional swipe at Pal's film: "Mankind [used to be] separated into white, black, and yellow races before the United Nations. Trust, honor, and cooperation were the qualities that brought us together."

Honda follows a large ensemble of characters, many played by mainstays of his revolving-door troupe. Ryo Ikebe and Ken Uehara are astronomers marshaling the world's scientists to the crisis response, while Takashi Shimura is their elder colleague. There are young, eager astronaut cadets and modern, independent young women who talk of marriage and money. There's a precocious kid brother whose innocent banter about bombs and rockets inspires the solution to the threat, international eggheads who bicker over the use of nuclear energy to move Earth off its orbit—but not about the wisdom of actually *moving Earth off its orbit*—and politicians (played by respected actors from the Kurosawa camp, such as Seizaburo Kawazu,

Takamaru Sasaki, and Ko Nishimura), who defer to the scientists for answers. Familiar faces such as Hirata and Kenji Sahara (the latter acting in severe pain, with a broken ankle) are the heroic captains and officers of the space program. In this big tableau, Honda includes everyday people "just waiting for the end to come," from a happy-go-lucky cabbie (Ikio Sawamura) to a cynical nightclub-goer (Hideyo Amamoto) who tells an astronaut, "If you get to outer space, you can watch Gorath run us over."

"The common folk cannot be at the forefront of big problems, but there are so many more of them. . . . so, those scenes create depth for the story," said Honda. "These are the types of people that I want in my films. This is the very foundation of my films."

There is no widespread panic. "People crying out loudly, getting angry, it just wouldn't seem real," he added. "If something like this happens, people would think seriously about how to deal with it. It's a much more natural style rather than over-reacting, a style that the audience can take more seriously."[4]

The dialogue is heavy on scientific terminology and mathematical formulas. At one point, Ikebe uses a large blackboard of calculations to support his theories. It gets a bit dry, but it's part of Honda's dedication to scientific plausibility, if not possibility. While writing, Honda and Kimura spent a week at Tokyo University, consulting with Takeo Hatanaka, renowned professor of astrophysics, who crunched the numbers appearing on the board.

"We learned a lot from him," said Honda. "I first heard the term 'escape velocity' from his team. At 11.2 kilometers per second, that's the speed to escape Earth's gravitational field. At more than [618 kilometers per second] you can escape the Sun's gravitational pull."[5]

"Ikebe's lines are all based on real scientific data. Everything was precisely calculated by Prof. Hatanaka's people. For example, at the South Pole base, the kind of buildings that should be constructed, or creating a power source from hydrogen. Whether or not it was possible . . . we always made sure that there was some actual scientific basis."[6]

By now, the aesthetics of Honda's genre films were well established. Cameraman Hajime Koizumi employs big, wide-angle views of the expansive sets and tracking shots of a rocket ship's interior, and groups are arranged in democratic formations. The musical score by Kan Ishii, a noted composer of ballets, operas, and choral music who dabbled in film, is stirring and nationalistic in flavor, if not particularly memorable. Eiji Tsuburaya's ample and impressive miniatures include detailed models of a rocket port and the South Pole construction site, and the special effects again support the story without distracting from it.

Tsuburaya's requisite destruction occurs as Gorath approaches Earth. Saturn's rings are sucked away; and when Gorath eerily passes across Tokyo's night horizon, the city goes into civil-defense posture. People flee by car and evacuees camp in the hills. The Moon is destroyed, then all hell breaks loose: worldwide floods, storms, landslides. Honda knew he was playing faster and looser than usual with science here, and it made him uncomfortable. "If the Moon was pulled away by Gorath, then theoretically the Earth would be similarly affected," Honda said. "I wondered what we should do about this. Of course, [producer] Tomoyuki Tanaka's reaction was, 'The truth doesn't make a good movie.'"

The giant walrus Magma, whose name remains unspoken, was Honda's regret.

Tanaka pushed Honda to include a monster; it was originally written as a "dinosaur-like creature," but Honda didn't want to remind viewers of Godzilla. *Gorath* is set in a world without Godzillas and Mothras, and the creature's sudden and brief appearance is an outlier in an otherwise straight sci-fi story; and in hindsight Honda would wish he had refused to include the scene. "That was definitely the human weakness of Ishiro Honda," he said. "That idea came from above. They make more profit with monsters [in the movie]. I think that left a scar on this film."[7]

Gorath ends by asking, "If we can come together to cooperate, to overcome the dangers that threaten us, can't we take this opportunity to work together for all eternity?" Still, the controversial Japan-America alliance casts a shadow over the movie's appeal to universalism. Other than videophones and spaceships, the Japan of 1980 looks like the post-Occupation Japan of 1962: American cars, Christmas carolers, burgeoning materialism, and square dancing, a then-popular fad. Japan and America are above reproach; though in this world, Japanese scientists are more advanced, while fictional nations such as Crenion and the USSO offer mild dissent before acquiescing. A reviewer for *Kinema Junpo* rejected Honda's fantasy of global harmony. "All the main scientists leading things are Japanese, and there are only two countries which can be identified clearly—Japan and America. All the others are unknown countries with unknown flags, unknown people. This becomes a realistic reflection of Japanese politics. This so-called UN-ism, or the concept of 'all mankind together,' is like a cheap side dish of 'free world' ideology. It looks so phony."

Honda retains some humanity in his big, impersonal, tech-heavy story. Tough-

and-gruff Jun Tazaki, in his first of many roles in Honda's genre films, is quietly yet powerfully emotional as captain of the ill-fated JX-1, forced to lead his men to their deaths. The story's spine is the relationship between impetuous cadet Kanai (Akira Kubo) and beautiful, heartbroken Takiko, whose astronaut fiancé was killed on the JX-1. Kanai tries to prove his worth as both spaceman and suitor, but is stricken with amnesia after flying too close to the deadly star. The would-be hero is nursed back to health by his friends.

A half-hearted monster cameo didn't guarantee success after all. *Gorath* had a relatively modest budget of ¥126 million (about $350,000, though it looks more expensive), yet it did not recoup its production costs, failing to crack the top twenty-five in the annual *Kinema Junpo* box-office rankings. An English-language version, which received a limited release in the United States in 1964, had numerous editorial changes—the giant walrus was deleted; a narrated prologue, introducing the astronauts and their mission to investigate a disturbance in the solar system, was added; and many scenes were recut.

For Honda's next project, the studio would double down on giant monsters, with blockbuster results.

King Kong vs. Godzilla. © Toho Co., Ltd.

It was such an entertaining film. The house was packed, you know? We could barely get a seat.
— Masaaki Tezuka, film director

In April 1962, a match pitting Japanese pro wrestling superstar Rikidozan and tag-team partners Toyonobori and Great Togo against American challengers Freddie Blassie, Lou Thesz, and Mike Sharpe aired nationally on Japanese television. During the bout, Blassie bit Great Togo on the forehead, opening a horrible bloody gash. Two elderly viewers, shocked by the gory sight, collapsed and died, casualties of a media war that saw networks and sponsors producing outrageous programs and stunts to grab the audience. Released later that year, Honda's *King Kong vs. Godzilla* is pop art imitating life, with two gargantuan wrestlers of Japanese and American pedigree tussling on live TV, raising ratings while razing cities. It's monster-movie-as-satire, a biting critique of the banal programming that dominated television, prompting widespread debate over the ascendant medium's effect on Japanese culture. The social critic Soichi Oya warned that TV was creating "a nation of 100 million idiots."

"People were making a big deal out of ratings," said Honda. "But my own view of TV shows was that they did not take the viewer seriously, that they took the audience for granted . . . so I decided to show that through my movie."[8]

King Kong vs. Godzilla was one of five banner releases for 1962 to commemorate Toho's thirtieth anniversary, along with

Kurosawa's *Sanjuro* (*Tsubaki Sanjuro*), Hiroshi Inagaki's *47 Samurai* (*Chushingura*), Mikio Naruse's *Lonely Lane* (*Hourou-ki*), and Yasuki Chiba's *Born in Sin* (*Kawa no hotori de*). By far Honda's most commercially successful film, *King Kong vs. Godzilla* was a runaway hit and the bedrock of the long-running Godzilla franchise that followed. Though Godzilla was a household word, this was the monster's first appearance in seven years.[9] Only after Godzilla battled "the eighth wonder of the world"—Kong, the more popular monster, received top billing—did Toho truly begin producing its long and legendary series of monster-versus-monster sequels.

This is also perhaps Honda's most infamous effort, thanks to a poor imitation of the great King Kong and an inept, reworked American version that, as with *Godzilla*, was distributed to many more territories than Honda's cut. Most troubling for Honda, though, was how Godzilla, in only its third film—and the first in color and scope—transformed from nuclear protest monster into outsized Rikidozan, engaging in comic wrestling antics. "[The studio] thought it would be interesting to make these two monsters fight," Honda later reflected. "That was all there was to it. Still, when you are the director, it is your film, so you still have to do your best. So I sucked it up and worked as hard as possible."[10]

The project originated in Hollywood several years earlier, when stop-motion animator Willis O'Brien developed a proposed project titled *King Kong vs. Frankenstein* (later *King Kong vs. Prometheus*). O'Brien envisioned a battle in the streets of San Francisco between Kong and a monster created by Victor Frankenstein's grandson; the creatures would be animated via O'Brien's signature effects work. O'Brien partnered with independent producer John

Beck, who failed to attract a Hollywood studio but eventually hit paydirt in Japan. Beck brokered a deal wherein Toho purchased the right to use King Kong in a film; however, O'Brien's ideas were jettisoned and he would have no involvement in the production. Toho made *King Kong vs. Godzilla* instead, with Beck retaining the film's lucrative overseas distribution rights.

RKO's fee for King Kong was reportedly ¥80 million (about $220,000), inflating the budget and forcing Honda to cut costs. At the last minute, he canceled plans to film scenes set on Faro Island, Kong's home, on location in Sri Lanka. Instead, the crew shot at Oshima Island near Tokyo and on studio sets. "King Kong took all the money!" said actor Yu Fujiki.[11]

Shinichi Sekizawa's script is light and quickly paced. Tako (Ichiro Arishima), the excitable advertising chief for Pacific Pharmaceutical Co., is desperate to shake up the low-rated TV science program that his company sponsors. He sends a cameraman, Sakurai (Tadao Takashima), and a sound man, Furue (Fujiki), to the Solomon Islands archipelago to investigate reports of a *majin* (demon god) worshipped by natives of tiny Faro Island. They return with King Kong literally in tow, but Kong breaks free en route and runs wild in Japan. Meanwhile, Godzilla bursts out of an iceberg in the Arctic and instinctively heads south toward its Tokyo stomping grounds. The Japanese military can't stop either creature, so a plan is hatched to pit them against one another, a monster matchup tailormade for the TV cameras.

King Kong vs. Godzilla takes a page from the *keizai shosetsu* (business novels) and films of the late 1950s and early 1960s that spoofed ruthless Japanese business practices. There are also similarities to Yasuzo Masumura's excellent *Giants and*

Toys (*Kedamono no yado*, 1958), a satire about two candy companies engaged in an over-the-top media war, though where Masumura is cynical and heavy-handed, Honda is lighthearted. "The reason I showed the monster battle through the prism of a ratings war was to depict the reality of the times," said Honda. "When you think of King Kong just plain fighting Godzilla, it is stupid. But how you stage it, the times in which it takes place, that's the thought process of the filmmaker. Back then, Sekizawa was working on pop song lyrics and TV series, so he really had a clear insight into television."[12]

The film gets its farcical energy from three main actors. Arishima, as the ad man, is an agitated physical comedian with manic energy and a knack for sight gags, and best known as the exasperated father in Toho's *Young Guy* series. His eager accomplices Takashima and Fujiki, a straight man–funny man duo in the Japanese *manzai* comic tradition, had previously appeared together in salaryman comedies. They loosely based their characters on the Hollywood "Road" films with Fujiki as the bumbling Bob Hope sidekick to Takashima's cocksure Bing Crosby. The dialogue is peppered with wrestling and baseball references; the year 1962 was legendary slugger Sadaharu Oh's breakout season, thus the two rival drug companies are named after Japanese pro baseball's Pacific and Central leagues.

There are memorable funny bits, such as Kong imbibing narcotic jungle juice and passing out cold, and Tako's gag with a dynamite lever. The first meeting between the explorers and the islanders recalls Abbott and Costello's safari parody *Africa Screams* (1949), with dark-skinned natives in stereotypical jungle garb and a gruff tribal chief (Yoshio Kosugi) and a cowardly interpreter (Senkichi Omura) speaking a mix of Polynesian, pidgin English, and backward phrases. The natives are bribed with tobacco and a radio that receives Japanese stations from afar. The song it plays is a politically incorrect number about a native family on a palm-treed island: "Dad is Rumba, Mom is Mambo, and the kids are Conga and little Bongo."

When Arishima, Takashima, and Fujiki are offscreen, Honda and Sekizawa revert to monster-movie tropes and the tone abruptly shifts. Damsel-in-distress Fumiko (Mie Hama) is caught first in Godzilla's path and then in Kong's hand (a full-scale but rather unconvincing prop), both monsters attack trains, and scenes from *King Kong* and *Godzilla* are revisited when Kong easily scales the Diet Building—somehow, without crushing it—and an electrical barrier is erected to keep Godzilla out of the city. By the final act the mood has darkened and the satire is over; and despite Honda's intent to expose television's moral bankruptcy, there is no one watching the monster battle at home, no public reaction to the crass spectacle, no one who questions the insanity. Tako walks away free, despite indications that he would be held accountable for the destruction. Ultimately Honda pivots to a theme of harmony with nature. "Humans must change how we treat plants and animals," concludes the defense minister (Akihiko Hirata). "It's time to learn from them."

Even if the approach is broader overall than *Mothra*, Honda did not direct differently than before. "I picked [actors] with those types of personalities," he said. "But I did not ask them to play it as a comedy." Instead, Honda lets his cast find humor in the absurdity of it all. "Rather than a straight comedy, my point was that there was this one guy in the advertising section.

He tried to do the best job he could, but because of the company's orders, whatever he tried to do became a joke," Honda said. "That's the kind of satire I wanted . . . The person himself is serious, but the harder he tries, the funnier it gets."[13]

"When Arishima descends onto the ship from the helicopter, the acting of that scene is excellent," added Koji Kajita. "Tripping and hitting the switch—only Honda-*san* could direct a scene that way. There are different ways to direct. Kurosawa's way was to fit everyone into the mold he wanted. But Honda-*san*'s way was to work with everyone's character" and build the film around the actors. "That was the Honda style of directing." The actors had experience ad-libbing, but they were told to stick to the script. "[Honda] really didn't like that, so we tried not to do it," recalled Fujiki.

This is neither the Kong of 1933 nor the Godzilla of 1954, and the monsters inspire little of their original pathos. Instead of moody monochrome, they are photographed in bright, revealing Eastmancolor and often framed at waist level, betraying any illusion of size. Godzilla has an improved design and blue-hot radiation breath; but Kong, played by stuntman Shoichi Hirose, is too obviously a man in a furry costume with lumpy facial features. Curiously, RKO reportedly required Toho not only to distinguish its Kong with a different face, but also to depict the ape snatching a female and scaling a building, recalling the original. Mie Hama does an excellent job shrieking in Kong's clutches, though one wishes Honda had borrowed even just a bit of the tragic romance of Merian C. Cooper's film. Godzilla mocks its opponent, Kong beats his chest and scratches his noggin, and both monsters employ slapstick fighting moves—Godzilla kicking boulders, Kong swinging its foe by the tail, and so on.

Kong appears outmatched, but the odds are evened in the final battle via a deus ex machina, a thunderstorm that gives Kong a jolt of strength-inducing electricity.

Comedic human drama was one thing. But when it came to the monsters, Honda felt Toho went too far. From the early drafts of the script, the studio had made notes regarding the monsters, asking, "Make it as funny as possible, please."[14]

"To me, what happened was not acceptable," Honda said. "Personally, I didn't want to do it, but the company demanded it. When you have to do it, then you have to do it . . . I did the best I could with it, and Mr. Tsuburaya did his best as well. It was about that time that Godzilla movies started to move toward a younger audience. [But] the fact that they decided to make Godzilla act like a human, it was not a good decision . . . This showed off the fact that it was a man in a suit. Bad idea."[15]

While Honda was uncomfortable with this change, Eiji Tsuburaya embraced it. According to assistant effects director Sadamasa Arikawa, some members of Tsuburaya's own crew felt he went "overboard" to appeal to young children and "couldn't believe" he had Kong and Godzilla volleying boulders and performing silly stunts.[16] Still, Honda never spoke of friction with Tsuburaya, only with the front office.

———

Many of Honda's science fiction films required mountain locations, and by now his favorite destination was the area around Gotenba, a town in Shizuoka Prefecture on the southeastern side of Mount Fuji, and the place where Akira Kurosawa shot *Seven Samurai* and other films. There were snow-capped peaks in winter and rugged forest in summer, and easy access by rail or highway. For this film, Honda shot the live-action portions of Godzilla's train assault, the military's Godzilla-trapping operation, and the final monster battle there.

"One of the big deals in directing is how to manage the time and budget properly," said Kajita. "Considering all this, picking a location was very important, and Gotenba got to be his favorite. It's rather close to the studio, and the place has a lot of variety. There are mountains, valleys, small towns, plains, rivers, and railroads—everything he needed. Also, a lot of his films required the cooperation of the Self-Defense Forces, and there was a base at Fuji-Gotenba. Picking the right location, getting people's cooperation, making people move, meeting the requirements, all to get a film done—it all came down to the director's skill."

Honda still enjoyed hiking and climbing from his soldiering days, and his crew often had trouble keeping up with him on location—"He just goes zoom, zoom, zoom, walking so fast," Kajita remembered. "The mountains were nothing for him." Nevertheless, while filming near the mountain town of Yamakita, about thirteen miles from Gotenba, Honda suffered a potentially serious hiking accident.

Kajita continued: "We borrowed a fire engine from the Yamakita fire department. We were moving [to a new location], and we had to go fast so we could return the truck on time. [Honda] was rushing . . . the rest of us took the longer, safer route through the valley to get from point A to point B, but only Honda-*san* took the mountain road as a shortcut—the cliff route. The mountain was very dry, so there were dangerous spots with loose gravel. Along the way, he disappeared from our sight. 'Oh my God, did he fall off the cliff?' Everyone started looking for him. Sure enough we found him, injured. I understand why he needed to hurry, but it turned into a huge ordeal. [Laughs.] We took him to Numazu Hospital.

Filming was called off for the day. The next day, I took over filming for him, just for one day." Honda suffered a sprained left arm and wore a cast and sling for a while. "Imagine if something really serious had happened to him and the whole movie had to be canceled."

Kajita directed most of the sequence wherein Fujita (Kenji Sahara) races along mountain roads in a jeep to rescue girl-friend Fumiko (Hama) from Godzilla. It was trial by fire, a test of Kajita's readiness to eventually become a director himself. Sahara wrote in his autobiography: "[Honda] had told me to imagine that my girlfriend really was in that situation. But the staff, especially assistant director Kajita, who directed that scene, told me not to speed too much . . . I couldn't help myself but to get into the character, and I couldn't help but think I really had to go save my girlfriend, so I sped really badly . . . One slip of the tire or one small mistake with steer-ing, and you could just fall off the cliff. After the scene, Kajita ran up to me with a red face, yelling at me. 'What the hell are you doing, speeding like that? Don't you know how dangerous that is?' But I thought that my acting was very realistic."

After playing heroes in *Rodan*, *The Mysterians*, and *The H-Man*, Sahara was transitioning into supporting parts, and in Honda's next three films he would become the most versatile member of the director's ensemble. Sahara's role in *King Kong vs. Godzilla* isn't terribly memorable, but he recalled it fondly because of the trust that Honda showed in him. Sahara was at home, enjoying a day off from shooting, when an unexpected call summoned him to the studio. That day, Honda was filming the live-action portion of Kong's climb atop the Diet Building, when he realized that something was lacking. Sahara's character was quickly written into the scene, the young man screaming for Kong to release his girlfriend.

"As soon as I arrived at the studio, director Honda said to me with a really serious face, 'Ken-*bo*, you know what to do,' and he gave me the script," Sahara recalled. "As short as his words were, the script was equally short . . . It was the scene where I yelled at King Kong, 'You bastard, give her back to me! What are you going to do with her?' Whether it's a fictional monster or an actual, powerful institution like the government, as a little commoner all you can do is yell and scream. [Honda] was always saying that you have to approach the situation as if it were really happening . . . I understood him. It was just one short scene, but it meant a lot to me."[17]

The domestic scenes and prominent female characters recall Honda's 1950s comedies. The banter inside Fumiko's apartment allows the young cast to briefly shine, with Takashima as the overprotective older brother and Sahara the eager boyfriend trying to impress with his new invention, a superstrong thread. Hama and Akiko Wakabayashi, as Fumiko's neighbor, are charming and chaste, revealing little of the sex appeal they would exude as Bond girls in *You Only Live Twice* (1967). More alluring is beautiful Akemi Negishi, leading the native dance that lulls Kong to sleep. Students from a performing arts school, wearing bright costumes and dark body makeup, formed the tribal chorus line. They were choreographed by Kenji Aoki of the Nichigeki Theater dance company.

The score by Akira Ifukube is perhaps the film's greatest strength, a stirring sonic backdrop that transcends the material. Ifukube's Faro Island chant, which also serves as the main title theme and Kong's motif, is a deceptively simple rhythmic piece with a chorus vocalizing Ifukube's chromatic phrases. This film also marks the debut of an early version of Ifukube's signature Godzilla motif, an ominous chromatic piece. Ifukube would remain Honda's primary composer, scoring all but three of the director's future genre films.

Because it was made not long after the AMPO protests, *King Kong vs. Godzilla* is sometimes interpreted as a critique of the Japan-US alliance, the monsters representing their respective countries. Studies such as Cynthia Erb's excellent *Tracking King Kong* make this analogy, but Honda had no such intent and, in fact, he portrays Kong as something of a proxy Japanese monster, with no apparent American origins.[18] Unlike *The Mysterians, Battle in Outer Space, Mothra,* or *Gorath,* there is no involvement by the West in averting the crisis, and unlike Honda's 1950s dramas, the trappings of imported American culture (steaks and fries eaten with fork and knife, jazz albums decorating Fumiko's apartment) are benign. Kong unintentionally helps expel Godzilla from Japan, playing the hero-by-default role that Godzilla would adopt a few years later. The fight ends in an apparent draw, then the monsters swim away—an ending to be repeated often, with variations. This is also the first of several Honda-Tsuburaya films wherein monsters battle beneath majestic Mount Fuji, another sign of the *kaiju eiga*'s evolution into a uniquely Japanese sci-fi subgenre.

This is far from a masterpiece. Take, for example, the scenes of a nuclear submarine trolling the Arctic, a nod to the USS *Nautilus*'s 1960 voyage under the polar ice cap. The sub inexplicably crashes into an iceberg after a long, drawn-out sequence choppily edited into the picture. Plot holes are ignored (why do the natives allow Kong to be taken, and how did they get Kong on that raft?) and contrivances put characters in harm's way. The special effects are not always up to snuff, and the natives' battle with a giant octopus features some of Tsuburaya's poorest composite work.

And yet, *King Kong vs. Godzilla* proved an entertaining mash-up of corporate comedy and monster melee. It sold approximately 11.2 million tickets in its theatrical run, plus an additional 1.3 million when rereleased in the 1960s and 1970s, and remains the most highly attended live-action Japanese science fiction film of all time. According to *Kinema Junpo* it grossed ¥352 million (roughly $972,000) and was fourth in the 1961–62 domestic box-office rankings behind Shigeo Tanaka's historical epic *The Great Wall* (*Shin shikotei*), *Sanjuro*, and Hiroshi Inagaki's *Chushingura*. Toho released four of Japan's top five movies that year, and Honda was now among the studio's most successful directors. However, his importance to Toho was largely outside Japan.

————

"When it comes to Japanese cinema," the American critic Judith Crist wrote in 1964, "that means Akira Kurosawa." More than a decade after *Rashomon*, Kurosawa remained the only renowned Japanese director in the West. Works by Kinugasa and Ichikawa and Kinoshita appeared intermittently, but only Kurosawa's films were anticipated by influential critics; old masters such as Ozu and Naruse, or New Wave auteurs such as Oshima, would not be discovered for several years. Still, Kurosawa's exposure was usually limited to art-house theaters and screenings on college campuses.

Nobody realized it, but the Japanese director whose works were most widely seen and most profitable around the world in the early 1960s was not Kurosawa. It was Ishiro Honda.

Several factors obscured Honda's feat. Critics who viewed Kurosawa's work as high art saw science fiction films as low culture. There was also a belief that most things made in Japan—then infamous for inexpensive exports—were junk. ("And a Japanese transistor radio" was the refrain of a 1962 hit song by comedian Allan Sherman about cheap Christmas gifts.) Bosley Crowther's *New York Times* review of *King Kong vs. Godzilla* was typically dismissive. Viewers of this "ridiculous melodrama" would "get what they deserve." Crowther focused on the "[horribly] dubbed diction" and "sloe-eyed" cast members, but like many American reviewers, he considered neither Honda's direction nor name deserving of mention.

In truth, the film Crowther reviewed was only partly Honda's. John Beck created an English-language version employing a mock newscast format a la Orson Welles's *War of the Worlds*, with no-name actors playing anchormen on threadbare newsroom sets in segments edited into the Japanese film. Though most of Tsuburaya's effects remained, much of Honda's footage was excised; and Ifukube's excellent score was replaced with library cues, changing the lively feel and rhythm into an often dull, halting film. Regardless, the spectacle of Kong and Godzilla fighting reportedly earned $2.7 million at the American box office and millions more in Europe, Latin America, and other territories. During this time, the first-ever licensed Godzilla merchandise, a model kit and a board game, appeared in the United States, several years before Godzilla goods were sold in Japan.

Since Toho International opened for business in 1953, many dozens of Toho films had been made available for export to the West, including comedies, dramas, war movies, and other pictures popular in Japan. However, with few exceptions, only the works of Akira Kurosawa and Honda's science fiction films were sought after by American distributors and consistently brought in foreign money. In February 1960, when Toho International published its periodic "List of Leading Pictures Exported Abroad," the top six movies included were all Honda's: *Varan, Rodan, Godzilla, The Mysterians, The H-Man,* and *Battle in Outer Space;* of the remaining ten, three were by Kurosawa: *The Hidden Fortress, Seven Samurai,* and *Drunken Angel.* The $25,000 that Toho reportedly netted for *Godzilla* would grow to $90,000 per title by the time American International Pictures (AIP), a distributor of exploitation films, acquired Western territorial rights to Honda's *Atragon* in 1964.[19] And in the second half of the decade, five of Honda's films would be cofinanced by American companies, offsetting much of Toho's negative cost. In exchange for this windfall, Toho continued to give foreign distributors wide latitude "to cut, edit, alter, rearrange" films as they saw fit.[20]

Honda had neither the respect of critics nor the protection of his studio. Yet, his films were moneymakers in Japan and overseas, the latter increasingly important as domestic box-office numbers declined. And after *King Kong vs. Godzilla,* Honda's value to the company was never greater.

It was a position of leverage, but he was not one to wield it.

—————

After making films constantly in the late 1950s, Honda took two roughly yearlong absences from directing, first in 1959–60 after *Battle in Outer Space* and again in 1962–63 following *King Kong vs. Godzilla.* Despite his success, he still longed for more

than science fiction. Kimi Honda recalled, "There seemed to be a moment when he became quite uncertain about his career, wondering, 'When will I finally have an opportunity to make the kind of films I really want to make?' Of course he never said this out loud, but he did have this feeling inside . . .

"There would be times where he would lose his cool, drink heavily, and sometimes pick quarrels with me. He was never, ever violent of course, but this gentle man began to start arguments over the littlest things. Where he should have stopped at a few drinks, he would finish an entire bottle. So I'm sure there was something quite heavy going on, internally."

Kimi added: "One may think he was living a spectacular life as a film director, but in reality his spirits were often very low around the time he turned fifty [in 1961]. The film industry was losing its audience to television . . . The *tokusatsu* films that Ino-*san* was making, which required large budgets, were the target of blame and attack by corporate management" when they failed to turn a profit. "Ino-*san* was not the only one feeling resentment and dissatisfaction."[21]

In April 1959, Akira Kurosawa had formed Kurosawa Productions, hoping to gain independence from the studio system and to keep more of the box-office revenues. "To enable a movie director to live a comfortable life, this is the only option available," he said. Toho executive Sanezumi Fujimoto went further: "Kurosawa has performed a distinguished service for Toho . . . We want him to make more money."[22] The move was considered bold, and it received much media attention, though Kurosawa wasn't totally bucking the system. His company maintained an exclusive production and distribution agreement with Toho, and finances were covered by a complex profit-sharing arrangement. Under this framework, Kurosawa would make some of his greatest films.

Kurosawa offered to help Honda go independent as well. Kimi recalled, "When Kuro-*san* was launching Kurosawa Productions, he came over and said 'Ino-*san*, you should form Honda Productions. Your films are much more successful [internationally] . . . Let's work together with my lawyers.' Had [Honda] done that back then, it would have been a big deal. But he was not that kind of man."

Eiji Tsuburaya, in contrast to Honda, was eager to parlay the success of his work on special-effects films into something bigger; and in April 1963 he formed Tsuburaya Visual Effects Productions (later Tsuburaya Productions) to create visual effects for television and film productions, domestic and foreign, and to develop original films and TV programs. Tsuburaya would now divide his time between his own company and Toho, where he remained head of the special-effects department.[23] The startup was a family affair—its staff included Tsuburaya's wife and two sons—and Tsuburaya wanted Honda to join them.

"There was the idea of me doing something in management, but I still wanted to be actually making films," said Honda. "I don't know what position [Tsuburaya] had in mind for me but I pretty much turned that offer down because I wasn't quite the right material for that kind of thing."[24]

———

Honda remained active even when he was not directing. He went to his office on the lot each day and attempted to alter his career trajectory with numerous proposed projects. Perhaps the biggest of these was *Today I Am in the Skies* (*Kyo mo ware ozora ni ari*), which Honda presented to Toho in or around 1960. Honda envisioned a collaboration with Eiji Tsuburaya far different from that of their sci-fi films, a semidocumentary dramatization of the history of Japanese aviation. It would focus on pioneers in the field including Kokichi Ukita, who built artificial wings and was "the first Japanese person to fly"; Chuhachi Ninomiya, who designed a three-engine aircraft earlier than the Wright brothers; and Yoshitoshi Tokugawa, who flew Japan's first successful powered aircraft in 1910. Honda's research included interviews with early aviators, and he collaborated with prolific Toho writer Katsuhito Inomata on a screenplay, but the studio canceled the project when it was nearing the production phase. "[The reason] was never communicated to me," Honda later said. The project was later taken up by director Kengo Furusawa, whose 1964 film of the same title (and also known as *Tiger Flight*) starred Tatsuya Mihashi, Makoto Sato, and Yosuke Natsuki. Honda was not pleased at the turn of events. "I had a lot of things I wanted to say to [Tomoyuki Tanaka] about that," he recalled. "My version was nothing like the film that was made."

Honda also proposed a semidocumentary drama about fishermen in the Okinawan port of Itoman, where the locals practice an old style of fishing in which underwater divers drive the fish into nets. It was a familiar Honda story, a la *The Blue Pearl*, of young people trapped in a traditional, regional community and longing for an escape. Honda traveled to Amami Oshima, an island in Kagoshima, to scout locations, and a screenplay was completed. "The company was 100 percent ready to make this film, but for whatever reason [it fell through]," Honda remembered. "At the time, they tended not to like films that were too serious, but I did. And I really loved stories involving the sea . . . I had thought about establishing myself in the sea genre, and underwater filming, expanding my repertoire." The idea was later picked up by Nippon Newsreels Co. and made into a documentary.

Honda had many projects, originating during this retrenchment period or earlier in his career, which never materialized. "[The studio] urged me to submit ideas, so I did and they [were all rejected]," Honda remembered. "For some, they said it just wasn't the right time; for others, they said the idea wouldn't make any money." Two of his stories were inspired by the war years. *Naked Spring* (*Hadaka no izumi*) was about Japanese and Chinese soldiers stationed at nearby bases, both reliant on the same spring for their water supply. The two sides agree to share the spring and not to attack each other. "When one troop had musicians visit them, the other troop asked them to play for them, too," Honda said. "It was never reported . . . but this kind of thing actually happened at the front." Another idea was titled *Meeting Again* (*Sai-kai*), about a Japanese troop befriended by Chinese villagers. "When the war was over and the soldiers had to leave, both sides expressed their wish to meet again," Honda said."[25]

There were several stories that took place in Hokkaido, Japan's largest and northernmost prefecture. One was *Cross of the Iron Rail* (*Tetsuro no Jyujika*), based on a novel by Akutagawa Prize–winner Kotaro Samukawa, about the construction of a railroad line through the area's rugged mountains during the early Meiji era to transport coal from Sapporo to the port town of Otaru. Honda saw Takashi Shimura and Toshiro Mifune as his lead characters,

rough-and-ready men overseeing the construction and competing for power and the affections of a woman, but the project was deemed too expensive. Another, inspired by artist Naoyuki Sakamoto's *Frontier Journal* (*Kaikon no ki*), was to be a semidocumentary film about early Japanese settlers on Hokkaido, showcasing the area's natural beauty.

There were others. Honda wanted to adapt a novel by Shugoro Yamamoto, whose books inspired Kurosawa's *Sanjuro* (*Tsubaki Sanjuro*, 1962) and *Red Beard* (*Akahige*, 1965), among other films. He wrote a film treatment titled *Violin Duet* (*Violin kyosokyoku*), a romantic tragedy centered on a concert violinist. And shortly after the war, Honda had proposed a project entitled *The Remains of Sanpei* (*Ikotsu Sanpei-kun*), about a soldier's ghost returning to Japan. He also, uncharacteristically, proposed a historical drama, the true story of a member of the powerful Otomo Clan—which ruled parts of Kyushu for about four hundred years—who scandalously set fire to the Imperial Palace gate and was banished during the Heian period. Many proposals would remain unfinished because of a lack of time and momentum. "I have more [ideas] in my notebooks," Honda later recalled. "Looking back, I was working hard back then."[26]

At the same time, Honda did not distance himself from science fiction films. In 1961 he participated in a symposium on the subject for *SF Magazine* with Eiji Tsuburaya and novelist Kobo Abe (*The Face of Another*). He directed the Japanese-language dubbing for a 1962 release of *Sampo*, a Finnish-Soviet fantasy film, and wrote an essay about its special effects for the theater program book. But his reluctance to challenge or leave the studio system, coupled with the film industry's hastening decline, would limit his opportunities to do other things.

———

One day, Honda jumped into a taxicab. When the ride was over, he handed the driver a wad of bills. The cabbie was confused; Honda didn't realize he had overpaid the fare and didn't seem concerned.

Honda remained disconnected from mundane financial details. As was typical of Japanese households, his wife continued to manage the family budget and stocked his wallet with spending cash. "Whenever he would take me out, my father would pay, but it was me who retrieved the change. He would simply pay and be on his way," Ryuji remembered. "Once, my mother forgot to refill his wallet. He went to see movies and do things. You'd think he'd check his wallet, but he didn't, and he took a cab home. When it was time to pay the fare, he was broke. I remember him yelling from the street, 'Money! I need money!'"

While Honda was attempting to develop his projects, he also may have declined to direct one or more studio assignments. This decrease in production had repercussions at home, for although Honda earned a comfortable income, it was not guaranteed. Toho directors were expected to be productive. "[*King Kong vs. Godzilla*] was only my second film of the year after *Gorath*," said Honda. "If you didn't make at least two movies a year, you couldn't support yourself."[27]

Directors failing to meet this quota could find themselves in arrears. Kimi, acting as Honda's agent, asked the studio to spread out her husband's wages in order to help balance the family books. "There was no monthly salary once [a director] became a formal employee," Kimi said. "This sort of contract was very unstable. So I asked Toho to take the director's pay . . . and prorate it into monthly payments throughout the year instead of a lump sum. So, he got paid every month, but if he were to decline a project, the pay he received would become debt. Then, for example, if he made two films the following year, he might only get compensated for one."

The family had moved into their "mansion" not long before, and expenses were high. But Kimi shielded Honda from the financial stress. "He had absolutely no idea I was up to my neck in debt, so he declined work," she said. "I think that period was when he cleared his mind."

In 1963, Honda would return to directing with renewed energy, and over the next several years he and Tsuburaya would collaborate on some of their most entertaining and popular films.

19

DANGEROUS WATERS

Matango (1963),
Atragon (1963)

Kumi Mizuno worked for many fine directors, such as Naruse, Taniguchi, Inagaki, Okamoto, and Makino. But for Ishiro Honda, she became more than an actress. Into the modest, chaste reality of Honda's science fiction and fantasy films, Mizuno brought sex appeal, eroticism, and a feminine danger that excited. They made just a handful of films together, but Mizuno was, briefly, Honda's muse. "She always seemed genuine," Honda would say. "She would just step right into her role."[1]

"Honda-*sensei* was so shy," Mizuno remembered. "He was always smiling. I never once felt scared of him. If I talked to him, looking into his eyes, he would look away, feeling awkward and shy. That's a strong memory I have of him. I also got an impression that he was very much like a young boy in a way. Sometimes I would go ask him questions about the scene, but he would just smile and say, 'Just do it like that. Do as you please.' He tended to like more realistic performances, so if we overacted or exaggerated too much, he would say something like, 'I don't quite think that was right.' But he never really said much, especially to us women."

Mizuno played urbane, fashionable, assertive women. And those eyes—they were large, deep, expressive, and seemingly non-Japanese in their directness. Once, she played an alien temptress; twice, she allowed a giant monster to fall in love with her, not to mention her male costars. In science fiction, the roles were smaller, the characters less complex; the actors had to be able to do more with less. Mizuno could, and then some. Was that why Honda chose her, again and again?

"I'm not your typical good-looking type. Among the Toho actors, I'm more sort of . . . not unrefined, but I 'smell buttery.'[2] I don't know if you would have called me modern, but I really did enjoy fashion and getting dressed up. And I was more masculine . . . If I started to like a guy, I would go up to him myself and tell him so . . . I'm also very clear about what I like and dislike. I never make compromises. Maybe I was a man in my past life. But when I was young, I had many love encounters so in that way, maybe I'm a female after all. Things are different now, but back then, I loved to fall in and be in love."

In Honda's *Matango* she was the femme fatale, eating the forbidden fruit of mutated mushrooms. She was a star, but had no quarrel with making genre pictures. "It was fun. I was still very young, so my heart was pounding and it was really thrilling."

Honda directing Yoshio Tsuchiya (center) and Kumi Mizuno (left) in *Matango*.
Courtesy of Honda Film Inc.

[W]e enter the abandoned ship, and upon opening the door to the captain's cabin, the mold [is everywhere]. I asked [Honda], "*Sensei*, I'm in this eerie place for the first time . . . What exactly shall I do here?" He said, "Hmmm. In cases like this, the first thing one would notice is the smell." He told me, "Smell the air. People sense things by smelling." I remember that well.
– Akira Kubo

The 1950s malaise and the political protests that had begun the 1960s were by now largely forgotten. Upon taking office in 1960, Prime Minister Hayato Ikeda introduced his Income Doubling Plan, spurring rapid economic growth fueled by Western-style consumerism. An emerging middle class now coveted lifestyle items previously beyond reach, such as refrigerators, vacuum cleaners, and washing machines, while more upwardly mobile citizens owned sports cars and expensive luxuries. Meanwhile, Tokyo was undergoing a makeover, with new stadiums, highways, and other facilities sprouting up for the 1964 Tokyo Olympics; this construction is depicted in Kon Ichikawa's impressionistic documentary *Tokyo Olympiad* (1965). Nearly twenty years after the war, Japan's people and its capital were rejoining the modern world.

Matango (1963) is a taut, tense horror film rooted in psychology and proto-psychedelia, and a critique of the shallow materialism and self-centered attitudes that accompanied Japan's new prosperity. "Around this time, there were people who started to be Americanized, or have a very modern lifestyle," recalled Honda. "There were rich people who sent their kids to school in foreign cars, that kind of thing. We tried to show that type of social background in this film."[3] Honda was inspired by a headline-making story about thrill-seeking rich kids who took their father's yacht far out to sea and had to be rescued. Early drafts featured characters mirroring the incident, spoiled young sons of the moneyed class. Reports of vanishing ships and aircraft in the Bermuda Triangle were another influence. Honda also managed to embed his antinuclear message into the film with a mysterious research vessel of unknown nationality that becomes yet another facsimile of the Lucky Dragon.

Like *Mothra*, *Matango* has a literary pedigree. It was loosely based on "The Voice in the Night," a 1907 story by British writer William Hope Hodgson, a disciple of Poe, Wells, Verne, and Doyle. Hodgson's tale concerns a shipwrecked couple, who drift onto a foggy island in the Pacific, where they find an abandoned ship. A hideous, immortal gray fungus covers nearly everything, and the man and woman struggle to survive on what little food they can muster. Soon the fungus grows on their bodies, creating ugly deformities. Starving, they eat the mold and find it intoxicating, but resign themselves to the same fate as the derelict ship's crew, now grotesque fungus-men living in the forest.

With Hodgson's plot, setting, and flashback motif as inspiration, producer Tomoyuki Tanaka commissioned an original story from genre writer Masami Fukushima, editor of *SF Magazine* and the man often credited with popularizing science fiction literature in Japan. Fukushima's story, published in magazine form in August 1963, received a polish from acclaimed novelist Shinichi Hoshi before Honda and Takeshi Kimura wrote the adapted screenplay. (Michelangelo Antonioni's *L'Avventura* [1960], in which a beautiful woman disappears on a mysterious island in the Mediterranean, may have also provided inspiration.)

In Honda's film, the castaways are a cross section of 1960s Tokyo: Kasai (Yoshio Tsuchiya) is a greedy capitalist whose recklessness puts everyone in danger. Sakuda (Hiroshi Koizumi) is the gruff captain, whose authority is usurped. Mami (Kumi Mizuno) is a carefree singing starlet, who relishes the role of temptress. Yoshida (Hiroshi Tachikawa, a Kurosawa regular and a pilot in *Gorath*) is a pretentious mystery novelist. Koyama, the boatswain (Kenji Sahara), is a crude, low-class ruffian driven by misogyny, envy, and survival instinct. Murai (Akira Kubo), a conscientious psychology professor, is powerless to stop his friends' self-destructive behavior. His girlfriend Akiko (Miki Yashiro) is shy, afraid, and chaste until the forbidden fungus liberates her id.

Matango's themes of dehumanization and societal collapse resemble the dystopian film and literature cycle that began in the 1950s and eventually inspired later efforts such as *Battle Royale* and *The Hunger Games*. The film also recalls William Golding's 1954 novel *Lord of the Flies*, wherein schoolboys stranded on an island devolve into murderous savages in the absence of British authoritarian rule. The transformations in *Matango* are less extreme; from the start, no one is particularly admirable, and when the flirtatious Mami opens things with a ditzy pop song (with the men leering at her), the group's shallowness is apparent. The island is a claustrophobic hell, where Honda and Kimura magnify the Freudian impulses normally suppressed by the unspoken respect, authority, and hierarchy governing Japanese society. The novelist goes mad with lust, the rich man selfishly hordes provisions, the captain deserts the group, and the greedy boatswain extorts the rich man's money. Koyama is the worst of the lot, and yet the only one with a plan; he threatens to kill and rape, but he also bullies everyone to work together to find food. For his efforts he is murdered, his body strewn with now-worthless yen notes. Before the nightmare begins, Yoshida declares, "We are completely free from the problems of man"; but in this misanthropic Kimura script, and arguably Honda's darkest film, the opposite is true.

Thematically and visually, *Matango* is uniquely dark among Honda's films; its eerie imagery and atmosphere are a radical departure from the brightly lit and light-hearted *Mothra* or *King Kong vs. Godzilla*. The breezy mood at the outset is shattered by a storm that wrecks the yacht and leaves the group helplessly adrift. The sun rarely appears again, and the foreboding fog follows the castaways onto the island. Bad omens persist—ghost ships real and imagined, frightened birds, a graveyard of shipwrecks, an unsettling feeling of being watched. The abandoned research ship, with its rotting sails, a patina of slippery, stinking fungus, and cabinets of mutated animals, is a haunted house marooned in the sand. Aboard it, Honda effectively uses overt horror-movie tricks to good effect, from creaking doors and sudden screams to oblique angles and intense colors that create an unsettling imbalance. The stark look was designed by art director Shigekazu Ikuno, working with Honda for the first time. "The shipwreck set was tilted, so filming in there all day made me feel sick," remembered Koji Kajita. "Ikuno was [*Godzilla* production designer] Satoru Chuko's apprentice and was a very studious person, a research enthusiast. He was known for set designs that were the vanguard, experimental sets." *Matango* is also the first Honda film to utilize an Oxberry optical printer—purchased by Toho from the United States at Eiji Tsuburaya's behest—which allows for improved image compositing, evidenced in the misty jungles and many other scenes.

This was Honda's first film after a long layoff, and he showed a renewed determination. "He got so into it," remembered Tsuchiya. "Honda was so enthusiastic about the project. There was a rare moment, when he gathered everybody before filming started and told us all, 'This is a serious drama picture, so please keep this in mind and work accordingly.' I totally agreed, and the actors were all united in this concept."

With meatier roles, the actors immersed themselves. "Director Honda wanted to challenge me with a different kind of character," Sahara said. To portray the rough-and-tough bosun, he worked out rigorously and wore a tank top; Honda suggested he cover one of his front teeth in black, but Sahara reportedly went further and had a dentist pull it. "I desperately wanted to make him happy."[4]

Likewise, Kumi Mizuno is wholly believable as the flirtatious diva. Like Tallulah Bankhead in Alfred Hitchcock's similarly themed *Lifeboat* (1944), she remains fashionable and attractive, no matter how harsh the conditions. In the final act, as everybody's foibles and faults intensify, Mizuno seems to become only more alluring. The original plan was for Mizuno to grow keloid bumps, like the others, but instead Hajime Koizumi's camera pans upward to show her munching a mushroom and smiling seductively; at that brief instant, her beauty radiates. "I was told to lure and tempt in that scene, so I had to think hard as to what exactly that meant," Mizuno said.

"It was Honda-*san* who asked, 'Is the keloid the only way to portray her transformation?'" remembered assistant effects director Teruyoshi Nakano. "I think that was not only his creativity, but also his kind heart. 'Rather than messing up a beautiful face, wouldn't it be better if she gets more and more beautiful, and for that to signify her transformation?' This is all he had to say. We'd been trying to come up with a good idea for days until then. Tsuburaya-*san* said, 'That's it!'"

Honda lamented that *Matango* suffered

a disconnect between the location shooting on beautiful Oshima Island and Ikuno's surreal sets. "Those scenes aren't cut together in a completely smooth manner," he said. "I think it was too choppy."[5] By the final act, the film plunges into a semihallucinatory state owing to the artificial, dreamlike look of the mushroom rainforest. Small mushrooms sprout up in real time, an effect created with a primitive liquid Styrofoam, and oversized toadstool men lurch from the shadows, emitting a cacophony of insane laughter. The bizarre effect is underscored by the sparse, jazzy soundtrack by Sadao Bekku, a classical composer. When Kasai eats the mushrooms, Bekku's music-box-like melody accompanies a mind-bending trip of Tokyo neon and exotic dancers. After addressing drugs literally in *A Man in Red*, now Honda creates a metaphor for hallucinogens. "Here we did it as mushrooms, but showing the same kind of thing, that you can get completely addicted and cannot do anything about it. It destroys you. Also, how people can become so ugly and selfish in certain situations."[6]

The final scene appears to be influenced by Hitchcock's *Psycho* (1960), with the lone survivor under observation in a psychiatric ward. The climactic moment when Akira Kubo turns to face the camera, revealing his scars, is also likely inspired by "Mujina," a story from Lafcadio Hearn's 1904 collection of Japanese ghost tales, *Kwaidan*. ("Mujina" ends with the shock of a man suddenly revealing his ghostlike face.) However, actor Tsuchiya claims—though it is unconfirmed—that another, more ambiguous ending was shot at his suggestion, in which Kubo's face was normal. "I told Honda-*san* . . . 'It will be more interesting if you leave his looks alone,'" Tsuchiya said. "'Make the audience believe that he's gone nuts—but

in actuality, this really did happen.' They ended up using the bumpy version. But we filmed it two ways."

Matango fell short of *Kinema Junpo*'s list of annual top performers and languished in obscurity for many years after its release. "This wasn't really a typical Japanese mainstream movie at all," said Honda. "When critics saw it, [they] didn't like it, so that was pretty much the end of that film."[7] This was Honda's first picture to bypass a theatrical release in the United States and go straight to TV, where American International Pictures rebranded it *Attack of the Mushroom People*.

Years later, both Tsuchiya and Sahara recalled having strong misgivings about the project. "We felt something was off with the mushrooms," said Tsuchiya. "We felt they looked cheap, like something from Disneyland . . . I actually complained to Honda-*san* and Tsuburaya-*san*, saying I had no intention of acting in such a cheap-looking film." They were also concerned that their performances were too over the top. But their fears were allayed by the finished film.

"It still is really entertaining if you watch it now," said Tsuchiya. "That's Honda-*san* for you. He's so good. There weren't many directors like him, though."

There were some Japanese people who felt like Jinguji. However the world turns, even when confronted with their wrongdoing, they still cannot shake loose their pride . . . I can understand him very well because I was also in the war . . . But instead of thinking, "What about Japan?" what I got from my war experiences was, "What about humanity?"
– Ishiro Honda[8]

In the late 1950s Toho began making war epics with all-star casts and elaborate effects from Eiji Tsuburaya. Following the example set by Honda's *Eagle of the Pacific*, these films contrasted heroic battles with tragic stories of military men facing the futility of war and its human cost. They were helmed by Honda's colleagues such as Shue Matsubayashi, a World War II Imperial Navy veteran, whose big-budget *Storm over the Pacific* (*Hawai Middowei daikaikusen: Taiheiyo no arashi*, 1960)—an unsympathetic and sober look at combat, and Matsubayashi's memorial to fallen comrades—was the best of the lot. Despite Honda's previous success in the war genre, he was not assigned to these projects; but he still made one final, overt antiwar statement in *Atragon*, a sci-fantasy that, at its core, is about the uneasy legacy of World War II. Though conceived and shot quickly, this was Honda and Tsuburaya's last truly ambitious collaboration, an entertaining blend of traditional science fiction and contemporary influences, imaginative production design, and political ideas, backed by Akira Ifukube's stirring martial music.[9] *Atragon* is loosely based on *The Undersea Warship* (*Kaitei Gunkan*), a militaristic adventure novel written in 1899 by Shunro Oshikawa, a pioneer of Japanese science fiction.[10] Published at the height of the Meiji era, amid a conservative backlash against Western influence and between military victories over China and Russia, *The Undersea Battleship* reflects the nationalistic spirit of its time. The novel's protagonist Capt. Sakurai is an exiled naval officer and idealistic engineering genius, devoted to the samurai ethic and dedicated to establishing Japan as a major world power. At a secret base on a small Pacific island, he and his forces construct a supersubmarine

that rams pirate ships with a drill in its bow. Oshikawa borrowed liberally from Capt. Nemo's adventures in Jules Verne's *Twenty Thousand Leagues under the Sea* (1869) and *Mysterious Island* (1874).

Screenwriter Shinichi Sekizawa and Honda took Oshikawa's idea and contemporized it; in their version, the naval officer is holding out on a remote island two decades after World War II, refusing to acknowledge Japan's surrender. Aided by devoted sailors, Capt. Jinguji has built the Gotengo submarine warship to restore the glory of the Japanese empire, to restart and win the war. Thus, Jinguji becomes a cautionary figure against resurgent nationalism, even as his technical feats recall Japan's wartime supremacy. There are clear allusions to three "monster submarines" built near the end of the war, dubbed the I-400, I-401, and I-402, which carried and launched bomber planes. The legend of Mu, a sunken continent in the Pacific, was popularized by British occult writer James Churchward in the 1920s; but Sekizawa and Honda took the idea from a secondhand source, *The Undersea Kingdom* (*Kaitei Okoku*), a children's story by production illustrator Shigeru Komatsuzaki. In the film, Mu is a fascist mirror of Imperial Japan, an ancient civilization with modern weaponry and science, blindly convinced of its own superiority and unwilling to negotiate even when facing catastrophic defeat.

Atragon begins with several intersecting mysteries. Fashion photographer Susumu (Tadao Takashima) and his assistant Yoshito (Yu Fujiki) witness a taxicab driving off a pier and the appearance of a "vapor man." A police detective (Hiroshi Koizumi) investigates the kidnappings of several prominent marine engineers. Kosumi (Ken Uehara), a shipping magnate

Kosumi (Ken Uehara, left, in suit and tie) urges Captain Jinguji (Jun Tazaki, center) to use his supersubmarine to defend the world in *Atragon*. © Toho Co., Ltd.

and former navy admiral, is hounded by an oily, bearded, beatnik-looking reporter (Kenji Sahara, again effectively playing against type), who insists that Kosumi's war comrade Capt. Jinguji (Jun Tazaki), long believed dead, is still alive and secretly building a new, high-tech submarine. Kosumi raised Jinguji's daughter Makoto (Yoko Fujiyama) after the war, and now the girl's hope of reuniting with her father is rekindled. In short order, the kidnappings are revealed to be the workings of the Mu Empire, an ancient undersea civilization that aims to conquer the earth's surface. Mu demands mankind's surrender, escalating the threat by attacking ships and causing earthquakes. The world is on alert; the H-bomb is debated. The UN is powerless, and Jinguji's supersub may be the only hope. In the second act, the heroes head for Jinguji's island hideout, a time-warped war outpost, to plead for help.

Dignified Kosumi, gruff Jinguji, and melancholy Makoto are the pivotal characters in Honda's large ensemble. Through their confrontations, Honda reveals his parallel themes: the uniquely Japanese ideals of nationalism and personal honor represented by Jinguji, contrasted with Kosumi's regret over the vanity, foolishness, and horror of war. Kosumi served his country well but has accepted Japan's defeat and, through his work, has helped rebuild Japan as a peaceful and prosperous nation. Jinguji's fierce determination to reclaim Japan's empire is compounded by the shame of having deserted the navy during the war's last days. His desire to salvage national and personal honor makes Jinguji oblivious to the current crisis, and he refuses to help. When told that the world has changed since the war's end, Jinguji retorts that he'll "change it again!"

Jinguji likely resonated with Japanese audiences, for he represents actual right-wing extremism and ghosts of the war. The year 1963 saw publication of *Affirmation of the Greater East Asian War*, a controversial tract by novelist Fusao Hayashi that reaffirmed the old belief that Japan's brutal military conquests were a just and noble effort to, as a wartime slogan declared, "liberate the Asian people from the Western powers." This catalyzed a fringe of high-profile conservatives that included the writers Yukio Mishima and Shintaro Ishihara.[11] Meanwhile, newspapers reported stories of military stragglers just then returning home from South Seas islands and other war territories. Some of them had been left behind accidentally, others were prisoners of the Soviet Union, but a number were misguided loyalists, like Jinguji. As historian Beatrice Trefalt writes:

These individuals missed the end of the war altogether; fear, shame and disbelief . . . caused them to hide on the periphery of battlefields and on the edge of survival for years and sometimes decades . . . They had had little or no contact with the outside world. They were thus mostly unaware of developments in the postwar world and within Japan. The stragglers were "preserved," as it were, as wartime figures: they dressed in makeshift uniforms, spoke a stilted military language . . . They often cited . . . the importance of loyalty to ideals that had long since been abandoned by the population as a whole.[12]

In their first heart-to-heart in twenty years, Jinguji is tearfully rebuked by Makoto, not only for refusing to help the world and to abandon the war, but also tacitly for the betrayal and loss felt by a generation of postwar orphans. The role of Jinguji would have been well suited to Toshiro Mifune, who was now dividing his career between Kurosawa's projects and a variety of program pictures; Jun Tazaki underplays the scene much as Mifune might have, with the pain of a regretful father beneath the captain's steely façade. Tazaki was one of Toho's great character actors, with a screen presence that was simultaneously dignified and intense, and he often played military men, bosses, fathers, scientists, and other authority figures. *Atragon* offers Tazaki a rare featured role, and he gives his best and most complex performance for Honda here. Fujiyama, whom Honda described as an "authentic Japanese beauty," was a relatively inexperienced actress but well cast as the doleful daughter. This is the most emotionally resonant scene in a Honda genre film since Serizawa's torment in *Godzilla*.

While Honda's dramas and comedies were often personal character studies, his effects pictures could be impersonal and plot-driven. *Atragon* offers insight into Honda's approach to the human drama

because it is structured somewhat differently, with only one major action scene, the Gotengo's test run, during the first two-thirds of the film. There was room to flesh out the characters and raise emotional stakes; in fact, Sekizawa wrote a scene that would have done so, but Honda cut it out. In it, Jinguji decides to attack the Mu Empire, only to learn that his daughter and Susumu are held prisoner there. Jinguji is prepared to sacrifice Makoto to save the world, but Kosumi objects and an argument ensues. Honda, however, saw his story as a parable of global problems and purposely avoided details that, in his view, created "smaller personalities for the characters." Thus, Makoto's kidnapping goes unmentioned, and the ensuing rescue and father-daughter reunion doesn't tug the heartstrings.

"I wanted to concentrate on the larger-scale problem of mankind versus the Mu and ignore the personal problems in that scene," said Honda. "If they talk about their personal problems, unless you really express it deeply . . . the audience will not be satisfied."[13]

The final act is action-packed, highlighted by Mu's geologic attack on Tokyo, causing Ginza and Marunouchi to collapse from below—one of Tsuburaya's great miniature feats—followed by a fiery attack on ships in Tokyo Bay. *Atragon* includes the somewhat perfunctory giant monster Manda, a guardian sea serpent that the Mu people worship with ritualistic chants. Honda builds anticipation and dread before the creature's appearance, but it proves to be rather unformidable, a spindly marionette. Manda was included at producer Tanaka's insistence, a la *Gorath*.

Mu seems unstoppable, yet it fears Jinguji's submarine. And for good reason: when the Gotengo makes its grand entrance, it becomes the star of the movie and arguably the greatest of the super-weapons designed by Komatsuzaki (who, as in *The Mysterians* and *Battle in Outer Space*, worked uncredited). It can hover and fly above the ocean's surface and is equipped with a massive drill, high-voltage shocks, and freezing jets, all of which it employs to penetrate and destroy Mu's massive reactor, which harvests the earth's energy.

Things also perk up with the late arrival of the youthful, regally evil Empress of Mu, adorned with fire-red wig, makeup, and flashy garb. Honda initially had no idea whom to cast, as none of his usual actresses fit the mold. By chance, twenty-two-year-old Tetsuko Kobayashi, a newcomer, was working in a TV show on the Toho lot. Honda instantly knew she was perfect. "She was hard working and a very energetic actress, and she even went so far as to do all of her makeup by herself," said Honda. "Usually, a young girl like her would just follow the director and not do much else, but she had more guts and initiative."[14]

The empress's minions include thirty-seven-year-old Hideyo Amamoto as an old priest with shock-white frock and beard, and two Caucasian ladies-in-waiting, played by American military wives. The rest of the large cast features Honda regulars and semiregulars. Funnymen Takashima and Fujiki provide occasional comic banter, though this film is much more straightforward overall than *King Kong vs. Godzilla*. Takashima, playing the boyfriend this time, gets the best dialogue, calling Jinguji "a ghost wearing rusty armor." Sahara and Akihiko Hirata go shirtless in Phoenician-style costumes. Some characters stay too long; Koizumi, noticeably, is reduced to standing in the background during the last reel.

The schedule was shorter than normal. Production officially began on September 5, 1963, and Toho pegged the release for December 22, during the holiday box-office season, just three and a half months away. Tsuburaya had to omit or scale back some effects—the Mu's destruction of New York is mentioned but not shown, for instance—and the rushed pace is evident in some of his work. For Honda, the challenge was to show the Mu Empire as a vibrant civilization and contrast its advanced technology with ancient architecture and iconography. There are brief views of a city, with modern transportation systems and statues of gods, although the citadel where the empress presides over her genuflecting subjects is obviously a façade and is visibly smaller than those in the Hollywood historical epics that inspired it. Honda felt his depiction of Mu lacked depth. "I wanted to show something like its towns or residential areas," Honda said. "Those kinds of things were a necessity, but we didn't have the budget."[15]

Toho had only two films in the *Kinema Junpo* top ten for 1963–64, both *Station Front* salaryman comedies. *Atragon* was the thirteenth highest-grossing domestic film, earning ¥175 million. Foreign films were now taking a huge share of the Japanese box office: the top grosser overall was Joseph L. Mankiewicz's *Cleopatra* (¥504 million), while Stanley Donen's *Charade* and the James Bond film *From Russia with Love* also outperformed most domestic releases. Given Toho's interest in foreign sales, *Atragon*'s theme of defiant nationalism would seem ill-advised, but the film nevertheless reached the United States in 1965. American International Pictures marketed it in the vein of Irwin Allen's popular *Voyage to the Bottom of the Sea* (1961).

Honda said he identified with Kosumi, but he also had empathy for Jinguji. "[He] would restart the war, so I could not express my film through his viewpoint. [But] I understood his feelings, his thoughts, and how he talked."[16] Thus, Honda grants the old captain one last victory even while defusing his nationalism, walking a fine line between lamenting war's horror and preserving the honor of those who fought. In turn, Jinguji allows the empress to die honorably, sharing the fate of her people. As flames rise spectacularly from the ocean's surface, the story ends on a somber note, similar to *Godzilla*. The threat at the bottom of the ocean is defeated, but at great cost, and there is no rejoicing.

20

MONSTERS AND GANGSTERS

Mothra vs. Godzilla (1964),
Dogora (1964), *Ghidorah, the
Three-Headed Monster* (1964)

**Demonstrations against nuclear bombs
don't make news anymore.**

— Sakai

When Godzilla destroyed Tokyo in 1954,
the dreary city still resembled the one
firebombed by America less than a decade
earlier. In the intervening years, however,
the construction boom preceding the 1964
Olympics had transformed Tokyo into a
modern, vibrant place. Memories of the war
were fading and, like much of the world,
Japan had compartmentalized the threat of
nuclear annihilation. In this new environment, postwar Japan historian Yoshikuni
Igarashi observes, "The critical power of
Godzilla was proportionately diminished,"
as Toho recalibrated its monster films for
younger and younger audiences, attempting to keep the *kaiju eiga* viable. Over
the course of the decade, Godzilla would
evolve from bad guy to good and behave in
increasingly humanlike ways.

"In 1960s Japan, a place overflowing with
optimism inspired by economic growth,
the monsters could not find a place other
than as caricatures," Igarashi writes. "The
darkness that prevailed in . . . the mid-1950s
had vanished from the screen and Japanese
society . . . [Godzilla] was tamed and transformed into a guardian of postwar Japan's
prosperity."[1]

But before that transformation began,
Honda and Tsuburaya gave Godzilla one
more destructive rampage. *Mothra vs. Godzilla* revisits the spirit of 1954 if not the substance, along with the bright-colored fantasy of *Mothra* and the monster battles of
King Kong vs. Godzilla, Honda's two biggest
recent monster hits. With a lighthearted
message of goodwill among mankind, a
snarling Godzilla, and big, widescreen set
pieces showcasing the monsters, the fourth
Godzilla film is a standout in the genre.

A massive typhoon dislodges Mothra's
egg from Infant Island. It floats to Japan,
where shifty promoter Kumayama (Yoshibumi Tajima) builds an amusement park

around it, with a big incubator. The twin fairies of Infant Island (The Peanuts, Emi and Yumi Ito) appear in Japan pleading for help bringing the egg back home; they are aided by cynical journalist Sakai (Akira Takarada), greenhorn photographer Junko (Yuriko Hoshi), and scientist Murai (Hiroshi Koizumi), but Kumayama and his greedy financier Torahata (Kenji Sahara) refuse to relinquish it. When Godzilla awakens and tramples Nagoya, the heroes plead for Mothra's help, but the Infant Islanders—scorned by Japan and irradiated by American nuclear tests—decline. Then, just when Godzilla is about to attack the egg, Mothra arrives and dies defending it. The military batters Godzilla unsuccessfully until the egg—in a third-act surprise— hatches not one, but a pair of giant caterpillars, which encase Godzilla in a silk cocoon, triumphing in a titanic battle.

As originally conceived, Shinichi Seki-zawa's screenplay picked up where *Mothra* ended, and Godzilla was to attack the fictional nation of Rolisica before heading to Japan. As the script was revised, Honda made his ideal of a social contract among all peoples the central theme, illustrated by the characters' actions throughout. An unscrupulous politician (Kenzo Tabu) tries to steamroll an industrial development without testing for dangerous radiation. Kumayama swindles the fishermen, then gets swindled himself. The greedy capitalists refuse to help the Infant Islanders. The public is apathetic—a headline screams, "Faith in humans shattered"—and so the islanders return the favor, turning a deaf ear to Japan's cry for aid. The heroes' impassioned plea sounds as if Honda himself is speaking: "We, too, want a world without distrust," says Sakai. The words stir the compassionate monster Mothra, which sacrifices itself to save both its progeny and mankind; the caterpillars likewise selflessly risk their lives against Godzilla. "Mothra's

Godzilla advances on its foe in *Mothra vs. Godzilla*.
© Toho Co., Ltd.

role was a messenger of peace," actor Hiroshi Koizumi observed. "I think the idea of Mothra showed what Honda-*san* was like at heart better than Godzilla did."

The flow between Honda's drama and the special effects is mostly effortless. Tsuburaya delivers numerous money shots, starting with the roaring typhoon that opens the picture. A wide view of Mothra's egg on the beach is stunning, the adult Mothra in flight is near lifelike, and the Tohoscope vista of its battle with Godzilla is quite ambitious for a film of this type. Godzilla's entrance is memorable, with the beast rising out of the mud flats, as is its destruction of the Nagoya Castle and surrounding city. The Oxberry optical printer that Tsuburaya introduced on *Matango* enables near-seamless compositing of the twin fairies into the picture, and oversized furniture props further add to the illusion of their size.

The final twenty-plus minutes hint at the genre's impending tilt toward young boys. It's a near nonstop barrage of military hardware and monster action, as Godzilla is assaulted by tanks, bombers, napalm, and "artificial lightning." Impressively, Godzilla can now fire its radioactive breath from all angles with intense heat, turning tanks to molten metal. There is no *King Kong vs. Godzilla*–style clowning, however. Godzilla is a lizard-out-of-water in this fast-modernizing Japan; it stumbles and catches its tail on a broadcast tower, but not for laughs—these accidents only make the monster angrier. At the same time, Honda seemed to know that kids were now rooting for Godzilla, and so the film never gets too scary. The overall tone is family friendly, played straight with occasional comic relief from the cast. Kenji Sahara recalled that, before production started, Honda had discussed the demographic shift: "Now that

movies are being overtaken more and more by TV, [Toho] is targeting kids, not just adults, so we have to make something that all ages will find interesting." Honda didn't want to condescend to youngsters, saying, "Kids are more mature than we think."[2]

As in *Mothra*, Sekizawa's writing moves briskly and doesn't stop for lengthy pseudoscientific exposition. It's a simple good-versus-evil story with appealing heroes and shady villains. Akira Takarada, ten years removed from his boyish appearance in *Godzilla*, was by now a major Toho leading man. He never musses his hair or his tailored tan suit, not even in the tropics, yet he's not above suffering a silly bump on the head or dribbling the islanders' ceremonial drink for comic effect. The real scene stealers, though, are the archscoundrels. Tajima, a versatile character actor in his mid-forties, had worked with Honda since the *Night School*, *H-Man*, and *Seniors, Juniors, Co-workers* days. The oily, grinning Kumayama gets outmaneuvered by the younger and slicker Torahata, played by Sahara, again relishing an unsavory role. Torahata wears tinted glasses, expensive clothes, and a constant smirk; he smokes cigars and is doted on by servile women. "Producer Tomoyuki Tanaka said he wanted a villain with impact," said Kenji Sahara. "I thought this was a big chance for me, so I was going to be the best villain in the history of Godzilla movies." Researching his role, Sahara hung out with pushy real-estate agents, posing as a buyer, and imitated their supreme self-confidence. "Money was everything to him," Sahara said of his character. "He was a symbol of greed."

Sahara recalled shooting the fight that ends with both antagonists dead, an uncharacteristically violent moment. "I talked to the director about this scene, how this villain should meet his end, and we came up with the idea that we'd make my face all bloody and then I [would] try to escape with all the money. Honda said, 'Ken-*bo*, are you sure that you want to get a bloody nose? You'll ruin your cool-guy image.' . . . But once we decided to do it this way, we all got into it." Torahata, nearly knocked out on the floor, regains his senses only to be startled by the sight of Godzilla approaching outside the window. He shoots Kumayama through the back of the head, then greedily gathers the cash and tries to flee, but too late: Godzilla, playing judge and jury, destroys the hotel. It's a memorable sequence, though the villains' early exit defuses the human tension in an already thin plot. For the rest of the movie, the heroes are reduced to carrying around the Small Beauties in a box, then saving a group of schoolchildren. While this follows Honda's do-the-right-thing theme, it's a manufactured crisis to keep the stars on camera during the finale. The suspense of act 3 is all about whether Godzilla will be defeated—first by the military, then by the Mothras.

When she made her film debut in Honda's *Inao: Story of an Iron Arm*, actress Yuriko Hoshi had spent a month stranded on location in a far-off part of Kyushu, waiting for her scene to be shot. It was just few lines, and she was ultimately cut out of that film. "When I made *Mothra vs. Godzilla*, Honda apologized for making me wait so long," Hoshi said in 1996. "I was surprised he even remembered."[3] Hoshi was twenty-one at the time of *Mothra vs. Godzilla*, and she was now popular for costarring as a pure-hearted Annette Funicello type in Toho's *Young Guy* movies. Her banter with Takarada has a warm, big brother–kid sister appeal. Jun Tazaki, the nationalistic sub captain of *Atragon*, is pitch-perfect as

the exasperated newspaper editor, and his byplay with Yu Fujiki as a goofy, egg-eating reporter is funny.

With an eye toward the Western market, Honda and Tsuburaya filmed a sequence specifically for the English-language version of *Mothra vs. Godzilla* in which the American military comes to Japan's defense, unsuccessfully attacking Godzilla with missiles. The footage does not appear in the Japanese cut, and this difference points up Honda's evolving portrayal of the Japan Self-Defense Forces and their alliance with the United States. The joint military operations of *Mysterians*, *Battle in Outer Space*, and *Mothra* were now over, and the JSDF would fend for itself in the 1960s. Moreover, *Atragon* and the forthcoming *Dogora* would be the last Honda sci-fi films to offer a purely military solution; future conflicts would be resolved by the monsters or by an act of God, with the occasional human assist. Honda's fictional version of the Self-Defense Forces would nevertheless continue mounting big defensive operations with imaginary high-tech weapons, though this would seem more an appeal to children's fascination with models and military hardware than a political comment on the nation's massive defense buildup during this period, which did not always enjoy wide domestic support. By 1970, Japan would be the twelfth-largest military power in the world.[4]

This film marks a high point of Honda's work with composer Akira Ifukube, who contrasts the brash, raw power of Godzilla and the grace and beauty of Mothra in an operatic clash of chromatic and diatonic themes, stirring emotions even when the thin human drama doesn't. It was here that Ifukube perfected his chromatic Godzilla motif, which would become a highly recognizable piece of genre film music; he also

Watching through the viewfinder as Infant Island natives dance in *Mothra vs. Godzilla*.
Courtesy of Honda Film Inc.

incorporated the melody of Yuji Koseki's familiar *Song of Mothra* into the score. The final battle between Godzilla and the caterpillars is propelled by Ifukube's thundering, eight-minute opus accompanying it. Ifukube also composed *Holy Spring*, a lovely and mournful vocal piece sung by the Small Beauties while standing at the last green, unspoiled spot on Infant Island. The song underscores Honda's antinuclear, prounity themes and provides an emotional turning point.

By now, Honda and Ifukube had an established routine in which they would hold planning sessions to decide which scenes would have music and other details. A rare conflict occurred between the two men while making this film. "Honda-*san* asked me to use attack music as a bridge for an up view of Godzilla's appearance [over a ridgeline]," Ifukube recalled. "I said, 'Well, Honda-*san*, no music is necessary there. Godzilla is very impressive enough.'

'Yes, you are right. I agree,' he told me. So I did not write any music for that sequence. But when I saw the final print at a staff screening, it had the kind of music that Honda-*san* had asked for . . . he had taken attack music from the tapes for another scene and used it there anyway. It was used without my permission. So I glared very hard at Honda-*san* and he just shrugged his shoulders kind of innocently and said 'sorry' very softly.

"Our relationship was very good," continued Ifukube. "Of course there were small things . . . but really there was never any quarrel between us, and I enjoyed working with him very much. He always told me, 'Mr. Ifukube, I am totally ignorant about music, so I'll give you total freedom with it.' But in truth, Honda-*san* was quite knowledgeable about music. He very much enjoyed the recording sessions for the score. All other directors confined themselves in the recording booth, but

Honda-*san* came right up to me, listening and watching. Especially I remember in recording the dance music of *King Kong vs. Godzilla*, I told him, 'Honda-*san*, I'll add much more percussion here.' But Honda-*san* replied, 'No, it's not necessary. It's perfect.' He knew very well. We had this kind of conversation all the time."[5]

The film shows evidence of Japan's prosperity—burgeoning infrastructure, a postwar amusement park boom, working women—but also of studio cost cutting. Infant Island looks nothing like the lush place glimpsed in *Mothra*; instead it's a threadbare set of artificial rocks, with unconvincing whale and turtle skeletons on the beach. Honda had intended to show a former paradise devastated by nuclear testing. "I wanted to visualize the terror and the power of the atomic bomb," he said in the early 1980s. "The first island scene was supposed to be more graphic and realistic [but] the art department didn't have enough budget to make the set that I wanted. As a director, I should have been more stubborn. The proper way of making a movie is to visualize the director's idea [but] the business people thought the scene was not important because you could still follow the story without seeing that."[6]

Mothra vs. Godzilla was released on April 20, 1964, just prior to the Golden Week holidays, a prime movie-going season. Still, it did not make *Kinema Junpo*'s list of top earners for 1963–64, selling 3.5 million tickets, less than half of *King Kong vs. Godzilla*. But its reputation grew, and its theatrical rerelease in 1980 sold nearly 3 million more tickets. A reviewer for *Kinema Junpo* praised the special effects, but like many Japanese critics covering the genre, was dismissive overall: "As soon as Godzilla starts walking around, just as in every single monster movie, the people still try attacking it with electricity, which is sure to fail. It's strange that the people don't learn from the past. From the Self-Defense Forces on down, every single person just plain looks stupid."

————

Japan's criminologists know the years between the early 1950s and the early 1960s as the "period of gang wars." Economic growth gave rise to big-city red-light districts, the playgrounds of gangsters involved in extortion, prostitution, and drug rackets.[7] In the 1950s Nikkatsu Studios turned this material into popular *yakuza* films, which would acquire a cult following in the West decades later. Toho likewise made a good number of gangster pictures, and Honda's next two science fiction films would borrow ideas and talent from them. *Dogora* and *Ghidorah, the Three-Headed Monster* (both 1964) would mix monsters with mobster types, and both featured a pair of young action-film regulars: handsome Yosuke Natsuki and stunning beauty Akiko Wakabayashi.

Dogora opens with a luminous blob-monster destroying a Japanese TV satellite. It would be tempting to interpret this as a sly comment on the banality of television, or to view the monster's appetite for coal as concern about Japan's industrial pollution problem, a trade-off of postwar growth. There is also the specter, still lingering high above Japan, of radioactive isotopes from Hiroshima and Nagasaki that mutate the monster into a gigantic cross between the Aurora Borealis and a jellyfish, which floats in the sky and threatens to consume everything made of carbon, including diamonds—and the human race. But *Dogora* never probes these ideas much. Instead, befuddled detectives and inept diamond thieves play cat and mouse while the monster wreaks havoc. The film has an interesting cast, another fine Ifukube score, and a dash of superlative effects, but its various parts don't click.

The sci-fi plot came from a treatment by Jojiro Okami, while screenwriter Sekizawa and Honda added the cops and crooks. Okami was never consulted about the screenplay, which was unusual. "We just got his original story and took it from there," Honda said. Tsuburaya lamented that his budget was lower than normal, thus Dogora's destruction of the Wakato suspension bridge in Fukuoka, rendered with models and cel animation, is the only standout effects sequence. Honda enjoyed shooting the picture because the emphasis was on making a suspenseful drama rather than a monster extravaganza, but the screenplay is too unfocused to generate much tension. Some plot points are half-baked—Dogora levitates the occasional drunkard, safecracker, or garden rock for no apparent reason—and the story flits from crime caper to long scientific investigation to drawn-out military deployment and back again.

Some of the characters are fun to watch. Robert Dunham, an American expat actor, has a romp playing Mark Jackson, an international diamond insurance investigator who outsmarts both the gangsters and the cops. Jackson is fleet-footed and quick-witted, and speaks decent Japanese, though his vulgar social graces receive some priceless reactions from the Japanese cast. Among his quirks is the phrase "Oh, kami-sama!" ("Oh, God!"), a decidedly Western use of the language. Honda creates an appealingly adversarial buddy relationship—unique among his films involving the police—between the glib Dunham and Yosuke Natsuki as Komai, the harried

junior detective. The scientist Dr. Hanakata, a role that might normally go to Takashi Shimura or Ken Uehara, is played by Nobuo Nakamura, a distinguished stage actor who had significant parts in Yasujiro Ozu's films. In his forties but appearing much older, Nakamura has an unusual, clipped speaking style that gives his playful berating of the young policeman a certain charm. The mobsters are another matter. Clad in stereotypical bad-guy attire of flashy suits, shades, and white gloves, they behave more like cartoony castoffs from old James Cagney and Edward G. Robinson movies than recent *yakuza* flicks. Wakabayashi, with jet-black hair and a slinky dress, is underused as the double-crossing gun moll.

Dogora has an underlying feeling of retraction, as if the budget cutting that Honda often lamented is happening before the viewer's eyes. When the world unites to produce mass quantities of synthetic wasp venom to defeat the monster, Honda illustrates this with what appears to be stock footage of a laboratory, chemical plant, and thousands of steel drums. While Dogora is an interesting deviation from the standard man-in-suit, it's more an extreme weather event than a monster, and its coal-inhaling trick is obviously done by pouring debris onto a set and reversing the film. Some effects are plainly unconvincing, such as when the dying monster hurls huge, fake-looking boulders down on the heroes and villains, while they shoot it out on a beach below. An especially phony rock wipes out the crooks—a convenient, unlikely, and laughable end.

An early version of the *Dogora* plot, which was storyboarded, promised a more ambitious sci-fi story without the cops-and-robbers shenanigans. This unfilmed version began with several luminous monsters attacking a space station, then New York;

consuming diamonds at jewelry stores; and swiping necklaces off rich ladies' necks. The monsters levitate a cruise ship and the Golden Gate Bridge, then attack a Russian coal mine before finally wreaking havoc in Tokyo. Japanese authorities capture a small monster and, assisted by international scientists, learn the creatures can be killed with beta rays. The ending was hopeful, with global reconstruction under way. By comparison, the film that Honda and Tsuburaya made was modest and unspectacular; even more than in *Battle in Outer Space*, the bean counters forced them to scale back. Years later, Honda would recall the increasing pressure to succeed with less money. He told Tsuburaya, "It's getting harder and harder, isn't it?"[8]

Released August 11, 1964, this was Honda's second straight effects film that failed to make *Kinema Junpo*'s annual box-office rankings. It apparently made little impression on some cast members, as well. Asked about *Dogora* by an interviewer in 1996, actor Natsuki could not remember having appeared in it.[9]

———————

The transformation of Godzilla, Mothra, and their monster cohorts into Japan's defenders happened rather abruptly in Honda's *Ghidorah, the Three-Headed Monster* (*San daikaiju chikyu saidai no kessen*). In this follow-up to *Mothra vs. Godzilla*, Honda's theme of social responsibility is now articulated not by the human cast but by Mothra, a gigantic Winston Churchill that encourages Godzilla and Rodan to settle petty differences and unite for the common good of monsters and mankind. The role of villain is assumed by an outsider, King Ghidorah, a golden space dragon with an enormous wingspan and three wiggling heads that spit magnetic force beams. *Ghidorah* was the fourth-

International poster for *Ghidorah, The Three-Headed Monster.* © Toho Co., Ltd.

highest-grossing domestic movie of the 1964–65 season, and its success effectively severed any meaningful connection remaining between Godzilla and its atomic origins.

Ghidorah's plot resembles that of *Dogora*, though the cops and criminals are better integrated with the monster action this time. Yosuke Natsuki again plays a detective combating overdressed thugs and international assassins out to kill the beautiful Princess Salno (Akiko Waka-bayashi) before she can inherit the throne of the tiny kingdom of Selgina. Having somehow escaped an assassin's bomb that exploded her plane high above the ocean, the princess wanders Japan in a catatonic, amnesiac state, claiming to be from Venus and prophesying the world's destruction by Ghidorah.

As in *Mothra vs. Godzilla* there is a

Honda shows Hisaya Ito how to aim his rifle in *Ghidorah, The Three-Headed Monster.*
Courtesy of Honda Film Inc.

pleasant cast of regulars and semiregulars. Both Yuriko Hoshi, as a radio reporter, and Hiroshi Koizumi, as a scientist, essentially reprise their previous roles. Akihiko Hirata has a brief supporting part as chief of detectives, and Takashi Shimura is similarly underused as a doctor attempting to restore the princess's memory with shock treatments. The knife-wielding killer Malness is played with steely malice and a Ray-Ban stare by Hisaya Ito (the heavy in *A Rainbow Plays in My Heart* and *A Man in Red*). Malness and his goons sport gangster fashions and have vaguely non-Japanese features suited to foreign assassins. The Peanuts make their final appearance as the Small Beauties, who now perform on Japanese TV and embrace their celebrity status.

However, the opening-credits montage—Godzilla, Rodan, and Mothra fight-ing, backed by Ifukube monster motifs—makes clear that the creatures are now the stars. There are more monsters than ever, and their antics surpass *King Kong vs. Godzilla* in humanized behavior and humor. Godzilla and Rodan play volleyball with boulders (the Japan women's team had just won an Olympic gold medal, and the sport was wildly popular), the monsters guffaw at one another, and Godzilla takes some painfully funny shots to the tummy and rump. As in *King Kong vs. Godzilla*, Tsuburaya was further anthropomorphizing the monsters, a change that made the company happy and Honda uncomfortable. Honda would regret that with two crews working in tandem he could not watch the filming of every special-effects scene, thus "it was possible for different ideas [from mine] to emerge."[10]

But the most troubling development for Honda was the monster summit scene, wherein Godzilla, Mothra, and Rodan converse in a cross-species dialect. "I used The Peanuts as Mothra's interpreters, but even that was something I had to force myself to do," Honda would later say.[11] And though he could stomach the Earth monsters defending their turf, he thought it ridiculous that they would join forces to do it. Honda again carried out the studio's wishes despite his misgivings. "The producer liked how it turned out," he would recall. "It was a big success."[12]

Ghidorah was rushed into production after Kurosawa's *Red Beard* fell behind schedule and Toho needed a replacement for its New Year's holiday slate. Thus 1964 would be the only time two Godzilla pictures were released in one year. Production values don't appear to suffer greatly because of the short schedule, however. As in *Mothra vs. Godzilla*, Tsuburaya stages monster battles on big landscape sets that fill the widescreen frame, and there is a bit more emphasis on urban destruction as well as impressive landslide and forest fire effects. Ghidorah's demolition of a shrine gate demonstrates creative shot composition, reminiscent of eighteenth-century traditional Japanese woodblock prints. Godzilla makes another memorable entrance, surfacing to chase a school of whales and then destroying an ocean liner that interrupts its meal. And in one of Tsuburaya's most imaginative moments, King Ghidorah emerges from a meteor via a spectacular, animated fireball. However, *Ghidorah* is the first Honda giant-monster film with no visible military mobiliza-

Directing Yuriko Hoshi in *Ghidorah*. Courtesy of Honda Film Inc.

tion, another possible sign of budgetary restraint. The defense minister laments that the only way to kill the beasts is the atomic bomb, a nonstarter. He leaves Japan's fate in the monsters' hands: "My state of mind . . . is to accept God's will."

King Ghidorah is an homage to *Yamata no orochi*, the eight-headed dragon of Japanese mythology. Though a man-in-suit monster, it required numerous puppeteers to operate its three heads, two tails, and wings. "It wasn't easy at all to move," Honda recalled. "It was so bulky, and not so smooth in the air . . . but the kids liked it a lot. It is probably one of our best monsters, and it has an oriental feeling, too."[13]

While Honda was making *Ghidorah*, the People's Republic of China successfully tested its first atomic bomb on October 16, 1964. It has been speculated that King Ghidorah symbolized China's nuclear threat, but Honda doubted that Shinichi Sekizawa (*Atragon* aside, an apolitical writer) had such an intent. "[*Ghidorah*] is basically *Yamata no orochi*. It is . . . an old folktale, and we wrote it as a creature from outer space. It is fine for the audience to think that way, but I do not believe it was written with such a political notion."[14]

Honda did a lot of location shooting. Rodan's emergence terrifies a group of tourists at steaming Mount Aso, Japan's largest active volcano, the same site where Kurosawa filmed Kamatari Fujiwara's attempted suicide in *The Bad Sleep Well* (*Warui yatsu hodo yoku nemuru*, 1960). Other locations included Yokohama, Gotenba, and Tokyo's Ueno Park, where Tokyoites heckle the prophetess. Some of Honda's sets again appear to have been made on a strict budget. Infant Island is even smaller than last time, and the kingdom of Selgina consists of one small room outfitted with rattan furniture and Asian statues, where the

ruling class wear Renaissance-era garb with ruff collars.

The screenplay has the usual brisk Honda-Sekizawa pacing, but it might have benefited from another polish. Early plot points are later dropped entirely: a winter heat wave, an outbreak of encephalitis, a search for flying saucers. A UFO expert returns briefly, midmovie, for a strange monologue delivered to the camera. Some scenes become repetitious—the prophetess issues warnings again and again—and others are recycled from recent films. Japan again asks Mothra for help, the Small Beauties sing another dreamy song to beckon her, inept gangsters are again foiled by falling rocks, including a big, phony boulder that Hisaya Ito impossibly *catches* before it carries him to his death. Mothra's silk is again the unlikely coup de grace.

Though Honda rarely made overt homages to Hollywood films, *Ghidorah* borrows a conceit from William Wyler's romantic comedy *Roman Holiday*, perhaps the most perennially popular foreign film in Japan since its release there in 1953. Honda's film pretends that, just as Audrey Hepburn did, a gorgeous foreign princess can hide in plain sight with only a slight change in appearance. What's more, the final scene in *Ghidorah* is something of a tribute. As her highness bids farewell to the shy policeman who thrice saved her life, Honda instructed his actors to recall the ending of Wyler's film. Unlike Hepburn and Gregory Peck, these two characters have no shared secret, no forbidden love; it's been all business between them. And yet, a hint of feeling in Wakabayashi's eyes and Natsuki's stammer gives the scene a certain charm.

Wakabayashi devoted herself admirably to playing the monotone princess, ditching her glamorous looks and royal gown for an old fisherman's jacket and cap. The actress

Honda (far right) directing the final scene of *Ghidorah, The Three-Headed Monster*, shades of *Roman Holiday*. Courtesy of Honda Film Inc.

went temporarily blind after staring at an arc light representing a Venusian spirit beckoning the princess, and she filmed the shock-therapy scenes after pulling an all-nighter on another gig; Honda allowed her to sleep on the gurney between takes. Wakabayashi had appeared in several European films in the early 1960s, and she spoke bits of Italian and German, traces of which can be briefly heard as the princess reads from a book about amnesia.

Wakabayashi later recalled how the princess's character and wardrobe came about:

Princess Salno is supposed to be the Venusians' descendent; they were destroyed by King Ghidorah 50 million years ago. I wasn't quite sure if she just noticed this inside of her, or if she was possessed, but I tried to play the charac-

ter as someone who was sleepwalking . . . I tried not to look at each person's face. [The princess] had the look of a homeless person . . . she really had a boy's style; that was actually my favorite kind of look in private. One day, I was walking around Toho Studios with jeans and a big guy's hat on, and director Honda spotted me and said, "I like that! Let's go with that." That's how we came up with that style.[15]

The 1964–65 box-office year was the biggest to date for Japanese movies. Toho, which released the top eight domestic films, was at the peak of its postwar dominance. *Ghidorah* earned ¥375 million (just over $1 million), technically more than even *King Kong vs. Godzilla* and an impressive feat in context. The only domestic films with bigger numbers were the documentary *Tokyo Olympiad* (¥1.3 billion); the comedy *Great Adventure* (Daiboken, ¥420 million), the tenth anniversary extravaganza from the megapopular Crazy Cats comic troupe; and Kurosawa's *Red Beard* (¥400 million). And so *Ghidorah's* finale, with Japanese villagers cheering as the good monsters expel Ghidorah, became the shape of things to come. Honda and Tsuburaya's once mysterious and dangerous creatures were shedding the mythology that spawned them a decade ago, and for the first time, Godzilla remains on Japanese soil. The monster was not yet a true superhero; in the infamous *kaiju* confab, Godzilla professes no sympathy for mankind. For now, it was simply protecting its turf from outside threats, a necessary if unpredictable guardian.

IV
GOOD-BYE, GODZILLA
1965–75

Monsters are tragic beings. They're not bad [willingly]. They're born too tall, too strong, too heavy; that's their tragedy. They don't attack [mankind] voluntarily, but because of their physical dimensions they cause danger and grief; therefore man defends himself against them. After several stories of this type, the public finds sympathy for the monsters.
— Ishiro Honda

He had a warm heart, and paid delicate attention to people. I cannot understand why he was always shooting Godzilla movies.
— Tatsuo Matsumura, actor

21

EAST MEETS WEST

Frankenstein Conquers the World (1965), *Invasion of Astro-Monster* (1965), *The War of the Gargantuas* (1966), *Come Marry Me* (1966)

In the mid-1960s, several Honda films competed against works by Joseph Losey, Jean-Luc Godard, and others in the International Science Fiction Film Festival in Trieste, Italy, an event founded by, among others, novelists Kingsley Amis and Umberto Eco. At home in Japan, however, recognition came from a much younger and less discerning audience.

The copious fan mail that Honda was now receiving seemed to validate Toho's business strategy. In February 1965, he reprinted several letters, all from children, in a studio newsletter.

"I really enjoyed [*Ghidorah*], especially when Godzilla laughs, holding his stomach," wrote a child from Shizuoka. "I love the monster films by Toho much more than those teen films by Nikkatsu or Daiei," wrote another from Ibaraki. A kid from Fukuoka rejoiced, "We students have long vacations during the summer and winter. And almost always, there is a monster film showing by Toho."

Honda would praise the youngsters for their "pure-hearted" imagination, but he was clearly conflicted. He expressed resignation about the genre's inexorable changes and worry that management was condescending to children.

"There are those who feel that humor should be excluded from the creative process, opposing the idea of giving humanlike characteristics to an animal . . . The original *Godzilla* is a prime example of this. The creators wrote the story from this viewpoint. However, [since then] we have continued to create monsters from a variety of perspectives.

"Looking back on *Ghidorah*, I feel that [most fans were] elementary and middle school students . . . We, however, have never once made a film . . . just for children. I am . . . concerned that we are drifting toward taking the easy route, believing a silly storyline is OK—though it might be mocked by adults—simply because the film is made for children. Kids will not tolerate nonsense."

Honda resolved to continue working with his usual seriousness. "I feel that the filmmakers, first and foremost, must be surprised and astonished. What would happen if Godzilla really appeared? What if Rodan actually hatched in today's world? "[1]

————

Somewhere high above the American Midwest, Honda surveyed the checkerboard farmland, the rivers and mountains dividing the territory below. "America is *huge*," he later wrote. "Just one state is bigger than all Japan . . . I looked down at the ground from the airplane and realized that the size of America on the map was real."

Honda made at least two trips to the United States between 1964 and 1966, and enjoyed sightseeing in New York, San Francisco, Las Vegas, and especially Washington, DC, but his main purpose was to help finalize a Hollywood deal. In 1964, United Productions of America (UPA), a small animation studio that produced the popular *Mr. Magoo* cartoons, proposed a joint project with Toho. UPA was headed by Henry G. Saperstein, the original buyer of the US rights to *Mothra vs. Godzilla*, though he had quickly flipped that film to AIP. UPA entered feature film production with the animated musical *Gay Pur-ee* (1962, featuring the voices of Judy Garland and Robert Goulet), and now it would cofinance, in short order, three Toho science fiction pictures, all directed by Honda. It was Saperstein's idea to hire Hollywood stars—albeit fading ones—to lead Honda's cast. "I would put up half the budget for territorial rights, and we would consult with them on the script," Saperstein said of the arrangement,

but UPA's involvement went much deeper and was not without friction. Though they made only three films together, Saperstein's association with Toho would last decades, and his questionable business moves would further compromise and marginalize Honda's work abroad.

The first Toho-UPA venture was announced in August 1964 with the working title *Frankenstein vs. Godzilla*. By the time the film hit Japanese cinemas the following summer, Godzilla was gone and the picture had become *Frankenstein vs. the Subterranean Monster Baragon*; it would later be released in the West as *Frankenstein Conquers the World*. Honda went to Los Angeles for meetings. Wary of on-set meddling by the Americans, he insisted that Saperstein honor the Japanese system and grant the director "the right of final decision."[2] Even so, things would not always go smoothly on this joint Japanese-US collaboration, nor on similar projects that followed. During the second half of the decade, five of Honda's nine films would have American backers. Foreign capital reduced Toho's negative costs, but large strings were attached. Despite having the "final decision," Honda would nonetheless intermittently contend with ridiculous demands, prima donna stars, and flakey Hollywood types. Though his approach was unchanged, Honda was now directing for the American market as well as for Japan. The huge country across the Pacific had helped spawn Godzilla with bombs, and now it was sustaining Toho's monsters with dollars.

————

Nick Adams was a big fish again. Back in Hollywood he'd fallen on hard times. After a promising start as a supporting player in *Rebel Without a Cause* (1955) and other films, a stint as a primetime TV star in a series he cocreated, *The Rebel* (1959–61),

Directing Nick Adams in *Frankenstein Conquers the World*. Courtesy of Honda Film Inc.

and a supporting actor Oscar nomination, his career had slipped toward low-budget genre movies. Adams was Saperstein's pick to play the leading man in *Frankenstein Conquers the World* and, arriving in Tokyo in summer 1965, he became the life of the Toho party, entertaining costars and crew members with Hollywood stories.

A constant jokester, Adams teased his director. "Adams said they called him 'Hondo' in America, not 'Honda,'" remembered Koji Kajita. "He would say, 'Honda, not *honto*' ["Honda, not really"], or 'Hondo, Hondo, he and I are *tomodachi* [friends].' He was a very nice guy." Honda teased back, calling the actor "skeleton Nick" because Adams was always dieting.

Adams nicknamed himself "Horny Nick," and though his wife and kids were in Japan, he was openly infatuated with leading lady Kumi Mizuno. "He was kind of a headstrong guy, who'd come at you straight on," Mizuno said. "He called me every single night. I would tell him, 'But you have such a nice wife.' I [had] to get out of that situation, but working with him was fun." Adams would recall his Japan adventures fondly in an article titled "A Kind Word for Those Monster Movies," which he wrote for a Los Angeles newspaper. Adams was

pleased when he learned, "[T]he film was going to be directed by Ishiro Honda and the special-effects wizard was to be Eiji Tsuburaya. These two geniuses have earned the well-deserved title of the world's greatest directors of science fiction films."[3]

Honda remembered Adams being "completely passionate about movies" and "the type of guy who would come up with ideas on his own, one after another." Adams was Honda's guinea pig, the first foreign actor to speak his lines in English while his costars spoke Japanese. Adams's dialogue would later be rerecorded by a Japanese actor for the domestic release, while the others would be dubbed into English for the US cut. This method could have proved a confusing disaster—the actors often didn't understand each other at all—but with Adams's enthusiasm and the help of interpreters, Honda pulled it off. The dual-language script would become his standard system for directing multinational casts.

"When the actor is speaking in English, I had them show emotion and feeling fully in English. Language and words are such that even if you do not understand what the other is saying, if they act and truly emote feelings, [they can understand one another]. Especially in scenes with Kumi Mizuno-*kun*. She understood English just a little, but they acted with full emotions, one in English and the other in Japanese . . . You can . . . see how their eyes glimmer when they interact.

"If you have them perform over and over during the filming, the movements of the human emotions start feeling very natural. They all start to naturally come out . . . There are rhythms to the performances of actors."[4]

————

The idea for *Frankenstein vs. Godzilla* apparently came not from inside Toho, but from Saperstein's camp. Television writer Jerry Sohl and Saperstein associate Reuben Bercovitch would receive credit for a synopsis and story, respectively, though it is unclear how much of their work remained in the final cut. The first draft screenplay by Takeshi Kimura, dated July 3, 1964, began much the same as the film that Honda would eventually make, with the Nazis sending the beating, undying heart of Frankenstein's monster to Imperial Japan during the last days of the Third Reich. The heart is irradiated by the Hiroshima blast and regenerates into a boy, who grows into a giant-sized Frankenstein monster. The military attempts to fix things by freeing Godzilla from an iceberg and luring it to Japan to fight Frankenstein. Kimura's script introduced three main characters: Dr. James Bowen, his assistant Sueko, and a second scientist, Dr. Kawaji; the trio would be played by Adams, Kumi Mizuno, and Tadao Takashima in the film that was eventually made. However, in a subsequent draft dated March 1965, Godzilla was replaced by Baragon, a floppy-eared reptile that can tunnel underground. By the final draft, dated May 10, 1965, the characters had developed compassion for Frankenstein, portrayed as less a monster than a gigantic man-child.

Released on August 8, 1965, just two days after the twentieth anniversary of Hiroshima, *Frankenstein Conquers the World* contains Honda's only reenactment of the nuclear attack on Japan, eerily rendered with a siren, a long shot of the Enola Gay flying above, and an impressionistic display of smoke and fire by Eiji Tsuburaya. Images of the famous Atomic Bomb Dome, a structure located at ground zero that survived the blast, are featured prominently. And Honda again alludes strongly to Japan's wartime fascist militarism, when a doctor

(Takashi Shimura in a brief cameo) says the Nazis have sent Frankenstein's immortal heart to help Japan create a race of unkillable supersoldiers.

Numerous intriguing ideas are introduced. The 1945 prologue begins with a dialogueless scene in a German laboratory; only the clicking of Nazi boot heels and the smashing of test tubes are audible. Later, there are homages to James Whale's *Frankenstein* (1931) and shadows on walls recalling F. W. Murnau's *Nosferatu* (1922). The story begins fifteen years after the war, in Hiroshima—where ninety thousand people still suffered from radiation-related illness, and about fifty were dying annually from the bomb's lingering effects.[5] The compassionate Dr. Bowen (Adams) is discouraged by his inability to help the victims, and he contemplates abandoning his work. Meanwhile, Bowen and his assistant Sueko openly develop a relationship, teaching one another American and Japanese customs. This appears to be one of the first romances between a *gaijin* (foreigner) and an *onna* (woman) depicted in a Japanese film, a taboo pairing that had been scandalized in Japanese literature. Honda shows a modern, equable couple, far different from the overbearing Yank and his "kimona girl" [*sic*] in Samuel Fuller's *House of Bamboo*. The relationship between man and monster is also deeper than in any previous Honda picture, as Bowen's team adopts the homeless Frankenstein youth. Sueko affectionately calls the creature *boya* (boy) and develops maternal feelings for him, but the scientists struggle to decide whether he is human, animal, a research specimen, or a dangerous predator. They could determine whether or not he's the Frankenstein monster by amputating a limb to see if it regenerates, but would it be right?

Regrettably, these premises are not fully

explored. Less than halfway through, the now fugitive Frankenstein appears at the second-story window of Sueko's apartment, a nice special effect. He grunts an apparent plea for help and then wanders away, pitiable and hopeless. Hereon, the film falls back on formulaic army deployments, evacuations, and a monster wrestling match for the finale. Frankenstein spends long stretches hiding in the forests and being blamed for deadly attacks committed by the carnivorous Baragon. The pace slows during talky meetings where everyone usually sits around a table. Bowen maintains Frankenstein's innocence but, puzzlingly, doesn't protest much when the military tries to exterminate the creature. Despite being hunted, Honda's tragic figure holds onto humanity: even after Kawaji breaks rank and attempts to harvest Frankenstein's heart for research, the monster saves the scientist's life.

The latter scene includes one of many impressive visuals. As Bowen and Sueko drive through the mountains, Frankenstein emerges from the forest, and huge legs and feet straddle the road, a startling sight; and the creature sets down Kawaji's limp body. Urban destruction is deemphasized in favor of lush forest sets and an enormous fire encircling Mount Fuji, a bold display of color and light. But much of Tsuburaya's contribution is the long, repetitive monster fighting, again filmed from angles that create little illusion of size; some scenes are closer to American B movies such as *The Amazing Colossal Man* or *The Crawling Hand* than to Tsuburaya's best work, and the puppets of livestock eaten by Baragon are especially poor. Honda would later regret that he "felt the limits of special effects," because the Frankenstein monster is too obviously a man standing in a miniature set, whereas Godzilla is more accept-

able because it is "an artificial thing in an artificial place."[6] This problem is apparent when Frankenstein startles revelers aboard a party boat on Lake Biwa, recalling a similar scene in *Godzilla*. The boat is a large, well-detailed miniature, but it's suddenly less convincing when Frankenstein wades into the frame.

Honda was honored to pay tribute to Whale's iconic *Frankenstein* and to Boris Karloff's tragic monster, and he was pleased to learn that Adams had appeared with Karloff earlier that year in the horror film *Die Monster Die!* (1965). First-time actor Koji Furuhata, a student, won the role of Frankenstein through open auditions. Furuhata wore green contact lenses for a Caucasian look, was outfitted with a flat-head prosthetic and exaggerated brow resembling Karloff's creature, and wore impossibly large shirts and loincloths.

Furuhata gives the monster surprising emotional range. In the most tensely charged scene, the adolescent Frankenstein grabs Sueko roughly and appears ready to assault her; but it turns out he is attracted to a shiny necklace, not the girl. Frankenstein exhibits innocent, childlike behavior, from violent tantrums (rock music and television are particular peeves) to fear, sadness, and guileless wonder. He is not unlike a human Godzilla, another tragic spawn of man's scientific hubris. Honda would have liked to examine Frankenstein's affliction and revisit the science-gone-wrong theme more deeply, but the studio's focus on monsters precluded it. "The story completely changes in the middle," he recalled. "Suddenly, [Baragon] appears in an oil field and then it leads to a battle. How convenient can you get?"[7]

The final scenes of *Frankenstein Conquers the World* were the subject of confusion among genre enthusiasts for many

The Frankenstein monster (Koji Furuhata) threatens Sueko (Kumi Mizuno) in *Frankenstein Conquers the World.* © Toho Co., Ltd.

years. The film ends after Frankenstein kills Baragon at the foot of Mount Fuji and then is killed himself via a deus ex machina, sinking into a fissure that spontaneously opens below. However, an alternative ending was filmed at Saperstein's request exclusively for the overseas version. In this scenario, after defeating Baragon, Frankenstein is then coaxed into another fight with a giant octopus that suddenly appears nearby; the pair tumble into a lake and disappear underwater, and the film ends. Not only was Saperstein's idea nonsensical (what's an octopus doing on dry land?), but it forced Honda and Tsuburaya, after wrapping production and postproduction on schedule for the Japanese release, to quickly build a new set, create the octopus (a large, awkward prop with wire-controlled tentacles), reassemble cast and crew, and shoot the scene. Adding insult to inconvenience, Saperstein ultimately changed his mind. "The [octopus] wasn't that good, so we cut it out," he later recalled.

Honda remembered, "There was never any official plan to ever utilize the sequence [in Japan], but an alternative print with that ending was accidentally aired on television, surprising many Japanese fans."[8] The infamous octopus footage eventually resurfaced and was screened at a Japanese fan convention in 1982, and was later released as bonus material on home video.

Honda's comments about the episode were typically diplomatic. "We added [the scene] because of an order from the American side. Putting the octopus in a lake in the mountains was very awkward."[9] Though Saperstein didn't change the ending, he nevertheless reedited the film for US release using alternate takes and unused footage from several scenes. Saperstein's American version shows Frankenstein throwing a police car and portrays the creature as somewhat more violent.

Nick Adams is genuinely likeable onscreen, and the three main scientists have a nice rapport. Toho's publicity corps touted this as the first science fiction film coproduced by Japan and the United States, and prominently advertised "Hollywood star Nick Adams" in the lead role. The film earned ¥93 million (about $258,000), not enough to dent the box-office charts. Still, in September 1965 Tomoyuki Tanaka flew to Los Angeles for more meetings with

Off-camera moment with Nick Adams on location near Mount Fuji. Courtesy of Honda Film Inc.

Saperstein, and a sequel was announced in December, tentatively titled *The Franken-stein Brothers* (*Frankenstein no kyodai*).

———

"When they made Godzilla do that '*shie*' thing," Ryuji Honda said, "I knew how pissed my father was. He didn't say a word, but he was beyond angry."

Godzilla's penchant for comedy reached a new level in Honda's next effort, *Invasion of Astro-Monster* (1965), in which Godzilla celebrates a victory by jumping up and down while flexing its arms and legs. This silly dance was borrowed from the award-winning manga *Osomatsu-kun*, wherein it was performed by a bucktoothed character who shouted, "*Shie!*" (or "shee-eh"). The postwar manga boom was under way, and the *shie* was briefly a pop-culture phe-nomenon, with people everywhere striking the pose. One day, a Toho exec approached Eiji Tsuburaya and said Godzilla should do it, too. "Tsuburaya-*san* . . . came back and asked, 'Hey guys, do you know about this *shie* thing?'" remembered Teruyoshi Nakano, assistant effects director. Tsubu-raya liked the stunt so much, he filmed Godzilla repeating it several times. "It was very familiar, and fun to see it on the screen," Nakano said. "But the audience's opinion was divided."

The *shie* was yet another turning point in Honda's relationship with Godzilla, one that would eventually lead Honda to put some distance between himself and his monster ego. "My father found it humili-ating," Ryuji Honda said. "I am sure he was telling himself, 'We did not create Godzilla for that. It is not right.'"

Astro-Monster was Toho's second coventure with Henry Saperstein and UPA, who again contracted Nick Adams to star. Shinichi Sekizawa's fast-paced script com-bines the giant-monster and alien-invasion

Invasion of Astro-Monster: Honda with Nick Adams (left) and Akira Takarada (right) on the Planet X control room set. Courtesy of Honda Film Inc.

genres, and revisits a number of ideas from Honda's previous films. Once again, Tokyo is a key partner in the space race, with buddy astronauts Glenn (Adams) and Fuji (Akira Takarada), representing America and Japan, leading the way. Duplicitous aliens from Planet X, newly discovered in our solar system, use their advanced technology to control Godzilla, Rodan, and King Ghidorah in a bid to conquer Earth and its precious water supply, a plot that would be rehashed, with variations, in numerous movies and television shows produced by Toho and others. The story has a simple, naïve logic to it; the aliens could simply attack, but first they concoct an elaborate ruse—pretending to offer Earth a cancer cure in exchange for the mon-sters—because that's what bad guys do. They could simply bump off nerdy inventor Tetsuo (Akira Kubo, playing against type), but instead they set up a sham corporation to keep his Lady Guard buzzer—which emits a sound that's deadly to the aliens—off the market. The climax has the heroes disabling the aliens' monster controller, allowing Godzilla and Rodan to expel Ghidorah from Earth in much the same way as they did before, though without Mothra's help.

The third-act monster rampage noticeably includes shots recycled from *Rodan* and *Ghidorah*. Honda lamented the increased use of stock footage, or "dupes," from previous films to pad the special-effects sequences. "The more dupes we used, the cheaper we could produce the effects parts," Honda later remembered. "Then [fans] started saying, 'Something's funny, it isn't new' . . . There was criticism that special-effects movies were no good anymore; a good movie could not be made this way. That period is a sad part of our history."[10]

Invasion of Astro-Monster appears to be a direct sequel to *Ghidorah*, though it takes place sometime in the future, when the Japanese military possesses state-of-the-art weapons, such as the A Cycle Light Ray cannon, and space travel is commonplace.[11] The aliens rule their civilization by computer-controlled fascism, and the women are subservient clones or replicants, all of them identical to alien temptress Namikawa (Kumi Mizuno). Scientists had successfully cloned frogs and fish in the 1950s and 1960s, and Honda offered the X-*seijin* (Planet X people) as another warning about the misappropriation of science; he had wanted to make his point by having astronaut Adams find hundreds of identical Namikawas on Planet X, but settled for only two because of budget limits. "The trick was much smaller and cheaper than we hoped," Honda said.[12]

The production design possesses a charming artificiality. Unlike the glorious space vistas of *Battle in Outer Space*, the views of the P-1 rocket flying through the cosmos, with Earth in the rear-view mirror, are attractive if obvious models; and the simple rockets and flying saucers are throwbacks to sci-fi films from decades earlier. There is little location footage, but a flying saucer's landing at beautiful Lake Myojin in the Japan Alps is nonetheless stunning. Honda's crew held a "weather festival" the night before filming, praying for clear skies, and they were rewarded. The resulting composition of the actors and saucer on the beach are finely achieved with Eiji Tsuburaya's Oxberry optical printer.

The X-*seijin* are more human-looking than Honda's previous aliens; and in their body-hugging vinyl uniforms and wraparound sunglasses, the males are coolly menacing. Honda took particular interest in the appearance of Namikawa, who poses as a Japanese femme fatale but is actually a femalien in a mop-top, nylon wig. Honda helped design Namikawa's alien makeup, and he instructed actress Kumi Mizuno to "fall in love with [Adams] like a human being, not as an alien," the actress recalled.

The relationship between Adams and Mizuno has more heat here than in *Frankenstein Conquers the World*. In one scene, the camera catches the couple just after a kiss; in another, Glenn confides that he and Namikawa spent a night together at an inn. Their final scene, in which Glenn implores Namikawa to defect from Planet X and help stop an interplanetary war, has the intense close-ups and back-and-forth cuts that were the stock-in-trade of old Hollywood. Adams channels Bogey, even referencing the "hill of beans" speech from *Casablanca* (1942).

Adams is less a leading man in *Astro-Monster* than an anchor of Honda's ensemble, which also includes the eccentric

Yoshio Tsuchiya as the despot of Planet X. Tsuchiya typically came with creative suggestions; he improvised the Controller's quirky hand gestures and, at Honda's request, combined French, German, and Ryunosuke Akutagawa's *Kappa* language to devise the aliens' odd dialect, which he mutters in a few scenes.[13] Newcomer Keiko Sawai, who had a bit part in Honda's Frankenstein film, is the inventor's fiancée. Though Sawai might appear demure compared to Western actresses of the day, the character was forthright for a young Japanese woman, speaking her mind to elders and pushing back against her domineering older brother and her wimpy beau. Sawai recalled, "From the start I was told by director Honda, 'You are a gentle and quiet type, but your character is propping up a weak guy and giving him a kick in the butt, so you must be assertive.'"[14] She would later star in Honda's *Come Marry Me*.

Nick Adams would appear in a third Toho film, a minor spy thriller costarring his friends Tsuchiya and Mizuno, and directed by Senkichi Taniguchi. But of all the friends he made, it was Honda that Adams admired most, and Koji Kajita believed the brash actor had become "emotionally attached" to the quiet director. The Hondas invited Adams to their home for dinner several times, and they hosted a farewell party when he returned to the United States. They had become so close that Adams offered to host Honda's son Ryuji in a postcollege homestay program. But on February 6, 1968, Adams, aged thirty-six, was found dead at his Los Angeles home of an apparent suicide.

The domestic audience for Japanese films continued to decline, while American films dominated the box office and TV viewership grew. The top-grossing films overall for 1965–66, according to *Kinema Junpo*, were *Thunderball* (¥1 billion) and *Mary Poppins* (¥428 million). Released December 19, 1965, *Invasion of Astro-Monster* was the year's no. 10 domestic release, earning ¥210 million (about $580,000) against a budget of ¥132 million. It would be the last Honda-Tsuburaya genre picture to crack the yearly top ten.

————————

In spring 1964, Honda paid a rare social visit to Eiji Tsuburaya on the Hawaiian island of Kauai. Tsuburaya was on location, directing the effects for a plane crash scene in Frank Sinatra's war drama *None But the Brave* (1965). A joint project of Sinatra's production company with Toho and Toei studios, the film featured several Toho actors playing Japanese soldiers, including Tatsuya Mihashi (*The Human Vapor*) and Kenji Sahara. Tsuburaya confided to Honda that he was having trouble finding a leading man for his company's first television show, tentatively titled *Unbalance*. Honda convinced a skeptical Sahara to take the role of Jun Manjome, leader of a team of paranormal investigators tracking giant monsters. The show debuted in January 1966 with the new title *Ultra Q*, and Sahara became a bigger star on TV than he'd ever been in film.

Tsuburaya Productions' entry into television was a massive success. *Ultra Q* was watched by 30 percent of television-owning households; the follow-up series *Ultraman* commanded a 40 percent viewership in 1967.[15] Because children could now watch monsters at home on a weekly basis, there was less incentive to beg their parents to take them to the cinema for the occasional feature. Thus, Tsuburaya Productions' good fortune in TV was, in effect, diverting box-office money away from Toho's genre films.

At the same time, Tsuburaya was creating new and exciting job opportunities in the growing field of TV, and a number of Toho staffers began moving from big screen to small.

Honda remained focused on film, but he did not discourage others from making the transition, not even trusted colleagues. After directing three episodes of *Ultra Q* for Tsuburaya, Koji Kajita was offered a job as a producer in Toho's emerging television department. "I consulted with director Honda for advice," Kajita recalled. "He said, 'The future will be in TV, so do the best you can.'" Kajita would serve as Honda's chief assistant once more, on *The War of the Gargantuas*, before departing.

Clearly Honda understood that television was supplanting film, for he even arranged for his son to launch his professional life in the new medium. "I had told my father I'd take it easy for six months after finishing college. But one day, when both my father and I were home, we got a phone call from old man Tsuburaya. 'Why don't you come to the [Tsuburaya Productions] studio today?' he said. My father was never around when I answered the phone, but I noticed he was behind me, smiling. Obviously something was fishy . . . At the studio, there was a name plaque that said, Third Assistant Director: Ryuji Honda, and everybody was waiting for my arrival. I felt, 'I guess I am also destined for this business.'" Ryuji began his long career in television production on the staff of Tsuburaya's *Monster Booska* (*Kaiju Booska*, 1966–67), a comedy about a friendly, teddy bear-like monster.

At the end of 1965, Toho informed Honda that his annual director's contract would not be renewed. With box-office numbers falling, the studio began discontinuing certain guaranteed jobs and cutting costs, a process that would extend into the next decade as hundreds of directors, actors, and other personnel were gradually removed from the payroll.

Honda was taken aback. "Iwao Mori told me, 'From now on, you have to talk to Tomoyuki Tanaka for each assignment.' In other words, Toho didn't need my films anymore."[16] As things turned out, Honda would continue working for Toho, but strictly on a project-by-project basis.

He remained the studio's primary director of science fiction films but, for a time, not those starring Godzilla. Toho briefly put the Godzilla franchise in the hands of skillful action director Jun Fukuda, whose *Godzilla vs. the Sea Monster* (1966) and *Son of Godzilla* (1967) were markedly different from Honda's films in style and tone. Fukuda had no qualms about having Godzilla play volley-boulder with a giant shrimp, or parenting a baby Godzilla. It remains unclear, however, whether Honda explicitly declined these projects or if the studio sensed Honda's frustration and tapped Fukuda instead.

Years later, Honda recalled, "Frankly, there is a part of me that felt I [had] made too many of these films. There were certain projects I would not have wanted to make. *Son of Godzilla* is something that I probably would have not been able to do. As you take a look back at my past works, you can see that I [resisted] personifying and giving humanlike characteristics to the monsters . . . Those are things I truly had a difficult time making and filming."[17]

I remember seeing a film called *The Gargantuas* [sic] . . . At the end of it, the good gargantuan [sic] had to sacrifice

himself to defeat the bad gargantuan and rid the world of evil.
— Brad Pitt[18]

As Koji Kajita prepared to leave the fold, a fiery young understudy was groomed as his replacement. Seiji Tani took tremendous pride in serving as Honda's chief assistant in the challenging times of the late 1960s, regarding Honda not only as a teacher but a pillar of strength. Decades later he recalled, mincing no words, how that strength was repeatedly tested on *The War of the Gargantuas*, a film in which Honda contended not only with the demands of Hollywood coproducers but also, for the first time, with the on-set friction created by a Hollywood attitude.

"Honda-*san* had to hold back and bear so much during that one. [Russ Tamblyn] was such an asshole," Tani said. "He was exactly like that character he played [in *West Side Story*]. Like a hoodlum turned actor. Raw, very selfish, rebellious, and disobedient. The director told him to come and walk from this side to the other, not giving any specific acting instructions, just explaining the scene. And [Tamblyn] said that he usually does the exact opposite of what the director says. What a punk. He pissed me off."

The third and final Toho-UPA collaboration would prove the most difficult. Nick Adams was gone, and Saperstein replaced him with another star on a downward trajectory. Tamblyn, a former child actor turned MGM contract star, and a onetime Academy Award nominee, had peaked in *West Side Story* (1961) as singing-and-dancing gang leader Riff, but now he was slumming through TV guest spots and small films. He reportedly showed little enthusiasm for the project and made no friends with his above-it-all attitude.

From left to right, Russ Tamblyn, Kenji Sahara, Kumi Mizuno, and Honda, in *War of the Gargantuas*. Courtesy of Honda Film Inc.

"Even [Honda] looked pissed," Tani continued. "On top of that, [Tamblyn's] acting sucked. Afterwards, we complained, 'Why the hell did they bring over a guy like that?'"

Saperstein, the man responsible, concurred. "Nick Adams . . . was a consummate pro and blended in very easily," he said. "Tamblyn was a royal pain in the ass."[19]

The War of the Gargantuas certainly helped to stereotype Japanese monster movies as campy, cult cinema. It's known for a nightclub scene in which an American chanteuse warbles an ear-splitting, faux Burt Bacharach number with the refrain "the words get stuck in my throat," and then a monster grabs her off the stage. Tamblyn sleepwalks through his scenes, mumbling jokes about bad LSD trips and toy poodles, dialogue he reportedly improvised. "There was one interpreter that spoke English, and he interpreted between myself and [Honda], and myself and the actors," Tamblyn later recalled. "Lucky for me, they didn't know what I was saying half the time

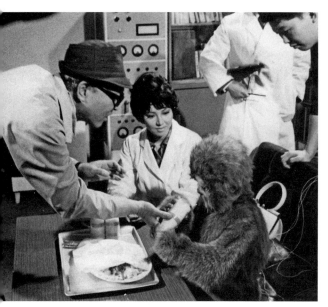

Directing the baby gargantua and Kumi Mizuno in *War of the Gargantuas*. Courtesy of Honda Film Inc.

so I changed all my lines. My lines were so bad in the original script, and I changed them all."[20]

Originally announced as *The Franken-stein Brothers* and rebranded *The Two Frankensteins*, *Frankenstein vs. Franken-stein*, *Frankenstein's Decisive Battle*, and *Frankenstein's Fight* during the scriptwriting process, the film was eventually released in Japan as *Frankenstein's Monsters: Sanda vs. Gailah*. Though originally intended as a sequel to *Frankenstein Conquers the World*, continuity between the films is somewhat fuzzy. Tamblyn plays Dr. Paul Stewart, a "Frankenstein expert" who has raised one such creature in captivity; in a flashback scene, the creature looks not like the previous film's young Frankenstein, but like a kid in a teddy bear suit. Nevertheless, Stewart says, "The Frankenstein we raised . . . died at Mount Fuji," seemingly implying that it's the same creature studied by Nick Adams's character. Kumi Mizuno reprises the role of the professor's assistant, now named

Akemi, while Kenji Sahara is Dr. Mamiya, second-fiddle scientist.

The film opens with a fishing boat under attack by a giant octopus (the prop from the unused alternate *Frankenstein Conquers the World* ending), but suddenly the octopus is ambushed by a second creature, a hideous, green, hairy, scaly giant, which then feasts on the fishermen. From there, the plot somewhat resembles the previous film. The creature's rampage culminates in a horrific attack on an airport, where it gruesomely devours an office lady, then spits out her clothing like sunflower seed shells, the first Toho monster to graphically eat humans. The press believes Dr. Stewart's Franken-stein is the culprit, but the scientists insist the creature is gentle natured. It turns out there are two monsters: the violent, green "sea Frankenstein," called Gailah, and a larger, nicer, brown "mountain Frankenstein," or Sanda. (In an early script draft, Gailah was gray and Sanda white; it is not known why the monsters' colors were changed.) Despite their obvious dif-ferences, everyone still has trouble telling the monsters apart—even Akemi, who is almost killed because of it. The story is very loosely inspired by the tale "Umihiko and Yamahiko" (The Sea Boy and the Mountain Boy) from the *Kojiki*, a collection of ancient Japanese myths.

Kitschy pop song and Tamblyn's detach-ment aside, *Gargantuas* is a viscerally enjoyable monster movie. Screenwriter Takeshi Kimura starkly contrasts good and evil and creates a simple, compelling reason for the creatures to fight. Sanda has no quarrel with humanity, and its bond with surrogate mother Akemi runs deep: when she falls off a cliff, Sanda is there to rescue her, suffering a broken leg in the act, a rare and touching moment between mon-ster and human. After discovering that its sibling dines on civilians, Sanda becomes outraged and the third-act battle begins. Sanda is stronger, but its hobbling injury gives the swifter, meaner Gailah the advantage. Facial casts were used in creating the monster suits, and Haruo Nakajima gives an expressive performance as the slimy Gailah; the body-conforming costumes enabled Nakajima to run at a full clip, and the monster's distinctive roar is chilling.

The monsters are roughly half as tall as Godzilla; and because they are smaller, the miniature sets are larger and more detailed, which pleased Honda. "Once the filming was done, we would watch the rushes along with the director," remembered special-effects art director Yasuyuki Inoue. "Afterwards, Honda-*san* grabbed my shoulders and expressed how content he was. Back then, the art department had about 32 people, but at that time we were down to about 14 [because of cost-cutting moves] . . . I guess Honda-*san* was totally shocked."

Accommodations to the American side increased. An undated English-language script, bearing the imprint of both Toho and Benedict Productions (Saperstein's banner for overseas distribution), indicates that Honda and his crew shot at least nine scenes in two different ways, once for the domestic release and again for a separate American edit. Some of these "favor cuts," as the Japanese crew called them, introduced Tamblyn earlier, to more clearly frame him as the star in the US edit. But the script also shows that Saperstein wanted various scenes, such as those involving press conferences, to be shorter in his version. "We would edit the films and make such additions or deletions as we felt would make for a better progression," Saperstein later said.[21]

Playing the nearly devoured cabaret singer is Kipp Hamilton, a onetime Fox contract actress who'd had guest-starring roles on many popular TV series, including *Perry Mason*, *Rawhide*, and *Bewitched*; this would be her last film appearance. According to certain sources, Saperstein insisted on the unnecessarily long nightclub number, and on casting Hamilton because, as Tamblyn recalled, she was "the girlfriend of [Saperstein]."

But it was Tamblyn who tested Honda's patience most. At one point, the production went on location to Mount Ichinokura-dake in Niigata Prefecture, in a treacherous mountain range where climbers often perished, to shoot Tamblyn and his team hiking in search of Sanda and discovering giant footprints in the snow. During a break, Tamblyn wandered off by himself, scaling alongside a cliff in an area prone to rockslides. Honda's crew pleaded with Tamblyn to descend, but he refused, even when it was time to resume work. "I'm sure [Honda] was furious, but he didn't have time to get angry," Tani said. "It was a great learning experience for me, watching from the sidelines. It showed me how a director should be."

Tamblyn didn't socialize; when work was done, he'd go back to his suite at the Imperial Hotel, and tension eventually developed on set between the actors. Tamblyn would later say he had "learned to love" the film, though he was embarrassed by it at the time.

"I never thought anybody was going to see it," Tamblyn said. "I was offered money . . . my wife at that time said, 'I've always wanted to go to Japan.' So I said, 'All right, let's go . . . Unfortunately for me . . . when the movie was released they ran it on [a Los Angeles TV station] every single night . . . [I thought] that's it, I'll never work again." Tamblyn did, however, pay Honda a compliment of sorts: "I liked working with

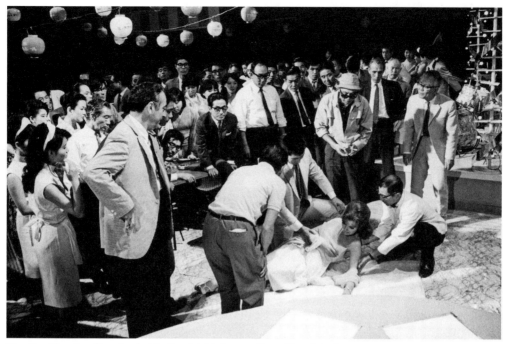

Directing Kipp Hamilton (center) in the nightclub scene from *War of the Gargantuas*. US coproducer Henry G. Saperstein (far left) looks on. Courtesy of Honda Film Inc.

him because he didn't give me too much direction. The best directors I worked with gave me very little direction."

In contrast to Tamblyn, Kenji Sahara was grateful for his first sizeable role in a Honda film since *Mothra vs. Godzilla*. Sahara regarded the part of Dr. Mamiya as a "prize" for having, at Honda's urging, taken the leap to television in *Ultra Q*. Sahara said *The War of the Gargantuas* made him nostalgic for Toho's golden days, though he now realized that TV, not film, was where "everyone had a passion for creating something new."[22]

Screenwriter Kimura was now using the pseudonym Kaoru Mabuchi because of, some sources indicate, disillusionment with his work. It's true that, other than allusions to the dangers of cloning, *War of the Gargantuas* lacks the interesting themes of earlier Honda-Kimura efforts. It feels padded during a long military deploy-

ment, and the contrived ending, with the monsters buried by a sea volcano, recalls both *Rodan* and *Frankenstein Conquers the World*. Even so, the film has a strong Honda feel, with haunting Ifukube themes, beautiful scenery, and Mizuno's memorable rendition of the folk song *Furusato* during a mountain hike.

————

The War of the Gargantuas was made quickly. Kimura's third and final draft screenplay was dated April 23, 1966; Honda shot the dramatic footage from May 9 to June 4; Tsuburaya's crew finished the effects in mid-July; and Ifukube's score was recorded July 22. The film was released across Japan a little over a week later, on July 31, 1966. Toho marketed the film to children via numerous television shows, including a "Toho Kaiju Festival" with appearances by Tomoyuki Tanaka, Tsuburaya, and Honda and a reenactment of the fight between Sanda and Gailah, broadcast live on *Yomiuri Children's News*.[23]

It would be four years before Saperstein released his American cut. Sometime during preproduction, Saperstein and UPA decided that the US version would omit all references to *Frankenstein Conquers the World*, calling the creatures Green Gargantua and Brown Gargantua instead. In addition to having Honda shoot scenes twice, UPA required Toho to deliver negatives and prints of outtakes and other footage from several scenes, plus music and sound elements. The biggest demand was for "all camera angle outtakes and trims of Kipp Hamilton" and of the monster grabbing her. Little of this material was apparently used; Saperstein's cut differs from Honda's in numerous ways, including the partial replacement of Ifukube's score with library music, but overall the two versions are substantially similar.[24]

Saperstein had partnered with American International Pictures to release *Frankenstein Conquers the World* to US theaters in the summer of 1966. But for reasons that remain unclear, Saperstein failed to obtain a theatrical distribution deal for both *Invasion of Astro-Monster*, which was retitled *Monster Zero*, and *War of the Gargantuas* for four years. UPA finally released both titles through a tiny distributor in summer 1970, when they played on a double bill and had a profitable run in drive-in theaters and matinees. By this time, Nick Adams was dead, thus his name was excluded from posters and trailers; Tamblyn's star had fallen further in the interim. Saperstein then sold both films into heavy syndication to independent US TV stations during the 1970s, and they became cult classics. *Gargantuas* has been cited as an influence by Brad Pitt and Quentin Tarantino.

Yuzo Kayama was one of the biggest celebrities in 1960s Japan, with a string of megapopular films and a parallel career as a top recording artist. From 1961 to 1971 Kayama starred in Toho's *Young Guy* film series, escapist fantasies filmed in far-off locations such as Hawaii or New Zealand, where he excelled at skiing, sailing, judo, and other diversions. He was handsome, well dressed, and prone to breaking into song, while ladies swooned. Culturally equivalent to the Elvis Presley films, the *Young Guy* series was a touchstone for working-class young adults, who watched Kayama live the carefree life they only dreamed about.

Honda never directed a *Young Guy* movie, but he came close with *Come Marry Me*, a romantic dramedy starring Kayama that was made quickly and released on October 20, 1966—less than three months after *Gargantuas*—and closer to the director's 1950s films than his recent output. The story revisits old dilemmas of following traditions versus following one's heart and old questions of how class and social standing help or hinder one's prospects for happiness. Familiar archetypes return; the love triangle, arranged marriage, funny father (in this case, grandfather), parental meddling, and the storybook ending all make one final bow before Honda's camera.

Kayama plays Tamotsu, the playboy scion of a shipbuilding magnate. He designs luxury boats for a living and relaxes by singing and strumming a guitar on his yacht.[25] In a meet-cute involving a broken-down convertible, Tamotsu meets lovely, tomboyish Masako (Keiko Sawai of *Invasion of Astro-Monster*), a poor waitress from an old, ramshackle neighborhood of Tokyo. She is resentful of the rich and suspicious of Tamotsu at first; she's also attracted to quirky cab driver Noro (Toshio

Come Marry Me: with Yuzo Kayama (left) and Keiko Sawai (right). © Toho Co., Ltd.

Kurosawa). Aided by his scheming little sister (Yoko Naito), Tamotsu woos Masako even as his disapproving parents push him to marry a business associate's daughter, whose nose job signifies fakeness, contrasted with the pure-hearted Masako. As the story climaxes, Tamotsu and Noro fight for the girl, a comical nonbrawl on the beach set to spaghetti-Western music. Kayama wins easily, but Masako chooses the working-class cabbie. Jilted Tamotsu, a nice guy through and through, sails away, strumming and singing.

Come Marry Me is a tale of two Tokyos. Tamotsu's family lives in Yamanote, the high city of sprawling, Western-style houses. They have servants and a grand piano. Masako helps support her mother and younger siblings in a wooden row house in Shitamachi, the low city. She passes a smoky factory on her way to work and prefers to spend her hard-earned money on a bowl of noodles than a high-priced cup of coffee, a luxury item in those days. Working with new cinematographer

Shinsaku Uno, Honda uses modern transportation modes to show this divide, opening with a long montage of commuter trains arriving in Tokyo followed by the stampede of salarymen and office ladies. The movie is constantly moving, shot mostly on location in the city streets, in cars, and on boats. Contrasts of working- and upper-class transit become a theme: convertible versus taxicab, lobster fishing versus yachting, the street trolley below and bullet train overhead. As in earlier Honda films, the characters are well aware of their economic station. When Masako discusses her meager salary with Tamotsu, and when Tamotsu buys Masako a much-needed pair of shoes, screenwriter Zenzo Matsuyama is echoing scenes from *Good Luck to These Two*, which he also wrote, and *An Echo Calls You*. The difference is that a decade later, American-style consumerism and money's allure are strong, thus Masako is not content with her meager means.

Toho's *Come Marry Me* ad campaign touted the faces of Kayama and sixteen-year-old Yoko Naito, who made an auspicious debut in *Red Beard* and Kihachi Okamoto's *The Sword of Doom* (*Dai-bosatsu toge*, 1966) and was being groomed for major stardom. Naito is cute, fashionable, and quick-witted; her repartee with Kayama makes for some of the best moments. Meanwhile twenty-one-year-old Sawai more or less carries the film, though she lacks the charisma of Honda's earlier leading ladies. The "Japanese Chaplin," Ichiro Arishima—the crazy ad man in *King Kong vs. Godzilla*, by now better known as Kayama's irascible dad in the *Young Guy* movies—provides comic relief as the nervous, breath mint–popping restaurant boss; and regulars Senkichi Omura and Ikio Sawamura have funny bits as a trainer and a cabbie, both obsessed with Jack LaLanne-style calisthenics, popular at the time.

This is Honda's only film with the great actor Chishu Ryu, who was famous for playing the kind of fathers and authority figures for Yasujiro Ozu that Takashi Shimura often did for Kurosawa, and occasionally for Honda. Ryu shines as Tamotsu's grandfather, who moves from abject opposition to complete support for his grandson's love for Masako, despite their caste differences. Ryu needs few words to convey humor and warmth, and is particularly charming when snooping around Masako's grubby neighborhood, investigating her background. As in *Song for a Bride* and *Seniors, Juniors, Co-workers*, Honda finds common ground between the generations, and the younger folk only push the boundaries so far; Masako finds true love within her own social strata.

Honda didn't recall the project with much fondness, saying only that it originated from "headquarters" and that the studio forced him to use a different crew and to shoot on location, making things difficult. Though he liked the script, he felt he'd gotten the job because he was a "safe bet" and could complete it cheaply. Still, this is very much a Honda film, with his trademark optimism, light comedy, and musical flourishes courtesy of jazzy composer Kenjiro Hirose, working with Honda for the third time.[26]

By now, many people could afford a television, and Masako's family has one sitting prominently in their home—a tacit recognition of why the movie business was changing. Toho had begun producing television programs in 1964, and many of the studio's film actors were now appearing regularly on the small screen; a number of Honda's fellow directors were likewise moving into the new medium, including Toshio Sugie, Seiji Maruyama, and Motoyoshi Oda.

Following *Come Marry Me*, Honda would follow suit, working briefly on *The Newlyweds* (*Shinkon san*, 1966–67), an anthology-style dramedy produced by Toho Television for the TBS network. Honda directed two episodes. "The Woman, At That Moment" (January 7, 1967) was about an ex-couple that keeps bumping into one another on a group honeymoon tour, featuring Honda regulars Yoshio Tsuchiya and Akira Takarada, and newcomer Kyoko Ai, whom Honda would cast as the villainess in *Destroy All Monsters* a year later. "Forgive Me, Please, Mom" (February 4, 1967), written by the trailblazing female screenwriter Kuniko Mukoda, starred Hiroshi Koizumi and Yumi Shirakawa as a couple who stir up family conflict when they decide to have a modest wedding, devoid of formalities.

22

MONSTERS OR BUST

King Kong Escapes (1967),
Destroy All Monsters (1968),
Latitude Zero (1969),
All Monsters Attack (1969),
Space Amoeba (1970),
Terror of Mechagodzilla (1975)

Japan's monster movie boom peaked in 1967, when all five major studios produced at least one *kaiju eiga*. Daiei released *Gamera vs. Gyaos*, its third film starring the popular giant turtle, while Toei introduced *The Magic Serpent*. Shochiku had the most ridiculous one in *The X from Outer Space*, and Nikkatsu's *Monster from a Prehistoric Planet* borrowed the plot of *Gorgo*. Toho made two: Fukuda's aforementioned *Son of Godzilla* and Honda's *King Kong Escapes* (*King Kong no gyakushu*). This coventure with Rankin/Bass Productions, the American company whose puppet-animation holiday classic *Rudolph the Red-Nosed Reindeer* (1964) was filmed in Japan, is more directly targeted at children than Honda's previous works, even while incorporating the theme of nuclear proliferation more than anything since *Godzilla*, though not in a serious way.

King Kong Escapes is loosely based on the Rankin/Bass cartoon *The King Kong Show*, which debuted on ABC-TV in September 1966 and featured the villain Dr. Who—no relation to the British science fiction hero—who aims to capture Kong for his evil schemes, and the robot Mechani-Kong; both would feature prominently in Shinichi Sekizawa's script. The story is even more outlandish than the typical Honda-Tsuburaya film, taking place in a brightly lit world influenced by manga and James Bond, with islands inhabited by prehistoric monsters, a caped supervillain, rogue nations bent on nuclear domination, and giant robots that do their bidding. The film also has something of a Western flavor, as Honda trades his typical Japanese settings for an international backdrop, spending much time at the villain's North Pole hideout and at Kong's home on fictional Mondo Island before the inevitable showdown in

King Kong Escapes: Honda (lower right) with Eiji Tsuburaya (lower left), cameraman Hajime Koizumi (upper left), and assistant director Seiji Tani (upper right). Courtesy of Honda Film Inc.

Tokyo. Rhodes Reason, a prolific American television actor, is a more dominating presence than Nick Adams or Russ Tamblyn, and there are numerous non-Japanese background players. Another significant change is the relationship between the monster and its human love interest, which Honda handles more affectionately than ever before. There is no singing or dancing; and Akira Ifukube's score is comparatively subdued, offering a love theme for Kong and the heroine but no military marches because, in another atypical change, the big countermonster offensive is called off, to avoid antagonizing Kong.

Toho and Rankin/Bass had originally planned a coproduction titled *Operation Robinson Crusoe: King Kong vs. Ebirah.* Shinichi Sekizawa turned in a script on July 13, 1966, but the project was rejected by the American side. Toho salvaged the project by subbing Godzilla for Kong, and it became Fukuda's *Godzilla vs. the Sea Monster* instead. On September 8, 1966, Toho sent Rankin/Bass a proposed synopsis for *King Kong Escapes.* The story was all new, though it shared two key themes with *Sea Monster*: exaggerated villains of unspecific nationality, secretly creating fuel for nuclear weapons, and a South Seas setting. *King Kong Escapes* was shot in spring 1967, with a break in late April to observe the

Golden Week holidays, and released July 22. It had a reported production budget of over ¥170 million (about $472,000), nearly double that of *Godzilla*; and with costs rising and box-office numbers falling, Toho was holding Honda and Tsuburaya more accountable. "The early [science fiction] films . . . did really well, so we were able to walk with our heads high," assistant director Seiji Tani remembered. But now "If the movie was not successful, the company would really come down hard on us."

Once again, foreign involvement brought friction. Arthur Rankin Jr. was concerned that Honda and crew would "make the picture sillier than it already is," and he assigned Reason to "keep an eye on things."[1] To that end, Reason asked Honda's art department to redress sets, some of which were so loaded with props it was "like a garage sale," he complained. Reason rewrote his own dialogue and worried that his makeup made him look "like a geisha girl." Reason was not impressed with the "primitive" Japanese way of filmmaking, nor with Honda, telling an interviewer three decades later:

He knew how to make those films for his audience . . . He was always very intro- spective, very thoughtful. But to me, I hate to say it, Honda-*san* was a hack. I've worked with hundreds of hack TV direc- tors, and he could fit beautifully over here doing a number of motion pictures and things. He knows his craft, but there was nothing special about Honda-*san* as a director . . . He would direct me in strange and exotic ways that only the Japanese would appreciate. Everything was exaggerated; everything was so styl- ized there was no reality in it. [Translator Henry] Okawa would say, "Honda-*san*

wants you to run through the door." And I would say, "Thank Honda-*san* for me. I just think it would be more appropriate [to do it differently]." His direction was, a little bit, from outer space . . . You can tell from the other actors in the film; everybody's bigger than life, you know, with the mugging and it gets to the point where it's ridiculous. I had to work to underplay, to bring the film some credibility.[2]

Reason said he "knew [the film] was very bad before we made it. But I couldn't turn down the trip to Japan." Honda was unfazed by his star's condescending attitude and enjoyed working with Reason regardless. Assistant director Tani remem- bered that Honda had previously handled Nick Adams just like he did the Japanese cast, but Reason was "a class above," and "[Honda] treated and used him accordingly, confidently. The way these two were treated was clearly different.

"Reason had a similar personality to [Honda]. They were the same type of people. I think Honda-*san* really liked him. However, at the same time [Reason] was also a bit brusque . . . It helped him act with great confidence and showed his skills off, so he had the director's trust."

During a preproduction visit to Japan, Rankin had seen nineteen-year-old beauty Linda Miller on the cover of a fashion magazine. Miller was a military brat living with her family in Japan, who had recently begun modeling professionally; she had no acting experience except for an English- instruction program for Japanese schools. Rankin chose her immediately; early deal memos show Miller was set to play the ingénue, nurse Susan Watson, well before any of the other actors were chosen.

From left to right, Rhodes Reason, Honda, Linda Miller, and Akira Takarada on the set of *King Kong Escapes*. Courtesy of Honda Film Inc.

Thrust before the cameras, Miller was overwhelmed. She recalled: "I had never acted before in my life. The very first scene we shot, I'm walking through the submarine and saluting people. It's one of the first scenes in the movie. All I ever did was modeling. You stand and you strike a pose; there's no movement . . . You'd think walking would be an easy thing to do, but I was so stiff . . . I remember being very embarrassed; I just couldn't get it. Honda shot it quite a few times. Honda-*san* was very much a gentleman, and he never looked at me like, 'God, that was awful.' But you could tell he was thinking, 'Well, it could have been better.' [Laughs.] I was sure that at the end of the day, I was going to be [fired]. It was so bad." But Miller settled down and, with some coaching from Reason and Takarada, delivered

a reasonably good performance as the screaming damsel in frequent distress. This was Miller's only major part; she quit acting a few years later.

————

Japan's fascination with giant robots can be largely credited to Mitsuteru Yokoyama's manga, *Tetsujin 28*, about a ten-year-old boy who uses a robot to fight evil, which debuted in 1956 and became an animated TV show in 1963. Mechani-Kong, however, was built for evil deeds; it's essentially a gorilla-shaped earth mover, a wonderfully ludicrous rationale indicative of the continuing shift toward younger, less discerning audiences. The entire story is something of a juvenile-level lark, propelled by the madman Dr. Who (Hideyo Amamoto, sporting arched eyebrows and gray frightwig), whose evil-genius schemes go comically awry again and again. Mie Hama, who'd recently played a bikini-clad Bond girl in *You Only Live Twice*, dons an assortment of Audrey Hepburn fashions as the conflicted, seductive villainess Lady Piranha. There are hints of interracial attraction between Reason and Hama, and Miller and Akira Takarada, but the scenario never demands to be taken seriously.

Though Honda was resigned to working within the genre's narrowing constraints, his idealistic young assistant resented having to "kiss ass and accommodate the kids."

"Toward the later years, the human drama aspect got thinner and thinner," said Seiji Tani. "We had this discussion. [Producer Tomoyuki] Tanaka was there with us, and I asked him directly, 'Why can't we make the same sort of films, but geared more toward adults?' Honda-*san* didn't say anything; maybe he *couldn't* say anything. [Tanaka] looked at me with a very troubled face. He replied, 'The company keeps telling us to target the kids' market, and if we don't attract the kids, we can't get enough box office.' . . . Honda-*san* had a very bitter smile on his face."

————

This would be the last time Honda and Tsuburaya directly collaborated on a giant monster film, and the results are mixed. Kong, played by Godzilla actor Haruo Nakajima, is better proportioned than in *King Kong vs. Godzilla*, but its furry brown hide (Toho's publicity materials proudly announced that Kong was made using dog fur) and plastic eyes aren't convincing. Honda and Tsuburaya reference Merian C. Cooper's original film with a well-staged fight between Kong and a kangaroo-kicking dinosaur, a tense sequence with helicopters attacking Kong, including impressive flyover point of view shots and an amusing finale atop a big model of Tokyo Tower, where Kong saves the girl and sends its doppelganger crashing to the ground, reduced to a heap of scrap metal.

In another sign of the times, Toho pressed Honda and Tsuburaya to show a bit of gore in the monster battles. Children's television programs were depicting increasingly violent content, and Tsuburaya's own programs had heroes Ultraman and Ultra Seven slicing, dicing, beheading, and otherwise mutilating their monster foes. However, Tsuburaya reportedly felt that such bloodshed was inappropriate on the big screen. "[Executive Producer Iwao Mori] pushed Tsuburaya-*san* to the edge," recalled assistant effects director Teruyoshi Nakano. "[Tsuburaya] said, 'These movies are for kids. It's nonsense. Why do you enjoy showing them blood?'" Tsuburaya met the studio halfway: When Kong snaps the dinosaur's jaw, the dying beast vomits a bubbly white foam. "They wanted it to get all bloody after getting beat by King Kong . . . But Tsuburaya-*san* said, 'I don't want to do that!' [He asked Honda], 'What do you think, Ino-*san*?' 'I absolutely agree.'"

Japanese critics by now regarded domestic science fiction films with patronizing disdain. But *Kinema Junpo* writer Chieo Yoshida had some positive words for *King Kong Escapes*, noting the "sad atmosphere" of Kong's unrequited love and the "interesting" juxtaposition of the primitive ape and its technological duplicate. "I see this as the filmmaker's [satirical] view of the modern world, where everything must be mechanized," Yoshida wrote. "But if they are aiming for kids, what's Mie Hama's irrepressible sex appeal doing here? Perhaps that's a little present for the dads who have to bring the kids to the theater?"

The four top-grossing Japanese films of 1967 were all Toho productions: Kihachi

Okamoto's war epic *Japan's Longest Day* was no. 1, and the next three consisted of two Crazy Cats comedies and the latest *Young Guy* movie. Monster-fighting heroes were thriving on television—Tsuburaya Productions' new *Ultra Seven* was another hit—but *kaiju eiga* were fading on the big screen. Of the many released that year, only two cracked *Kinema Junpo*'s top grossers: *Gamera vs. Gyaos* (no. 25) and *The X from Outer Space* (no. 27). *King Kong Escapes* did not rate a mention. Just five years after *King Kong vs. Godzilla* had been the biggest-selling *kaiju eiga* ever, Japanese moviegoers showed little interest in the great ape. With the genre's future in doubt, Toho would pull out all the stops for a grand finale.

This force of giant monsters with Godzilla at its head is truly a sight to behold.
— Newscaster

In March 1968, Toho announced a slate of thirty feature films for the coming year, and not a single monster movie was among them.[3] For this reason, Honda's next film, which was already in production, was expected to be a final bow for Godzilla and company. *Destroy All Monsters* (1968) recycles the basic premise of *Invasion of Astro-Monster*, with space aliens using Godzilla and other creatures to conquer Earth; but what the film lacks in originality it makes up for in spectacle. In the tradition of *House of Frankenstein* (1944) and *House of Dracula* (1945), which featured a gallery of Universal's monsters, this film would star eleven of Toho's *kaiju*. With its audacious and simple story, a bounty of monsters and destruction, and a memorably booming soundtrack from Akira Ifukube, *Destroy All Monsters* would become a cult favorite,

remembered as the last truly spirited entry from Toho's original cycle of giant-monster films.

Japanese antiwar sentiment surged in 1968 as thousands of students protested America's involvement in Vietnam. There were renewed calls to dissolve the US-Japan security pact, and concerns that Washington would maintain nuclear forces on Okinawa beyond the island's scheduled return to Japanese control in 1972. Averting nuclear war was now a global effort, and the United States, USSR, and other nations signed the Treaty on the Non-Proliferation of Nuclear Weapons (Japan would become a signatory in 1970). Against this backdrop, *Destroy All Monsters* looks like Honda's greatest antiwar allegory, with space invaders deploying Godzilla, Rodan, and the rest against the capitals of all the then-current nuclear weapons states: Paris, London, Beijing, and Moscow—with one exception. In this imaginary future of 1999, Honda sees the United Nations as the seat of world power, a governmental-diplomatic-scientific body that leads military operations and a global space program, thus becoming the villains' primary target. Godzilla attacks New York, not Washington, and destroys the UN headquarters. Reminders of war abound: Monsterland, a penal colony for Godzilla and friends, is located at the Ogasawara Islands (aka the Bonin Islands), seized by the United States after the war and returned to Japan in 1968.[4] Notably, this is Honda's only film in which Godzilla attacks America, and his last in which the monster attacks Japan. Afterward, the camera tracks through decimated Tokyo, recalling a similar moment in *Godzilla*.

Political protests aside, Japan was celebrating the innocence of youngsters coming of age in peace and prosperity. A pop song titled "We Are the Children Who Have No Memory of War" would soon be a major hit, and it is these kids for whom the unthreatening *Destroy All Monsters* was made.[5] The monsters are now domesticated, easily manipulated by remote control, and it's fun to watch the harmless, bloodless destruction when they're let loose. Honda creates an exciting popcorn picture, with interstellar fighter pilot Katsuo (Akira Kubo) pursuing the aliens in a series of chases, confrontations, and ultimatums. The Kilaaks—rocklike beings who take the form of beautiful Japanese women—have no stated agenda other than a hostile takeover, though they build their base near hot springs and a volcano, implying that they covet earth's geothermal heat.

The main attractions are introduced early, during an entertaining flyover of Monsterland, each creature getting a brief walk-on while a narrator explains the island's ecosystem and security apparatus. Then follows a series of action sequences, as Honda ups the ante with more and more monsters; just when it seems Godzilla, Rodan, and Manda have Tokyo vanquished, Mothra arrives to make things even worse. The climax is a melee between Earth's monsters and the Kilaak attack-dog King Ghidorah, with a TV newscaster providing dramatic running commentary. The battle is staged on wide-open plateaus beneath Mount Fuji, alleviating the need for costly miniatures. The budget was increased to a reported ¥200 million ($550,000), yet the overabundance of monsters and big set pieces noticeably stretched the money thin at times. There are bits of stock footage, and most monsters are refurbished costumes from previous films. Honda returns to his theme of international cooperation, but

The monsters assemble for the climactic battle of *Destroy All Monsters*.
© Toho Co., Ltd.

although the stakes are global, the story remains Japan-centric. Military-aerospace operations carry the UN banner but are run by the Japanese. Caucasians play minor roles, but there are no American stars; and there is less of an attempt to appeal to overseas audiences than in Honda's recent genre efforts. Ironic, then, that *Destroy All Monsters* would be one of Toho's most internationally popular Godzilla films, distributed in numerous territories around the world.

The film was developed under the title *Monster Chushingura*, referencing the historical tale of the forty-seven ronin that avenged their master's unjust death. A first-draft script was completed on January 9, 1968; Honda and screenwriter Kaoru Mabuchi (Takeshi Kimura) sequestered themselves to write together. As Honda explained to an interviewer in 1992, the studio had given them a simple premise: "show all of the monsters."

"[Kimura] and I . . . agreed it would be crazy to make each of the monsters just somehow appear. Eventually, we came up with an island on which all of the monsters had been collected for scientific study. We imagined that undersea farming would be required to feed all of the monsters . . . What would happen if that got developed on a superscale? I thought about the idea of a marine ranch . . . scientifically, it would be what we now call aquaculture . . . From there, we started to develop the storyline.

"Initially, I had a lot more underwater scenes in the script. I was going to use special effects and set filming to depict them. But because of . . . financial as well as time constraints, what you ultimately see is what we were able to do, the bare minimum. In a way, those things [that I could not do] were the scenes I wanted to film the most. Back

then, the notion of aquaculture and bio-technology was already there, and we knew that things were going in that direction in the future."

Honda indicated that early concepts had the monsters being "raised" on the island as part of a biotechnology research project. He cited the island of genetically engineered dinosaurs in Steven Spielberg's *Jurassic Park* (1993). "Our idea was one of the first along those lines," he said.

————

With Eiji Tsuburaya no longer exclusively devoted to feature-film productions, Toho tacitly promoted his protégé Sadamasa Arikawa to the role—if not the title—of special-effects director on Jun Fukuda's *Godzilla vs. the Sea Monster* and *Son of Godzilla*. *Destroy All Monsters* marked Arikawa's first official credit as special-effects director, while Tsuburaya remained attached as effects "supervisor." Behind the camera it was mostly business as usual, for Arikawa and Honda were already well acquainted. On-screen, Arikawa's work has fresh energy and some new ideas. He often positions the camera at or above the monster's height, providing a Godzilla's-eye-view effect. He favored wire-operated monsters, and thus the final battle includes four of them—Ghidorah, Rodan, Mothra, and the giant spider, Kumonga—a logistical and choreographic feat. Meanwhile, the humanizing and hero-making of Honda's monsters continues: they punch and kick like barroom brawlers, Godzilla rallies the troops, and the camera positioning does little to make the men in suits look like gigantic creatures.

Honda's longtime cameraman Hajime Koizumi had joined the TV exodus to direct three episodes of Tsuburaya's *Ultra Q* in 1966, and stopped working on feature films altogether after *King Kong Escapes*. Here, Koizumi was replaced by Taiichi Kankura, a veteran shooter of Toho's commercial programmers. Kankura had shot Honda's *The Man Who Came to Port*, but this was his first science fiction film. Honda's drama scenes are crowded with actors and extras playing reporters, military men, astronauts, and civilians, and Kankura's framing is more static and stagy than his predecessor's. Most of the film is shot on sets, giving it an artificially bright look, though Kankura and Honda do include one of the director's customary outdoor hiking scenes, when the heroes discover the aliens' forest hideout.

Coming immediately after the Shinichi Sekizawa-penned *King Kong Escapes*, with its swaggering American hero and sneering villain, it's worth noting how comparatively joyless, in typical Takeshi Kimura style, *Destroy All Monsters* is. Most everything is played completely straight, and the film's considerable charm comes less from its characters than from the monster-filled, comic-book world that Honda and Tsuburaya create. Made just months before Apollo 8 became the first manned lunar orbiter, the movie envisions a technologically advanced though not terribly farfetched future in which moon travel is common, as are videophones and miniature televisions, and the military engages in remote-controlled warfare. As in *Invasion of Astro-Monster* and *The War of the Gargantuas*, conventional forces are ineffective, but another superweapon, the SY-3 fighter rocket, helps defeat the enemy. As before, experts were consulted to help lend credibility to the film's imaginary technology. "[The science] in *Destroy All Monsters* . . . was all thought up by the staff," Honda later wrote. "Those who work on these films take pains to establish grounds for truth or possibility . . . [We]

search through science books, visit labs and factories of electronics makers, gather facts and opinions."[6]

Within the thin story, Honda includes a number of familiar ideas. Scientists, as usual, are more prominent than politicians, and commanders again bear the burden of sending troops into battle. When the astronaut-soldiers risk their lives to destroy the aliens' transmitter, contact with Earth is lost and the men are feared dead, mirroring similar moments in *Battle in Outer Space* and *Gorath*, though the tension in this sequence is undermined by drawn-out pacing and the silly-looking transmitter device.

There is a who's-who of Honda's character actors, with gruff Jun Tazaki as the stalwart Dr. Yoshida; Yoshibumi Tajima as a buttoned-down general; Yoshio Tsuchiya as a man driven by aliens, as in *Battle in Outer Space*, to evil deeds and an early death; Kenji Sahara again lending star power in a small role; and Kubo leading the group as the brave astronaut. A somewhat intriguing performance is turned in by twenty-one-year-old newcomer Yukiko Kobayashi as Kyoko, the demure girlfriend who briefly transforms into a femme fatale. Kobayashi had made her debut as a waitress in Honda's *Come Marry Me* and was one of Toho's rising actresses in the late 1960s. When Kyoko is under alien control, her hairstyle suddenly gets hip, her fashions become bolder, and her personality turns ice cold. One of the best scenes has Kyoko walking through Tokyo, with a sinister smile as she seems to silently direct the urban assault by Godzilla and the rest. Regrettably, Kyoko is soon rescued and reverts to her far less interesting self.

Kinema Junpo critic Chieo Yoshida's review was typically dismissive. "They put almost all their star monsters together,"

Yoshida quipped, "including ones I thought were already dead." Yoshida found the film bemusing, while pointing up an unanswered question regarding the relationship between man and monsters. "At the end, the Kilaaks are defeated and the monsters go back to Monsterland . . . But why do the humans keep the monsters there? As far as I can tell, it's not just for preserving endangered monsters. It looks like they're raising them as weapons."

Though box-office numbers continued trending downward overall, Toho had a good year in 1968 with six of the top ten domestic grossers, including Seiji Maruyama's war epic *Admiral Yamamoto* (*Rengo kantai shirei chokan—Yamamoto Isoroku*), starring Toshiro Mifune and with effects by Tsuburaya, which was no. 2 at ¥400 million. *Destroy All Monsters* was the twelfth highest-grossing domestic release with ¥170 million; this would be Honda's last genre film to make the *Kinema Junpo* rankings. Two notable Hollywood genre films far outperformed it: *Planet of the Apes* (¥288 million) and *2001: A Space Odyssey* (¥266 million). These films intelligently addressed nuclear war, space travel, and other themes; despite Toho's tunnel vision, clearly children were not the only movie-goers interested in science fiction.

Around this time, a French periodical asked Honda whether he made films for children or adults. Honda answered in his usual diplomatic way, but again made clear that his objectives were compromised by economic reality. "When I make a monster film, I never think that it will be for children. As a director, I'm a man who wants to imagine and express a story. But when it's distributed to the theaters it's always the children who are the most interested . . . particularly those in the primary schools."

With peace restored, *Destroy All Mon-*

sters ends with another flyover of Monster-land, set to a melancholy Akira Ifukube coda. The final shot has Godzilla and its son, Minilla, appearing to say good-bye. And yet, when asked about future projects, Honda nonetheless sounded optimistic that these films might continue and thrive, while repeating his desire to break free. "I would like to do futuristic . . . science fiction. I would like to do a documentary without monsters. And also to do monster films with an enormous budget."

————

After going independent, Akira Kurosawa had spent the first half of the 1960s making numerous commercially and critically successful films, the last of which was *Red Beard*, the highest-grossing production of 1965 and Kurosawa's last film to top the *Kinema Junpo* critics' poll. But even if Kurosawa and Honda had followed very different career paths in recent times, the two friends nevertheless fought parallel battles against an unlikely adversary: Holly-wood's money men.

Kurosawa had found that his exclusive distribution arrangement with Toho gave the studio tremendous financial leverage over him, and so he cut ties in July 1966 and shifted his focus to America, where he believed his ambitions might find enthusi-astic support. Producer Joseph E. Levine, who had imported Honda's *Godzilla* to the United States a decade earlier, sub-sequently agreed to finance Kurosawa's *The Runaway Train*, a $5.5 million thriller based on an actual railroad accident, to be filmed on location in upstate New York with an American crew and cast. However, Levine canceled the project after Kurosawa, feeling rushed into production, made a last-minute request that filming be delayed one year.[7] Soon thereafter, Twentieth Century Fox hired Kurosawa to write and direct half of

Tora! Tora! Tora!, a war epic about Pearl Harbor alternately told from the Japanese and American perspectives. For two years Kurosawa toiled to the point of exhaustion, rewriting the screenplay twenty-seven times. Filming began in December 1968, but after unscheduled delays and reports of his erratic behavior, Kurosawa was fired by Fox. Humiliated, Kurosawa threatened to "commit *hara-kiri* and die."[8]

———————

While Kurosawa's Hollywood adventures unraveled, Honda was beginning work on another Japan-US coventure, an undersea sci-fi fantasy titled *Latitude Zero*. It was to be Honda's most ambitious project yet, and the first Japanese movie with an all-English-speaking cast and an English-language script written by an American. It would star the great Joseph Cotten of *Citizen Kane* (1941) and *The Third Man* (1949) fame, and the villain would be played by Cesar Romero, at the peak of his popularity as The Joker on the *Batman* TV series. In June 1968 a deal was announced between Toho and Ambassador Productions, with the two companies evenly splitting the production cost of ¥360 million ($1 million) and dividing the worldwide rights. With box-office returns declining, Toho saw this as an opportunity to expand internationally. "We want to export the film overseas as much as possible and raise foreign currency," said studio executive Tadashi Yonemoto. "That's why we're making it in English."

This was intended as the first in a series of coproductions with Ambassador Productions' owner Don Sharpe (no relation to British genre filmmaker Don Sharp), all with American casts. Shooting began on October 28, 1968, and was scheduled to wrap December 28.[9] It appeared Honda would fulfill his hopes of making a serious science fiction picture with a larger budget, but once again the Americans came with attitudes and issues, causing numerous delays and the near-collapse of the production.

Latitude Zero originated as a radio serial, created by writer Ted Sherdeman, running for seventeen episodes on NBC radio network in 1941. Sherdeman—whose screen credits included *Them!* (1953), *A Dog of Flanders* (1959), and episodes of *Gilligan's Island* and *My Favorite Martian*—had partnered with producer-agents Sharpe and Warren Lewis and unsuccessfully pitched *Latitude Zero* as a TV show in the late 1950s. Now, a decade later, this same trio was behind Honda's feature film version. Sherdeman would write the screenplay, while Sharpe's Wall Street–financed production company would cover the salaries and expenses of Cotten and costar Romero, who reportedly were paid $100,000 and $50,000 respectively—enormous figures by Japanese standards, and far more than Japanese stars were paid—as well as those of Cotten's wife, the actress Patricia Medina, character actor Richard Jaeckel,

Rehearsing a scene from *Latitude Zero* with Lucretia (Patricia Medina) and Dr. Okada (Tetsu Nakamura). Translator Henry Okawa assists; Joseph Cotten looks on. Courtesy of Honda Film Inc.

and twenty-year-old newcomer Linda Haynes. Lewis would be the hands-on producer for the American side; and to that end he prowled Honda's sets and made complaints, demands, and criticisms of Japanese filmmaking methods. Concerned about how the film would play in the United States, Lewis "was bitching until the end," recalled assistant director Seiji Tani. (In early script drafts, the villain Malic's [Romero's] menagerie included a caveman-like humanoid that was dropped into an acid pool and killed; the creature was nicknamed "Warren.")

Sharpe and Lewis were television veterans. They had developed numerous shows together; Sharpe also had ties to Desilu Productions and *I Love Lucy*. This might explain why they initially insisted Honda shoot *Latitude Zero* using a television-style, multiple-camera setup, with a central camera for the master shot and side cameras for close-ups. This wasn't like Akira Kurosawa's method of using numerous cameras to capture the spontaneity of the actors' performances. Sharpe and Lewis thought they could cut costs and time by eliminating separate takes and setups. The Japanese crew disagreed.

"We'd never done anything like that, so everyone was opposed," remembered Teruyoshi Nakano, assistant special-effects director. "But Honda-*san* said, 'It sounds fine . . . If they insist, I am sure there are merits in doing it this way.' Any other Japanese director would have had a fit, saying, 'How stupid! It's just a waste of time!' As we were filming, Honda-*san* explained to them one day, 'For this cut, if you calculate and plan well, there is really no need to have all of these cameras rolling wastefully.'" Lewis then "did a 180" and realized the Japanese were not incompetent, Nakano said. The experiment reportedly lasted about a week,

Latitude Zero: Coaching Joseph Cotten (center) as Henry Okawa (left) translates. Courtesy of Honda Film Inc.

then Honda resumed shooting with the studio's usual single-camera setup.

The project proceeded smoothly until about three weeks into production, when Sharpe defaulted on his share of the costs. Cotten later said the producer "had omitted to tell us that he was bankrupt."[10] Cotten and the others wanted to quit and go home; but a Toho production executive, whom Cotten identified only as "Mr. Yoshimura" (though he was possibly referring to producer Tomoyuki Tanaka), begged them to remain in Japan and finish the movie, implying that he, as the man responsible for the agreement with Sharpe, would otherwise lose face, lose his job, or—as Cotten understood it—even commit *hara-kiri*.[11]

Filming was canceled for four days in late November 1968 as details were ironed out. Toho assumed the entire production cost and the actors stayed on; Lewis remained on set and would be credited as "creative adviser," as did Sherdeman, who assisted with on-set rewrites and was considered agreeable and flexible by the Japanese crew. Sharpe's name would be absent from the credits. The delay forced Honda to shoot on Christmas Eve and Christmas day to ensure the Americans were dismissed by New Year's, as contractually required. The budget was reduced to ¥289 million (about $800,000).[12]

The friction between the two sides wasn't only financial. Filming was interrupted briefly when Lewis berated Mari Nakayama for misplacing an earring; Honda had to console the bawling actress. When a stunt coordinator suggested Cotten use the villainess Lucretia (Medina) as a human shield in the climactic fight, Lewis gave Honda's crew a condescending lecture, insisting that a hero never behaves this way.

"[Lewis] was there to ensure the film would appeal to an American audience, so I don't think it was wrong for him to make requests, but he talked as if the Japanese knew nothing," Tani recalled. "Honda-*san*'s facial expression at this moment didn't look too amused. He didn't speak to Warren directly for a while after that. He was pretty pissed off." The scene was instead filmed as Sherdeman had written it. Cotten pushes away Medina in self-defense, and she is impaled on Romero's knife. Tani, in turn, schooled the Americans on the Japanese system, which put the director in charge of production once filming began. The young A. D. was a buffer between the two sides, extinguishing minor conflicts before they could reach Honda and "[turn] into a true fight." He was so stressed by the experience that he lost weight. "I was made to lay on a bed of nails . . . almost every day."

The biggest disagreement concerned the "bath of immunity," where the heroes gird themselves for battle in a jacuzzi that makes them temporarily impervious to gunshots. After the men have immersed themselves, beautiful Linda Haynes enters, silhouetted against a backdrop. With the

lifting in 1968 of the Motion Picture Production Code, female nudity was exploding in Hollywood films, thus Lewis insisted that Haynes be naked. In Japan, nudity was accepted in art and "pink" films, but not general-audience features, and Honda refused.

Tani recalled, "They wanted to show that there is no shyness here, there should be no element of embarrassment between men and women . . . But Honda-*san* said, 'No. We have to show this film in Japan, as well.' There were talks about shooting an alternate version, but the director was against it. What he came up with eventually was to make it seem like she is completely nude—we shot her entire body, but backlit so that you can't really see the details. You might call this skirting the issue, but the Americans had a look on their faces, like, 'Man, he got us on this one.'" Sherdeman's early drafts also had more heat between Dr. Anne Barton (Haynes) and Dr. Jules Masson (Masumi Okada), but the film shows only a chaste kiss.

It's easy to see why *Latitude Zero* appealed to Honda, with its Gene Roddenberry–esque vision of a utopian civilization governed by reason, cooperation, and selflessness. Cotten plays Capt. Craig MacKenzie, a Nemo-like hero who commands the Alpha, a high-tech, swift-moving, flying submarine created for scientific research. MacKenzie hails from a city beneath a geodesic dome at the sea bottom, where peaceful pursuit of science has trumped politics. Many of Earth's leading scientists, believed dead, are actually living and working there in secret; the place has an artificial atmosphere and no pollution, enabling people to live hundreds of years. There are bucolic surroundings, fine art, great architecture, and groovy fashions made of gold and see-through plastic.

Greed is nonexistent; diamonds are used as potting soil.

Sherdeman's screenplay has neither the levity of Shinichi Sekizawa nor the gravity of Takeshi Kimura, however. There is an entertaining submarine chase, with the Alpha pursued by the ominous Black Shark sub, captained by Malic's vaguely sado-masochistic henchwoman, Kroiga (Hikaru Kuroki). After that, the script is padded with exposition about life in MacKenzie's Shangri-La and inert scenes of people watching action on video monitors; Taiichi Kankura's camera work and shot framing is sometimes even more static and flat-footed than in *Destroy All Monsters*. Things go from sublime to silly, with Malic kidnapping Japanese scientist Dr. Okada (Tetsu Nakamura) and threatening to steal his antiradiation formula by extracting it from his brain. Within his Batcave-like hideout, Malic operates his own Island of Dr. Moreau, surgically grafting condor wings onto a lion and implanting Kroiga's brain in its skull, creating a subservient flying gryphon. The compound is guarded by giant rats—costumed men walking on their knees—and man-bats that fly on wires. The heroes, wearing "helio-elevation belts" and impenetrable gold bodysuits, and shooting lasers from their fingertips, invade the madman's lair and rescue Okada in a melee resembling an old Buck Rogers serial.

The shooting script was in English, with a Japanese translation on the facing page. Tani, who spoke English, assisted Honda with shooting dialogue. "I'd tell Honda-*san*, 'If you cut it here, what they are saying comes out backwards.' 'Why?' he'd ask. It's because the grammar is flipped around in English, and the sentence is the reverse of that in Japanese. I advised him on where to cut so that the scenes would make sense."

Honda again relied on interpreter Henry Okawa when directing the English-speaking actors, and got along best with the hardworking Jaeckel, who had starred in Kinji Fukasaku's *The Green Slime* (*Gamma sango uchu daisakusen*, 1968) and was familiar with Japanese methods. Jaeckel, as the skeptical photographer Perry Lawton, gives the most credible performance, while Cotten, Medina, and especially Romero are broad and theatrical. Cotten's only comment about Honda was a tad patronizing, calling him "charming and artistic, and I'm sure that had he been able to speak English, or we Japanese, he would have had some very interesting ideas."[13] Haynes was more appreciative. "He had a way of communicating with us," she said. "When you looked him in the eye and watched his hand motions, you understood . . . I really liked him a lot. He was a really sensitive, gentle person." Along with the photographer, two scientists are rescued from their wrecked bathysphere and taken to Latitude Zero. They're played by Okada, a prolific Danish-Japanese actor, and Akira Takarada, acting quite competently in English, though playing an atypically marginal role. These two men embrace the undersea utopia and decide to stay.

Though Tani remembered Honda directing with unusual enthusiasm, ultimately *Latitude Zero* doesn't resemble a typical Honda-Tsuburaya effort. Sherdeman's writing is rooted in the fantasy adventure serials of the past, with noble good guys and over-the-top villains and their dastardly plots; the film should have been made a decade or two earlier. Sherdeman tries to contemporize his story with vague commentary on late 1960s unrest. A news montage shows the Tet Offensive, the Nigerian civil war, and Japan's student riots but, inexplicably, none of the biggest events that shook the United States in 1968: the assassinations of Martin Luther King Jr. and Robert F. Kennedy and the Democratic National Convention riots. Eiji Tsuburaya's effects include some impressive model work (the submarines are reminiscent of Gerry Anderson's *Thunderbirds* teleseries) and matte renderings of the undersea city. The monsters, normally one of Tsuburaya's strengths, are crude and laughable, however—evidence, perhaps, of budget cuts made necessary after Sharpe bailed out.

And what of Honda's *The Wizard of Oz*–like twist ending? Perry is rescued at sea by a ship awaiting a NASA capsule splashdown. He's greeted by the captain (Cotten) and first officer (Romero), spitting images of MacKenzie and Malic. Perry tries to prove his outlandish story, but his film has been erased and his booty of souvenir diamonds has vanished. The captain's last name is MacKenzie—according to the script, he's a distant descendant of the undersea hero, though this is unsaid—and the déjà vu also includes a naval officer played by Akira Takarada, suggesting the entire story is a hallucination, including the bathysphere expedition. But then, Perry receives an anonymous cache of diamonds, apparently confirming it was all true. This head-scratching ending appears as an "alternate" take in Sherdeman's final draft, dated October 25, 1968. Sherdeman's original ending had Perry presenting a slide-show of his Latitude Zero photos to a group of journalists, but the images are blurry and the reporters believe him mad. In the back of the room, Perry spots a man who looks just like MacKenzie. After everyone leaves, the man turns the slide projector back on, and crisp images of the undersea city now appear.

Problems persisted during and after production. Cotten was stricken with Asian flu in the last days of filming and is noticeably pale in certain scenes. Dr. Okada was originally played by the esteemed actor and writer Takamaru Sasaki, who quit the production early because of illness, forcing Honda to reshoot his scenes. Toho continued sorting out issues resulting from Sharpe's divestment for months. When the picture was released on July 26, 1969, advertising ironically boasted it had "five of Hollywood's top stars," but the picture made ¥170 million (about $472,000), far less than its reported cost and not enough to make the *Kinema Junpo* rankings; and it received only a minor US release. Producer Tanaka implied that Honda was responsible for its failure: "It was a fun story, but it turned out [boring]. Honda couldn't get ahold of how to use Cinemascope properly, and the project only showed how difficult it was to make a coproduction with another country."[14] Honda lamented that he "[felt] like we got tricked" by Sharpe. The additional costs, he said, "[really] affected our filming . . . It was really stressful. I wish we could have done more, and under better circumstances."[15]

———

Following *Latitude Zero*, Honda made a second foray into primetime TV on the family comedy *Husbands, Men, Be Strong* (*Otto yo otoko yo tsuyokunare*), a one-hour anthology series produced by Toho Television for the Nippon Educational Television (now TV Asahi) network. Its title reflected the rise of women's rights, and stories routinely satirized gender roles. Honda directed two episodes, both airing in October 1969. The first, "Honey, It's a Presidential Order" (*Anata shacho meirei yo*) had a company boss ordering his male employees to do household chores, with *jidai-geki* TV star Asahi Kirizuka playing against type as a timid husband.

Honda was hired for the job by his old

protégé Koji Kajita, one of the show's producers. It was a learning experience; Honda was still accustomed to a larger screen, and Kajita had to ask his old mentor to reshoot some close-ups more tightly. One script was in poor shape, and Honda had to quickly make significant changes before filming.

About television, Honda said, "The first three minutes is key. You have to grab the hearts of the audience within this time frame. Since the tempo is very different from film, you must keep this in mind as you write the script as well as direct." But Honda remained committed to feature films and wasn't interested in a new career as a TV director.

**The company wanted a lot of monsters, but they told us that they had no money . . . We decided to take on one of the social problems of that time, the latchkey kid. We set it up that the kid liked monsters, so he pretends and makes it all real [in his dreams]. This one got to be really popular and made a lot of money, and it is one of my favorites as well.
– Ishiro Honda[16]**

Toho's unofficial Godzilla moratorium was over before it started. In April 1968, while *Destroy All Monsters* was in production, an agreement was reached with Hollywood-based Filmation, the production company behind *The Archie Show* (1968) and other television programs, for a Godzilla cartoon series. It was to air on Japanese and American television in 1969–70, and Toho would reedit episodes into a feature for theatrical release. The two companies also may have planned a companion live-action Godzilla film.[17] The deal collapsed, but it was clear that Godzilla was now considered a chil-

dren's entertainment property, and too valuable to keep under wraps.

National box-office numbers for 1968–69 fell approximately 21 percent versus the prior year. When Toho executives met on September 9 and 10, 1969, to finalize the New Year's holiday film slate, they apparently took these gloomy economics into consideration. Among the projects approved was a different kind of Godzilla movie proposed by Shinichi Sekizawa, a children's fantasy that would repurpose monster scenes from prior films, thus requiring a very low budget. The project was fast-tracked, and Sekizawa turned in his first screenplay draft of *All Monsters Attack* on September 17. In the span of less than a month, child actors were auditioned, Sekizawa turned in his final draft, and live-action and special-effects sets and props were built. Honda's cameras began rolling October 11, and the film was released just over two months later, on December 20.[18] Despite this accelerated pace, Honda managed to create a uniquely personal monster movie, a warmhearted story reflecting the harsh trade-offs of Japan's high-speed economic growth. Long dismissed for its heavy use of stock footage, *All Monsters Attack* is actually a modest, sixty-nine-minute masterpiece of children's entertainment.

If Honda's earlier sci-fi films were made for general audiences with an eye toward children, then *All Monsters Attack* is the first made expressly for kids, a change allowing Honda and Sekizawa to ditch standard formulas and make a radical departure, a Godzilla story that takes place outside the "Toho universe." There is no apparent continuity with previous films. Instead of stock characters, the story is a day in the life of a single, sympathetic protagonist, the good-natured but diminutive Ichiro (Tomonori Yazaki), a boy harassed by the

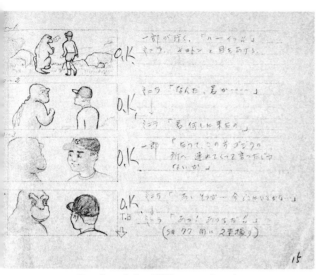

Storyboards for *All Monsters Attack*.
© Toho Co., Ltd.

neighborhood bully and his gang. There is no urban destruction, no actual sci-fi or fantasy premise; instead Honda's backdrop is an unvarnished side of late 1960s Japan, an industrial city blighted by smoke-belching factories, traffic congestion, dusty railroad yards, and crime, reflecting a growing discontent with the trade-offs of the rapid postwar recovery. A subplot about two bumbling, stumbling bank robbers, Senbayashi (Sachio Sakai, in gangster garb and swigging booze) and Okuda (Kazuo Sukuki), is inspired by a notorious ¥300 million armored car robbery, then the biggest theft in Japan's history, which dominated headlines in 1968. The robbers kidnap Ichiro, mirroring a spate of child abductions that occurred in Tokyo during the 1960s, which previously influenced Kurosawa's *High and Low*.[19]

All Monsters Attack introduces the term "Monster Island," which would become synonymous with Japanese science fiction film. This island is different from the penal colony of *Destroy All Monsters*, however;

here, the monsters run free. The place exists only in Ichiro's dreams, a refuge from reality. *Kagikko* (latchkey kids) became a social issue in the mid-1960s as families struggled to afford rising housing costs, and more women were forced to take jobs outside the home. After-school care was uncommon, so kids like Ichiro had to fend for themselves until their mothers returned.[20] Ichiro spends lonely afternoons searching condemned buildings, collecting junk electronic parts for a homemade "computer" that, in his vivid imagination, teleports him—via psychedelic effects—to the home of Godzilla's offspring, Minilla (pronounced "Minya" in the English-dubbed US version).[21] The little monster is likewise harassed by a bully, an ogre resembling a cross between a Tsuburaya creature and the beasts of *Where the Wild Things Are*.[22] Ichiro's nemesis and Minilla's tormentor are both called Gabara; the normally apolitical Sekizawa supposedly borrowed the name, originally "Gebara," either from Marxist revolutionary Che Guevara or the German word *gewalt* (violence), both popular with Japanese student protesters at the time.[23]

Little boys in shorts and yellow caps who befriend giant monsters were already a genre cliché.[24] Daiei's *Gamera* films routinely featured precocious children befriending the titular monster. But Ichiro is different, a true reflection of the audience, so obsessed with movie and TV monsters that they seem real to him. In turn, timid Minilla—speaking Japanese, assuming human size, and facing similar childhood problems—is a reflection of the boy, making for a self-reflexive *kaiju eiga*. Ichiro longs for quality time with his parents: his overtime-working railroad engineer father (Kenji Sahara) is never home, and whenever dad and Ichiro are together on-screen, the camera emphasizes the distance separating them. Ichiro's neighbor and surrogate parent is Minami (Hideyo Amamoto), a kindly, odd-looking toy inventor, who encourages Ichiro to stand up for himself. In dreamland, this advice is exemplified by Godzilla, as Ichiro watches the monster dispatch foes the old-fashioned way, with fisticuffs. Minilla learns courage, inspiring Ichiro to do the same.

Godzilla's battles with a giant tarantula, condor, lobster, mantises, and a squadron of fighter planes are all taken, in edited form, from Jun Fukuda's *Godzilla vs. the Sea Monster* and *Son of Godzilla*. Sekizawa had penciled Rodan and a giant octopus into his original draft, presumably via footage from Honda's previous films; but Honda decided to use the Fukuda material instead because its island settings suited the story.[25] (Curiously, a charming *Son of Godzilla* scene in which Godzilla teaches Minilla to exhale radiation was re-filmed here; this version shows Godzilla to be a more stern parent.) Other than some noticeable changes in Godzilla's appearance or an abrupt shift from day to night, these stock scenes are almost seamlessly inserted, with cutaways showing Ichiro and Minilla watching from a distance. Godzilla's fights are part of Ichiro's tutelage; they support the story without seeming like filler, even if they do help pad the running time.

For much of 1969, Eiji Tsuburaya and many of Toho's effects technicians were busy making *Birth of the Japanese Islands*, an audiovisual exhibit that used film, mirrors, and effects to simulate earthquakes and volcanoes, to be exhibited at Expo 70, the upcoming world's fair in Osaka. Because of this commitment, and because he was away on sick leave for part of the year, Tsuburaya did not direct the special effects for *All Monsters Attack*. For the first time, there was just one crew, working under Honda, to film both the human drama and monster scenes.

"I directed almost [everything]," Honda remembered. "The two reasons why I did were the limited size of the production budget and time constraints. In addition, the movie was shot on a very small sound stage, so it was decided not to separate the filming of the special effects and the standard footage as was usually done."

"The difference was that there was only one schedule . . . based on the entire film," added Teruyoshi Nakano, assistant effects director. "Honda-*san* would say to me, 'I do not know how to go about directing the effects, so please, go ahead and do it for us.' So I did, but the rest of the staff was the same for both segments.

"Honda-*san* was behind me, watching . . . He just told me to freely do my thing. Maybe he was expecting to get the quality of work he had gotten from Tsuburaya-*san*, but unfortunately I was not as talented."

The new effects sequences are limited mainly to Ichiro and Minilla talking, and a pair of monster fights, simply shot on a small island set. Still, with a single crew filming everything, Honda wanted a cinematographer accustomed to shooting monsters. Without knowledge of necessary camera angles, lenses, lighting, and other details, Honda feared they would "just look like men in suits, no matter what you do in post-production." Mototaka Tomioka, a Tsuburaya protégé and the effects cinematographer on Fukuda's two Godzilla pictures, became Honda's director of photography. Tomioka's camera gives the film a visual theme and continuity across its disparate settings and sources. A dirty river

Directing Tomonori Yazaki (as Ichiro) and wrestler Marchan the Dwarf (as Minilla) in *All Monsters Attack*. © Toho Co., Ltd.

where kids fish, barren lots where they play, and the filthy, shadowy interior of a condemned factory are the backdrops of real life; in contrast, the dream world is lush and bright. A symbolic "rabbit hole" on Monster Island and a parallel hole in the floor of an abandoned building form a minimotif, with each leading Ichiro into, then out of danger.

Honda tells the story almost entirely from Ichiro's point of view, and everything in the boy's world, real or imagined, is well thought out. There are roaring, industrial-urban sound effects and a jazzy, Neal Hefti–like score, heavy on horns, drums, and electric guitar from Kunio Miyauchi, composer of Honda's *The Human Vapor*, and more recently, Tsuburaya's *Ultraman* teleseries. References are made to the recent Apollo 11 lunar landing and numerous pop-culture slogans kids would recognize. When Ichiro cries, "*Okaasan!*" ("Mommy!"), it's a riff on a popular miso

soup commercial. The kids repeatedly exclaim, "*Yattaze baby!*" ("Yeah, baby!"), a then hip catchphrase, and Minami quotes a gasoline company's advertising tagline.

Honda had previously expressed reservations about directing children. "Usually, kid actors just forget about their character right after they speak one word. Of course, they are saying something they do not want to say, so as soon as they finish speaking, they start looking somewhere else."[26] Here, however, Honda gets a remarkably natural and consistent performance from Yazaki, who portrays Ichiro's loneliness and fear without wallowing in sentimentality.

"[Honda] would explain the scene to him, have him do it once or twice, then film it," said assistant director Koji Hashimoto. "He didn't say too much, just let the child act. This allowed him to get the purity of the child's performance as well as [his] expressions and feelings." Little is known about

Yazaki, who made only a few other acting appearances.

The other children are good too, particularly the sneering, bully with cap askew. The adult cast of familiar Honda regulars is led by Sahara, whose biggest memory of making the film was being allowed to drive a train. Honda joked that the actor should go work for Hankyu Railway. "That's the sense of humor he had," said Sahara. "He made working enjoyable."

The adults are preoccupied with money—earning it, stealing it, recovering it, and so on—but ultimately Honda does not moralize about this or the other issues raised. The story concludes with three big fights, all seen from a child's idealized viewpoint, with good prevailing over evil. Ichiro dreams of Minilla bravely confronting the bully monster, and papa Godzilla steps in to finish the job. The emboldened boy then confronts his real-life villains, with Honda using pratfalls and creative editing to depict violence in harmless terms. Senbayashi chases Ichiro with a knife, but the kid uses a fire extinguisher to blind him with "radioactive breath." Next morning, the bully and his gang confront Ichiro in the street—like a Western showdown—but he's not a wimp anymore. Their shoving match is shown with freeze-frames resembling comic-book panels and music that sounds like a superhero theme. Triumphant, Ichiro pranks a nearby sign painter, something he was too "chicken" to do yesterday, resulting in some slapstick humor. The lonely little boy's story ends with optimism and hope: Ichiro is a media star for nabbing the criminals, and his bravery earns the neighborhood kids' respect. He apologizes to the bedraggled painter, showing that he's still good-hearted; and there are hints that his father, who comes to his son's aid as Godzilla did, and mother will do better. The

Honda with child actors from *All Monsters Attack*. Courtesy of Honda Film Inc.

social problem is acknowledged, but there is a sense that everyone will persevere.

————

Destroy All Monsters was the last of Toho's original wave of sci-fi movies to receive a standard theatrical release. Beginning with *All Monsters Attack*, such films became part of the Toho Champion Festival, a recurring children's entertainment marathon. These hours-long events, modeled after the popular Toei Manga Festival, typically featured a monster movie accompanied by cartoons, short subjects, and sometimes an episode of *Ultraman* or a similar TV show. There were three per year, when kids were out of school: during New Year's, spring break (in March, just before the start of the school year), and summer vacation. More often than not, the main attraction was an older *kaiju* film, heavily reedited to emphasize the monster action. The first was *King Kong vs. Godzilla*, shortened to just seventy-four minutes in March 1970. Since he could not prevent the films from being recut, Honda did it himself, albeit reluctantly. "I can't say that they were made better by editing them a second time," he said, diplomatic as always.[27] The Champion Festival would continue until 1978, with reedited classic films often drawing audience numbers as good or better than Toho's latest sci-fi features.

————

Honda hadn't seen Eiji Tsuburaya much in the past year, as Tsuburaya was busy developing TV shows and directing special effects for Toho's Russo-Japanese war epic *Battle of the Japan Sea* (*Nihonkai daikaisen*), directed by Shue Matsubayashi and released in August 1969, as well as working on the Expo 70 project. *All Monsters Attack* would be Tsuburaya's last big-screen credit; and though he didn't take part in the shoot, it was more than honorary. "He was personally involved with the editing," Honda remembered. "The film may have been generally put together [by others], but he definitely looked it over and instructed the staff to shorten certain scenes, and so on."[28]

In early November 1969, Tsuburaya paid an unexpected visit to Honda's home. It wasn't a mere social call. Sitting in Honda's living room, Tsuburaya made it clear that he wanted to restart their creative partnership and end the monotony of monster movies. He was eager to revive the proposed historical drama about Japan's early aviators, which they'd discussed making years earlier. Tsuburaya was already working on an outline. He told Honda, "Let's . . . make special-effects films not just about monsters destroying buildings but more fantastic and entertaining. Something to give children a sense of dreams and hope." Honda enthusiastically concurred, and as Tsuburaya said good-bye, they pledged to begin working together the following March.[29]

It would be the last time Honda saw the Old Man. Though Tsuburaya had often mentioned his deteriorating health, he'd

maintained the speed and drive of youth. To friends and colleagues, he appeared healthy; but Tsuburaya had been diagnosed with angina, and years of overwork were taking their toll.[30] Soon, Honda learned that Tsuburaya was hospitalized with a heart ailment. "He was instructed to be in complete rest; and so I chose not to go visit and bother him because, knowing how we get when we are together, I could picture us getting into conversations about topics such as the future of Japanese cinema and indignant lamentation over the evils of the times."

Tsuburaya refused to recuperate in hospital, but he nevertheless reduced his workload. He stepped down as head of Tsuburaya Productions and was replaced by his son Hajime; and in December, after completing work on the Expo 70 film, Tsuburaya retreated to his summer villa on the Izu Peninsula.[31] He was reportedly recovering well, even telling others of his plans to reunite with Honda. But on January 25, 1970, a day before his scheduled return to Tokyo, Tsuburaya was found dead of a heart attack. He was sixty-eight.

Honda learned the next morning. "I was still at home and was totally caught off guard by the sudden, shocking news. The tragedy was confirmed once I went to the studio, but I was not able to believe and process it for a while." There was a funeral in a Catholic church and a memorial service at Toho, inside a large stage where Tsuburaya had filmed many of his illusions. Honda was among the mourners who spoke, and he also paid tribute to Tsuburaya in an essay published shortly thereafter:

"He was not only my great *senpai* but an inseparable partner at the workplace," Honda wrote. "He was still filled with ambition to practice his craft, and we all wished he would work for many more years. This team we had formed, however, has come to an end. A gaping hole has opened where Eiji Tsuburaya stood . . . It would take great time and effort for even his skilled successors, to whom he gave disciplined training, to fill it.

"Tsuburaya cultivated his skills and demonstrated them on a grand scale. This is not something that can be so easily mimicked. He was a master who proved his greatness within the boundaries of Japanese cinema."

One of the last things Tsuburaya had said to Honda was, "Conditions in the film business are getting harsher and harsher, but let us both do our best."

"These words," Honda wrote, "still linger in my ears."[32]

———————

Two days before Tsuburaya's death, Honda began shooting *Space Amoeba* (1970), a project stuck in the creative rut that the two men had hoped to escape, and symptomatic of the harsh conditions they aspired to overcome. Though it was made at the start of the new decade, the project actually originated with a script written in 1966, *Invasion of the Monsters* (*Kaiju daishugeki*), which was part of a package of film and television coproductions between Toho and Henry Saperstein's UPA Productions that were announced but never completed. As originally written, the script by Ei Ogawa (a prolific, veteran Toho action specialist, whose credits also include a trio of cult-favorite vampire movies) was a global sci-fi yarn on the scale of *Gorath*, with Earth invaded by alien monsters that wreak havoc, submerging continents and threatening man's survival. When Toho revived the project three years later, the script was heavily revised so that everything takes place on a South Seas island.[33]

Made just before Toho and its competitors would undergo major corporate upheavals, *Space Amoeba* was an attempt to recapture the old magic, rehashing plot points from past Honda pictures. Some scenes and ideas are so familiar—a man struck with amnesia after seeing a monster (a la *Rodan*), alien possession of monsters and people (*Destroy All Monsters*, etc.), a giant squid destroying a thatch hut, body-painted natives attacking the monster with spears (*King Kong vs. Godzilla*), and so on—that it seems like a greatest-hits reel. Tomoyuki Tanaka was busy with the Expo 70 project and did not produce the film, but he nonetheless complained it was too much of a retread.[34]

At the same time, Toho injected this film with new blood, though the results were poor. Ogawa's script is an unsuccessful facsimile of the pessimistic writing of Takeshi Kimura. Neophyte producer Fumio Tanaka (no relation to Tomoyuki Tanaka) allowed some rather shoddy special effects to pass muster. The cast is a mix of Toho's new, younger talent and members of the classic Honda family, appearing together for the last time. There are no kids; but this was a Champion Festival release, and the film caters to a young audience. As in *All Monsters Attack*, Honda shows the monsters right away, during the opening credits, and the situations and dialogue are appropriately simple.

Helios 7, an unmanned space probe headed for Jupiter, is hijacked by an amoeba-like alien being and returns to Earth, crashing into the sea near fictional Selgio Island in the South Pacific. The island is the site of a vacation resort planned by Japanese investors, who send an expedition there to survey the terrain. The standard lineup includes macho photographer Taro Kudo (Akira Kubo), stoic scientist Dr. Kyochi Miya (Yoshio Tsuchiya), and his plucky assistant, Ayako (Atsuko Takahashi). They're joined by Obata (Kenji Sahara), a sleazy anthropologist who turns out to be an industrial spy. Their visit is interrupted by three giant monsters: Gezora (a giant squid), Ganime (giant crab), and Kameba (giant turtle), each created and manipulated by the alien, intent on overtaking Earth. After the humans repel the monsters with World War II guns and gasoline left behind on the island by the Japanese military, the alien takes possession of Obata, who throws himself into a volcano to save his friends and mankind.

Some members of the production team suggested an on-screen dedication to Eiji Tsuburaya during the opening credits, but the studio declined, causing hard feelings among the staff. Tsuburaya protégé Sadamasa Arikawa, again serving as effects director, was deeply offended and refused to speak about the production in later years. Viewed with the benefit of hindsight, *Space Amoeba* suffers greatly from Tsuburaya's absence, with poorly designed monsters and rougher-than-usual transitions between Honda's live-action footage and the effects. The requisite monster battle at the film's climax is a long, uninspired tussle between the turtle and crab, the stuntmen visibly struggling inside their bulky monster costumes. Honda and other members of the production team visited scientists, as in the past, to learn about ultrasound waves emitted by dolphins and bats, a major plot point in defeating the alien menace. But sometimes the film disregards science completely. The giant squid leaves the ocean and walks upright on dry land, using its rubbery tentacles as legs.

"Tsuburaya had more influence within Toho than [Sadamasa] Arikawa did, so the special-effects staff were given less time

to do their work after Tsuburaya died," recalled Fumio Tanaka. "This made them work a little less carefully than they previously had. I remember that at one point the giant squid's eyes stopped working, but shooting was not stopped. That wouldn't have happened if Tsuburaya had still been in charge."[35]

"The company was pressing us hard about the budget, budget, budget," said assistant director Seiji Tani. "The schedule was pretty tight. We were forced to rush through filming." *Space Amoeba's* script was finalized in January, and the film was shot in the cold of winter, though the actors are dressed for the tropics. Plans to shoot the live-action scenes in Guam were canceled because of budget restrictions; and Honda was forced to shoot at Hachijo Island, the "Hawaii of Japan," about 170 miles south of Tokyo.

Space Amoeba is notable for allusions to the legacy of Japan's occupation of the Marianas, Carolines, Marshall Islands, Palau, and other South Pacific islands roughly from 1914 until the end of World War II. The setting is a fictional island formerly held by Japan, and tension remains between the indigenous people and the Japanese visitors who now wish to recolonize the place with a luxury hotel—alluding to the multimillion-dollar vacation resorts, some of them controversial, built by Japanese developers in Hawaii, Fiji, and other territories beginning in the mid-1960s.

For those involved, *Space Amoeba* was an unmemorable experience. Honda hardly spoke or wrote of it, and others would recall little about it in later years. No one realized its significance at the time, but this was the final Toho science fiction film made under the traditional studio system, which had reached a crossroads.

Honda was fifty-nine when *Space Amoeba* was released on August 1, 1970. Nearly forty years had passed since he had entered Toho. It was becoming difficult to stay.

The film industry's steady decline had been slowed by occasional blockbusters or the success of long-running film series, but between 1960 and 1970 national attendance had dropped from one billion to about 250 million annually, and it was still falling. Toho was once a powerhouse of movie stars, famous directors, and a mix of commercial films and prestige pictures, but now it would drastically remake itself in order to survive. The studio was split into several smaller subsidiary companies, including Toho Eiga (Toho Film), its main production arm, and Toho Eizo (Toho Visual), which would make special-effects films under Tomoyuki Tanaka's supervision. The number of actors under contract, which had exceeded two hundred as recently as 1965, would fall to eleven by 1972; over roughly the same period, the number of Toho-produced films fell about 50 percent. Longtime contracts were ended, and crew members would be hired on a per-project basis. The special-effects department founded by Tsuburaya was disbanded. These moves were designed to weaken the labor unions, which were blamed for rising costs. Other studios were retrenching as well: Daiei declared bankruptcy and closed; Nikkatsu, which had dominated the youth market with popular gangster films, began exclusively making soft-core "Roman Porno" features.

Amid this sea change, in late 1970 Honda's employment contract came up for annual renewal. When it was time to negotiate terms for the following year, he took stock of his future.

"Ishiro was already thinking about quitting Toho, but he didn't mention this to me just yet," said Kimi. "It takes guts to tell the company, 'I quit,' and there was absolutely no guarantee that he would have gotten work as a freelance director afterwards.

"He ultimately asked me if it would be OK if he quit. The children were older by then . . . so I said to him, 'Let's go back to our old lifestyle, just the two of us like back in the day.' Then he said to me, 'I am sorry, but can you please go speak to [Toho] on my behalf?' He didn't even want to negotiate or talk anymore, he was so determined to end it . . . But at the same time, he had gained such a big fan base that he had stayed until he could no longer tolerate it.

"Everyone said it would be a shame to see him go, and people encouraged him to sign a TV contract so he could continue to earn money. But his pride wouldn't allow it. For him, TV shows were things that simply got made, viewed, and disappeared. Keep in mind that the reputation of TV . . . back in those days was completely different from now.

"He always gave his absolute all when making something, so it was difficult for him to switch to TV at the time. He was clueless about making a living and had no concept of money, so maybe that enabled him to follow his heart in making this big decision.

"When he told interviewers that the studio 'just stopped bringing him projects,' that was his way of avoiding the details of [how he left] the company. But it was also not completely untrue, because Toho . . . could no longer assign him to projects like he was used to making."

It was an unceremonious departure. There were no farewells, no recognition for accomplishments, and no golden handshake. "He didn't get any retirement allowance or anything, because he was [an independent contractor]," Kimi said. "I told them . . . the least you could do is pay him a merit bonus or something." With income prospects uncertain, the "Honda mansion," where the family had thrown so many parties and received innumerable guests, would have to be sold. Honda's old mentor Kajiro Yamamoto suggested an available parcel of land in his Seijo neighborhood, where the Hondas built a comparatively small, two-story, Western-style home. It was not unlike a suburban American house, with a small front yard, living room and dining area with adjoining kitchen, and bedrooms upstairs. "Before we knew it, this little house became an extremely warm and cozy home," said Kimi.

———

The "big fan base" that Kimi spoke of now extended beyond Japan, as Honda's films had been distributed across Asia, Europe, Latin America, and other parts of the world. In the United States, the drive-in era was ending, but Toho's sci-fi films now received even greater exposure, airing repeatedly on independent television stations across the country. Honda now had time to indulge his passions for reading and playing an occasional round of golf, and he made a point of answering all fan letters, mailing out scores of autographed *shikishi* (traditional square paper) boards. He continued to welcome admirers arriving at his door, or he'd accept their phone calls, even the occasional collect call from overseas.

It was also a time for family. On August 29, 1971, the Hondas became grandparents when a daughter, Yuuko, was born to Ryuji and his wife Kuniko. Ryuji was now spending as much as eight months per year overseas, producing documentary television programming, and so Yuuko would grow closer to her grandfather than her own father during her formative years.

———

Following his *Tora! Tora! Tora!* debacle, Akira Kurosawa moved to restore his career and reputation. With fellow auteurs Kon Ichikawa, Keisuke Kinoshita, and Masaki Kobayashi, Kurosawa cofounded an independent production company and directed his first film in five years, *Dodes'ka-den*, released on October 31, 1970. Shot in one month on a comparatively low budget, the film was a stylistic departure, and Kurosawa's first without star Toshiro Mifune since *Ikiru* (1952). This was Kurosawa's first color film; and with daring visuals and a free-form narrative, *Dodes'ka-den* told an emotionally uplifting story of people living in abject poverty. Kurosawa mortgaged his home to finance the project, but it was a critical and commercial failure, leaving him with large debts and, at age sixty-one, dim work prospects. His disappointment culminated a year later, on December 22, 1971, when Kurosawa attempted suicide by slashing his neck and wrists with a razor.[36]

Uncharacteristically, Honda was not moved by the outpouring of support for Kurosawa, particularly from the film community, that followed. Watching television coverage showing well-wishers gathered outside Kurosawa's home, Kimi spotted old friend Senkichi Taniguchi among the crowd, and asked her husband why he didn't visit Kurosawa himself. His answer surprised her. Having endured his own setbacks as a filmmaker, he did not sympathize with Kurosawa's plight.

"At one time or another, everyone feels they want to commit suicide and end it all," he told Kimi. "I have been through many such hard times. He should stop being such a baby. I will not go." Eventually Honda's feelings softened, and he wrote Kurosawa a long letter of concern.

In truth, Honda was only semiretired. Between 1970 and 1978, he continued with the intermittent work of reediting movies for the Toho Champion Festival. *Mothra vs. Godzilla*, *Invasion of Astro-Monster*, *Ghidorah*, *Destroy All Monsters*, *King Kong Escapes*, *Latitude Zero*, *Mothra*, and *The Mysterians* would go under the knife. He also supervised the recutting of Fukuda's *Godzilla vs. the Sea Monster* and *Son of Godzilla*.

And despite Honda's ambivalence toward television, he was eventually drawn in—ironically, to direct the type of programming that contributed to the box-office demise of his films. At the beginning of the new decade, an explosion of genre programming hit Japanese TV, inspired by manga, anime, and the *Ultraman* phenomenon. Over a two-year period, Honda would direct episodes of five different science fiction TV series for kids, largely out of loyalty to colleagues and friends.

In early 1971, Tsuburaya Productions launched *Return of Ultraman* (*Kaettekita Urutoraman*), the fourth incarnation of the *Ultra* franchise and first since Eiji Tsuburaya's passing. Hajime Tsuburaya personally asked Honda to direct the debut episode, to lend credibility and authenticity to the show.

"We had Honda-*san* come in on [Eiji Tsuburaya's] behalf," recalled Minoru Nakano, an optical-effects technician who'd previously worked at Toho. "We specifically asked him to direct the first episodes because of his expertise and the vibe he creates." Despite his prior aversion to the small screen, Honda accepted, in deference to Tsuburaya's memory. In his self-deprecating manner, Honda told Hajime Tsuburaya, "I will do it, if you think I would suffice."

Return of Ultraman follows a racecar driver who becomes the "new Ultraman" and joins the Monster Attack Team to defend the world. Recalling the experience in a 1987 magazine essay, Honda said there were many challenges—a shorter schedule, lower budget, half-hour format, and shooting on sixteen-millimeter film—but as always he fully immersed himself in the work. "In those days . . . television works were considered lower quality than movies. However, I always felt that each had their unique qualities," he wrote. "I considered this job an opportunity for me to study and learn what sort of visual images I could create through the [medium] of television." Working out of Tsuburaya Productions' small studios near Toho, Honda stressed advance preparation, especially when taking his crew out on location. He was mindful that the characters were beginning a long arc that was already plotted out and directed the actors accordingly. In working with twenty-three-year-old lead actor Jiro Dan, who played the hero Ultraman Jack, Honda "thought about how to capture his youth, his movements, and his physique . . . I did not ask him for many difficult performances."[37] The half-hour show debuted April 2, 1971, in the 7:00 p.m. Friday slot. The premiere episode, "Charge of the Monsters" (*Kaiju soshingeki*), was a relatively elaborate production that featured Honda's signature crowd-evacuation scenes. Honda directed four of the first ten episodes, then returned to direct the fifty-first and final episode, "The Five Ultra Pledges" (*Urutora go-tsu no chikai*), which aired on March 31, 1972.

Honda also helped launch Tsuburaya Productions' *Mirrorman* by directing the first two episodes, aired in December 1971, and by establishing a straightforward tone for this series about a hero born to a human mother and a father from the "mirror dimension." The premiere, "Birth of Mirrorman" (*Miraman tanjo*), was also shown in theaters during the March 1972 Toho Champion Festival.

Even when he wasn't working directly on *Return of Ultraman* or *Mirrorman*, Honda visited the set of both productions. Minoru Nakano recalled Honda advising the crew on maintaining continuity between the drama and effects footage, and optical composition. "I think Honda-*san* was asked to be there, to oversee things . . . that he had experience with. He never [critiqued] the work. He simply guided us."

His third and final assignment from Tsuburaya was *Emergency Command 10-4, 10-10* (*Kinkyu shirei 10-4, 10-10*), a sci-fi mystery series in the vein of Tsuburaya's *Ultra Q*, with a child protagonist and no giant monsters. The main character, described as a "science boy," and an investigative team probe strange phenomena caused by the abuse of science. The team uses ham radios in their sleuthing, hence the show's title. Honda directed four episodes, broadcast from July to November of 1972 on NET.

As his TV résumé grew, more offers arrived. In summer 1972, Honda was approached by Hiromi Productions, a small outfit developing a superhero show based on Osamu Tezuka's new manga *Thunder Mask*. One of the show's directors was Akira Okazaki, an old family friend who had briefly lived with the Hondas years earlier. Honda accepted the work at Okazaki's request, though *Thunder Mask* was a decidedly low-budget project with barebones sets, crude effects, and a storyline about a teenage boy who transforms into a heroic alien. Honda looked at the job as an opportunity to teach young crew members their craft. He directed the premiere

episode, which aired on October 3, 1972, on the NTV network, plus five more during the show's twenty-six-episode run. *Thunder Mask* would eventually fade into obscurity because of rights disputes.

———

More than six years after the debut of *Ultraman*, Toho introduced its own monster-fighting giant alien hero. *Meteor Man Zone* (*Ryusei ningen zon*, aka "Zone Fighter") was the first teleseries produced by subsidiary Toho Eizo, and Tomoyuki Tanaka recruited veteran studio directors Honda, Jun Fukuda, and Kengo Furusawa to help launch it. These three men would split the majority of the twenty-six episodes that aired from April to September 1973 on Nippon Television, and their presence helped shepherd the largely young, less-experienced crew.

The typically juvenile *Meteor Man Zone* follows a family from planet Peaceland, who flee to Earth and pose as a Japanese household after their world is destroyed by the evil Baron Garoga aliens. Three of the children have superpowers; and when the aliens send giant "terror beasts" to conquer Earth, the eldest son transforms into Zone Fighter, an Ultraman-style hero. Though not among the most popular genre programs of its day, *Meteor Man Zone* was notable for five guest appearances by Godzilla, as well as foes King Ghidorah and Gigan, bridging the worlds of Toho's monster films and the *henshin* (transforming) hero shows that overtook them in popularity. Honda directed eight episodes, including Godzilla's first appearance on April 23, 1973.

———

In *Meteor Man Zone*, Godzilla the "justice monster" resides in a cave and comes to Japan's aid whenever monsters strike. Godzilla's transformation into a true superhero was now complete, and it had happened immediately after Honda's exit from Toho.

Although *Young Guy*, *Company President*, *Station Front*, and other long-running film series that defined the Toho brand in the 1960s had ended with the company's restructuring, the Godzilla franchise had continued with lower budgets and lower expectations. Five Godzilla movies would be produced from 1971 to 1975, each released via the Champion Festival.

The first was *Godzilla vs. Hedora* (1971), a singularly bizarre film by first-time director Yoshimitsu Banno, a former chief assistant to Kurosawa, Naruse, and others. Inspired by the environmental movement and Japan's mounting pollution problem, Banno's story of Godzilla battling an industrial sludge monster ran the gamut from a James Bond–style credits sequence, psychedelic rock, and cartoon animation segments to grim images of toxic death. In the climax, the hero Godzilla flies through the air using its breath as jet power.

Banno met with Honda to formally greet and pay respects to Godzilla's founding father. Honda never publicly commented on the film, but if he had any quarrel with Banno's handling of the character, he nevertheless came to the neophyte's assistance.

"Since this was my first film as a director, producer Tomoyuki Tanaka wanted Honda to watch the rough edit and give his advice," said Banno. "I had only been given about half of the budget of past films and was only given thirty-five days to shoot the whole film, so we'd written the script with all of that in mind . . . When Honda watched the rough edit, I told him I needed a few more days to finish shooting. I asked Honda to ask Tanaka if he could extend our shooting schedule for the film, and thankfully it worked."[38]

Even so, Banno's film would eventually be labeled one of the worst of all time.[39] Tanaka reportedly accused Banno of having ruined the Godzilla franchise, and attempted to restore order by assigning Jun Fukuda to direct the next three films, but arguably things got worse. *Godzilla vs. Gigan* (1972) featured a Godzilla that "talks" with comic-book word balloons, and *Godzilla vs. Megalon* (1973) was a depressingly cheap production pitting a Muppet-like Godzilla against a giant beetle, and utilizing large amounts of stock special-effects footage. The twentieth anniversary film, *Godzilla vs. Mechagodzilla* (1974), had aliens building a Godzilla-like robot a la *King Kong Escapes*; it sold 1.3 million tickets, less than one-third that of Honda's *Ghidorah* a decade earlier.[40]

Toho simultaneously experienced a resurgence with bigger-budgeted disaster movies. Shiro Moritani's *Submersion of Japan* (*Nippon chinbotsu*, 1973) was highly successful, and Toshio Masuda's *Prophecies of Nostradamus* (*Nosutoradamusu no daiyogen*, 1974) was another major release, while the Godzilla films were now second-tier productions. As if to restore lost luster to the franchise, in mid-1974 Tomoyuki Tanaka approached Honda with a formal request to direct the next Godzilla movie.

The project would reunite Honda with Tanaka and composer Akira Ifukube for the first time since *Destroy All Monsters*, but otherwise the circumstances for his return to feature films were less than ideal. Most of his crew members and actors no longer worked for Toho. Even Haruo Nakajima, the original Godzilla, had lost enthusiasm after Tsuburaya's death and retired in 1972. The 1973 Middle East conflict and resulting climb in oil prices had caused an economic panic; there was no chance the budget would approach those of the 1960s films. What's more, Honda was being asked to make a sequel to a film by another director, one of his former assistants.[41]

Ryuji Honda was surprised when his father accepted. "I believe that by now, part of him really didn't want to make any more [monster] films. So for him to have gone back to make another one is a question mark," he said. Loyalty may have again guided Honda. "He was . . . thankful to have worked for Toho all that time," said Ryuji. "Maybe [he] wanted to pay them back, or maybe he simply desired to make a film once again."

Terror of Mechagodzilla was the winning entry in a Toho contest soliciting story ideas for a sequel to Fukuda's *Godzilla vs. Mechagodzilla*. Its author was Yukiko Takayama, a student at an independent Tokyo screenwriting school and daughter of renowned fine artist Tatsuo Takayama. In her treatment, Takayama infused the usual alien invasion and giant-monster plot with a romantic tragedy. Tomoyuki Tanaka liked it so much that, rather than hire Shinichi Sekizawa, he commissioned Takayama for a full screenplay, making her the first and only female screenwriter in the entire Godzilla franchise. Takayama may have had some influence on Tanaka's choice of director. "She wanted [Honda], no matter what," Kimi remembered. Honda, meanwhile, was pleased to learn the young screenwriter was from Yamagata, his birthplace. "He decided to take it on," said Kimi.

———

In August 1974, word came that Honda's mentor Kajiro Yamamoto was bedridden with a grave illness. Though once a premier Toho director, Yama-*san* was among those left behind during the studio's decline; his last film was one of Toho's *Company President* comedies in 1967. The "three crows," his protégés, lately weren't faring much better. Honda hadn't made a film in four years, Senkichi Taniguchi's career had ended in 1968, and Kurosawa now had to find backers outside Japan. After visiting Yamamoto on his sickbed, Kurosawa left for Russia to shoot *Derzu Uzala* (1975), financed entirely by Mosfilm, the Soviet film agency.[42]

Yamamoto died at age seventy-two on September 21, 1974. It was a difficult loss for the Hondas, for Yamamoto was not only a mentor and family friend since the 1930s, but also a neighbor who had counseled Honda on life after Toho. Honda would pay respects not only for himself, but also for Kurosawa, who sent a letter from the Soviet Union asking Honda to act on his behalf.

———

Takayama finished the customary third draft of *Terror of Mechagodzilla* on December 5, 1974; a fourth draft, with revisions requested by the studio to curb costs, was finished on Christmas day. While Takayama's original story had two dinosaur-like monsters called Titans that fused together to form a single monster, the final version had just one creature, Titanosaurus. Takayama's destruction sequences were also scaled down, but the neophyte writer was not discouraged. "My original [screenplay] focused on Katsura Mafune, the girl who had been turned into a cyborg by aliens," Takayama said. "Even after she had been altered, she [still] had emotions. As long as this idea was not removed from the script, I didn't care all that much about what was done with it."[43]

Katsura is not one of Honda's typical, modern women. She lives a cloistered life, dominated by male authority figures. Like a samurai woman in feudal Japan, she is expected to be loyal, to take revenge on enemies, and even to fight and, if necessary, sacrifice herself. Bound by obligation, Katsura submits to serving her mad-scientist father and the aliens who've twice saved her life by replacing her heart with an electronic gizmo, rendering her a cyborg. She walks and talks without emotion, yet the embers of Katsura's heart are reignited by Ichinose, a caring young scientist and Romeo. Even more dramatically than Namikawa in *Invasion of Astro-Monster*, Katsura is torn apart by love and duty; her internal struggle between ice queen and lovelorn young woman makes this one of Honda's most compelling sci-fi characters.

Honda chose twenty-year-old actress Tomoko Ai for the part. At the time, Ai was a regular cast member on *Ultraman Leo* (1974–75), the last "Ultra" series from Tsuburaya Productions made in the 1970s. She auditioned during a break in shooting the TV show, still in wardrobe.

"When I got there, the auditions were already finished. There were only director Honda, [assistant producer] Kenji Tokoro, and some others. I didn't even read lines or anything. They just asked me a lot of questions," Ai later recalled. "They were surprised at how weird I looked, on top of the fact that I was late for my audition . . . The staff told me later on that Honda-*sensei* liked how I looked back and bowed to him when we passed by in the hallway after the audition."

This was Ai's first feature film, and Honda's direction was much more specific than what he usually gave his actors. "His way of directing, his manner of speaking was so precise, so I hardly showed any energy at all," she said. "I recall especially that he told me to speak without changing my facial expression . . . [Katsura] isn't supposed to smile. That's so unlike me. So pretty much my acting was to talk without

any emotion, but sometimes, you have to put some kind of feeling in. How to switch between those modes was pretty hard."[44] The role required Ai to expose her breasts—or rather, plastic prosthetics—during a surgery scene; the actress dozed on the operating table. "Everyone told me not to move," she said. "I got nice and cozy, so I just fell asleep."

Honda again introduces the monsters immediately, recapping the battles from Fukuda's *Godzilla vs. Mechagodzilla* via stock footage under the opening credits. The story begins with a submarine searching for the wreckage of Mechagodzilla, which Godzilla tore apart in the previous film. The sub is attacked and destroyed; an SOS recording of the captain screaming "dinosaur!" offers the only clue. An investigation leads biologist Ichinose (Katsuhiko Sasaki) and Interpol agent Kusugari (Katsumasa Uchida) to a rundown mansion. They seek advice from the discredited marine biologist Dr. Shinzo Mafune (Akihiko Hirata), but instead the men meet the mysterious Katsura, who says her father is dead. In truth, the deranged Mafune is living in seclusion, developing an electronic

Directing *Terror of Mechagodzilla*.
Courtesy of Honda Film Inc.

device to control the actions of Titanosaurus, an undersea dinosaur; the sub attack was a test run. The financiers of Mafune's project—who've apparently been funding his work for many years—now reveal themselves to be the space aliens who built Mechagodzilla. They invite the revenge-mad scientist to join their world-invasion plan, enlisting him to build a control device for their robot, which they've rebuilt inside a hangar deep in the mountains. But when Mafune unleashes Titanosaurus on Tokyo prematurely, he sets off events that result in Katsura's death. While surgically resuscitating her, the aliens hide the Mechagodzilla controller in Katsura's chest, turning the girl into a walking remote control and seemingly killing what remained of her humanity. Katsura becomes a coldhearted surrogate alien, donning a sleek silver suit. Her eyes blazing green, she unleashes Titanosaurus and Mechagodzilla. Godzilla battles the monsters for the earth's fate.

Moody and deliberate, *Terror of Mechagodzilla* doesn't resemble the childish and action-packed Godzillas that immediately preceded it. Similarities to *Invasion of Astro-Monster* and *Destroy All Monsters* are obvious, but the humorless tone and gloomy themes are closer to *The Human Vapor*. Honda reteams with Mototaka Tomioka, his *All Monsters Attack* director of photography, who again supervises the live-action and effects cameras and brings a similarly gritty visual style. The cheaper production values, muted color palette, day-for-night scenes, and generally drab visuals lend a depressing vibe; and Honda and Tomioka employ unphotogenic locations and ordinary looking interiors instead of the lush outdoor locales and bright, imaginative sets of the old days; even the villains' hideout looks more like an industrial facility than an alien base.

All this is compounded by Takayama's writing, as pessimistic as Takeshi Kimura's. The alien commander engages in sadistic whippings and executions; the invaders keep slave laborers, their vocal cords slashed, in a dungeon-like cell. Then there is the normally cherubic Ikio Sawamura playing Mafune's creepy servant, a gaunt mute whose job involves spying on Katsura. Sawamura was reportedly ill during filming and died a short time later; his atypical appearance epitomizes Honda's shift to a darker, misanthropic tone here. It doesn't feel much like a children's matinee film, and Godzilla—the nominal main attraction—doesn't appear until fifty minutes into the picture, reduced to acting as Japan's guard dog.

Still, there are Honda touchstones, from the fleeing Tokyo hordes to Akira Ifukube's brash, melancholy score. It's the maestro's best genre work in a decade, with a foreboding Mechagodzilla theme and a reworking of the original Godzilla melody, not heard since 1954. Honda's stock characters populate the background: Ichinose's perky female sidekick, scientist Yamamoto (Tomoe Mari), is a role that might have been played by Yuriko Hoshi a decade earlier. There is a stoic Interpol commander (Tadao Nakamaru) and a detective (Uchida), parts once played by Jun Tazaki and Tadao Takashima. Chameleon Kenji Sahara, graying at the temples, cameos as a military commander.

However, the two star-crossed lovers at the story's center are atypical of Honda's monster films. Ichinose's undying attempts to draw the guarded Katsura out of her shell create a character-based drama; and although it hardly carries the same emotional impact, Katsura's suicide is a Serizawa-like act of redemption to save both her paramour and the world from a deadly threat. There are cheers for Earth's victory over the invaders, a la *Battle in Outer Space*, but the happy ending is tempered by the grim sight of Ichinose carrying the body of his would-be bride.

"The idea, from the planning stages of the project, was to bring back Godzilla to its origin," said effects director Teryuoshi Nakano. "The character had been a children's idol for quite some time, but we started to question if that should continue." It was producer Tanaka who urged the filmmakers to get back to basics, but there were conundrums: Godzilla was now a superhero, and the themes of the 1954 original no longer resonated. "We thought about what we could do instead, and came up with something like *Beauty and the Beast*," Nakano said. While that might be a stretch, there are interesting parallels between Katsura and the two monsters she controls: Titanosaurus, forced to fight against its will, and Mechagodzilla, the heartless mechanical war machine.

As if to draw a through line from 1954 to the present, Honda cast Akihiko Hirata as Dr. Mafune. Unfortunately, the character becomes the film's biggest liability, and a 180-degree reversal from Hirata's role in *Godzilla* twenty-one years before: where Serizawa was a conflicted recluse, quiet and sensitive, Mafune is cackling and vengeful, eager to use science for mass destruction. Hirata was forty-eight but, wearing a poorly designed Einstein wig and makeup, he appears much older; Mafune's banishment from academia occurred about fifteen years ago, but he has aged at least thirty years. Honda's paradox of scientific overreach and morality is present, but Mafune never ponders it. After his reckless actions rob his daughter of her very soul, the old man cries yet has no change of heart. This lack of self-reflection coupled with Hirata's

Honda and crew on location for *Terror of Mechagodzilla*. Courtesy of Honda Film Inc.

hammy performance reduces Mafune to a cartoonish madman with a God complex.

Honda had spent the past few years shooting mindless sci-fi TV shows, and he may well have known that this would be his last feature. One can almost sense his struggle to carve out an entertaining and meaningful story—even incorporating a few trendy cinematic tropes for the adults, such as a Peckinpah-style, slow-motion shooting death and nonsexual female nudity—all while making another children's film and again struggling with production limitations. The entire film was shot by a single crew in early 1975, in the span of about one month, for a March release. There are ample special effects, but few spaceships and none of the ambitious superweapons of vintage Tsuburaya; and some of the composite shots are grossly out of scale.

In an essay for the film's program booklet, Honda cited the comparative lack of detail in the miniature work as one indication of the genre's economic decline. In the old days, there were typically three sizes of miniatures for long shots, medium shots, and full-scale portions for close-ups, but "Nowadays, there are times when we try to film everything using only one miniature due to . . . increases in material costs," he wrote. "When we compare these to the older works . . . you cannot help but feel that something is missing."

Even more telling were Honda's comments—still tempered, but worded more strongly than usual—on the studio's condescending to kids and the genre's resulting slide into irrelevance:

The fear and terror that people felt toward Godzilla [in 1954] was actually that toward nuclear weapons, something human beings should have never gotten our hands on.

In *Terror of Mechagodzilla* Dr. Mafune exclaims, "I have invented a device that will control any and all animals!" Can we not see the conceited nature of man in this character? Recently, people have begun contemplating threats such as pollution, but I feel that perhaps we have become overconfident in our own ability [to control our own destiny], and it is now time for us to rethink and reevaluate ourselves once again.

Of course, I have no intention of voicing these . . . arguments in any of my films. The truth is that Godzilla has transformed from a creature of terror into a hero. This is because of the children who say, "Poor Godzilla, it does nothing wrong, it is simply gigantic," or they see Godzilla as their hero because no matter how fierce the opponent, it fights without fear, is strong and very courageous. On the other hand, there are those who say, "It's boring, because Godzilla has become way too much of a good guy." And I believe these opinions are all valid. There are those who say,

"Monsters that are not scary are boring," and others who wish to see monsters that are more comical. However, it is awfully difficult to try to incorporate all of this into one movie.

He again criticized a trend that had bothered him since *King Kong vs. Godzilla* and had now overtaken the genre: "One thing we must be very careful about is when the monsters mimic human action and feelings. This rarely succeeds. For those works that have monsters doing silly, ad-lib-like actions, it is important to write the story that way from the very beginning."

Despite their intent to return the franchise to its roots, the filmmakers couldn't resist having the monster act the clown just a little; and when Godzilla appears dead and buried, it gets off the mat and comically brushes off its shoulders. But Nakano handles the monsters in a mostly straightforward manner, while introducing some creative new ideas. Mechagodzilla and Titanosaurus employ movements borrowed from Noh drama in their attack on Tokyo, and the camera's vantage point is constantly changing—there are ground-level shots amid fleeing civilians, a helicopter pilot's point of view above the monsters on a huge landscape, a dramatic dolly-tracking shot around the monsters fighting in a miniature set, and even a Busby Berkeley–style overhead view of the battle. Godzilla's entrance scene is the most dramatic since *Mothra vs. Godzilla*, the monster rising behind a building and silhouetted against the night sky. Nakano's effects and Honda's actors are wed dramatically; instead of watching the monsters fight from afar, the hero Ichinose overtakes his alien captors with an assist from his Interpol buddy, and the action is mirrored by cutaways to Godzilla fighting its foes.

In a 2010 interview, Nakano recalled how Honda and he designed the look of the film:

[Honda's] generation thought camera angles were better if shot a bit from above . . . By showing a portion of the floor and table in the frame, it gives a sense of everyday living. Where this actually comes from is the *Tales of Genji* scrolls. So you see the floor, the tatami mat, from the toe to the top of the head. By doing this, one can get a very good idea of what life was like back then . . . Honda-*san*'s angles tend to be a little pulled back and from atop. If you watch . . . the laboratory scenes, for example, you can see this angle being used, unlike other films. You can see all the way down to the floor; that was the Honda viewpoint. So I had to match my angles to his . . . but then it's a lot of work because this angle reveals everything. We'd lift the camera up a bit, so that the monster's feet don't show and we don't have to complete the set all the way to the floor. [Laughs.] That was actually my little trick. In this film I tried to incorporate the Honda directing style into the effects shots.

Though certainly flawed, *Terror of Mechagodzilla* is an unusually compelling *kaiju eiga*, with more complex characters and themes than any Honda sci-film since *Atragon* or *Matango*. It was nevertheless the lowest-attended film in the entire Godzilla series, selling less than one million tickets. Japan's monster boom was over, both in film and television; even Tsuburaya Productions had ceased making *Ultraman* spinoffs. Toho would continue to reduce in-house film production, and its genre out-put would come to a near halt. Its only true science fiction film of the late 1970s would be Jun Fukuda's poor *Star Wars* knockoff, *The War in Space* (*Wakusei daisenso*, 1977). The Champion Festival was also winding down and replacing Godzilla with old Disney movies and animated films starring Doraemon, a blue cat, which performed much better at the box office than the recent Godzillas.

Although several Godzilla projects would be rumored or announced in the late 1970s—*Rebirth of Godzilla* (a proposed color remake of the original), *Godzilla vs. the Devil*, *Godzilla vs. Gargantua*, and possibly others—none came to fruition. Godzilla's popularity in America was down, too. *Terror of Mechagodzilla* received a small, spotty matinee theatrical release and went into TV syndication.

Still, Honda sounded as optimistic as ever after making *Terror of Mechagodzilla*. "I plan to continue to make a variety of special-effects films into the future," he wrote. "I also wish to make films that allow the audience to forget everything, [to] lose themselves in the world on the screen." Given the reality, this may have been merely sweet lemons. Years later, Honda would say it had become more difficult to make films because the crews were now made up of freelance specialists rather than a collaborative team. "In my time, everybody had so much energy for making movies, and all the staff had ideas." Now, he said, "everyone knew just their own department."[45] *Terror of Mechagodzilla* would stand unceremoniously as Honda's final directorial credit. Before long, however, he would discover a new and unexpected role behind the camera.

V

AT KUROSAWA'S SIDE

1976–93

I have unlimited memories of him. The period when we were assistant directors, when we lived together, when he went off to war, when we worked together every day, and the five movies from *Kagemusha* to *Madadayo*.

I can't finish it. I'll be sad if I try to remember more.

– Akira Kurosawa

23

RHAPSODY
IN AUTUMN

The Hondas' current residence was smaller than their former "mansion," but spacious enough for the quieter life they now lived. The two-story house stood on a corner lot in Setagaya, in a neighborhood of modern, suburban-style homes that wouldn't be out of place in middle America. It was an unassuming, gray stucco structure with a shingled roof, a driveway to the right, fronted by a cinderblock wall with a mailbox and metal gate, and "Honda" written in Japanese script. Pavestones led to the front door, and inside the *genkan* (entryway), above the shoes and slippers, were several Godzilla toy figures on shelves and framed drawings of Honda on the wall. These items, all gifts from fans, were the only visible evidence, anywhere, that the man behind the monster—or a filmmaker for that matter—lived here.

Entering the living room, on the right was a large wooden cabinet with brass lockets and framed family photographs on top. Decorative ceramic plates and vases were displayed throughout the room, with large glass ashtrays strategically placed. To the left was a cream-colored leather sofa set and a glass-top coffee table; on the opposite wall were built-in shelves with a TV, stereo, and as the years went by, a growing collection of VHS tapes and laser discs. There was a dining area with a large wooden table, big enough to host old Toho friends and other guests. The adjoining kitchen had custom low countertops putting everything within diminutive Kimi's reach; Honda rarely cooked at home, but when he bussed his dishes after a meal, he looked like a giant. Along one side of the house was a long sunroom filled with fresh flowers and plants, which Kimi and daughter Takako, both skilled in ikebana flower arranging, tended to daily. Each morning the sunroom blinds were opened, filling the house with light.

Upstairs, Honda and his wife shared a large bedroom, sleeping on full-size mattresses rather than futons. A second bedroom was occupied by Honda's daughter, Takako. Down the hall was Honda's study, smelling of the old books that lined the floor-to-ceiling shelves and the *sumi* ink from Honda's traditional calligraphy set. In one corner was an electric massage chair. Honda worked at a large, heavy, Western-style wood desk (as opposed to the Eastern, sit-on-the-floor type) neatly arranged with books, documents, pen holder, pencils, and Japanese brushes. Kimi had become an accomplished wood sculptor, and some of her creations—with decorative engravings and finished in a traditional Japanese lacquer—were used as paper holders or decorations. And always, atop the desk sat the unexploded mortar shell that Honda had carried home from China.

Rather than a shrine to his film career, Honda's home was now a refuge from it, a place to immerse himself in private life. He cared for the plants and trees outside, tolerated the family dogs, and welcomed visitors. The neighborhood was still largely undeveloped and heavily wooded; and the Hondas took frequent walks to scenic spots where the trees parted for a clear view of Mount Fuji, or they would descend the stone steps to the bank of the Nogawa River for a stroll. The train station, post office, and family doctor were all within walking distance; sometimes the entire family would eat at a local restaurant, and even if his daughter insisted on a taxi or bus, Honda always preferred to walk.

Without a set schedule, Honda had time to read, listen to classical music (he collected the works of Vivaldi and recordings by the Austrian conductor Herbert von Karajan, among others), play golf, and be a grandfather. His son Ryuji, by

now a producer of documentary television programming, lived with his family in an apartment complex in the adjacent town of Komae. Every Saturday morning, granddaughter Yuuko would walk a long, wooded, uphill path that connected the two neighborhoods, and at the top of the road her grandparents would be waiting. Beginning in 1974, when she was three years old, Yuuko spent weekends at the Honda house; and those days often turned into playdates with grandfather. They pretended the sofa was a fort or a bath, played games, and took walks. Once, they got caught in the rain and Kimi opened the front door to find them both standing there, the tall old man and the tiny girl using big *fuki* leaves as umbrellas, like the iconic image from *My Neighbor Totoro*. Honda had a playful side, but even so, he spoke to the child as he would anyone else, never treating her like a kid. "I gave him the nickname *iki jibiki* [living encyclopedia] because whatever I asked him, the answer would always come right back, about everything," Yuuko recalled. "I used to [make] fun of him because he was like a dictionary."

He was an A-level director; even so, he decided to assist Mr. Kurosawa. That's why I really respected him.
— Kyoko Kagawa[1]

By now Honda had become a halfway decent golfer, and he frequented the Fuji Heigen Golf Club and Tomei Country Club, both located in the Fuji-Gotenba area; and it was on the links that Honda soon bumped into Kurosawa, himself an avid golfer for decades. The two men had rarely socialized during the heady days of the 1950s and 1960s, and even after both had parted ways with Toho, they seldom crossed paths. Kurosawa was now living near the Hondas, but he still never visited; then there were the matters of Honda's absence in the wake of Kurosawa's suicide attempt, and Kurosawa's absence at Yama-*san*'s funeral. And yet, none of it mattered. Instantly, the two men reestablished the deep friendship that had been put on hold roughly twenty-five years earlier.

"It goes all the way back to their days at the Musashi-so dormitory [at PCL], sharing a room, a pot of rice, drinks, and laughter," said Ryuji Honda. "It was fate how they met back then, and [they picked up where they left off] from back in those days. I don't think they ever got off track."

At first it was all about golf. They would meet up at a local driving range after dinnertime, take some practice swings, then wind down by chatting at Honda's house before Kurosawa went home. Sometimes they'd play eighteen holes. Each man's game reflected his temperament. Kurosawa was a hacker—he'd walk up to the ball and hit it hard, then jump back on the golf cart, ready to go. Honda was serious and deliberate, quietly gauging each shot.

Kurosawa had time to play golf largely because he was, once again, unable to find backing for his next film. He'd spent recent years eking out a living, starring in whiskey commercials while developing three screenplays, all historical epics set in feudal Japan: *Kagemusha*, *Ran*, and an adaptation of Edgar Allan Poe's "The Masque of the Red Death." Kurosawa wanted to direct *Ran*, the most ambitious of the three, but Toho viewed *Kagemusha* as more commercially viable and offered to finance it instead. *Kagemusha* was a comic tragedy about a petty thief who is a dead ringer for Shingen Takeda, lord of a mighty

clan. When Shingen dies, the clan conceals his death and installs the lookalike, or "shadow warrior," as its pseudochief, maintaining a façade of stability. The story, based on actual events, ends in an epic, bloody battle that wipes out the entire clan. However, Toho soon balked at the $5.5 million budget, more than five times what the studio then typically spent on a feature. Kurosawa thought he might never make the film, but the project was rescued by one of his admirers, director George Lucas, who'd paid homage to Kurosawa's work in *Star Wars* (1977). Lucas pressured Twentieth Century Fox to make a substantial investment, essentially shaming Toho into funding Kurosawa's film. Fox and Toho jointly announced the production of *Kagemusha* in December 1978, with cameras set to roll the following April.[2]

As his project came together, Kurosawa shared the news with Honda during a round of golf. But on this day, Kurosawa had something more in mind.

"Ino-*san*," Kurosawa said, "let's work together again. Just like the old days, when we were under Yama-*san*."

Honda's reply, as usual, was unpresuming, even self-effacing. "If I can be of any assistance to you, sure. Anytime."

With these few words, the two men entered into a cinematic pact of great significance, yet one without precedent. Kurosawa was implicitly asking Honda to become his right-hand man, one of his most trusted advisers and confidants. And by invoking their mentor Kajiro Yamamoto, Kurosawa was reaching back to a time of shared ideals, optimism, and promise, a time when—as Kurosawa surely remembered—Honda was forced to sacrifice his ambitions while Kurosawa's flourished. It was only because of this shared history that Kurosawa, a director of tremendous ego

At Toho Studios during preparation for *Kagemusha*. Courtesy of Honda Film Inc.

coordinator on *Kagemusha*, but his actual function, according to Kurosawa biographer Stuart Galbraith IV, was a unique hybrid of roles. Honda was simultaneously a chief assistant director who oversaw major second-unit shooting, including ambitious battle scenes, and a consultant whose opinion Kurosawa highly valued. Honda "would quietly make suggestions, and many of his ideas were incorporated in their films together"; and because Kurosawa suffered from serious vision problems during his later years, "to some extent, Honda was also Kurosawa's eyes," Galbraith noted. Additionally, Honda would advise on special-effects scenes, help Kurosawa communicate with his crew during filming, and work with the actors. Kurosawa called Honda his "mental support" and said Honda enabled him to concentrate on other tasks without worry.[3]

In 1985, Honda described his working relationship with Kurosawa:

and a man not known to display humility or empathy, would ask Honda—himself a veteran director of international renown—to join his innermost circle. Perhaps never has another filmmaker of Kurosawa's stature invited a colleague to collaborate in quite the same way.

For his part, Honda was being asked to make a huge commitment. The demands of a Kurosawa production far exceeded those of the old days at Toho. There would be weeks and months away from home, shooting on location. But in a way, the timing was perfect: Ryuji Honda and his family would move to New York in 1979, so there would be no more weekends with grandpa and granddaughter. Still, the low-key life that Honda had enjoyed after *Terror of Mechagodzilla* would be disrupted while *Kagemusha* was in production. Knowing this, Kurosawa visited Honda's wife and asked her permission to "borrow" Honda to make a film together. Kimi enthusiastically approved.

Honda was credited as production

We get along really well. Kuro-*san* . . . uses three cameras at once, so I would supervise Camera B and Camera C. For scenes that have a lot of people, it's impossible to direct the whole picture by yourself. Especially things like scenes with soldiers, I handled their movements. I have experience in the military, so it's kind of like the same thing, moving an entire crowd. I know how to organize them, how to move them, acting as the leader or captain. I worked with the actors and assistant directors like that.

I was just giving him advice . . . like how to use the guns or how to make it look [good], that kind of thing. He could ask me anything, like if he should cut something out, or how to make someone sit, or whatever. Any old little thing. It wasn't quite about director and assistant director. I think that some people thought it was weird. One guy came from France and asked me, "Why is the guy who directed *Godzilla* working on Kurosawa's movie?" It's not that we needed two directors, but it was easier if I was there for him. At least, he thought it would be a positive thing to work with me, that's why he asked me to do it. Pretty much I could do anything, so I was very useful for him.

[Our positions were] exactly the same as when we were both assistant directors. To understand and make good movies, it's not about my position, our positions. Instead, just me and him . . . "Want to do it? Can you?" "Yeah, OK." "Let's do it." That's pretty much how it went.[4]

Kurosawa informed his staff that there would be two directors on set and instructed them to treat Honda with the same respect and deference as himself. At the same time, Honda was not interested in a director's credit; in fact, Honda seemed to have had little concern about his on-screen title, which would change to associate director, creative consultant, special adviser, adviser to the director, and other variations on subsequent Kurosawa films, though Honda's role remained largely the same. Honda made it clear that he would not usurp Kurosawa's position, telling him, "A movie will not succeed if there are two directors." He was even unconcerned about his salary, urging Kurosawa to instead spend the money on additional quarter horses for the big action sequences. For Honda, the opportunity to make a film with his best friend was all that mattered.

"He told [Kurosawa], 'Instead of making films myself, it would be a greater benefit

to cinema if I just helped you,'" recalled Kurosawa's son, Hisao. "That's how sincere Honda was . . . Sometimes people say things that they really don't mean. But he meant it."

Once filming began, both men appeared reinvigorated, moving about with the energy of their days as twentysomething assistant directors. Kurosawa rebounded from recent health problems and directed with new energy, while Honda alternated between working at Kurosawa's side and roaming the expansive locations on the plateaus beneath Mount Fuji, overseeing parts of vast combat sequences that filled the screen with hundreds of warriors on horseback. Honda was just shy of seventy, with a thinning head of jet-white hair, big glasses, and a wizened, lined face. Even though Kurosawa was the older man, crew members began to see Honda as a mature, reassuring presence capable of calming the volatile Emperor, whose quick, fierce temper they feared. When Kurosawa would occasionally erupt and storm away, it was only Honda who could approach and talk him off the ledge so work could resume. If the director was troubled by something, he sought Honda's advice; when Honda noticed something wasn't right, he would pull Kurosawa aside and discuss it. These conversations occurred when the pair were alone, out of earshot from the cast and crew. "Everything went so much smoother," remembered Hisao Kurosawa. "Those two had such a wonderful relationship." During off-days, Kurosawa would come over to Honda's to watch sumo matches on TV, or they'd hit the golf range.

The Kurosawa-Honda alliance required each man to suppress part of his professional pride. Their seemingly contradictory personalities meshed smoothly and fully, puzzling those around them. "Those two were so close, it even baffled me at times," Kimi Honda said. "Maybe they were brothers in another life." Honda himself couldn't explain it—"This is something only Kurosawa and I truly understand," he told friends—and he eventually grew tired of trying. Once, he angrily hung up on an inquisitive *Kinema Junpo* writer, telling him to butt out of private matters. It was one of the few times Kimi saw Honda get truly mad.

When Kurosawa was asked about their compatibility, he credited Honda's patience and tolerance:

> Male friends, no matter how close their relationship is, [sometimes] they fight. But with [Honda], we never fought. That's because of him, not me. He is so nice and gentle, we never fought. I am sure I did some things that were a pain in the ass to him, but he never got angry.
>
> When we are shooting in different groups, I can rely on him 100 percent. He can create the scene exactly how I ask. For instance, when we were shooting *Kagemusha*, I got sick with pneumonia and I couldn't move. But I didn't have to worry a bit because I knew he could substitute for me exactly as I would want.[5]

"My father trusted him so much," Hisao Kurosawa said. "That was the key point."

In the words of Teruyo Nogami, Kurosawa's longtime script supervisor, Honda was Kurosawa's "sworn friend."

————

It was a pivotal scene that Kurosawa, stricken with a high fever and unable to work, asked Honda to direct in his stead. Lord Shingen's ambitious son, resentful of living in the shadow of his dead father, recklessly leads the clan into battle against rival forces. After nightfall, enemy soldiers approach on their horses, but the sight of the impostor lord, surrounded by his troops atop a hill, fools and intimidates the attackers, who retreat. Disaster is avoided, but these events foreshadow imminent doom. The impostor is soon discovered and ousted; Shingen's son, assuming full control of the Takeda clan, leads the army into an unnecessary, ill-advised war and the entire faction is bloodily destroyed.

Decades earlier, it would have been unthinkable for Kurosawa to allow another director to shoot scenes for him, but Honda continued to be tapped on subsequent projects whenever Kurosawa fell ill. For *Ran*, Honda would direct an important and emotional scene in which the king's estranged son, after reuniting with his father, is shot by a sniper and falls from his horse. And in *Rhapsody in August*, Kurosawa asked Honda to shoot a symbolic scene of ants invading a blooming rose; Kurosawa simply lacked the patience to film the insects, so he sent his even-keeled friend.

Shooting *Kagemusha* stretched to nine months, the budget inflated to $7 million, and the release was briefly delayed, all of which might have signaled a troubled production. However, after it opened in Japan on April 27, 1980, *Kagemusha* was a big hit, earning more than $12 million in its domestic theatrical run. It would share the coveted Palme d'Or at Cannes with Bob Fosse's *All That Jazz*, and be nominated in the Best Foreign Film category at both the Academy Awards and the Golden Globes. *Kagemusha* was seen as Kurosawa's return to epic form, a comeback effort that opened a new career chapter. And Honda, a stabilizing force on the Kurosawa team, had rediscovered his love of making movies.

"I think [Honda] enjoyed filmmaking the most then," said Ryuji Honda. "Before that, he had to obey company orders and make films he didn't necessarily agree with . . . There was always some kind of restriction, handcuffs and shackles getting in his way or holding him back, being forced to work only within the given parameters. To have all of this removed, to be completely free to do as he pleased, to be able to be on the set of a movie that he really liked, [directed by] his closest and best friend . . . there was nothing more liberating and fun for my father than this."

———

On October 22, 1982, a Mercedes Benz sedan pulled up in front of a two-story house in Seijo. Out of the car emerged Akira Kurosawa, then Ishiro Honda, and finally assistant director Takashi Koizumi. Soon they would be joined by other members of Kurosawa's inner circle: cinematographers Takao Saito and Asazaku Nakai, and sound recordist Fumio Yanoguchi, a veteran of numerous Kurosawa and Honda films. The team convened in this rented house to begin preproduction work on *Ran*, the film Kurosawa had longed to make for a decade. When Honda joined the *Kagemusha* production, he and Kurosawa pledged to work on five films together. It seemed an impossible goal: both men were approaching seventy, and Kurosawa was still struggling for support; he hadn't made a film wholly financed by a domestic film company since *Red Beard*. Even after the success of *Kagemusha*, Japanese studios balked at the projected $10 million cost of Kurosawa's next project. Kurosawa initially found support from France, but because of economic instability in that country, the financing of *Ran* would have to be rescued by a complex partnership of Japanese financiers and backers from the film and TV industries.[6] The start of filming was delayed; but nevertheless, here were Kurosawa, Honda, and

Contemplating a scene from Kurosawa's *Ran*.
Courtesy of Kurosawa Productions

the rest, launching Kurosawa's last epic period masterpiece, the artistic apex of his late period.

Inside the house, the team worked Monday through Saturday from 9:00 a.m. to 5:00 p.m. They broke down the script, written by Kurosawa with Hideo Oguni and Masato Ide, into individual scenes and, using detailed storyboards hand-painted by Kurosawa, developed a detailed shooting schedule. Casting, locations, sets, props, and costumes were finalized. Even during these routine days, Honda would serve as a buffer between Kurosawa and the staffers walking on eggshells around him. Just as on set or location, there was a codified hierarchy in the house: Kurosawa, Honda, and the other core team members worked on the ground floor, while a couple of support staff, rarely if ever spoken to or acknowledged, worked upstairs. One of these was Masahiko Kumada, a young production assistant sweating his way through his first Kurosawa film, who had the unenviable task of informing the director that he couldn't shoot at the historic Azuchi Castle near Kyoto. Kurosawa wanted the location for an important scene in which the protagonist, the exiled Lord Hidetora Ichimonji (Tatsuya Nakadai), hides in the ruins of a castle he long ago destroyed. However, Azuchi Castle's overseers had barred further filming there after Kurosawa spattered fake blood on the walls while shooting *Kagemusha*. Kumada delivered the bad news, expecting to be fired on the spot. But Honda, who'd been researching other locations in Kyushu, suggested Nagoya Castle—which Godzilla knocked over in *Mothra vs. Godzilla* two decades earlier—as an alternative. Kurosawa was understanding, Kumada kept his job and would go on to become Kurosawa's unit manager, and Honda cemented his role as the level-headed, mature "brother" quieting Kurosawa's fiery tempest. "Once Kurosawa-*san* starts to get irritated, his face changes, and everyone around him starts to . . . get uncomfortable," Kumada said. "It was so much easier to deal with someone like Honda-*san*, who was more patient."

Ran, loosely inspired by Shakespeare's *King Lear*, tells the story of an aging tyrant who divides his rule among three sons. Soon after abdicating, Lord Ichimonji's reign of bloodthirsty totalitarianism comes back to haunt him: the memory of his horrific deeds drives him mad, while two of the sons turn against him and prove even more ruthless than their father, weaving a complex web of rivalry, revenge, and war that ends with the tragic destruction of the entire clan. Shooting began in June 1984 and took thirty weeks, and Honda again supervised camera work on Kurosawa's sweeping battle sequences on the vast, gorgeous, pristine plains of Kyushu, with hundreds of armored cavalry and infantry bearing color-coded banners that identified the warring factions and filled the frame with stunning hues and movement.

By contrast, the dark, bleak, third-act landscapes, where Ichimonji and his one loyal son meet their deaths, were filmed near Kurosawa's and Honda's stomping grounds around Mount Fuji and Gotenba; and it was there that Honda again helped the crew weather Kurosawa's stormy temper. One day, while shooting at the black volcanic ash slopes of Tarobo, at the southeast foot of Mount Fuji, Kurosawa became infuriated—no one seems to remember exactly why—and suddenly stormed off, demanding to be driven to his villa in nearby Gotenba, where he stayed during filming. Once there, Kurosawa was so upset that he took a swig of whiskey and went straight to bed. The crew members stood by on location, wondering what to do. Honda called the house and, after learning that Kurosawa was out cold, sent everyone home. "It was a difficult call to make," recalled production assistant Kumada.

Honda (left) and Kurosawa (right) review the script of *Ran*. Courtesy of Kurosawa Productions

Consulting with Kurosawa's longtime scripter Teruyo Nogami on the set of *Ran*.
Courtesy of Kurosawa Productions

"What if Kurosawa-*san* changed his mind and went back to the location and no one was there?"

From the time of *Kagemusha*, Kurosawa and Honda had begun staying for extended periods at the villa. When Kurosawa was shooting on location in and around Gotenba, this vacation house provided a cost savings and a sanctuary away from the cast and crew, lodged at hotels. Other times, it was simply where Kurosawa and Honda went to unwind—"a place where two fully-grown men could escape the everyday world, be away from family, and where they could play, just like children," said production assistant Kumada. Midway through the making of *Ran*, Kumada became responsible for tending to Kurosawa—waking him in the morning, getting him to and from the shoot, arranging meals—and so he became a fly on the wall, watching Kurosawa and Honda in their daily routine, witness to private details of their friendship that no one else saw. He accompanied the pair as they played golf, took a cab into the town of Gotenba for shopping, relaxed with drinks in the evening and reminisced about old times. Sometimes they'd work in the garden, clipping trees or pulling weeds, though

it was always Honda who actually did the clipping and pulling while Kurosawa sat and directed. Kurosawa was the free-spirited old man, staying up till morning and talking with friends, never cleaning up after himself. Honda was the disciplined one; he would usually excuse himself to bed by 10:00 p.m., rise early, and neatly make his bed. When the two men were alone, Honda did the cooking, precisely preparing one portion per man, even when Kurosawa wanted seconds. Honda preached the appreciation of food down to the last grain of rice; when he ate grilled fish, the bones were cleaned. Nothing was wasted; the soldier still conserved his rations.

"Kurosawa-*san* never had a human relationship with anyone else throughout his career," Kumada said. "Honda-*san* was the only human being that Kurosawa-*san* was truly able to trust until the very end . . . There are so many directors who are solely interested in being rich and famous; however, Kurosawa-*san* and Honda-*san* had no

Honda and Kurosawa on location at Gotenba for *Ran*. Courtesy of Kurosawa Productions

interest in those things. They simply and purely loved film . . . They wanted to run around the studio like they did when they were younger, and make movies together. That was it.

"For Kurosawa-*san*, [Honda] was somebody who [would never betray him]. This was their relationship. For Honda-*san*, Kurosawa-*san* may have been wilder in many ways, but the bottom line was that he absolutely believed in Kurosawa-*san*'s talent and abilities. I think this is where the two [were bound] together."

————————

Ran premiered in Japan in May 1985 and was the third-highest-grossing Japanese film of 1985. Its subsequent US release was met with rave reviews, and Kurosawa was nominated in the director's category at the Fifty-Eighth Academy Awards. *Ran* also received nominations for cinematography, art direction, and costume design, though the Japan Movie Producers Association inexplicably declined to submit *Ran* into competition for Best Foreign Film. Kurosawa attended the ceremonies in Los Angeles in March 1986. Costume designer Emi Wada took home the film's lone Oscar.

Kurosawa made just four films between 1966 and 1985. But with *Ran*, Kurosawa concluded this long and difficult career phase on a thunderous, albeit pessimistic, note. The film was a stunning achievement both visually and thematically, contrasting spectacular, epic battles with meditations on war, the end of empire, and the corruption of humanity.

In the next and final chapter of Kurosawa's career, this bleak vision would give way to deeply personal and reflective work that was altogether different from what came before. After a roughly five-year hiatus from the screen, and approaching eighty, Kurosawa would direct three

pictures within a four-year span, an accelerated pace at any age. Honda would maintain his role as wingman and counsel, and his influence would be more discernible in these final films, which addressed themes of concern to both men. On the eve of the Cold War's end, both *Akira Kurosawa's Dreams* (*Yume*, 1990) and *Rhapsody in August* (*Hachi-gatsu no kyoshikyoku*, 1991) would return to the horrors of nuclear radiation. The third film, *Madadayo* (1993), though set against war's backdrop, would be a quiet contemplation on aging and friendship.

————————

Though Godzilla disappeared after *Terror of Mechagodzilla*, nostalgia for the monster grew as children of the 1950s and 1960s reached adulthood. Toho sold $4.5 million worth of Godzilla toys from 1975 to 1979, books devoted to the genre were published, and in August 1981, Honda and *Godzilla* actor Akihiko Hirata were featured guests at the first annual SFX Convention, a fan-organized event in Tokyo. The next year, Honda would return as a guest speaker and to judge an amateur film contest. Meanwhile, Godzilla made the transition into the home video medium in the early 1980s, including a series of VHS tapes featuring highlight reels of the studio's genre films, supervised and edited by Honda.

Even with the Japanese film industry at its nadir, with Toho producing only a small number of movies per year, Tomoyuki Tanaka saw Godzilla as a potentially profitable franchise, "a world famous character, on par in terms of notoriety with Superman and *Star Wars*."[7] His first attempt to revive the monster was announced in August 1979, when the Associated Press reported that Honda was attached to direct *The Return of Godzilla*, with a story inspired by the meltdown at the Three Mile Island reactor in

Pennsylvania earlier that year. Godzilla was to battle a new monster foe against a timely backdrop of illegal nuclear waste dumping and the destruction of a nuclear power plant; it was to end with Godzilla's carcass washing ashore on the US coast. "We went downhill in the last five or six [Godzilla movies]," Honda told AP. "The first film was pacifistic in intent." Had *The Return of Godzilla* been green-lit, Honda would likely have started preproduction shortly after *Kagemusha*, and the final arc of his career might have been much different. But, like all previous Godzilla projects initiated in the late 1970s, it stalled in preproduction.

Tanaka's unflagging efforts were aided by the first US showings of Honda's original cut of *Godzilla*, in English-subtitled form, in a handful of art-house venues in summer 1982. These screenings confirmed what many American fans and cinephiles long suspected, that there existed a director's cut, far superior to the bowdlerized *Godzilla, King of the Monsters!* Soon thereafter, several Hollywood studios including Warner Bros. and Universal were in talks with Toho about a proposed *Godzilla* remake by director Steve Miner, in which the monster would lay waste to San Francisco. Miner was inspired by Honda's *Godzilla*, calling it "a beautiful movie [with] larger implications to society in general, and how we're the victims of our own reach, unleashing technologies and weapons without knowing really what the consequences are."[8] He envisioned a 3-D remake, with a budget of around $25 million and *Star Wars*–caliber special effects, but this project, too, lost momentum.

Hollywood's interest, along with pressure from the Godzilla Resurrection Committee, a group of Japanese fans that reportedly collected forty thousand signatures demanding Godzilla's return, eventually

provided the impetus to revive the monster; and in July 1984 a new Toho film simply titled *Godzilla* went into production. It was essentially a direct sequel to Honda's 1954 original, ignoring all previous sequels, and it contemporized Honda's antinuclear and antiwar themes by recasting Godzilla as a Cold War figure, caught between heightened US-USSR tensions pushing the world to the brink of World War III. It was the most expensive Godzilla film to date, with a budget of about $6 million, and featured several alumni of the Honda-Tsuburaya vintage, including Yosuke Natsuki (*Ghidorah*) as a Yamane-like scientist, Hiroshi Koizumi in a bit role, and Teruyoshi Nakano directing the special effects.

But Honda, now firmly ensconced in the Kurosawa fold, had declined Tanaka's request to direct the picture. "Godzilla is no longer mine, it has grown up into its own entity," he said of his decision. His wife, too, agreed it was time to move on: "I didn't want him to continue working on it just because [Godzilla] brings in money." Honda also felt an obligation to bequeath his monster to the next generation. The film was directed by one of Honda's former assistant directors, Koji Hashimoto.

Hashimoto's *Godzilla*, despite its admirable attempt to make the monster relevant again, had neither the pathos of the original nor the charm of the sequels. It was nevertheless the second-highest-grossing Japanese film of 1985, with box-office returns of about $11 million. It received a wide theatrical release in the United States the following year, heavily reedited and retitled *Godzilla 1985*. Raymond Burr reprised his journalist role from the 1956 US version, again via inserted footage.

Around the same time, Honda was approached about directing a remake of *Daimajin*, a period supernatural fantasy about a giant, Golem-like stone idol, which had appeared in three popular films from Daei Studios, all in 1966. Honda was reportedly interested, but the project never materialized. Thus, he had not completely turned his back on science fiction and fantasy film. And despite parting ways with Godzilla, Honda would continue to write and speak about the monster and the *tokusatsu* genre. Throughout the 1980s and until his death, he published magazine articles, appeared at conventions and on TV talk shows, lectured at film festivals, and granted interviews to numerous writers.

Beginning in 1989, Toho launched a new Godzilla series made by a younger generation, with stories influenced by the original *kaiju* films and Hollywood blockbusters, and touching on themes of bioterrorism, nuclear war, and Japan's "bubble economy" of the 1980s. But Honda, now fully untethered from the studio, was uncharacteristically frank in his assessment of them.

"The new films lack imagination," Honda told an interviewer in December 1992. "If they continue to make Godzilla films like they are now, where it simply . . . comes to Japan, I feel that the meaning of Godzilla will be greatly diminished. I think they should make [Godzilla] a global problem, [a threat to] planet Earth. . . . [S]cience fiction films [should be relevant] to today. Environmental concerns, a malfunction or accident at one of the nuclear reactors on the Eastern Sea, chemical weapons—horrific things like these are all Godzilla in my mind.

"In Japan, you can make money by just having Godzilla appear, and that is the sole reason why [Tomoyuki Tanaka] continues to make these films. Enough with such hackneyed thinking."[9]

Shortly after the release of *Ran*, the Hondas visited Ryuji and his family in New York.

When word got out that the *Godzilla* director was in town, there were invitations and requests for public appearances and interviews, but Honda declined them all. He and his wife spent a quiet vacation with family, visiting Niagara Falls, the Amish settlements in Pennsylvania Dutch Country, and other sites.

During the extended break between Kurosawa projects, Honda made a handful of minor on-screen appearances in films by director colleagues. Nobuhiko Obayashi, an experimental filmmaker who'd made his feature debut with the singularly bizarre horror-fantasy *House* (1977) for Toho, cast Honda and his wife in a brief, nonspeaking scene as grandparents in *The Drifting Classroom* (*Hyoryu kyoshitsu*, 1987). Then, in Obayashi's supernatural horror thriller *The Discarnates* (*Ijin-tachi to no natsu*, 1988), Honda had a cameo, with dialogue, as a street vendor selling skewers of yakitori. Shortly after Honda's death, Obayashi would pay tribute to his friend by posthumously casting him as a deceased grandfather, whose portrait sits atop the family hearth in the comic fantasy *Samurai Kids* (*Mizu no tabibito: Samurai kizzu*,

Honda playing a priest in *Come Back Hero*, with director Eiji Yamana (left).
Courtesy of Honda Film Inc.

1993). Honda also played a priest at a wedding ceremony in *Come Back Hero* (1987), a comedy directed by Eiji Yamana, who began his career making musical shorts featuring pop idols. Yamana's *A Gift from Agnes* (1975) was on the same Champion Festival bill as Honda's *Terror of Mechagodzilla*.

————

Winter 1945. The Japanese countryside. An Imperial Army captain, weary from years at war and demoralized by his time in a POW camp, makes his way home, walking mountain roads. Approaching the mouth of a dark tunnel, he is startled by the appearance of a hellhound, the rabid ghost of a military sentry dog. Its bark is a warning not to enter this passageway to the unknown, but the captain continues ahead. When he exits the other side, the sky is now darker, and the captain senses an unnerving presence. He turns to find, following close behind, the gray-faced apparition of a uniformed private. The young man died at the front, perishing in the captain's arms, but his disbelieving spirit roams Japan in postwar purgatory. Soon the captain is met by the ghosts of his entire platoon, all unaware they were killed in action, standing in formation and awaiting his command . . .

Akira Kurosawa's Dreams purports to be a cinematic tableau of eight of the director's visions, each presented from the point of view of a surrogate Kurosawa and rendered in expressionistic fashion. These vignettes weave together themes about the desecration of the environment, the resulting devastation of humanity, the tragedy of war, and the pursuit of art. Some segments reference events and places in Kurosawa's lifetime; but the most harrowing of all, "The Tunnel," instead mirrors Honda's autobiographical nightmare, the vision of fallen comrades that continued to awaken him decades after the war. Kurosawa

On location at the Daio Wasabi farm to film the "Village of the Watermills" sequence from *Dreams*. Courtesy of Kurosawa Productions

channels Honda's dream, the dead soldiers manifesting as a platoon of corpses standing at attention. Honda's terror becomes Kurosawa's lament for the war's legacy of millions of lives lost, families destroyed, and the unbearable guilt of those who survived and returned.

It has been rumored and implied that Honda ghostwrote, cowrote, or directed this sequence of *Dreams*. There is no conclusive evidence of this, but Kimi Honda believes her husband was the primary inspiration. "Since [Honda] was so close with Kuro-*san*, they had talked about these episodes, how he was still woken up by horrible nightmares," she said. "How he'd see all of his friends in his dreams, all of those who died fighting, all standing in a line."[10]

Kurosawa also relied on Honda's military background for authenticity. The more than forty actors who made up the Third Platoon rehearsed at Toho Studios prior to shooting, with Honda training the actors to march

Checking a waterwheel for the "Village of the Watermills" segment from *Dreams*. Courtesy of Kurosawa Productions

in formation, salute properly, and shout military commands. He taught them how to handle their rifles correctly and the posture for standing at attention.

His *Tora! Tora! Tora!* debacle aside, "The Tunnel" is the closest Kurosawa would come to making a film about World War II, and Honda helped him bring credibility to the segment. "Having Ishiro Honda, who served in the war, as a friend . . . I'd feel odd making a war movie," Kurosawa would say. "I don't know the reality of battle."[11]

Honda's influence is also visible in "Mount Fuji in Red," an apocalyptic dream informed by the horrors of the Chernobyl disaster of 1986 and presaging the Fukushima event of 2011. A nuclear plant adjacent to Mount Fuji melts down, its reactors exploding and filling the sky with crimson fire. Thousands flee toward the shoreline for safety, but clouds of deadly radioactive gases follow. The special effects, created by Industrial Light and Magic (ILM), the effects house founded by George Lucas, are more surreal than anything seen in the

Honda-Tsuburaya films, but the overall impact of this sequence is familiar. As Kurosawa scholar Stephen Prince notes:

"Throughout this dream, Kurosawa employs the visual rhetoric of his friend Ishiro Honda, who served as a creative consultant on the film and who is better known for his own series of Japanese science fiction films . . . The process photography and the shots of fleeing crowds recall similar, well-known sequences in Honda's films and make explicit the connection between Honda's popular monsters and Japanese nuclear anxieties."[12]

The next sequence, "The Weeping Demon," continues this post-*Godzilla* theme in an apocalyptic dream world, where radiation has destroyed the environment and plants and animals are mutated by fallout. And "The Blizzard," about a group of mountain climbers trapped in a raging snowstorm, may likely have been inspired by the long hiking trips taken by the "three crows" during their assistant director days; it resembles Honda's *Half Human* or Senkichi Taniguchi's *Snow Trail* more than any previous Kurosawa picture.

Dreams was financed with help from Steven Spielberg, who followed directors Lucas, Coppola, and Sidney Lumet (who campaigned for *Ran*'s Oscar nods) in supporting Kurosawa's recent work. A bit of this Hollywood adulation rubbed off on Honda, when Kurosawa cast filmmaker Martin Scorsese to play Vincent Van Gogh in the segment titled "Crows." During filming, Scorsese observed and admired how Honda worked alongside Kurosawa; and when the shooting on location in Hokkaido wrapped up, he asked the *Godzilla* director to pose with him for a photo. "Immediately after filming his scenes, Scorsese washed off his makeup and ran over to Honda," remembered filmmaker

Honda and Martin Scorsese on location during the making of *Dreams*. Courtesy of Martin Scorsese

Nobuhiko Obayashi, who captured the moment in the documentary film *Making of Dreams*. "They stood arm in arm and took a picture together. And Scorsese whispered to Honda, 'Actually, I came to Japan just to take this photo with you.'"[13] The American crew from ILM also took photos with Honda.

On March 26, 1990, three days after his eightieth birthday, Kurosawa received an honorary Oscar for lifetime achievement at the Sixty-Second Academy Awards. The presentation included a subtitled video message from the *Dreams* cast and crew, led by Honda, who told Kurosawa, "We've always known how important your films are to the world. Now the rest of the world knows. Congratulations. All of us are honored by your special Academy Award." They were joined by the Hollywood audience in a chorus of "Happy Birthday."

Though this segment appeared to be transmitted live, it was actually recorded in advance, with Honda and the others carefully keeping it secret from Kurosawa.

———

When *Dreams* premiered in May 1990, Kurosawa had already written the screenplay for his next project, *Rhapsody in August*, the story of a family still living under the cloud of the atomic bomb forty-five years later. This would be a simple and quiet film about the pain of remembering and the shame of forgetting a tragedy, an elegant and elegiac work of feelings and emotions, with themes tracing back to Kurosawa's *I Live in Fear* and Honda's *Godzilla*.

In 1954, Honda had critiqued Japan's postwar dependence on the United States by showing politicians afraid to reveal Godzilla's ties to American H-bomb tests for fear of damaging an important geopolitical and economic relationship. In *Rhapsody in August*, Kurosawa shows that, after generations of Japanese Westernization

During filming of *Rhapsody in August* (from left to right): Kimi Honda, Ishiro Honda, Akira Kurosawa, Yuuko Honda-Yun, and Richard Gere.
Courtesy of Kurosawa Productions

and a culture of materialism, this reticence is culturally ingrained and rooted at a personal level. A Japanese family is reluctant to tell their rich half-American cousins about an uncle who died at Nagasaki for fear of offending them and losing potentially lucrative relations. This and several other scenes in Kurosawa's film are like nods to *Godzilla*, three decades later. Child survivors of Nagasaki, now middle-aged adults, recall the kids orphaned by Godzilla's attack; and the grandmother, Kane (Sachio Murase), offers a distant echo to Dr. Yamane's warning about nuclear weapons: "People will do anything to win a war. Sooner or later, it will be the ruin of us all."

Rhapsody debuted at Cannes in May 1991; about a month earlier, Honda rather presciently observed to an interviewer that little had changed regarding the world's attitude toward the bomb. "Believe it or not," Honda said, "we naïvely hoped that the end of *Godzilla* was going to coincide with the end of nuclear testing."[14] *Godzilla*, made just after the Occupation, never referenced America by name, but enough time had passed for Kurosawa to allow his characters to plainly state the fact that America had dropped the atomic bomb. Though Kurosawa's dialogue was not accusatory or political, its directness offended some Western critics, who mistook it for anti-American polemics.[15] The pressures that may have undermined Honda's message when *Godzilla* was first imported to the United States remained, and so *Rhapsody in August* became one of the most controversial and misunderstood of all Kurosawa's films.

————

"When shooting a battle scene, Honda, the chief [assistant], oversees the shoot, and we can hear his voice in this vast, open space," Kurosawa told an interviewer while making *Rhapsody in August*. "But [nowadays] assistant directors all use the bullhorn, and it just isn't the same. Their voices just don't travel well . . . But when Ino-*san*, who's a quiet man, says, 'Charge!' everyone can hear it. That's a result of practice. It's actually an essential skill."[16]

By now, Honda's contribution included setting an example for the young assistant directors. People were again calling him by his old nickname, "keeper of the grain," and though one of the oldest, he was one of the most active people on the shoot. There was no standing around and waiting for orders; this was an old-school work ethic that Honda and Kurosawa were teaching.

"Honda-*san* was a very mobile guy," said chief assistant director Takashi Koizumi. "We'd get scolded by Kurosawa-*san*, saying, 'Ino-*san*'s running! What are *you* guys doing?' He would always take initiative to go fix something, even before us, and was always on the move."

The old studio apprenticeship program was history, and both Kurosawa and Honda bemoaned the difficulty of recruiting talented assistants because of the depressed state of Japan's film industry. Still, Kurosawa's assistants were considered among the elite of the business, and both Kurosawa and Honda were committed to preparing them to follow in their footsteps. And, in fact, two did just that. Takashi Koizumi would make his feature directorial debut with *After the Rain* (*Ame agaru*, 1999), from a script by Kurosawa; and assistant Okihiro Yoneda's first feature would be Toho's *Rebirth of Mothra*.

For most of 1992, Honda assisted Kurosawa with the shooting of *Madadayo*, a warm and understated drama based on the life of Hyakken Uchida, an eccentric academic and one of Japan's great literary figures. The film starred Kurosawa veterans

On the set of *Madadayo*.
Courtesy of Kurosawa Productions

Tatsuo Matsumura and Kyoko Kagawa—both of whom Honda had also previously directed—as Uchida and his long-suffering wife; and its simple story focused on the professor and a group of former students who remain dedicated to him through the years, regaled by his humorous, life-lesson stories. Much of the film takes place during the war years, when Honda was away for long stretches in China. If *Dreams* reflected Honda's wartime experience, then *Madadayo* is a glimpse of what Kurosawa and Kimi Honda remembered, of soldiers marching through the streets en route to the front and firebombs destroying Tokyo neighborhoods. Its central themes are friendship and mentorship, and perhaps it's not a stretch to see the main character as partly modeled on Kurosawa and Honda's old teacher, Kajiro Yamamoto. The title comes from a Japanese children's hide-and-seek game wherein the seeker shouts, "Are you ready?" and the hider replies, "*Mada da yo*" ("not yet"); in context, it represents the spirit of a man not yet ready to stop pursuing his art, yet an old man who recognizes the inevitability of death. As it turned out, it was a fitting finale for both Kurosawa, and Honda with him.

After retiring, I still went to visit the Honda home once a year, for New Year's. The last time I saw him [on New Year's Day 1993] he saw me to the door, so I told him, "Honda-*san*, please do go back inside, because it is freezing out." But he replied, "One has to breathe in some cold, fresh air from time to time," put on his *geta* sandals, and greeted me out. That was our last good-bye.
– Koji Kajita

Throughout his years with Kurosawa, Honda was always viewed as the more physically robust of the two, fleet of foot and possessed of stamina. Kurosawa was as big and imposing as ever, but he had a history of health episodes; while "Honda seemed like the type of man who would never get ill," said script supervisor Teruyo Nogami. "During *Madadayo*, there was absolutely no sign of such thing. I wonder if he was pushing himself through, feeling sick?"

After completing principal photography on *Madadayo* at the end of 1992, Kurosawa held a wrap party for the cast and crew. Honda was suffering from what seemed like cold symptoms, and perhaps because he was not quite himself, he drank more than usual. That night, he called his son in New York. "I had never heard or seen him that drunk, ever," said Ryuji. "But he was such a happy drunk, merry as a child: 'This film came out so great! It's just superb!'" Even so, Ryuji sensed something odd about the call.

Then, in mid-February 1993, Kurosawa, Honda, and Masahiko Kumada, the unit manager, attended a screening of *The Stranger*, the last film by Indian director Satyajit Ray, at an art-house cinema. As they took their seats, Honda said he had a cough and shared throat lozenges with his friends. When the film ended, Honda and Kurosawa were so moved by it that they clapped, and during the drive home they kept on singing its praises. Kurosawa invited Honda back to his place to continue talking over dinner and drinks.

"But Honda-*san* said, 'I think I am coming down with something, so I will go home,'" Kumada remembered. "Kurosawa-*san* offered to take him back to his house, but Honda-*san* declined and got out at Seijo station, and the [driver] took Kurosawa-*san* back home. That was the last time they saw each other."

Honda had received a clean bill of health after a December 1992 checkup, so at first there was no suspicion of a major illness. Even as his cough kept getting worse, the family doctor's diagnosis was a common cold with mild fever. Honda spent a week resting in bed, but after he began losing his appetite, he went for blood tests and X-rays. When the results came in, the doctor recommended that Honda be admitted to a hospital immediately; knowing something was seriously wrong, Honda already had his bags packed. The major hospitals were full, so he was placed in a tiny room at Kono Medical Clinic, a nineteen-bed facility in Soshigaya, a ten-minute drive from home.

Honda had coughed up blood, and believed his symptoms indicated a respiratory ailment. The reality was much worse. Tests had revealed late-stage lung cancer, and it had metastasized. Honda would never learn the true nature of his disease, because doctors and family members didn't want to upset him—shades of Takashi Shimura as the terminally ill man in Kurosawa's *Ikiru*.

Friends also didn't know how bad it was.

Kurosawa was concerned because he knew Honda hated hospitals, but there was no apparent need to worry. Honda was about to be transferred to a room in a bigger hospital, where friends could visit. But soon he developed pleurisy, an inflammation of the lungs that causes difficulty breathing; and on February 27 at about eight in the evening, shortly after returning home from visiting hours, Kimi and Takako received an urgent call: Honda's vital signs had taken a sudden turn for the worse. They returned to his bedside, and Honda clung to life through the night; but on Sunday, February 28, 1993, at 11:30 a.m., he died peacefully at Kono Medical Center. The official cause of death was respiratory failure.

————

Kurosawa didn't want to be a distraction, so he waited until the other mourners had all gone. He arrived at the Honda home at about eleven in the evening and sat silently beside his fallen friend, mourning into the wee hours. It is part of the Japanese funeral ritual for the deceased to spend one final night in his home, the body packed with ice and covered with a sheet, and so Honda lay on a futon in the living room. Family and close friends come to pay respects, an event that traditionally lasts one night before the deceased is taken to the funeral site and placed in a coffin; but Kimi extended the vigil several days while Ryuji traveled home from the United States, so that her son could view the body. About 350 people, most from the film industry, visited during that time. Kurosawa was devastated; he stayed each night until about two in the morning, then took his leave. Said Kimi, "It broke my heart, just watching him."

Traditional Buddhist funerals are the most common in Japan. But even if Honda was the son of a monk, he never cared much for Buddhist rites; and so the family held a more laid-back service, omitting the religious aspects. Some traditions were followed—mourners came forward to offer burning incense and bow before a large photo portrait of Honda—but instead of chrysanthemums, the traditional Buddhist funeral flower, there were white orchids. There was no Buddhist monk chanting sutras, and mourners did not ring the traditional bell upon paying respects before the casket. In the background, recordings of Vivaldi were played. "We toned it down and kept it not too strict and uptight, more fitting to my grandfather's personality," said Yuuko, his granddaughter.

The service was held on Saturday, March 6, at Joshoji Kaikan, an assembly hall in Setagaya. The turnout was larger than expected, with lines wrapping around the block. Family members were joined by several hundred colleagues, from the golden days of Toho to the latter-day Kurosawa team, from executives and filmmakers to actors and crew. The stars of Honda's films were there: Akira Takarada, Kenji Sahara, Kumi Mizuno, Yumi Shirakawa, and Kaoru Yachigusa, joined by nearly fifty supporting players from the extended "Honda family," some of whom hadn't seen Honda for many years. From the recent Kurosawa films, stars Akira Terao and Hisashi Igawa attended. A frail Toshiro Mifune exchanged a tearful embrace with Kurosawa; Honda's funeral would be their last meeting.[17] And there were fellow directors: from Honda's generation, Kihachi Okamoto and Shue Matsubayashi; from the new-wave movement there was Koreyoshi Kurahara, once mentored by Kajiro Yamamoto at Honda's referral; and younger filmmakers such as Nobuhiko Obayashi and Kazuki Omori.

The eulogy was read by an emotional

Kimi Honda at Ishiro Honda's memorial service.
Courtesy of Honda Film Inc.

Mourners gather to pay respects.
Courtesy of Honda Film Inc.

Kurosawa. "We had worked on film projects since we were assistant directors in our twenties," he said. "Recently, he was not only an executive staff of Kurosawa Productions but also a collaborator on my directorial projects, so we were always together. Now, I am at a loss for words, for I have suddenly lost my irreplaceable best friend. It's not just me, my entire staff are all in a daze."

Kurosawa and the Honda family visit Ishiro Honda's grave site at Tama Cemetery. Courtesy of Honda Film Inc.

"I was so surprised to hear the sudden news of his passing," said Tomoyuki Tanaka. "Ever since the very first *Godzilla* in 1954, it was all Honda-*san* and his meritorious deeds that made Tsuburaya-*san*'s works and techniques come to life. He had such a warm and sincere personality, a splendid filmmaker. May his soul rest forever in peace."

The family estimated that between two thousand and twenty-five hundred mourners showed up that day, most of them fans, but the hall wasn't large enough to accommodate everyone. "People were already standing outside the gates on the morning of the ceremony," said Ryuji, and "many were still there when the gates closed at the end of the day. . . . There were many who declined to come inside . . . [They said], 'I am in no position to [do so]. I am more than happy just to send him off from here, in the street.' I think many of my father's fans were like this, the very gentle and reserved type."

Honda's cremated remains were interred at Tama Cemetery, the largest municipal graveyard in Japan and the resting place of such notables as Isoroku Yamamoto and Yukio Mishima. Later, the family relocated the grave to the Fuji Cemetery, known for its abundant cherry blossoms, not far from Gotenba.

On the headstone is the inscription:

Ishiro Honda
February 28, 1993
Age: 81
Honda was truly a virtuous, sincere, and a gentle soul. He worked for the world of film with might and main, lived a full life and very much like his nature, quietly exited this world.
— Akira Kurosawa, February 28, 1993

Honda's passing brought numerous tributes and reminiscences from admirers and colleagues via the Japanese media. Most news outlets in the West, however, published only a very brief wire service death notice. One of the most thoughtful obituaries was a lengthy piece in London's *The Independent* by the poet James Kirkup. Although "Godzilla lives on," Kirkup wrote, toward the end of his life, Honda had "dropped out of the monster marathon and returned to his first love, pure cinema, happy to be of service to the Emperor Kurosawa. The title of that last film they made together now takes on an even more plangent note of lingering farewell: *Madadayo* . . . 'Not yet, not yet.'"

Madadayo was released about six weeks after Honda's funeral, on April 17, 1993. It would be Kurosawa's last film, though he had planned several more. After completing a new screenplay, *The Ocean Is Watching*, Kurosawa was again unable to acquire funding, so he began writing another, *After the Rain*. In 1995, after falling and suffering a spinal injury, Kurosawa was confined to a wheelchair for the rest of his life. He

本多は誠に善良で誠実で温厚
な人柄でした
映画のために力いっぱい働き
十分に生きて本多らしく静か
に一生を終えました
平成五年二月二十八日
黒澤明

Honda's gravestone. Courtesy of Kurosawa Productions

died of a stroke on September 6, 1998, aged eighty-eight.

————

In Japan, Honda's *Godzilla* has long been accepted as both the genesis of a multibillion-yen entertainment franchise and a historically, thematically, and technically important film. In 1984 it ranked no. 20 in *Kinema Junpo*'s *100 Best Japanese Films*, and it has bested films by Ozu, Mizoguchi, and even Kurosawa in this highly volatile, periodic poll of critics. Scholars and intellectuals have penned lengthy essays probing *Godzilla*'s meaning in publications such as *Bungei Shunju*, the literary journal associated with the prestigious Akutagawa and Naoki literary prizes. Honda's contributions as a director are also well recognized. He gave innumerable interviews in print and on television over the decades, and he was the subject of *My Life in Cinema: Ishiro Honda* (1990), one in a series of interviews with celebrated filmmakers produced by the Director's Guild of Japan for cable television. In 1992 the biography *Good Morning Godzilla: The Golden Age of the Movie Studio and Director Ishiro Honda* was published, and books about the man and his work continue to appear posthumously.

In the West, the original damage inflicted by the dubbing and reediting of Honda's films has been difficult to repair. Critical reappraisal of *Godzilla* and acknowledgment of Honda's direction has followed a gradual, decades-long groundswell of support for the film and for its genre among cinema fans, historians, and preservationists in North America, the United Kingdom, and elsewhere. Toho's second Godzilla film series, produced in the 1980s and 1990s, inspired many of these enthusiasts to revisit and reappraise the films of decades earlier.

They published fanzines, hosted revival screenings, and organized fan conventions with guest appearances by the genre's creators and personalities, including several of Honda's actors. Beginning in the mid-1990s, a handful of scholarly, trade-list, and underground English-language books devoted to Godzilla and Japanese science fiction films were published, some written by authors whose research had led them to Honda's doorstep prior to his death.

But it was the release of *Godzilla* in its uncut, original Japanese-language edition to art-house cinemas across the United States in 2004, marking the film's fiftieth anniversary, that was a major turning point, the first time the film was widely evaluated on its own merits in the West. The critical response was, on the whole, revelatory. In the *New York Times*, Terrence Rafferty praised the film's "distinctively haunted, elegiac quality," while highlighting Honda's nuanced themes:

> The most peculiar thing about *Godzilla* as a metaphor for the bomb is the creature's simultaneous status as a legendary beast of Japanese islanders' mythology: surely a more precise representation of the disaster that befell the country at the end of the Second World War would be an agent of destruction from far away, unheard of even in legend, not this native, almost familiar monster. Is Godzilla, then, also on some subterranean level a metaphor for Japan's former imperial ambitions, which finally unleashed the retaliatory fury that leveled its cities?
>
> Maybe. But the runaway metaphor of Honda's *Godzilla* isn't nearly so easy to pin down. It's more ambiguous, more generalized and perhaps more potent than that. And its significance can be

glimpsed only in the Japanese version of the movie, because what Honda's *Godzilla* is most fundamentally about, I think, is a society's desire to claim its deepest tragedies for itself.[18]

Over time, *Godzilla's* stature continued to improve, and interest in Honda's body of work grew. An academic conference titled "In Godzilla's Footsteps" was held at Kansas University in fall 2004, followed by a book of scholarly papers presented there; *Godzilla* has subsequently been taught in film studies programs at Johns Hopkins; Cornell; Columbia; Princeton; New York University; University of California, Berkeley; and other institutions in the United States and Europe. In 2006 the prestigious British Film Institute released the film on DVD with an essay by noted Japan scholar Ian Buruma. Later that year the film debuted on DVD in the United States, branded as *Gojira: The Original Japanese Masterpiece*. And between 2005 and 2007, American home video distributors released nineteen more Honda-Tsuburaya science fiction films in Japanese with subtitles, in their original aspect ratios; only *Half Human*, *The Human Vapor*, and *Gorath* were not included (the latter two because of rights issues), while *King Kong vs. Godzilla* remained available only in Americanized form. Many of the films were similarly released in Europe, Australia, and other territories.

Meanwhile, seeds of interest in Honda's nongenre films sprouted in Japan. The 2009 Yamagata International Documentary Film Festival, held not far from Honda's birthplace, hosted "The Man Who Shot Godzilla," the first retrospective of its kind. The documentary *Ise-Shima* and the rarely seen features *Night School*, *Song for a Bride*, and *Seniors, Juniors, Co-workers* were screened, and there were discussions about the films. Two years later, the same festival celebrated Honda's one hundredth birthday by screening *Skin of the South* and *Rodan*. Then, from April to June 2014, the famous Laputa revival cinema, located in Honda's childhood stomping ground of Suginami Ward, presented "Ishiro Honda: Exposure," a retrospective of nine nongenre pictures, including seven not seen at the Yamagata Festival: *Young Tree*; *Love Make-up*; *Mother and Son*; *Good Luck to These Two*; *People of Tokyo, Goodbye*; *An Echo Calls You*; and *Inao*.

Honda's two greatest posthumous milestones to date came in 2012. In January of that year, *Godzilla* joined the influential Criterion Collection, cementing its ascendance to classic film status. Criterion's Blu-ray disc treated the film as a landmark of postwar Japanese cinema, with a high-definition digital restoration of the image and sound. And on June 15, 2012, the respected cable television channel Turner Classic Movies hosted "Directed by Ishiro Honda," a tribute movie marathon featuring *Godzilla*, *Rodan*, *Mothra*, and *The H-Man*, all presented in Japanese with subtitles. TCM's Richard Harland Smith noted that, at the time of his death, Honda's "contributions to cinema had only begun to be appreciated, much less understood." Clearly that was changing; two years later, the TCM Classic Film Festival 2014 would honor *Godzilla's* sixtieth anniversary with a packed-house screening at the historic Egyptian Theater in Hollywood.

————

Late in life, asked if he thought *Godzilla* was his best film, Honda replied: "Probably. But let me say that I never said 'well done' after making any of my films. Eiji Tsuburaya and I would get together after filming, and our conversations would go: 'Well, what do you give this one? A seventy' 'No, maybe about a sixty.' And we'd get harder on ourselves as time went on because we were supposed to know more about filmmaking. Always in the back of your mind there's this realization that a film is forever and its influence is going to outlive you."[19]

The influence of the Honda-Tsuburaya films continues to reach across generations and cultures. Toho's third Godzilla series, made between 1999 and 2004, included contributions from two of Japan's most popular directors, both fulfilling a lifelong dream of making a Godzilla movie. Shusuke Kaneko's *Godzilla, Mothra and King Ghidorah: Giant Monsters All-Out Attack* (*Gojira, Mosura, Kingu Gidora: Daikaiju sokogeki*, 2001) revisited Godzilla's origin as a deadly metaphor for war, while Ryuhei Kitamura's over-the-top *Godzilla: Final Wars* (2004) brought back monsters, characters, and scenes from *Invasion of Astro-Monster*, *Atragon*, *Gorath*, *All Monsters Attack*, and others.

The iconic status of *Godzilla*—the film, and the monster itself—is best evidenced by Hollywood's attempts to remake it as a big-budget blockbuster, which finally culminated in Tristar Pictures' $130 million *Godzilla* (1998), directed by German-born Roland Emmerich. Rather than mimic the Japanese films and their cult appeal, Emmerich aimed to broaden Godzilla's reach to a wider, mainstream audience. The digitally rendered creature invading New York bore little resemblance to Tsuburaya's *kaiju*, and the light, often jokey story owed more to *Independence Day* and *Jurassic Park* than to Honda's antiwar allegory. The film grossed $379 million worldwide but was overwhelmingly panned.

However, by the time Hollywood inevitably "rebooted" Godzilla sixteen years later, Honda's 1954 film had been widely distributed in the Western hemisphere, and expectations had changed; any remake would now be judged against the original. Legendary Pictures' $160 million *Godzilla* (2014) portrayed the monster as a mythical force of nature and an inhospitable-yet-heroic guardian of Earth, while making somber-if-shallow allusions to Fukushima, climate change, natural disasters, September 11, and war.

Though British director Gareth Edwards's "jaw-dropping *Godzilla* may not have the depth of Honda's original, it exhibits an appreciation and understanding of what made that movie great," wrote Mark Kermode in London's *Guardian*. "Just as Gojira transmuted over the course of several movies from fire-breathing scourge to savage savior, so Edwards' lonely samurai dinosaur emerges from the depths as an avenging angel, safeguarding the natural order so blithely abandoned by man."

Some things hadn't changed. The subject of the atomic bomb remained uncomfortable, and so Edwards revised Godzilla's origin and underplayed Honda's theme of nuclear destruction. Nevertheless, critics generally considered the film a worthy successor; and after it earned $529 million internationally, work began on a sequel with more monsters from the Toho universe, and another big-budget film pitting King Kong against Godzilla was also planned. Somewhat ironically, America had become the steward of the Honda-Tsuburaya legacy. At the same time, Toho revived its own Godzilla franchise yet again with *Shin Godzilla* (2016)—a highly successful yet unconventional film that traded Honda's antinuclear pacifism for

a nationalistic theme, reflecting calls by present-day conservative politicians to revise Japan's US-drafted constitution and establish an autonomous Japanese military—and announced the first-ever anime Godzilla feature for 2017.

———

Honda lived for the joy of making movies, though his work was shaped by nightmares. In the hopelessness of war, it was the dream of directing that gave him hope; when the dream was fulfilled, it was a harrowing glimpse of Hiroshima's ashes and a lifetime of sleep disturbed by the souls of lost compatriots that haunted his films, from *Godzilla* to Kurosawa's *Dreams*. The boy raised amid natural wonders, the boy fascinated by the possibilities of science, became a director who feared the world's rapid technological advancements would spoil the environment and overtake humanity. And a director who was dedicated to his studio eventually found himself cast out, a relic of a former era, only to rediscover the love of film alongside one of cinema's giants, his closest friend.

His nightmares never ended, but behind the camera Honda found peace.

"My nightmares are almost always about war—wandering the streets, searching for something that's lost forever," Honda said in 1991. "But it's possible for me to will myself to have pleasant dreams. For me, the most wonderful fragrance in the world is new film. You open the canister for the first time and breathe deeply. That night, the same wonderful fragrance fills your dreams. It's grand."

AFTERWORD

From the time I was very young, my father taught me about the mysteries of life and how precious it is. These lessons can be seen in *Godzilla*—a film that, beneath the surface, is a depiction of nuclear holocaust, an image of meaningless killing and despoiling of the earth. As a lover of nature and a documentary filmmaker at heart, my father made a plea for world peace and protested the destruction of the planet through the metaphor of a giant monster. Sixty-plus years later, as climate change and constant warfare put our very survival in peril, the metaphor of *Godzilla* is even more powerful.

I hope this book gives the reader an understanding of how my father expressed his feelings and thoughts on a global level, through the medium of film. Ishiro Honda's works possess a visual flair, thanks to the imaginative illusions and unique aesthetics of Japanese special effects, achieved in partnership with the great Eiji Tsuburaya. Yet, at the core of every Honda film is a concern for Earth's future, a desire for peace, a compassion for the struggles within the human heart, and a fascination with science and technology. The audience is drawn into the story visually, then left with food for thought. With this formula, his films captured the imaginations of audiences worldwide, and continue to do so.

If Ishiro Honda were alive today, I know he would be supporting environmental causes to help save our planet and protesting against the wars that take the lives of innocent men, women, and children. This is the story of his life and work, and a testament to his legacy not only as the director of *Godzilla* and other iconic science fiction films, but also as a man of peace and humanity.

—Ryuji Honda

ISHIRO HONDA FILMOGRAPHY

Dates indicate original, official Japan theatrical release or broadcast date. The production company is Toho unless otherwise indicated. For detailed credits, see the official Ishiro Honda website (www.ishirohonda.org).

DOCUMENTARY FILMS

Ise-Shima (*Nihon sangyo chiri taikei dai ippen: kokuritsu koen ise-shima* [Japanese industry geographic survey part 1: Ise-Shima National Park]). 1949. 20 min.

Story of a Co-op (*Kyodo kumiai no hanashi*); alt. titles: *Co-op Way of Life* (*Seikatsu kyodo kumiai*), *Flowers Blooming in the Sand* (*Suna ni saku hana*). 1950. Approx. 30 min. (unconfirmed).

FEATURE FILMS

The Blue Pearl (*Aoi shinju*). August 3, 1951. 99 min.

The Skin of the South (*Nangoku no hada*). February 28, 1952. Mokuyo (Thursday) Productions/Toho. 95 min.

The Man Who Came to Port (*Minato e kita otoko*). November 27, 1952. 89 min.

Adolescence Part 2 (*Zoku shishunki*). July 1, 1953. 89 min.

Eagle of the Pacific (*Taiheiyo no washi*). October 21, 1953. 119 min.

Farewell Rabaul (*Saraba Rabauru*). February 20, 1954. 106 min.

Godzilla (*Gojira*). November 3, 1954. 97 min.

Love Makeup (*Koi-gesho*). January 9, 1955. 82 min.

Mother and Son (*Oen-san*). June 7, 1955. 100 min.

Half Human (*Ju jin yuki otoko* [Monster snowman]). August 14, 1955. 95 min.

Young Tree (*Wakai ki*). January 22, 1956. 92 min.

Night School (*Yakan chugaku*). April 18, 1956. Daiei/Nihon University College of Art. 44 min.

People of Tokyo, Goodbye (*Tokyo no hito sayonara*). June 28, 1956. 61 min.

Rodan (*Sora no daikaiju Radon* [Radon, giant monster of the sky]). December 26, 1956. 82 min.

Good Luck to These Two (*Kono futari ni sachi are*). February 19, 1957. 95 min.

A Teapicker's Song of Goodbye (*Wakare no chatsumi-uta*). July 2, 1957. 62 min.

A Rainbow Plays in My Heart (*Waga mune ni niji wa kiezu*). July 9, 1957. Part 1: 67 min.; Part 2: 68 min.

A Farewell to the Woman I Called My Sister (*Wakare no chatsumi-uta shimai-hen: Oneesan to yonda hito*). August 25, 1957. 67 min.

The Mysterians (*Chikyu boeigun* [Earth defense force]). December 28, 1957. 88 min.

Song for a Bride (*Hanayome sanjuso*). February 11, 1958. 87 min.

The H-Man (*Bijo to ekitai ningen* [The beauty and the liquid people]). June 24, 1958. 87 min.

Varan the Unbelievable (*Daikaiju Baran* [Giant monster Baran]). October 14, 1958. 87 min.

An Echo Calls You (*Kodama wa yonde iru*). January 22, 1959. 87 min.

Inao, Story of an Iron Arm (*Tetsuwan toshu Inao monogatari*). March 21, 1959. 106 min.

Seniors, Juniors, Co-workers (*Uwayaku, shitayaku, godoyaku*). September 13, 1959. 89 min.

Battle in Outer Space (*Uchu daisenso* [The great space war]). December 26, 1959. 93 min.

The Human Vapor (*Gasu ningen dai ichigo* [Vapor man number 1]). December 11, 1960. 91 min.

Mothra (*Mosura*). July 30, 1961. 101 min.

A Man in Red (*Shinku no otoko*). September 12, 1961. 89 min.

Gorath (*Yosei Gorasu* [Mysterious star Gorath]). March 21, 1962. 88 min.

King Kong vs. Godzilla (*Kingu Kongu tai Gojira*). August 11, 1962. 98 min.

Matango. August 11, 1963. 89 min. Alt. English title: *Attack of the Mushroom People*.

Atragon (*Kaitei gunkan* [Undersea warship]). December 22, 1963. 94 min.

Mothra vs. Godzilla (*Mosura tai Gojira*). April 29, 1964. 89 min. Alt. English title: *Godzilla vs. The Thing.*

Dogora (*Uchu kaiju Dogora* [Space monster Dogora]). August 11, 1964. 89 min. Alt. English title: *Dagora, the Space Monster.*

Ghidorah, the Three-Headed Monster (*San daikaiju—chikyu saidai no kessen* [Three giant monsters—the greatest battle on Earth]). December 20, 1964. 93 min.

Frankenstein Conquers the World (*Furankenshutain tai chitei kaiju Baragon* [Frankenstein vs. the subterranean monster Baragon]). August 8, 1965. Toho/Benedict Productions. 90 min.

Invasion of Astro-Monster (*Kaiju Daisenso* [Great monster war]). December 19, 1965. Toho/Henry G. Saperstein Enterprises. 94 min. Alt. English titles: *Monster Zero; Godzilla vs. Monster Zero.*

The War of the Gargantuas (*Furankenshutain no kaiju: Sanda tai Gaira* [Frankenstein's monsters: Sanda vs. Gailah]). July 31, 1966. Toho/United Productions of America. 88 min.

Come Marry Me (*Oyome ni oide*). October 20, 1966. 84 min.

King Kong Escapes (*Kingu Kongu no gyakushu* [King Kong's revenge]). July 22, 1967. Toho/Rankin-Bass. 104 min.

Destroy All Monsters (*Kaiju soshingeki* [March of the monsters]). August 1, 1968. 89 min.

Latitude Zero (*Ido zero daisakusen*). July 26, 1969. 89 min.

All Monsters Attack (*Oru kaiju daishingeki*). December 20, 1969. Alt. English title: *Godzilla's Revenge.* 70 min.

Space Amoeba (*Gezora-Ganime-Kameba: Kessen! Nankai no daikaiju* [Gezora-Ganime-Kameba: Showdown! Giant monsters of the South Seas]). December 20, 1970. 84 min. Alt. English title: *Yog, Monster from Space.*

Terror of Mechagodzilla (*Mekagojira no gyakushu* [Mechagodzilla's revenge]). March 15, 1975. 83 min. Alt. English title: *The Terror of Godzilla.*

TELEVISION

The Newlyweds (*Shinkon san*). Toho Television, Teatoru Pro; TBS network, Saturdays 9:30 p.m.; 30 min.
Episode 10, "The Woman, at That Moment" (*Onna wa sono toki*), January 7, 1967.
Episode 14, "Forgive Me Please, Mom" (*Yurushitene okasan*), February 4, 1967.

Husbands, Men, Be Strong (*Otto yo otoko yo tsuyokunare*). Toho Television; NET network, Thursdays 9:00 p.m.; 56 min.
Episode 2, "Honey, It's a Presidential Order" (*Anata shacho meirei yo*), October 9, 1969
Episode 5, "We're Going South-Southwest" (*Nan nan sei ni ikuno yo*), October 30, 1969

Return of Ultraman (*Kaettekita Urutoraman*). Tsuburaya Productions; TBS network, Fridays 7 p.m.; 30 min.
Episode 1, "Charge of the Monsters" (*Kaiju soshingeki*), April 2, 1971.
Episode 2, "Takkong's Great Revenge" (*Takkong daigyakushu*), April 9, 1971.
Episode 7, "Operation Monster Rainbow" (*Kaiju reinbo sakusen*), May 14, 1971.
Episode 9, "SOS Monster Island" (*Kaiju shima SOS*), May 28, 1971.
Episode 51, "The Five Ultra Pledges" (*Urutora go-tsu no chikai*), March 31, 1972.

Mirrorman (*Miraman*). Tsuburaya Productions; Fuji TV network, Fridays 7:00 p.m.; 30 min.
Episode 1, "Birth of Mirrorman" (*Miraman tanjo*), December 5, 1971.
Episode 2, "The Intruder Is Here" (*Shinryakusha wa koko ni iru*), December 12, 1971.

Emergency Command 10-4, 10-10 (*Kinkyu shirei 10-4, 10-10*). Tsuburaya Productions; NET network, Mondays 7:30 p.m.; 30 min.
Episode 5, "Japanese Beetle Murder Incident" (*Kabutomushi satsujin jiken*), July 31, 1972.
Episode 6, "Vampire of the Amazon" (*Amazon no kyuketsuki*), August 7, 1972.
Episode 20, "Assassin from Outer Space" (*Uchu kara kita ansatsusha*), November 13, 1972.
Episode 21, "Attack of Monster Bird Ragon" (*Kaicho Ragon no shugeki!*), November 20, 1972.

Thunder Mask (*Sanda masuku*). Hiromi Productions; NTV network, Tuesdays 7:00 p.m.; 30 min.

Episode 1, "Look! The Double Transformation of the Akatsuki" (*Miyo! Akatsuki no nidan henshin*), October 3, 1972.

Episode 2, "The Boy Who Could Control Monsters" (*Maju wo ayatsuru shonen*), October 10, 1972.

Episode 4, "Devil Freezing Strategy" (*Mao reito sakusen*), October 21, 1972.

Episode 5, "Merman's Revenge" (*Kyuketsu hankyojin no fukushu*), October 28, 1972.

Episode 14, "Monster Summoning Smoke" (*Maju wo yobu kemuri*), January 2, 1973.

Episode 15, "Degon H: Death Siren" (*Shi no kiteki da degon H*), January 9, 1973.

Meteor Man Zone (*Ryusei ningen Zon*). Toho Television, Mannesha; NTV network; Mondays 7:00 p.m.; 30 min.

Episode 3, "Defeat Garoga's Subterranean Base!" (*Tatake! Garoga no chitei kichi*), April 16, 1973.

Episode 4, "Onslaught! The Garoga Army: Enter Godzilla" (*Raishu! Garoga daiguntai–Gojira toujo*), April 23, 1973.

Episode 12, "Terrobeast HQ: Invade the Earth!" (*Kyoju kichi chikyu e shinnyu!*), June 18, 1973.

Episode 13, "Absolute Terror: Birthday of Horror!" (*Senritsu! Tanjobi no kyofu*), June 25, 1973.

Episode 18, "Mission: Blast the Japan Islands" (*Shirei: Nihon retto bakuha seyo*), July 30, 1973.

Episode 19, "Order: Destroy Earth with Comet K" (*Meirei: K suisei de chikyu wo kowase*), August 6, 1973.

Episode 23, "Secret of Bakugon, the Giant Terro-Beast" (*Daikyouju Bakugon no himitsu*), September 3, 1973.

Episode 24, "Smash the Pin-Spitting Needlar" (*Hari fuki kyouju Nidora wo taose*), September 10, 1973.

NOTES

INTRODUCTION

The epigraph is from Inuhiko Yomota, "The Menace from the South Seas: Honda Ishiro's Godzilla," in Japanese Cinema: Texts and Contexts, ed. Alastair Phillips and Julian Stringer (New York: Routledge, 2007).

1. Fauvism is a style of early twentieth-century modern art emphasizing painterly qualities and strong color, practiced by a group of French artists known as *les fauves* ("wild beasts").

2. "That Voice, This Face" (*Ano koe, kono kao*), *Nagoya Times*, August 7, 1951.

3. Notably, *Godzilla, King of the Monsters!* caused no significant anti-Japanese protest, despite being released in the United States fewer than ten years after World War II. By comparison, the German horror masterpiece *The Cabinet of Dr. Caligari* was withdrawn by some American exhibitors upon its 1921 release because of anti-German protests in the aftermath of World War I.

4. Carl Freedman, "Kubrick's 2001 and the Possibility of a Science-Fiction Cinema," *Science Fiction Studies* 75, vol. 25, pt. 2 (July 1998): 301.

5. Christopher Bolton, Istvan Csicsery-Ronay Jr., and Takayuki Tatsumi, *Robot Ghosts and Wired Dreams: Japanese Science Fiction from Origins to Anime* (Minneapolis: University of Minnesota Press, 2007), x.

6. Roland Lethem, "Inoshiro [*sic*] Honda Interview," *Midi-Minuit Fantastique*, no. 20 (Paris: October 1968).

7. Ishiro Honda, *Godzilla and My Movie Life* [*Honda Ishiro "Gojira" to waga eiga jinsei*] (Tokyo: Jitsugyo no Nihonsha, 1994).

8. Lethem, "Inoshiro [*sic*] Honda Interview."

9. Honda, *Godzilla and My Movie Life*.

10. Ibid.

11. Ibid.

12. Susan Sontag, *Against Interpretation and Other Essays* (New York: Farrar, Straus and Giroux, 1966), 213.

13. Donald Richie, "*Mono no Aware*: Hiro-shima in Film," in *Film: Book 2, Films of Peace and War*, ed. Robert Hughes (New York: Grove Press, 1962), 68.

14. Naofumi Higuchi, *Good Morning Godzilla: The Golden Age of the Movie Studio and Director Ishiro Honda* [*Guddo moningu, Gojira: Kantoku Honda Ishiro to satsueijo no jidai*] (Tokyo: Kokusho Kankokai, 2011).

15. Fumio Tanaka, *The Man Who Let the God (Godzilla) Loose: The Life and Times of Film Producer Tomoyuki Tanaka* [*Kami (Gojira) o hanatta otoko: eiga seisakusha Tanaka Tomoyuki to sono jidai*] (Tokyo: Kinema Junpo-sha, 1993).

16. Honda, *Godzilla and My Movie Life*.

17. More detailed information about Eiji Tsuburaya's life and work can be found in: August Ragone, *Eiji Tsuburaya: Master of Monsters: Defending the Earth with Ultraman and Godzilla* (San Francisco: Chronicle Books, 2007).

18. As of this writing, Honda's cut of *Half Human* was not officially available. The authors used an unofficial copy of the film for research.

19. Honda, *Godzilla and My Movie Life*.

20. Akira Kurosawa, *A Dream Is a Genius* [*Yume wa tensai de aru*] (Tokyo: Bungei Shunju, 1999).

21. Honda, *Godzilla and My Movie Life*.

1. A BOY FROM THE MOUNTAINS

1. Because of a common misreading of the kanji, Honda's given name is sometimes mistakenly translated as "Inoshiro."

2. Honda, *Godzilla and My Movie Life*.

3. Ibid.

2. TOKYO

1. Jordan Sand, *House and Home in Modern Japan* (Cambridge: Harvard University Asia Center, 2003), 256–57.

2. Joanne Bernardi, *Writing in Light: The Silent Scenario and the Japanese Pure Film Movement* (Detroit: Wayne State University Press, 2001), 98.

3. Honda, *Godzilla and My Movie Life*.

4. Steve Ryfle, *Japan's Favorite Mon-Star: The Unauthorized Biography of the Big G* (Toronto: ECW Press, 1999), 41.

5. Honda, *Godzilla and My Movie Life.*

6. *Jidai-geki* are typically set during the Edo Period and feature stories of samurai. The term is often interchangeable with *chambara* (swordfight) films, though the latter is a subgenre.

7. Honda, *Godzilla and My Movie Life.*

8. Tomoyuki Tanaka and Koichi Kawakita, *Encyclopedia of Godzilla—Mechagodzilla edition* [*Gojira daihyakka: ensaikuropedia obu Gojira—Meka Gojira hen*] (Tokyo: Gakken, 1993).

9. Honda, *Godzilla and My Movie Life.*

10. *My Life in Cinema: Honda Ishiro* (television program), interview by Yoshimitsu Banno, produced by Directors Guild of Japan, 1990, 58 min.

11. Ryfle, *Japan's Favorite Mon-Star*, 41.

3. FILM SCHOOL LESSONS

1. Tanaka and Kawakita, *Encyclopedia of Godzilla.*

2. Honda, *Godzilla and My Movie Life.*

3. Joseph L. Anderson and Donald Richie, *The Japanese Film: Art and Industry*, expanded ed. (Princeton: Princeton University Press, 1982), 82.

4. Honda, *Godzilla and My Movie Life.*

4. A RELUCTANT SOLDIER

1. Higuchi, *Good Morning Godzilla.*

5. FORGING BONDS

1. Stuart Galbraith IV, The *Emperor and the Wolf: The Lives and Films of Akira Kurosawa and Toshiro Mifune* (New York: Faber and Faber, 2002), 28.

2. Higuchi, *Good Morning Godzilla.*

3. Mette Hjort, *The Education of the Filmmaker in Europe, Australia, and Asia* (New York: Palgrave Macmillan, 2013), 176.

4. *My Life in Cinema: Kurosawa Akira* (television program), interview by Nagisa Oshima, produced by Directors Guild of Japan, 1993, 58 min.

5. Akira Kurosawa, *Something Like an Autobiography* (New York: Knopf Doubleday, 2011), 98.

6. Joan Mellen, *Seven Samurai* (New York: Macmillan, 2002), 9

7. *My Life in Cinema: Kurosawa Akira* (television program), interview by Nagisa Oshima.

8. Senkichi Taniguchi, interview by Stuart Galbraith IV, translated by Atsushi Sakahara, Tokyo, Japan, 1996.

9. Galbraith, *Emperor and the Wolf,* 27

10. Naoki Inose, *Persona: A Biography of Yukio Mishima* (Berkeley: Stone Bridge Press, 2012).

11. Toho is an acronym for "Tokyo-Takarazuka," the latter name taken from Kobayashi's female dance troupe. The kanji for "Taka" also can be read as "ho."

12. Daisuke Miyao, *The Aesthetics of Shadow: Lighting and Japanese Cinema* (Durham, NC: Duke University Press, 2013), 196–97.

13. In the 1930s, ¥1 was valued at approximately $0.25, according to historians Thomas E. Hall and J. David Ferguson in *The Great Depression: An International Disaster of Perverse Economic Policies* (Ann Arbor: University of Michigan Press, 2009).

14. Galbraith, *Emperor and the Wolf*, 30.

15. Anderson and Richie, *Japanese Film*, 131.

16. Higuchi, *Good Morning Godzilla.*

17. Ibid.

18. As opposed to an arranged marriage or a "love-match" marriage, the Honda marriage was a *shokuba shekkon* (company marriage), a union of two romantically involved coworkers.

6. WAR

1. Edward J. Drea, *Japan's Imperial Army: Its Rise and Fall, 1853–1945* (Lawrence: University Press of Kansas, 2009), 197–98.

2. Honda, *Godzilla and My Movie Life.*

3. "The Battle That Cannot Be Won—From the Creators of *Eagle of the Pacific*," *Movie Fan*, December 1953.

4. Robert B. Edgerton, *Warriors of the Rising Sun: A History of the Japanese Military* (New York: W. W. Norton, 1997), 323–24.

5. Honda, *Godzilla and My Movie Life.*

6. Ibid.

7. Vincent Canby, "*Uma* (1941); Film: 'Horse' from Japan," *New York Times*, May 9, 1986.

8. Miyao, *The Aesthetics of Shadow*, 196

9. Peter B. High, *The Imperial Screen: Japanese Film Culture in the Fifteen Years' War, 1931–*

1945 (Madison: University of Wisconsin Press, 2003), 382.

10. Ibid.

11. Ryfle, *Japan's Favorite Mon-Star*, 41.

12. Higuchi, *Good Morning Godzilla*.

13. Rana Mitter, *Forgotten Ally: China's World War II, 1937–1945* (New York: Houghton Mifflin Harcourt, 2013), 183–84.

14. Honda, *Godzilla and My Movie Life*.

15. Honda's memoirs indicate he was captured along the Yosuko River, as the Japanese called the Yangtze.

16. Ulrich Straus, *The Anguish of Surrender: Japanese POWs of World War II* (Seattle: University of Washington Press, 2004), 234.

17. Ibid., xiv.

18. Spencer Tucker, *Almanac of American Military History*, vol. 1 (Santa Barbara, CA: ABC-CLIO, 2012), 1727.

7. STARTING OVER

The epigraph is from Honda, *Godzilla and My Movie Life*.

1. Although Kurosawa was born in Tokyo, his father was from Akita Prefecture in the Tohoku region of northern Honshu. See Kurosawa, *Something Like an Autobiography*, 61.

2. Gary D. Allinson, *Japan's Postwar History* (Ithaca, NY: Cornell University Press, 1997), 43.

3. Joan Mellen, *The Waves at Genji's Door: Japan Through Its Cinema* (New York: Pantheon Books, 1976), 201.

4. Urashima Taro is a Japanese legend, akin to Washington Irving's *Rip Van Winkle*, about a fisherman who visits the land of the gods and, upon returning to his village, finds himself three hundred years into the future.

5. Straus, *Anguish of Surrender*, 236.

6. Honda, *Godzilla and My Movie Life*.

7. *My Life in Cinema: Honda Ishiro* (television program), interview by Yoshimitsu Banno.

8. Per Anderson and Richie, the average daily wage after the war was under a dollar; the average price of a movie ticket was about twenty cents.

8. ALLEGIANCES AND ALLIANCES

1. Higuchi, *Good Morning Godzilla*.

2. Sets for the black-market scenes in *The*

New Age of Fools films were reused in Kurosawa's *Drunken Angel* (*Yoidore tenshi*, 1948) and, years later, in Honda's *The H-Man*.

9. THE DOCUMENTARIES

1. EIRIN archival research was conducted by writer Nobutaka Suzuki and is used with permission.

2. Notably, *Ise-Shima* preceded two films considered landmarks in underwater cinematography: Robert D. Webb's Hollywood drama *Beneath the 12-Mile Reef* (1953), which received an Oscar nomination for Edward Cronjager's camera work, and Jacques-Yves Cousteau and Louis Malle's documentary *The Silent World* (1956).

3. Honda, *Godzilla and My Movie Life*.

4. Ishiro Honda, *Stray Dog* (*Nora inu*) laser-disc liner notes, Toho Video, 1993.

5. Honda, *Godzilla and My Movie Life*.

6. There is disagreement among various sources as to the film's title. Per researcher Nobutaka Suzuki, Japan Film Classification and Rating Committee records, which include the film's script, indicate the title as *Flowers Blooming in the Sand*; Toho public-relations material from 1951 calls it *Co-op Way of Life* (*Seikatsu kyodo kumiai*); in the *Kinema Junpo Japan Film Director's Encyclopedia*, it is listed as *Story of a Co-op*. As no film elements have been found, the on-screen title is unknown.

7. The credits for *Escape at Dawn* do not list Honda's name, but a copy of the screenplay found in Honda's archives indicates he was an assistant director on the film.

10. SEA, LAND, AND SKY

1 Shinobu Hashimoto, *Compound Cinematics: Akira Kurosawa and I* (New York: Vertical, 2015), 53.

2. The practice of sequestering screenwriters in seclusion at an inn was known as *kanzume* ("canning"). Writers were expected to complete the manuscript on deadline and were not allowed to leave the inn and its environs until then.

3. Higuchi, *Good Morning Godzilla*.

4. "That Voice, This Face" (*Ano koe, kono kao*), *Nagoya Times*, August 7, 1951.

5. *My Life in Cinema: Honda Ishiro* (television program), interview by Yoshimitsu Banno.

6. "Director Ishiro Honda's First Work in His Rise to Film Directing, a Screen Version of *Umi no haien*, an Underwater Spectacle Depicting Ama Divers!" *Eiga Fan*, June 1951.

7. Sakue Ise, "Toho *Aoi Shinju* location report," *Lucky* (Japanese periodical), July 1951.

8. In the Japanese studio system, "An editor [was] somebody in charge of simply . . . putting the cuts together" according to the director's instructions, Honda once said. However, rookie directors did not always have the final cut.

9. Honda, *Godzilla and My Movie Life*.

10. In the late 1950s and 1960s, a genre called *ama mono* (*ama* stories) emerged in which the divers were portrayed as racy sex symbols. These films may have been partly inspired by *Boy on a Dolphin* (1957), starring Sophia Loren as a Greek sponge diver who finds an ancient statue at the bottom of the sea (a plot vaguely and coincidentally similar to *The Blue Pearl*).

11. *My Life in Cinema: Honda Ishiro* (television program), interview by Yoshimitsu Banno.

12. Ibid.

13. Honda, *Godzilla and My Movie Life*.

14. August Ragone, *Eiji Tsuburaya: Master of Monsters* (San Francisco: Chronicle Books, 2007), 30.

15. Honda, *Godzilla and My Movie Life*.

16. According to Toho press materials for *Adolescence Part 2*.

17. Snack bars are a less expensive version of hostess clubs. Patrons, usually men, have drinks and conversation with women who serve them.

18. Akira Kubo, interview by Stuart Galbraith IV, translated by Atsushi Sakahara, Tokyo, Japan, 1996.

19. Stuart Galbraith IV, *DVD Review: "Admiral Yamamoto"* (1968), January 17, 2014. Retrieved from www.worldcineparadise.com.

20. Higuchi, *Good Morning Godzilla*.

21. "The Battle That Cannot Be Won—From the Creators of *Eagle of the Pacific*," *Movie Fan*, December 1953.

22. Galbraith, *Emperor and the Wolf*, 185.

23. "Yuko" was a friendly nickname for producer Tomoyuki Tanaka.

24. New Britain Island was an Australian possession until 1975, when Papua New Guinea became independent.

25. Tomoyuki Tanaka, ed., *Complete History of Toho SFX Movies* [*Toho Tokusatsu Eiga Zenshi*] (Tokyo: Toho Kabushiki Gaisha, 1983).

26. Killed In Action.

27. Don Niles, *Papua New Guinea: The Difficulties of Musical Diversity in an International Era* (Osaka: Osaka University of Arts, 1998).

28. Tanaka, *Complete History of Toho SFX Movies*.

11. NO LAUGHING MATTER

The first epigraph that opens Part III is from a supplemental video feature on *Godzilla* (Blu-ray), producer Curtis Tsui, Criterion Collection, 2011. The second epigraph is from Tanaka, *Complete History of Toho SFX Movies*.

1. The exchange rate was fixed at ¥360 to $1 from 1949 to 1971 under a postwar plan to stabilize Japan's currency.

2. *My Life in Cinema: Honda Ishiro* (television program), interview by Yoshimitsu Banno.

3. Toho Co., *Toho Special Effects Film Ultimate Collection* [*Toho tokusatsu eiga daizenshu*] (Tokyo: Virejji Bukkusu, 2012).

4. Eugene Lourie, *My Work in Films* (New York: Harcourt Brace Jovanovich, 1985), 241.

5. There are conflicting stories as to why Taniguchi did not direct Godzilla. "Most likely Sen-chan [Taniguchi] rejected it outright," Honda recalled. "I believe he said that no one could shoot something inhuman like that." Another version of events says Taniguchi was simply unavailable because he'd been assigned to direct *The Sound of Waves*.

6. Tanaka and Kawakita, *Encyclopedia of Godzilla*.

7. *Tsu-ka* describes an unusually close personal understanding between friends.

8. Higuchi, *Good Morning Godzilla*.

9. Toho Co., *Toho Special Effects Film Ultimate Collection*.

10. Ibid.

11. *Godzilla, King of the Monsters* (documentary film), producer Nick Freand Jones, BBC Video, 1998.

12. Ed Godziszewski, "The Making of God-

zilla," *Japanese Giants* 1, no. 10 (September 2004).

13. Nobutaka Suzuki, "Toho Special Effects Films and Their Expansions into Overseas Markets," in Toho Co., *Toho Special Effects Film Ultimate Collection* [*Toho tokusatsu eiga daizenshu*] (Tokyo: Virejji Bukkusu, 2012).

14. Hiroshi Takeuchi and Hideki Murata, *Gojira 1954* [Godzilla 1954] (Tokyo: Jitsugyononi-honsha, 1999).

15. Ibid.

16. Yuzuru Aizawa, interview by Stuart Galbraith IV, Tokyo, Japan, 2011.

17. Tanaka, *Complete History of Toho SFX Movies*.

18. Godziszewski, "The Making of Godzilla."

19. Ishiro Honda, interview by David Milner, translated by Yoshihiko Shibata, Tokyo, Japan, 1992.

20. Tanaka and Kawakita, *Encyclopedia of Godzilla*.

21. According to historian Gerhard Weinberg, "The United States had been developing atomic bombs, originally in what was believed to be a race with Germany, although it turned out ironically that Japanese scientists were further along than the Germans." See Nancy E. Rupprecht and Wendy Koenig, eds., *The Holocaust and World War II: In History and in Memory* (Newcastle upon Tyne, UK: Cambridge Scholars Publishing, 2012), 40.

22. Jayson Makoto Chun, *A Nation of a Hundred Million Idiots: A Social History of Japanese Television, 1953–1973* (New York: Routledge, 2006), 244–45.

23. Yoshikuni Igarashi, *Bodies of Memory: Narratives of War in Postwar Japanese Culture, 1945–1970* (Princeton: Princeton University Press, 2012), 116.

24. Suzuki, "Toho Special Effects Films."

25. Saburo Kawamoto, *Revisiting Postwar Japanese Film* [*Ima hitotabi no sengo Nihon eiga*] (Tokyo: Iwanami Shoten, 1994). Other Japanese scholars have noted that the route Godzilla travels through Tokyo would have taken the monster to the Imperial Palace, yet it is not shown or referenced in the film. However, even if Honda had wanted Godzilla to destroy the palace, it may have been difficult to obtain approval from EIRIN for such a scene. (The concept of Godzilla embodying the souls of Japanese soldiers killed in the South Seas was a major theme in Shusuke Kaneko's 2001 film *Godzilla, Mothra and King Ghidorah: Giant Monsters All-Out Attack*.)

26. Though not integral to the story, the influence of Western popular culture and fashion is seen in Emiko's outfits, which resemble those worn by Audrey Hepburn in *Roman Holiday* (1953).

27. Adoption of children unrelated by bloodlines remains relatively uncommon in Japan; Yamane's adoption of Shinkichi indicates the scientist has more liberal social views.

28. Honda, interview by David Milner.

29. Godziszewski, "The Making of Godzilla."

30. Tadao Sato interview.

31. Matthew Edwards, ed., *The Atomic Bomb in Japanese Cinema: Critical Essays* (Jefferson, NC: McFarland Publishing, 2015), 77.

32. Igarashi, *Bodies of Memory*, 116.

33. Suzuki, "Toho Special Effects Films."

34. Higuchi, *Good Morning Godzilla*.

35. Box-office data for *Godzilla* and subsequent films is compiled from archival issues of *Kinema Junpo* and from *Film 40 Years All Records* (*Eiga 40 nen zen kiroku*), a special edition published by *Kinema Junpo* in February 1986.

36. *My Life in Cinema: Honda Ishiro* (television program), interview by Yoshimitsu Banno.

37. Tanaka and Kawakita, *Encyclopedia of Godzilla*.

12. OBLIGATIONS

1. Ian Buruma, *Behind the Mask: On Sexual Demons, Sacred Mothers, Transvestites, Gangsters, Drifters and Other Japanese Cultural Heroes* (New York: Pantheon Books, 1983), 21.

2. In a traditional Japanese home, the bath is kept separate from the toilet, considered the dirtiest room in the house.

3. As of 2017, there were plans to close and relocate the Tsukiji Fish Market.

4. Toho Co., *Toho Special Effects Film Ultimate Collection*.

5. Ibid.

6. The history of Japanese censorship of discriminatory material in media is summarized in

Nanette Gottlieb, *Language and Society in Japan* (Cambridge: Cambridge University Press, 2005).

13. YOUTH MOVEMENT

1. *Enka* is a popular genre of sentimental ballad music that originated after World War II, with roots in traditional Japanese music forms.

2. Izu Oshima was the site of the epicenter of the 1923 Great Kanto Earthquake. The location figures prominently in many books and films.

3. *Anko tsubaki* is a term used in the Izu-Oshima region signifying local beauty.

4. Although *People of Tokyo, Goodbye* is Toho's English-language title for this film, a more literal interpretation of the Japanese title is "The One from Tokyo, Good-bye," as reflected in this unofficial translation of the song lyrics.

5. Camellia oil, or tea seed oil, is a foodstuff produced from the indigenous camellia flowers of Oshima and other Japanese islands.

6. Honda, *Godzilla and My Movie Life*.

7. Kuronuma's story, "Birth of Rodan," was published in the October 1956 issue of *Chugaku-sei no tomo* (Friend of middle schoolers), a boys' magazine. The Mantell incident helped inspire interest in flying saucers, including in many films, in the 1950s.

8. *Rodan* was originally planned as a black-and-white feature. It was decided during prepro-duction to film in color instead.

9. Joe Moore, *The Other Japan: Conflict, Com-promise, and Resistance Since 1945* (New York: M. E. Sharpe, 1997), 50–51.

10. Pradyumna P. Karan and Kristin Staple-ton, *The Japanese City* (Louisville: University Press of Kentucky, 2015), 10.

11. Toho Co., *Toho Special Effects Film Ulti-mate Collection*.

12. *My Life in Cinema: Honda Ishiro* (tele-vision program), interview by Yoshimitsu Banno.

13. The suffix *-bo* denotes a nickname given to a boy.

14. Miss Morinaga: a beauty pageant spon-sored by Morinaga Confectionery Company.

15. Tanaka, *Complete History of Toho SFX Movies*.

16. Toho Co., *Toho Special Effects Film Ulti-mate Collection*.

17. Honda, *Godzilla and My Movie Life*.

14. LOVERS AND ALIENS

1. Yasuki Hamano, *The Akira Kurosawa Archives* [*Taikei Kurosawa Akira*], vol. 2 (Tokyo: Kodansha, 2009–10), 684.

2. Honda's quote is taken from an article in *Studio Mail* (Toho Studios' internal publication), published 1957.

3. *My Life in Cinema: Honda Ishiro* (television program), interview by Yoshimitsu Banno.

4. "Mogera" is based on *mogura* (mole).

5. Honda, *Godzilla and My Movie Life*.

6. The extras on rooftops were filmed atop Toho's old headquarters building in Ginza.

7. *Toho SF SFX Movie Series*, vol. 5 [*Toho SF Tokusatsu Eiga Series*, vol. 5] (Tokyo: Toho Shup-pan Jigyoshitsu, 1986).

8. Ibid.

15. BRIDES, BLOBS, AND A BOMB

1. Barak Kushner, *The Thought War: Japanese Imperial Propaganda* (Honolulu: University of Hawaii Press, 2007), 71.

2. Donald Richie, *Japanese Movies* (Tokyo: Japan Travel Bureau, 1961), 91.

3. The script for *The H-Man* was based on a story idea by bit actor Hideo Kaijo.

4. "Staff Discusses *Bijo to Eikitai Ningen*," video featurette, *Bijo to Ekitai Ningen* DVD, TohoVideo, 2005.

5. Shirakawa's vocals were overdubbed by jazz singer Martha Miyake.

6. Toho Co., *Toho Special Effects Film Ultimate Collection*.

7. Ibid.

8. Ibid.

9. Ibid.

10. Ken Kuronuma, quoted in *Fantasy Litera-ture* [*Genso Bungaku*], no. 8 (1984).

11. Honda, interview by David Milner.

12. Tanaka and Kawakita, *Encyclopedia of Godzilla*.

13. Toho Co., *Toho Special Effects Film Ulti-mate Collection*.

14. Ibid.

15. Honda, interview by David Milner.

16. AB-PT Pictures had previously acquired Toho's *Godzilla Raids Again* and was in the pro-cess of reworking that film for American release when the company ceased producing films.

17. Kevin Heffernan, *Ghouls, Gimmicks, and Gold: Horror Films and the American Movie Business, 1953–1968* (Durham, NC: Duke University Press, 2004), 71.

16. MARRIAGE, MONEY, AND THE MOON

1. "Film *Tetsuwan toshu Inao monogatari* Starring *Sai-chan* Cranks in," *Sports Nippon Newspapers*, January 23, 1959. (Inao's nickname was *Sai-chan* [Little Rhino], a reference to his "rhinocerous-shaped eyes" as well as his strong build and slow gait.)

2. Tadao Sato, *Currents in Japanese Cinema* (New York: Kodansha/Harper and Row, 1987), 202.

3. Stuart Galbraith IV, *The Japanese Filmography* (Jefferson, NC: McFarland, 1996), 28.

4. Toho Co., *Toho Special Effects Film Ultimate Collection.*

5. Galbraith, *Japanese Filmography*, 468, 471.

6. Tanaka and Kawakita, *Encyclopedia of Godzilla.*

7. Toho Co., *Toho Special Effects Film Ultimate Collection.*

17. ACCIDENTAL MONSTERS

1. Jun Fukuda, interview by David Milner and Guy Tucker, translated by Yoshihiko Shibata, Tokyo, Japan, March 1995.

2. Postwar Japan income statistics are taken from several sources, including James Irving Matray, *Japan's Emergence as a Global Power* (Santa Barbara: Greenwood, 2001).

3. Ann Waswo, *Housing in Postwar Japan: A Social History* (New York: Routledge, 2013), 97.

4. The Bon Festival (*Obon*) is a Japanese Buddhist custom honoring ancestors; the date varies by region.

5. Galbraith, *Japanese Filmography*, 471.

6. Ibid.

7. Isolde Standish, *A New History of Japanese Cinema* (New York: Bloomsbury, 2003), 272.

8. Higuchi, *Good Morning Godzilla.*

9. Toho had already loosely adapted Wells's story in *The Invisible Man* (1954, d. Motoyoshi Oda).

10. Toho Co., *Toho Special Effects Film Ultimate Collection.*

11. Honda, *Godzilla and My Movie Life.*

12. Kitagawa Utamaro, a highly influential woodblock print artist from the Edo period.

13. Kaoru Yachigusa, audio commentary, *Gasu ningen dai ichigo* DVD, Toho Video, 2002.

14. Suzuki, "Toho Special Effects Films."

15. Samuel L. Leiter, *Kabuki at the Crossroads: Years of Crisis, 1952–1965* (Leiden, Netherlands: Martinus Nijhoff, 2013), 78.

16. *Toho SF SFX Movie Series*, vol. 2 [*Toho SF Tokusatsu Eiga Series*, vol. 2] (Tokyo: Toho Shuppan Jigyoshitsu, 1985).

17. Honda, interview by David Milner.

18. *Toho SF SFX Movie Series*, vol. 2.

19. Hajime Ishida, "Memories of Ishiro Honda," *Famous Monsters of Filmland*, no. 269 (September–October 2013).

20. *Toho SF SFX Movie Series*, vol. 2.

21. Japan's three nonnuclear principles have been national policy since the end of World War II and were officially adopted in 1971.

22. Ishida, "Memories of Ishiro Honda."

23. Ibid.

24. "Medicine: Sayonara, Heroin," *Time*, June 19, 1972.

18. GOING GLOBAL

1. Tanaka and Kawakita, *Encyclopedia of Godzilla.*

2. Andrew Oros, *Normalizing Japan: Politics, Identity, and the Evolution of Security Practice* (Palo Alto: Stanford University Press, 2009), 123.

3. Honda, *Godzilla and My Movie Life.*

4. *Toho SF SFX Movie Series*, vol. 4 [*Toho SF Tokusatsu Eiga Series*, vol. 4] (Tokyo: Toho Shuppan Jigyoshitsu, 1985).

5. Ibid.

6. Tanaka and Kawakita, *Encyclopedia of Godzilla.*

7. Honda, *Godzilla and My Movie Life.*

8. Tanaka and Kawakita, *Encyclopedia of Godzilla.*

9. Godzilla was already referenced frequently in Japanese popular culture. For instance, in Masaki Kobayashi's *I Will Buy You* (1956), a sports agent refers to a problem client as "just like Godzilla."

10. Honda, *Godzilla and My Movie Life.*

11. Yu Fujiki, interview by Stuart Galbraith IV,

translated by Atsushi Sakahara, Tokyo, Japan, 1996.

12. *Toho SF SFX Movie Series*, vol. 5.

13. Tanaka and Kawakita, *Encyclopedia of Godzilla*.

14. Toho Co., *Toho Special Effects Film Ultimate Collection*.

15. Tanaka and Kawakita, *Encyclopedia of Godzilla*.

16. Sadamasa Arikawa, in *Godzilla Days: 40 Years of Godzilla Movies* [*Godzilla Days: Gojira Eiga Yonjunen Shi*] (Tokyo: Shueisha Kabushiki Gaisha, 1993).

17. Kenji Sahara, *Wonderful SFX Life* [*Subarashiki Tokusatsu Jinsei*] (Tokyo: Shogakukan, 2005).

18. Cynthia Erb, *Tracking King Kong: A Hollywood Icon in World Culture*, 2nd ed. (Detroit: Wayne State University Press. 2009), 155–56.

19. Stuart Galbraith IV, "The Japan Files," *Stuart Galbraith IV's Cineblogarama* (online), June 9, 2012.

20. Galbraith, "The Japan Files."

21. Kimi Honda and Miyuki Nishida, *Godzilla's Trunk: The Love of Husband Ishiro Honda, the Friendship of Akira Kurosawa* [*Gojira no toranku: otto Honda Ishiro no aijo Kurosawa Akira no yujo*] (Tokyo: Takarajimasha, 2012), 141.

22. Hiroshi Tasogawa, *All the Emperor's Men: Kurosawa's Pearl Harbor* (New Jersey: Applause Theatre and Cinema Books, 2012), 37.

23. Ragone, *Eiji Tsuburaya*, 76.

24. Honda, *Godzilla and My Movie Life*.

25. Ibid.

26. Honda, interview by David Milner.

27. Honda, *Godzilla and My Movie Life*.

19. DANGEROUS WATERS

1. Honda, interview by David Milner.

2. Mizuno used the term *bata kusai* ("smells buttery"), meaning "Western looking."

3. Honda, *Godzilla and My Movie Life*.

4. Sahara, *Wonderful SFX Life*.

5. Honda, *Godzilla and My Movie Life*.

6. Ibid.

7. Ibid.

8. *Toho SF SFX Movie Series*, vol. 4.

9. Some sources indicate *Atragon* had only

one and a half months of preparation time and was shot in forty days.

10. For international release, Toho retitled the film *Atoragon*, apparently short for "atomic dragon." AIP changed the spelling to *Atragon* for its 1965 US release. In the English-language version, "Atragon" is also the name of the submarine.

11. John Lie, *Multiethnic Japan* (Cambridge: Harvard University Press, 2004), 132.

12. Beatrice Trefalt, *Japanese Army Stragglers and Memories of the War in Japan, 1950–75* (New York: Routledge, 2013), iii.

13. *Toho SF SFX Movie Series*, vol. 4.

14. Ed Godziszewski, "The Making of Atragon," *Japanese Giants* 1, no. 7 (April 1986).

15. Honda, *Godzilla and My Movie Life*.

16. *Toho SF SFX Movie Series*, vol. 4.

20. MONSTERS AND GANGSTERS

1. Igarashi, *Bodies of Memory*, 121.

2. Sahara, *Wonderful SFX Life*.

3. Yuriko Hoshi, interview by Stuart Galbraith IV, translated by Atsushi Sakahara, Tokyo, Japan, 1996.

4. Hiroshi Fujimoto, ed., *Fifty Years of Light and Dark: The Hirohito Era, by the Staff of the Mainichi Daily News* (Tokyo: Mainichi Newspapers, 1975), 312.

5. Akira Ifukube, interview by Ed Godziszewski, translated by Michiko Imamura, Tokyo, Japan, 1994.

6. Steve Ryfle and Ed Godziszewski, audio commentary, *Mothra vs. Godzilla* DVD, Classic Media, 2007.

7. Minoru Shikita and Shinichi Tsuchiya, *Crime and Criminal Policy in Japan: Analysis and Evaluation of the Showa Era, 1926–1988* (New York: Springer Science and Business Media, 2012).

8. Honda, *Godzilla and My Movie Life*.

9. Yosuke Natsuki, interview by Stuart Galbraith IV, translated by Atsushi Sakahara, Tokyo, Japan, 1996.

10. Honda, *Godzilla and My Movie Life*.

11. Honda, interview by David Milner.

12. Honda, *Godzilla and My Movie Life*.

13. Tanaka and Kawakita, *Encyclopedia of Godzilla*.

14. Honda, interview by David Milner.

15. *Toho SFX Actress Encyclopedia* [*Toho Tokusatsu Jyoyu Daizenshu*] (Tokyo: Yoshensha, 2011).

21. EAST MEETS WEST

The epigraphs that open Part IV are from Lethem, "Inoshiro [sic] Honda interview" and Matsumura's interview by Stuart Galbraith IV, translated by Atsushi Sakahara, Tokyo, 1996.

1. Ishiro Honda, "The Joy of Fantasy Films," *Toho Eiga* (studio newsletter), February 1965.

2. Honda, *Godzilla and My Movie Life.*

3. Nick Adams, "A Kind Word for Those Monster Movies," *Los Angeles Herald-Examiner,* August 22, 1965.

4. Honda, interview by David Milner.

5. Richie, "*Mono no Aware.*"

6. Honda, *Godzilla and My Movie Life.*

7. Ibid.

8. Ishida, "Memories of Ishiro Honda."

9. Higuchi, *Good Morning Godzilla.*

10. *Toho SF SFX Movie Series*, vol. 5.

11. An on-screen title indicates the story takes place in the year "196X."

12. Honda, *Godzilla and My Movie Life.*

13. *Kappa* is a 1927 satirical novel in the *Gulliver's Travels* tradition, about a man who travels through a subterranean land inhabited by water sprites.

14. *Toho SFX Actress Encyclopedia.*

15. Lie, *Multiethnic Japan*, 68.

16. Higuchi, *Good Morning Godzilla.*

17. Honda, interview by David Milner.

18 Brad Pitt appeared in a video segment in which Hollywood personalities described their first movie memories, in the ABC television broadcast of the Eighty-Fourth Academy Awards, Academy of Motion Picture Arts and Sciences, February 26, 2012.

19. Henry G. Saperstein, interview by Stuart Galbraith IV, Sherman Oaks, California, 1994.

20. Russ Tamblyn, Monsterpalooza (horror film convention), March 30, 2014, Burbank, California.

21. Saperstein, interview by Stuart Galbraith IV.

22. Sahara, *Wonderful SFX Life.*

23. Suzuki, "Toho Special Effects Films."

24. Paul P. Schreibman to Toho Co., August 29, 1966, Los Angeles. Letter courtesy of Honda Film Inc.

25. The film mirrors Kayama's well publicized, real-life passion for yachting.

26. The prolific Hirose previously had scored *Seniors, Juniors, Co-workers* and *A Man in Red* for Honda. Hirose never scored a Toho science fiction film, but he did score Daiei's *Gamera vs. Viras* (1968).

22. MONSTERS OR BUST

1. In the US version, Honda's credit reads: "For Toho Co., Ltd. . . . Directed by Inoshiro [*sic*] Honda." Rankin Jr.'s credit reads: "For Rankin/ Bass Productions . . . Producer/Director." Rankin Jr.'s is the final screen credit, giving the false impression he was in charge.

2. Rhodes Reason, telephone interview by Stuart Galbraith IV, Burbank, California, 1995.

3. Toho Co., *Toho Special Effects Film Ultimate Collection.*

4. A September 1968 *Kinema Junpo* review implied that the name "Monsterland" could have been inspired by Disneyland, though this is unconfirmed.

5. Igarashi, *Bodies of Memory*, 116.

6. Ishiro Honda, "Evolution of the Superman," *Toho Eiga* (studio newsletter), July 1968.

7. Tasogawa, *All the Emperor's Men*, 51.

8. Ibid., 18.

9. "Don Sharpe's Toho Deal," *Variety*, June 19, 1968.

10. It is not known exactly how long the film had been in production before Sharpe defaulted. Japanese interviewees typically said ten days, while Cotten, in his autobiography, said three weeks.

11. Joseph Cotten, *Vanity Will Get You Somewhere* (San Francisco: Mercury House, 1987), 169–70.

12. Suzuki, "Toho Special Effects Films."

13. Cotten, *Vanity Will Get You Somewhere*, 171.

14. Tanaka, *The Man Who Let the God (Godzilla) Loose.*

15. Honda, *Godzilla and My Movie Life.*

16. Tanaka and Kawakita, *Encyclopedia of Godzilla.*

17. Toho Co., *Toho Special Effects Film Ultimate Collection.*

18. Ibid.

19. Nagisa Oshima's *Boy* (*Shonen*, 1969), released six months earlier, also tells the story of a bullied and lonely boy who fantasizes about a world of monsters; like *All Monsters Attack*, the film also references a real-life criminal case. The two films are very different, however. Oshima, a leader of the Japanese New Wave film movement, depicts late 1960s Japan in starker, more pessimistic terms than Honda, evidence of the creative gulf between younger, independent filmmakers and the original, studio-based directors.

20. Sumiko Iwao, *The Japanese Woman: Traditional Image and Changing Reality* (Cambridge: Harvard University Press, 1993), 158.

21. Though transliterated as "Minilla," the character's name is pronounced "Minira," i.e., "Mini-Gojira."

22. Production notes indicate Gabara is a mutated toad.

23. Toho Co., *Toho Special Effects Film Ultimate Collection.*

24. With the proliferation of auto traffic, schoolchildren wore yellow caps to be visible to drivers.

25. Honda's script notes, in which he instructed Sekizawa to delete Rodan and the giant octopus from the screenplay and replace them with footage from Fukuda's films are referenced in Toho Co., *Toho Special Effects Film Ultimate Collection.*

26. *Toho SF SFX Movie Series*, vol. 5.

27. Tanaka and Kawakita, *Encyclopedia of Godzilla.*

28. Honda, interview by David Milner.

29. Ishiro Honda, "Magician of SFX," *Bungei Shinju*, April 1970.

30. Honda, interview by David Milner.

31. Ragone, *Eiji Tsuburaya*, 175.

32. Honda, "Magician of SFX."

33. Toho Co., *Toho Special Effects Film Ultimate Collection.*

34. Fumio Tanaka, audio commentary, *Gezora-Ganime-Kameba: Kessen! Nankai no daikaiju* DVD, Toho Video, 2005.

35. Ibid.

36. Tasogawa, *All the Emperor's Men*, 310.

37. Ishiro Honda, quoted in *Voice Last Issue* (Japanese fanzine), April 1987.

38. Yoshimitsu Banno, interview, *SciFi Japan TV*, episode 26, September 4, 2014, retrieved from www.youtube.com.

39. Harry Medved and Randy Dreyfuss, *The Fifty Worst Films of All Time (And How They Got That Way)* (New York: Popular Library, 1978).

40. Ryfle, *Japan's Favorite Mon-Star*, 200.

41. *Godzilla vs. Mechagodzilla* director Jun Fukuda was an assistant director on Honda's *Rodan.*

42. Galbraith, *Emperor and the Wolf*, 510.

43. Yukiko Takayama, interview by David Milner, translated by Yoshihiko Shibata, Tokyo, Japan, July 1994.

44. *Toho SFX Actress Encyclopedia.*

45. Higuchi, *Good Morning Godzilla.*

23. RHAPSODY IN AUTUMN

The epigraph that opens Part V is from Kurosawa's correspondence with Stuart Galbraith IV, 1996.

1. Galbraith, *Emperor and the Wolf*, 637.

2. Ibid., 548.

3. Ibid., 553.

4. Honda, *Godzilla and My Movie Life.*

5. Akira Kurosawa, quoted in the documentary film *Making of Dreams*, directed by Nobuhiko Obayashi, Pony Canyon Video, 1990.

6. Galbraith, *Emperor and the Wolf*, 571.

7. Ryfle, *Japan's Favorite Mon-Star*, 226.

8. Ibid., 221.

9. Honda, interview by David Milner.

10. It has also been misreported that Honda directed the sequences titled "Mount Fuji in Red" and "The Weeping Demon."

11. *My Life in Cinema: Kurosawa Akira* (television program), interview by Nagisa Oshima.

12. Stephen Prince, *The Warrior's Camera: The Cinema of Akira Kurosawa* (Princeton, NJ: Princeton University Press, 1991), 312.

13. Nobuhiko Obayashi, Japan Society, New York, November 21, 2015.

14. Ishiro Honda, interview by James Bailey, *Tokyo Journal*, April 1991.

15. For an account of the critical controversy surrounding *Rhapsody in August*, see Mitsuhiro

Yoshimoto, *Kurosawa: Film Studies and Japanese Cinema* (Durham, NC: Duke University Press, 2000).

16. Hisao Kurosawa, dir., *A Message from Akira Kurosawa: For Beautiful Movies* (documentary film), Kurosawa Production Co., 2000.

17. Galbraith, *Emperor and the Wolf*, 637.

18. Terrence Rafferty, "The Monster That Morphed into a Metaphor," *New York Times*, May 2, 2004.

19. Ishiro Honda, interview by James Bailey, *Tokyo Journal*, April 1991.

INDEX

Note: Page numbers in *italics* indicate illustrations.

ABOUT THE AUTHORS

STEVE RYFLE has contributed film journalism and criticism to the *Los Angeles Times, San Francisco Chronicle, Cineaste, Virginia Quarterly Review, POV,* and other publications. He is the author of a book on the history of the Godzilla film series.

ED GODZISZEWSKI is editor and publisher of *Japanese Giants* magazine. He has written for *Fangoria* and other publications.

Together, the authors have provided audio commentary tracks and produced supplemental material for numerous home video releases, including Ishiro Honda's *Godzilla* for the British Film Institute. They coproduced the documentary feature *Bringing Godzilla Down to Size* (2008).